DATE DUE

D0906757

TRACKING THE TEXAS RANGERS:

THE NINETEENTH CENTURY

edited by

Bruce A. Glasrud

and

Harold J. Weiss, Jr.

Number 10 in the Frances B. Vick Series

University of North Texas Press

Denton, Texas

10 9 8 7 6 5 4 3 2 1

Permissions:
University of North Texas Press
1155 Union Circle #311336
Denton, TX 76203-5017

The paper used in this book meets the minimum requirements of the
American National Standard for Permanence of Paper for Printed Library
Materials, z39.48.1984. Binding materials have been chosen for durability.

Library of Congress Cataloging-in-Publication Data
Tracking the Texas Rangers : the nineteenth century / edited
by Bruce A. Glasrud and Harold J. Weiss, Jr.
p. cm. — (Frances B. Vick series ; no. 10)
Includes bibliographical references and index.
ISBN 978-1-57441-465-3 (cloth : alk. paper)
1. Texas Rangers—History—19th century. 2. Law enforcement—Texas—History—
19th century. 3. Frontier and pioneer life—Texas. 4. Texas—History—Republic,
1836–1846. 5. Texas—History—1846–1950. I. Glasrud, Bruce A. II. Weiss, Harold J.
F391.T73   2012
976.4'05—dc23
2012017467

Tracking the Texas Rangers: The Nineteenth Century
is Number 10 in the Frances B. Vick Series

TRACKING THE TEXAS RANGERS:

THE NINETEENTH CENTURY

edited by

Bruce A. Glasrud

and

Harold J. Weiss, Jr.

Number 10 in the Frances B. Vick Series

University of North Texas Press

Denton, Texas

10 9 8 7 6 5 4 3 2 1

Permissions:
University of North Texas Press
1155 Union Circle #311336
Denton, TX 76203-5017

The paper used in this book meets the minimum requirements of the
American National Standard for Permanence of Paper for Printed Library
Materials, z39.48.1984. Binding materials have been chosen for durability.

Library of Congress Cataloging-in-Publication Data
Tracking the Texas Rangers : the nineteenth century / edited
by Bruce A. Glasrud and Harold J. Weiss, Jr.
p. cm. — (Frances B. Vick series ; no. 10)
Includes bibliographical references and index.
ISBN 978-1-57441-465-3 (cloth : alk. paper)
1. Texas Rangers—History—19th century. 2. Law enforcement—Texas—History—
19th century. 3. Frontier and pioneer life—Texas. 4. Texas—History—Republic,
1836–1846. 5. Texas—History—1846–1950. I. Glasrud, Bruce A. II. Weiss, Harold J.
F391.T73   2012
976.4'05—dc23
2012017467

Tracking the Texas Rangers: The Nineteenth Century
is Number 10 in the Frances B. Vick Series

To all the Ranger historians
who have gone before!!

CONTENTS

TIMELINE: 19TH CENTURY TEXAS RANGER HISTORY

Harold J. Weiss, Jr.

1823–1836 The formative era. Stephen Austin first used the word "ranger." Ranging companies took the field against Indian tribes and Mexican nationals. A Corps of Rangers was organized in 1835. Key Ranger leaders included Robert Coleman, John J. Tumlinson, Jr., and Robert "Three Legged Willie" Williamson.

1840 The Great Comanche Raid to the Gulf of Mexico. Ranging companies and other volunteers engaged and scattered the Comanches at the Battle of Plum Creek near present-day Lockhart.

1844 The Battle of Walker's Creek between the Comanches and the Rangers under John Coffee "Jack" Hays. In this engagement the Rangers maneuvered and fired five-shot Paterson Colt revolvers.

1846–1848 The war between Mexico and the United Sates. Ranging companies in federal service took part in the campaigns of Generals Zachary Taylor and Winfield Scott. Two Ranger images emerged from the war: a white-hatted fighter armed with six-shooters and bowie knives; and a black-hatted demon who pillaged and killed Mexican civilians.

1858–1859 Two noteworthy events. First, Rangers and Indian allies commanded by John S. "Rip" Ford crossed the Canadian River and attacked a Comanche village under Iron Jacket in 1858. Second, the raid on Brownsville by Juan Nepomuceno Cortina and his followers occurred in 1859. Thus began the troubles between Cortina and Texas officials that lasted for years.

1861–1865 American Civil War with Texas under a Confederate flag. Ranger units took the field and tried to defend frontier lands. Other forces, like Terry's Texas Rangers, fought elsewhere in the South.

1874 Formation of the Frontier Battalion of Rangers to protect frontier lands from Indian raiders and outlaw gangs. The new commander in chief was Major John B. Jones. At the same time a special force under Leander McNelly and Lee Hall was created. They went into South Texas to chase cattle thieves, even invading Mexico, and take into custody feudists and outlaws like John King Fisher. A forerunner to the troubles with Mexico was the Callahan expedition in the 1850s. These Rangers occupied a Mexican town and fought with Mexican troops, all in the name of chasing Indian marauders and looking for runaway slaves.

1877 Anglos and Mexicans disputed the use of salt beds near El Paso. In the ensuing violence a party of Rangers under John B. Tays surrendered, a blot on the record of the Texas Rangers.

1877–1878 In 1877, Ranger John Armstrong and other law officers subdued and captured John Wesley Hardin in Florida. In 1878, Rangers of the Frontier Battalion ended their pursuit of Sam Bass, as he was killed in his attempt to rob a bank in Round Rock, Texas.

MID-1880S Fence cutters, like the "Knights of the Knippers," arose and moved about at night to do their clandestine work. The doings of Ranger Ira Aten in trying to stop such actions became legendary.

1887 The Conner gang ambushed Captain William Scott and five Rangers in East Texas. When the smoke cleared, the record read: one Ranger killed, three more wounded, including future captains J. A. Brooks and John Rogers, one Conner brother dead, and another mortally wounded.

1892 In a chase after outlaws, Captain Frank Jones and several Rangers inadvertently crossed the Mexican border near El Paso. The Ranger captain did not survive the gun battle.

1896 In this year the governor sent the four Ranger companies into El Paso to stop an illegal heavyweight championship bout. The promoters staged the prizefight in Mexico opposite Langtry, Texas.

1901 Due to the legal dispute about making arrests, state authorities abolished the Frontier Battalion and formed the Ranger Force, which lasted until 1935.

ACKNOWLEDGMENTS

This book, *Tracking the Texas Rangers: The Nineteenth Century*, had its genesis at a meeting of the Texas State Historical Association where the two editors discussed the possibility of preparing an anthology on Texas Ranger history. Both concurred that it was a viable project, and subsequently spoke with Ron Chrisman, the director at the University of North Texas Press. With his initial encouragement we ventured forth. Thanks for all the help along the way, Ron. We received considerable additional support in preparing and publishing this book. For that assistance we wish to thank a number of people. Karen DeVinney's careful reading and editing of the manuscript greatly improved it. Without the scholarship and ability of the authors, of course, the book would not have been feasible. We are grateful for the cooperation of the eighteen authors whose studies are featured in our book. We also thank the publishers of their works who allowed us permission to use the essays. Two journals, the *Southwestern Historical Quarterly* and the *Journal of Big Bend Studies,* each allowed us to use two articles from their respective publications.

We acknowledge members of the historical community who examined the outline and contents of *Tracking the Texas Rangers.* That list includes notable historians such as Donaly Brice, Paul H. Carlson, Michael L. Collins, Mike Cox, Tom Crum, Arnoldo De Leon, Andrew Graybill, Stephen L. Hardin, Chuck Parsons, Louis R. Sadler, Paul N. Spellman, Charles Spurlin, and Robert M. Utley. All helped us consider what was included in this collection of Texas

Ranger articles. The staff at the Texas Ranger Museum in Waco has been especially helpful. In addition, the assistance of John Anderson of the State Archives in the selection of photographs should be recorded. Cecilia Gutierrez Venable located useable electronic files for us. Bonnie Tompkins, thanks for assisting with the preparation of the computer copy. Pearlene Vestal Glasrud read and reread our writings. Thanks Pearlene. Any errors or omissions we realize are our own for which we remain responsible.

Bruce A. Glasrud, Seguin, Texas
Harold J. Weiss Jr., Leander, Texas

IN PURSUIT OF THE TEXAS RANGERS: THE NINETEENTH CENTURY

Bruce A. Glasrud and Harold J. Weiss, Jr.

> The Rangers have both a black side and a white side but
> mostly, like all institutions composed of people, a range of
> grays separating the two. Sound history records the range
> as well as the poles.[1]

In Texas mythical history the Rangers exist as the saviors and protectors of Texas society. According to this story, the Rangers wore the white hats. They protected Anglo Texas from American Indians and from Mexican nationals, from peoples of color. They served as runaway slave catchers. They enforced white supremacy and Jim Crow laws and traditions. They made a stand against feudists. They arrested the bad guys. The task of determining the role of the Rangers as the state evolved and what they actually accomplished for the benefit of the state is a more difficult challenge. The actions of the Rangers fit no easy description. There is a dark side to the story of the Rangers; during the war with Mexico, for example, some murdered, pillaged, and raped. Yet these same Rangers eased the resultant United States victory. Even their beginning and the first use of the term "Texas Ranger" have mixed and complex definitions. It is not lack of interest that complicates the unveiling of the mythical force. With the possible exception of the Alamo, probably more has been written about the Texas Rangers than any other aspect of Texas history.

1

The historiography of Texas and its empire-building Ranger force can be approached from two different perspectives. Traditionalists have stressed a triumphal march of progress in the history of Anglo Texas. This mythic view contains a number of earth-shaking events and a pantheon of heroes in its creation story: William Travis, Jim Bowie and Davey Crockett at the fall of the Alamo; Sam Houston leading the Texas army against the Mexican army at the Battle of San Jacinto. The Texas Rangers, armed with six-shooters, rifles, and shotguns stood their ground and saved Texan settlements from depredations by Indian tribes, Mexican nationals, outlaw gangs, and modern-day gangsters. The basic account in the traditional line of reasoning is T. R. Fehrenbach, *Lone Star: A History of Texas and the Texans*. In these pages heroic Texan pioneers and fearless Rangers became a unique breed of men. To Fehrenbach, the "Texan history-mythology" explains the beginnings of the state. "It offers both inspiration and example while telling us how it all came about," he went on, it "gives even Johnny-come-latelies a feeling of shared experience."[2]

The second approach to the history of Texas has been called revisionism. Revisionists have taken a twofold course of action: (1) reexamine the myths and romantic landscapes that surround events in the Lone Star state; and (2) give coverage to the underclass in Texas history: blacks, Indians, Hispanics, women, and other underrepresented groups. For some epochs in the state's past, such as the Civil War and reconstruction, revisionists especially sought to debunk the traditional approach.

Revisionism brings to the forefront the Hispanic view of the Rangers as black hats. The classic example of this view is to be found in Americo Paredes, *"With His Pistol in His Hand": A Border Ballad and Its Hero*. In this perspective the Rangers exacerbated the conflict of cultures between Anglos and Mexican Americans on the border. A Hispanic ballad said it thus:

Then said Gregorio Cortez,

> With his pistol in his hand,
> "Ah, how many mounted rangers
> Against one lone Mexican!"[3]

This history-folklore in Hispanic culture has been passed from one generation to another.

Walter Prescott Webb became the dean of Ranger historians with the publication of *The Texas Rangers: A Century of Frontier Defense* in 1935. Since that date, all studies of the Ranger tradition begin with Webb's classic account. Two generations of Webb's disciples continued his approach to Ranger history, which he explained succinctly and clearly in his still unpublished autobiographical essay entitled, "A Texan's Story." As he acknowledged, the only "common thread" he could find in the writing of his seminal work on the Texas Rangers was that of the "great leaders," the "great captains" as he referred to them. Webb brought together a vast array of information from archival records and set the stage for future writers by stressing the work of these captains in the field. Yet the work becomes episodic after 1890, does not come to grips with the Hispanic-Ranger clash and, surprisingly, is not an overly readable book. Webb himself was more pleased with his other Ranger volume, *The Story of the Texas Rangers*.[4]

Webb's "top down" view of Ranger history has undergone changes recently. Many of the essays in our volume, *Tracking the Texas Rangers*, reflect the more recent approach of viewing the frontier institution from the "bottom up" as well as from varying vantage points. Less emphasis is placed on the traditional presentation of the "great captains" and more on the ranger majority in this compendium. We thus offer scholars and general readers alike not only a colorful and informative mosaic of scenes and stories but also accounts from well-recognized and established authors. The articles were all previously published, and bring a raft of scholarly insights to the study of this intrepid band of officers. The book focuses on central themes and events that amplify the complex story of the Texas Rangers, and provides access, in a single volume, to a wide-ranging spectrum of essays that capture the spirit and essence of the storied Rangers of the nineteenth century. The Rangers were complex and controversial and they left a legacy that is still being explored.

In recent decades attempts have been made to cram two centuries of Ranger moments into a single historical work. The best example is Charles M. Robinson III, *The Men Who Wear the Star: The Story of the Texas Rangers*. Nevertheless this valiant effort comes up short. Robinson used fewer archival records than Webb and ends in the early 1930s with the dramatic era of Bonnie and Clyde. In an important revisionist account, Julian Samora, Joe Bernal, and Albert Pena produced *Gunpowder Justice: A Reassessment of the Texas Rangers*. Stephen Hardin, in *The Texas Rangers*, puts together narration with black and color photographs to present a brief, appealing, and lively book of Ranger operations that covers two centuries.[5]

At the beginning of the twenty-first century, Webb's classic study has been replaced by several multi-volume histories of the Rangers. Two authors sit at the top of this list—Robert M. Utley and Mike Cox. Utley, a prominent historian of the American West, published a two-volume history of the Rangers—*Lone Star Justice: The First Century of the Texas Rangers* and *Lone Star Lawmen: The Second Century of the Texas Rangers*. Like Webb, Utley extensively used primary source records but, unlike Webb, his panoramic study is readable and objective. The other topnotch historical writer on the Rangers, especially on events in Texas, is Mike Cox. He considers himself to be a storyteller and readers agree. Cox has the ability to put a lot of data into his text and notes. His two-volume series is comprised of *The Texas Rangers: Wearing the Cinco Paso, 1821–1900* and *Time of the Rangers: From 1900 to the Present*.[6] The books by Cox and Utley have pushed into the background the works of Frederick Wilkins. This researcher of note provided a detailed account of Ranger service in the nineteenth century; his four volumes, including *The Legend Begins: The Texas Rangers, 1823–1845*, although uneven in their coverage, should be read in their entirety and not be overlooked by future Ranger historians.[7]

These general histories use photographs to give visual appeal to their narratives. Other studies reverse the process; they use narration as secondary to the extensive display of photos to tell the Ranger story. The best of the pictorial histories is John L. Davis, *The Texas Rangers: Images and Incidents*. Davis provides black-and-white camera shots by time lines and geographical areas. The more recent effort of Chuck Parsons, *The Texas Rangers*, a photo book with 200-plus pictures published by Arcadia Press, is an eye-catching collection of Ranger images.[8]

The types of Texas Ranger accounts proliferate; the advent of computers and online sites encourages the process. Secondary sources of value in addition to those already mentioned and those published in *Tracking the Texas Rangers* include well-written and lively stories in *Texas Ranger Dispatch Magazine*; its online site is http://www.texasranger.org/dispatch. Perhaps then visit *The Handbook of Texas Online* (http://www.tshaonline.org/handbook/online), begin with Ben Procter's article on "The Texas Rangers," followed by forays into essays on "John Coffee (Jack) Hays" or "Battle of Plum Creek" or "Leander H. McNelly" among numerous other possible Ranger-related entries. A multi-authored volume, led by Roger N. Conger, *Rangers in Texas*, also is recommended. Seven Rangers are featured—Jack Hays, Samuel Walker, Ben McCulloch, Rip Ford, Sul Ross, John B. Jones, and L. H. McNelly. The "Introduction" was written by prominent Texas historian Rupert N. Richardson. Mike Cox published two volumes of *Texas Ranger Tales*—they are informative and readable narratives from the storied writer.[9]

While Texas Ranger historians and writers search official records of the Ranger service for letters, telegrams, and reports, they also have used first-hand accounts by Rangers involved in the events and actions under study. These primary sources include diaries, memoirs, and autobiographies. The latter two, crafted long after the events have passed, can be selective, distorted, and self-serving. Yet all three sources reveal how individuals saw themselves and see those who worked around them. A number of these first-hand accounts by Rangers in the field have become classics, and have combined both subjectivity and objectivity.

Such accounts include coverage of Rangers as military figures: John S. Ford, *Rip Ford's Texas*, and Samuel C. Reid, *The Scouting Expeditions of McCulloch's Texas Rangers*. The accounts also portray Rangers as peace officers: George Durham (as told to Clyde Wantland), *Taming the Nueces Strip: The Story of McNelly's Rangers*; James B. Gillett, *Six Years With the Texas Rangers, 1875–1881*; and Daniel W. Roberts, *Rangers and Sovereignty*.[10]

As Walter Webb emphasized and other writers have accepted, Ranger captains were resourceful and important, especially when competent. As a result numerous biographies of Ranger leaders have been published. Biographers work with different formats in putting together a person's life. Characterizations may range from cradle-to-grave narratives and topical chapter headings to stories of human interrelationships and tell-all exposes. A few Ranger biographies published years ago have stood the test of time, such as James K. Greer, *Colonel Jack Hays: Texas Frontier Leader and California Builder*.[11]

More recent biographical studies have found additional source materials, using newer analytical tools, and connecting the subject matter to the wider world. In this vein mention should be made of Thomas W. Cutrer, *Ben McCulloch and the Frontier Military Tradition*; Chuck Parsons and Marianne E. Hall Little, *Captain L. H. McNelly—Texas Ranger: The Life and Times of a Fighting Man*, and Richard McCaslin, *Fighting Stock: John S. "Rip" Ford of Texas*. One would be remiss not to read Bob Alexander's first-rate Ira Aten biography, *Rawhide Ranger, Ira Aten: Enforcing Law on the Frontier*. The recent volumes of three of the "Four Great Captains": Paul N. Spellman, *Captain J. A. Brooks: Texas Ranger* and his *Captain John H. Rogers: Texas Ranger*; and Harold J. Weiss, Jr., *Yours to Command: The Life and Legend of Texas Ranger Captain Bill McDonald* add to our knowledge of effective Ranger leadership. So too does Chuck Parsons' insightful biography of the fourth, *Captain John R. Hughes: Lone Star Ranger.*[12]

Ranger historians have taken events in the lives of the Rangers and dissected and analyzed them. Traditionalists and revisionists have differed over the way to interpret the events and happenings. The Sutton-Taylor feud and the involvement of the Rangers in South Texas in the late 1800s is an example of the traditionalist and revisionist divide. Chuck Parsons, in his *The Sutton-Taylor Feud: The Deadliest Blood Feud in Texas*, sees the feud as a violent conflict between two families and their sympathizers, which lasted for several generations. This traditional view has been challenged by James M. Smallwood, *The Feud That Wasn't: The Taylor Ring, Bill Sutton, John Wesley Hardin, and Violence in Texas*. Smallwood posits the thesis that the feud should be seen in terms of a crime ring and the peace officers who pursued them amid the racial violence of Reconstruction Texas.[13] The two books, published within a year of each other, both won book awards.

To decipher the mystique of the Rangers we must look at their origins and their practices. The first mention of men who would ultimately become the Texas Rangers occurred in 1823 when Stephen F. Austin announced that he would hire ten men to serve as "rangers" in an effort to defeat a band of Indians. In 1835 the Texas legislature established a group known as Rangers to protect and help the settlers during the revolution. These and many other aspects of the formation and history of the Texas Rangers can be sought out in the first article in our book, *Tracking the Texas Rangers*.

The article, by one of the co-editors of this volume, Harold J. Weiss, Jr., introduces us to the subject in "The Texas Rangers Revisited: Old Themes and New Viewpoints," an article originally published in the *Southwestern Historical Quarterly*. Weiss effectively argues that understanding the Rangers can best be accomplished by viewing them through the perspective of three eras: (1) 1823–1874, the use of Rangers as citizen-soldiers; (2) 1874–1935, Rangers operating as lawmen who investigated crimes, pursued lawbreakers, and evaluated evidence; (3) 1935–present. In 1935 the Rangers became part of the Department of Public Safety (DPS), and operated as modern-day investigators. Weiss provides an overview of the complexity of understanding the role of Rangers, how they operated, and how they were interpreted historically.[14]

An evaluation of the nineteenth-century Texas Rangers must be viewed over time and in varied settings. Their use by their operators, the largely Anglo settlers, was often political. Stephen L. Hardin, a noted historian of the Texas revolutionary era, succinctly portrays the beginnings of Ranger operations in the Lone Star state. His article, the second in *Tracking the Texas Rangers: The Nineteenth Century*, provides fresh and intriguing analysis and interpretation of the first efforts of the Texas Rangers. Hardin argues, in "'Valor, Wisdom, and Experience': Early Texas Rangers and the Nature of Frontier Leadership," first published in *Osprey Military Journal*, that a vital element in the success of Ranger actions derived from their leaders. In another Hardin article (with Richard Hooks), "The Early Years, 1823–1839," taken from the book, *The Texas Rangers*, he especially stresses the first organized companies by Texan officials in 1835. A corps of Rangers, commanded by Robert "Three-Legged Willie" Williamson, moved into frontier lands and took part in the fight for control of the land between Anglos, Mexicans, and Indians.[15]

One of the first uses of the Rangers, as mentioned earlier, was to expel the Native Americans, such as the proud and daunting Comanche, and to encourage Anglo settlers to come to Texas. Donaly E. Brice, for many years a resource of import in the State Archives, clearly demonstrates in his article, "The Great Comanche Raid of 1840," the role of the Rangers, as well as other citizen-soldiers, in the struggle against the Comanche in 1840. Brice documents the reasons behind both the Comanche and the Anglo efforts and discusses the strategy and tactics precipitated by Rangers that ultimately led to Anglo Texas victory in 1840.[16] Brice's article is the third in our anthology.

Two key characteristics of the early Rangers were their horseback riding skills and their use of the six-shooter. As told in the entry by Stephen Moore, Jack Hays and a small company of Rangers demonstrated the value of the Colt revolver against a large Comanche party led by Yellow Wolf at the Battle of Walker's Creek in 1844. The Rangers maneuvered, attacked, and stood off counterattacks. In the end more Comanche were slain or wounded than Rangers. Hays declared about the Paterson five shots: "I cannot recommend these arms too highly." Moore's account is located in his book, *Savage Frontier*; the title of the article, the fourth in our volume, is "The Deadly Colts on Walker's Creek."[17]

Early Rangers were also called upon for work patrolling the border with Mexico and were present when the United States declared war on Mexico in 1846. As Stephen B. Oates, in "Los Diablos Tejanos," articulates so well, Texas Rangers joined the U.S. march into Mexico and in many respects were important elements, as scouts, spies, and fighters, of the United States' victory. They also became known as "los diablos Tejanos" due to some of their nefarious actions. The War with Mexico opened up opportunities for Rangers who disliked Mexicans to murder them with dispatch, as they did in a series of sordid incidents. Oates' classic account of the Rangers during the War, the fifth article in *Tracking the Texas Rangers*, is readable and dramatic.[18]

A little-known event in Texas Ranger history, and vitally important to antebellum Texas history, took place in South Texas in the middle of the decade of the 1850s. James H. Callahan and his Ranger company crossed the border between Texas and Mexico into the independent nation south of Texas. They engaged Mexican troops and occupied and burned Piedras Negras. Their motivation has been questioned by contemporaries as well as historians. Ostensibly Callahan's Rangers crossed into Mexico looking for Indian raiders, but more likely they were looking for some of the more than four thousand runaway slaves from the United States residing in Mexico. It was an attempt by slaveowners to reacquire former slaves. This episode has been covered by Ron Tyler in "The Callahan Expedition" in *The Handbook of Texas Online*, by Ronnie C. Tyler, "The Callahan Expedition of 1855: Indians or Negroes?" and by Ernest C. Shearer, "The Callahan Expedition, 1855."[19] The most recent explication of this controversial episode is Michael L. Collins' account from his thoughtful and readable book, *Texas Devils: Rangers and Regulars on the Lower Rio Grande, 1846–1861*. Collins' article is the sixth in our collection. In the end, the Callahan expedition rekindled old fears and hatred in people living along the border. To Anglo Texans the heroic Rangers stood as sentinels in the southern reaches of the Lone Star state. To those south of the border, these same fighters violated Mexican sovereignty and used scorched-earth methods.[20]

During the middle of the nineteenth century other skirmishes involving the Rangers took place. In the decade of the 1850s the Rangers continued their vigilant stand against Indian raids and Mexican incursions on the border. As explained in the seventh article in this anthology, W. J. Hughes points out in "Rip Ford's Indian Fight on the Canadian," that at one point in 1858 Rip Ford's ranging column, with his Indian allies, crossed the Canadian River and attacked a Comanche village under Iron Jacket. The ensuing battle took place over miles of open ground and showed that Indian country could be penetrated.[21]

Living on both sides of the Texas-Mexican border, Juan Nepomuceno Cortina was viewed by Anglo Texans as a cattle rustler and a killer and by Mexican Americans as a social bandit fighting for equality and justice. The first so-called Cortina War began in 1859 when Cortina shot a Brownsville city marshal who had been abusing a Mexican prisoner. Later, Cortina raided the town with a large body of men and killed several people. In time, pursued by the U.S. Army and Texas Rangers under the command of William Tobin and Rip Ford, Cortina retreated into Mexico after army regulars killed a number of his followers. In 1861 Cortina again appeared on the border in Zapata County and thus began the second Cortina War. This affair ended when Confederate soldiers killed and captured several of his men. Cortina, sometimes referred to as "The Red Robber of the Rio Grande," remained at odds with American and Mexican authorities until his death in 1894. The well-written eighth article in *Tracking the Texas Rangers*, "Rangers, 'Rip' Ford, and the Cortina War," is a segment from Richard B. McCaslin's first-rate biography of "Rip" Ford, *Fighting Stock: John S. "Rip" Ford of Texas*. McCaslin weaves the efforts of the United States Army and the Texas Rangers to track, capture, or defeat Cortina.[22]

Although the early Rangers, "los diablos Tejanos," treated Mexicans with disdain as in the war with Mexico, the Cortina wars, and later in the years from 1910 to 1920, in an intriguing study, "Hispanic Texas Rangers Contribute to Peace on the Texas Frontier, 1838–1880," David E. Screws discusses the use of Mexican American Rangers during the nineteenth century. In the ninth article in this collection, the author discovered records revealing that nearly four hundred men with Spanish surnames served in the Texas Rangers between 1838 and 1880, at least ten of them in the capacity of an officer. Some of the units were entirely composed of Hispanics but most of them consisted of both Mexican American and Anglo Rangers. The Hispanics who served in the ranks of the Texas Rangers made significant contributions to maintaining the peace along the border with Mexico. "They fought the same enemies," and as Screws notes, "their often brutal methods attested to the harshness of the times."[23]

Service with the Rangers, for well connected and ambitious individuals, was a great stepping stone to other offices and duties. As a result, the story of an incident sometimes could change over time. In a remarkable job of research and detective reasoning and writing, Paul H. Carlson and Tom Crum, in the tenth article in this book, "The 'Battle' at Pease River and the Question of Reliable Sources in the Recapture of Cynthia Ann Parker," compare accounts of the December 1860 struggle and how those accounts later were used by politicians such as Lawrence Sullivan "Sul" Ross. The authors reviewed the role of the Rangers in the battle and in the accounts. They investigated the so-called "Battle of Pease River," concluding that what became, in Texans' collective memory, a battle that broke Comanche military power was actually a massacre, primarily of women.[24]

Fighting against Native Americans and Mexican nationals was not the only function of Texas Rangers in the nineteenth century. They targeted outlaws in their role as peace officers. One of the more noted gunmen in Texas history was John Wesley Hardin. He took part in the Sutton-Taylor feud. He shot and killed more than one person, including a deputy sheriff in Brown County. Hardin then fled the state. In a dramatic encounter, as related by Leon Metz in "Capturing the Grand Mogul" from his biography of *John Wesley Hardin*, Ranger John Armstrong and other lawmen subdued and captured Hardin on a train in Florida in 1877. The next year he was sentenced to a prison term by a Texas court. After his pardon, Hardin went to El Paso in the 1890s and was shot and killed by John Selman. "Capturing the Grand Mogul" is the eleventh article in our anthology.[25]

In one other interesting episode the infamous outlaw, Sam Bass, was killed by the Rangers. In 1878, after committing several robberies and being chased by Texas Rangers, the Bass gang decided to rob a bank at Round Rock. As told by Bob Boze Bell and Rick Miller in a vivid account, "Bad Day at Round Rock" (found in our Encomium), a Ranger shot and killed the Texas Robin Hood in a wild melee.[26]

An unfortunate chapter in Ranger chronicles also occurred in the 1870s with the Salt War. Anglos and Hispanics disputed the control and use of salt beds near El Paso. Speculators entered the fray. In the ensuing violence the various groups committed acts of murder as well as other atrocious deeds, and a Ranger detachment serving under John B. Tays even surrendered to an opposing force. The Salt War has been covered exceedingly well by Paul Cool in his award-winning book, *Salt Warriors: Insurgency on the Rio Grande*.[27]

By the latter nineteenth century Texas Rangers, especially after the new organizational law of 1874 which created the Frontier Battalion, frequently were stationed in rural communities and found some of their focus on cattle. They were not alone. Farther north in Canada, the Northwest Mounted Police also found themselves with such duties. In a readable transnational approach, Andrew R. Graybill's article, "Rangers and Mounties Defending the Cattleman's Empire," compares the use of the two well-known police and law enforcement agencies. Originally published in *Agricultural History*, then revised and included as a chapter in *Policing the Great Plains: Rangers, Mounties, and the North American Frontier, 1875–1910*, Graybill's piece is a valuable study of the cattlemen who seized control of the range by fencing pastures and water holes and by evicting squatters. When less well-to-do homesteaders resisted this exclusion, government authorities dispatched their rural constabularies to protect the cattlemen. Graybill's article is the twelfth in *Tracking the Texas Rangers*.[28]

The Texas Rangers and the Northwest Mounted Police were not the only ranging units in the latter nineteenth, early twentieth century. Such units existed in both Arizona and New Mexico. Information on the Arizona Rangers can be located in Bill O'Neal's work, *The Arizona Rangers*, as well as in a well-done photo book, published by Arcadia, M. David De Soucy and Marshall Trimble, *Arizona Rangers*. For the New Mexico Rangers, see two works by Chuck Hornung, *New Mexico's Rangers: The Mounted Police* (another Arcadia publication) and *Fullerton's Rangers: A History of the New Mexico Territorial Police*.[29]

James M. Day, "Rangers of the Last Frontier of Texas," a study of the work of Company D in the Trans-Pecos region of Texas, includes information on Rangers Ira Aten, Frank Jones, John Hughes, and Bass Outlaw. In its law enforcement work in West Texas, Company D of the frontier battalion took part in violent operations and in plodding investigative work chasing outlaws. The last Indian "battle" in Texas took place in 1881 near Guadalupe Peak in the Diablo Moutains when Rangers killed four men, two women, and two children; the Apaches wore blankets and the Rangers allegedly could not tell their sex or age. Other duties followed; in El Paso in 1896 a large number of Rangers went to that city to prevent a prizefight and to restrict gambling. Day's study on these Rangers is the thirteenth in this anthology. For a more extensive treatment of Company D, Bob Alexander, *Winchester Warriors: Texas Rangers of Company D, 1874–1901*, is highly recommended.[30]

Some Texas Rangers gained national attention for their contributions to the establishment of law and order. In the rush to tell their stories, it is often forgotten that relatively unknown privates also contributed, acting bravely, following orders, and engaging outlaws in life-threatening situations. In a lively, well-written account of the death of a Ranger in Company D, Chuck Parsons investigated "The Jesse Evans Gang and the Death of Texas Ranger George R. Bingham." Bingham, a virtually unknown Texas Ranger, died in the line of duty while engaged in an 1880 gunfight against the Jesse Evans outlaw gang in West Texas. Jesse Evans first appeared in the Lincoln County War in New Mexico, then came to Texas, killed a Ranger, committed robbery, went to prison, escaped, and disappeared. Parsons' account is the fourteenth in *Tracking the Texas Rangers*.[31] Other Ranger privates, at the beginning also relatively unknown, avoided death and went on to outstanding non-Ranger careers. Born in 1871, Everett E. Townsend served as a Texas Ranger beginning in 1890 for three years and again at the end of the decade for two more years. After leaving the Rangers Townsend served as sheriff of Brewster County, as state representative, and became known as the "Father of Big Bend National Park" for his long and heroic struggle to make the park a reality.[32]

By the end of the nineteenth century new issues of law and order began to appear in Ranger reports. The rise of industrialization in the United States brought conflicts between labor and capital. Texas was no exception. In fact, the forces opposed to laborers' rights were more entrenched in Texas than in most other states. In a thorough study about coal mining at Thurber, Texas, Marilyn Rhinehart shows the ins and outs of the relations between a mining company, labor organizations, politicians, and Ranger Company B under Captains Samuel McMurry and Bill McDonald. Thurber's mines held the principal soft-coal deposits in the state. Today Thurber is a ghost town. Rhinehart's polished and well-written account derives from her chapter, "The Struggle for the Individual and the Union, 1888–1903" in her first-rate book, *A Way of Work and a Way of Life*; it becomes the fifteenth article in *Tracking the Texas Rangers*.[33]

In the nineteenth century the Texas Rangers had several distinctive characteristics that worked for and against their place in history inside and outside the Lone Star state. For the most part, they came from the common folk and had the stamp of approval of the majority of white Texans. To combat Mexican nationals and Indian tribes and go after outlaws and gunmen, the Rangers also made themselves into a courageous and generally hard-working outfit. They made horseback charges in battlefield formations. They adopted Colt revolvers. They used the telegraph and the railroads to cover vast distances in the state. They showed resolve in difficult situations. At the same time though, the Rangers in Texas in the 1800s had human frailties. They sometimes misjudged their opponents' strength or tenacity. At times they faltered in the face of the enemy. Most tragic of all, their biases and prejudices, which often reflected those of their generation, were used to wreak violence upon the powerless. They destroyed Indian villages, killed Mexican civilians, and employed the practice of *la ley de fuga* (the law of the fugitive) which meant to kill "escaping" prisoners. This chameleon-like attitude followed the Rangers even into the twentieth century.

The Texas Rangers have never existed in a vacuum and have always been viewed with a mixture of reality and myth. For many years the Rangers served as Indian fighters and peace officers on the frontiers of Texas. In the mythical world the role of the Ranger is inseparably linked to the use of the revolver and the image of the gunfighter. As Texas and its inhabitants grew and modernized, so too did the Texas Rangers. By the end of the nineteenth century the Texas Rangers sought to become new and respected lawmen.

With a further reorganization transpiring in 1901 Ranger duties and responsibilities changed, and the Rangers came under deeper scrutiny. A careful study of Ranger operations offers varied options. An individual Ranger might be a white-hatted hero, an intrepid individual, a heavy-handed officer, a black-hatted antihero, an organization man, a technology-oriented detective, or a modern pop culture icon. As noted earlier, Ranger actions occasionally made it difficult to determine who upheld the law and who violated it. These labels and behaviors help sum up the lives of the Rangers in the nineteenth century Lone Star state. They wore, depending on individuals and circumstances, white, black, and gray hats.

NOTES

1. Robert M. Utley, "Images of the Texas Rangers," in *The Way West: True Stories of the American Frontier*, ed. James A. Crutchfield (New York: Tom Doherty Associates, 2005), 263.

2. T. R. Fehrenbach, *Lone Star: A History of Texas and the Texans* (1968; New York: Da Capo Press, 2000); T. R. Fehrenbach, "Texas Mythology: Now and Forever," in *Texas Myths*, ed. Robert F. O'Connor (College Station: Texas A&M University Press, 1986), 219.

3. Americo Paredes, *"With His Pistol in His Hand": A Border Ballad and Its Hero* (Austin: University of Texas Press, 1958), 171–172.

4. Walter Prescott Webb, "A Texan's Story," Walter P. Webb Papers, Dolph Briscoe Center for American History, University of Texas, Austin; Llerena B. Friend, "W. P. Webb's Texas Rangers," *Southwestern Historical Quarterly* 74 (January 1971): 293–323; for a biography of Webb see Necah Stewart Furman, *Walter Prescott Webb: His Life and Impact* (Albuquerque: University of New Mexico Press, 1976).

5. Charles M. Robinson III, *The Men Who Wear the Star: The Story of the Texas Rangers* (New York: Random House, 2000); Julian Samora, Joe Bernal, and Albert Pena, *Gunpowder Justice: A Reassessment of the Texas Rangers* (Notre Dame: University of Notre Dame Press, 1979); Stephen L. Hardin and Richard Hook, *The Texas Rangers* (Oxford, Eng.: Osprey Publishing, 1991).

6. Robert M. Utley, *Lone Star Justice: The First Century of the Texas Rangers* (New York: Oxford University Press, 2002); Robert M. Utley, *Lone Star Lawmen: The Second Century of the Texas Rangers* (New York: Oxford University Press, 2007); Mike Cox, *The Texas Rangers: Wearing the Cinco Paso, 1821–*

1900 (New York: Tom Doherty Associates, 2008); and Mike Cox, *Time of the Rangers: From 1900 to the Present* (New York: Tom Doherty Associates, 2009).

7. Frederick Wilkins, *The Legend Begins: The Texas Rangers, 1823–1845* (Austin: State House Press, 1996); Frederick Wilkins, *The Highly Irregular Irregulars: Texas Rangers in the Mexican War* (Austin: Eakin Press, 1990); Frederick Wilkins, *Defending the Borders: The Texas Rangers, 1848–1861* (Austin: State House Press, 2001); Frederick Wilkins, *The Law Comes to Texas: The Texas Rangers, 1870–1901* (Austin: State House Press, 1999).

8. John L. Davis, *The Texas Rangers: Images and Incidents* (1991; Austin: University of Texas Press, 1993); Chuck Parsons, *The Texas Rangers* (Mt. Pleasant, South Carolina: Arcadia Press, 2011).

9. *Texas Ranger Dispatch Magazine* (http://www.texasranger.org/dispatch); *The Handbook of Texas Online* (http://www.tshaonline.org/handbook/online); Ben H. Procter, "The Texas Rangers," *The Handbook of Texas Online* (http://www.tshaonline.org/handbook/online); Ben H. Procter, *Just One Riot: Episodes of Texas Rangers in the 20th Century* (Austin: Eakin Press, 1991); Roger N. Conger, et al., *Rangers of Texas* (Waco: Texian Press, 1969); Mike Cox, *Texas Ranger Tales* (Plano, TX: Republic of Texas Press, 1998).

10. John Salmon Ford, *Rip Ford's Texas*, ed. Stephen B. Oates (Austin: University of Texas Press, 1963); Samuel C. Reid, *The Scouting Expeditions of McCulloch's Texas Rangers . . .* (Philadelphia: G. B. Zieber, 1847); George Durham (as told to Clyde Wantland), *Taming the Nueces Strip: The Story of McNelly's Rangers* (Austin: University of Texas Press, 1962); James B. Gillett, *Six Years With the Texas Rangers, 1875–1881* (Austin: Von Boeckmann Jones, 1921); Daniel Webster Roberts, *Rangers and Sovereignty* (San Antonio: Wood Printing and Engraving, 1914).

11. James K. Greer, *Colonel Jack Hays: Texas Frontier Leader and California Builder* (1952; College Station: Texas A&M University Press, 1987).

12. Thomas W. Cutrer, *Ben McCulloch and the Frontier Military Tradition* (Chapel Hill: University of North Carolina Press, 1993); Chuck Parsons and Marianne E. Hall Little, *Captain L. H. McNelly—Texas Ranger—The Life and Times of a Fighting Man* (Austin: State House Press, 2001); Richard McCaslin, *Fighting Stock: John S "Rip" Ford of Texas* (Fort Worth: Texas Christian University Press, 2011); Bob Alexander, *Rawhide Ranger, Ira Aten: Enforcing Law on the Frontier* (Denton: University of North Texas Press, 2011); Paul N. Spellman, *Captain J. A. Brooks: Texas Ranger* (Denton: University of North Texas Press, 2007); Paul N. Spellman, *Captain John H. Rogers: Texas Ranger* (Denton: University of North Texas Press, 2003); Harold J. Weiss, Jr., *Yours to Command: The Life and Legend of Texas Ranger Captain Bill McDonald* (Denton: University of North Texas Press, 2009); Chuck Parsons, *Captain John R. Hughes: Lone Star Ranger* (Denton: University of North Texas Press, 2011).

13. Chuck Parsons, *The Sutton-Taylor Feud: The Deadliest Blood Feud in Texas* (Denton: University of North Texas Press, 2009); James M. Smallwood, *The Feud That Wasn't: The Taylor Ring, Bill Sutton, John Wesley Hardin, and Violence in Texas* (College Station: Texas A&M University Press, 2008).

14. Harold J. Weiss, Jr., "The Texas Rangers Revisited: Old Themes and New Viewpoints," *Southwestern Historical Quarterly* 97 (April 1994): 621–640.

15. Stephen L. Hardin, "'Valor, Wisdom and Experience': Early Texas Rangers and the Nature of Frontier Leadership," *Osprey Military Journal* 4.2 (2002): 50–56; Stephen L. Hardin and Richard Hooks, "The Early Years, 1823–1839," in *The Texas Rangers* (London: Osprey Publishing, 1991), 3–7.

16. Donaly E. Brice, "The Great Comanche Raid of 1840," *South Texas Studies* (1996): 75–107. See also his book, Donaly E. Brice, *The Great Comanche Raid of 1840: Boldest Indian Attack of the Texas Republic* (Austin: Eakin Press, 1987).

17. Stephen L. Moore, "The Deadly Colts on Walker's Creek," in *Savage Frontier: Rangers, Riflemen, and the Indian Wars in Texas, 1842–1845* (Denton: University of North Texas Press, 2010), 4:139–154, 235–237.

18. Stephen B. Oates, "Los Diablos Tejanos," *American West* 2 (Summer 1965): 41–50.

19. Ron Tyler, "The Callahan Expedition," *The Handbook of Texas Online* (http://www.tshaonline.org/handbook/online); Ronnie C. Tyler, "The Callahan Expedition of 1855: Indians or Negroes?" *Southwestern Historical Quarterly* 70 (April 1967); Ernest C. Shearer, "The Callahan Expedition, 1855," *Southwestern Historical Quarterly* 54 (October 1951): 430–451.

20. Michael L. Collins, *Texas Devils: Rangers and Regulars on the Lower Rio Grande, 1846–1861* (Norman: University of Oklahoma Press, 2008), 79–88, 271–272.

21. W. J. Hughes, "Rip Ford's Indian Fight on the Canadian," *Panhandle Plains Historical Review* 30 (1957): 1–26.

22. Richard B. McCaslin, *Fighting Stock: John S. "Rip" Ford of Texas* (Fort Worth: TCU Press, 2011), 82–98, 294–297. On Cortina, see also Charles M. Robinson III, "The Cortina War," in *The Men Who Wear the Star: The Story of the Texas Rangers* (New York: Random House, 2000), 121–37, 303–305; Jerry D. Thompson, ed., *Juan Cortina and the Texas-Mexico Frontier, 1859–1877* (El Paso: Texas Western Press, 1994); Jerry D. Thompson, *Cortina: Defending the Mexican Name in Texas* (College Station: Texas A&M University Press, 2007).

23. David E. Screws, "Hispanic Texas Rangers Contribute to Peace on the Texas Frontier, 1838–1880," *Journal of Big Bend Studies* 13 (2001): 27–36, quote on 34.

24. Paul H. Carlson and Tom Crum, "The 'Battle' at Pease River and the Question of Reliable Sources in the Recapture of Cynthia Ann Parker," *Southwestern Historical Quarterly* 113 (July 2009): 32–52. See also their book, Paul H. Carlson and Tom Crum, *Myth, Memory and Massacre: The Pease River Capture of Cynthia Ann Parker* (Lubbock: Texas Tech University Press, 2010).

25. Leon Metz, "Capturing the Grand Mogul," in *John Wesley Hardin: Dark Angel of Texas* (El Paso: Mangan Books, 1996), 158–172, 320–321.

26. Bob Boze Bell and Rick Miller, "Bad Day at Round Rock," *True West* 40.5 (July 2002): 34–36. The authoritative work on Sam Bass is Rick Miller, *Sam Bass and Gang* (Austin: State House Press, 1999). For an older survey of note, see Wayne Gard, *Sam Bass* (Lincoln: University of Nebraska Press, 1964). The role of outlawry can be ascertained in Frank R. Prassel, *The Great American Outlaw: A Legacy of Fact and Fiction* (Norman: University of Oklahoma Press, 1993).

27. Paul Cool, *Salt Warriors: Insurgency on the Rio Grande* (College Station: Texas A&M University Press, 2008).

28. Andrew R. Graybill, "Rural Police and the Defense of the Cattleman's Empire in Texas and Alberta, 1875–1900," *Agricultural History* 79 (Summer 2005): 253–280. Graybill's book, *Policing the Great Plains: Rangers, Mounties, and the North American Frontier, 1875–1910* (Lincoln: University of Nebraska Press, 2007), covers more thoroughly the items raised in his article.

29. M. David De Soucy and Marshall Trimble, *Arizona Rangers, 1901–1909* (Charleston, SC: Arcadia Publishing, 2008); Bill O'Neal, *The Arizona Rangers* (Austin: Eakin Press, 1987); Chuck Hornung, *Fullerton's Rangers: A History of the New Mexico Territorial Mounted Police* (Jefferson, NC: McFarland, 2011); Chuck Hornung, *New Mexico's Rangers: The Mounted Police* (Charleston, SC: Arcadia Publishing, 2010).

30. James M. Day, "Rangers of the Last Frontier of Texas," *Password* 45 (Winter 2000): 159–174; Bob Alexander, *Winchester Warriors: Texas Rangers of Company D, 1874–1901* (Denton: University of North Texas Press, 2009).

31. Chuck Parsons, "The Jesse Evans Gang and the Death of Texas Ranger George R. Bingham," *Journal of Big Bend Studies* 20 (2008): 75–87.

32. Clifford B. Casey, "Everett Ewing Townsend," in *Mirages, Mysteries and Reality: Brewster County Texas: The Big Bend of the Rio Grande* (Hereford, Texas: Pioneer Book Publishers, 1972), 408–410. For various dates of Townsend's Ranger service, see Parsons, *Captain John R. Hughes*, p. 332, n. 99.

33. Marilyn D. Rhinehart, "The Struggle for the Individual and the Union, 1888–1903," in *A Way of Work and a Way of Life: Coal Mining in Thurber, Texas, 1888–1926* (College Station: Texas A&M University Press, 1992), 71–91, 134–138.

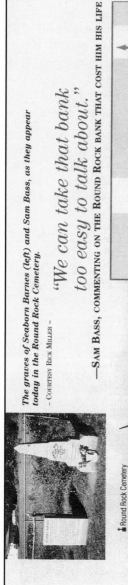

The graves of Seaborn Barnes (left) and Sam Bass, as they appear today in the Round Rock Cemetery.

— COURTESY RICK MILLER –

"We can take that bank too easy to talk about."

—SAM BASS, COMMENTING ON THE ROUND ROCK BANK THAT COST HIM HIS LIFE

The Bass gang's path after firing their horses in the alley

Bank

Highsmith's Stable

Saloon

Moore and Grimes

* * Connor, Herold and Highsmith

Lampasas Street

Dick Ware

Barber Shop

Koppel's Store

The gang's path after the shooting starts.

Maj. J. Jones and J.F. Tubbs

Georgetown Avenue

Mays Street

Alley

Round Rock Cemetery

The Sam Bass camp is believed to have been in this area and the gang returned here to fetch more rifles.

Bass was found approximately 3 miles north near the railroad.

First Baptist Church

Oatts home

OLD ROUND ROCK

Jim Murphy sitting in the Livingston and Mays store saw Bass and Jackson fly by as they raced through old Round Rock.

Quick house

Brushy Creek

The Georgetown spur of the International & Great Northern R. R. was under construction at this time.

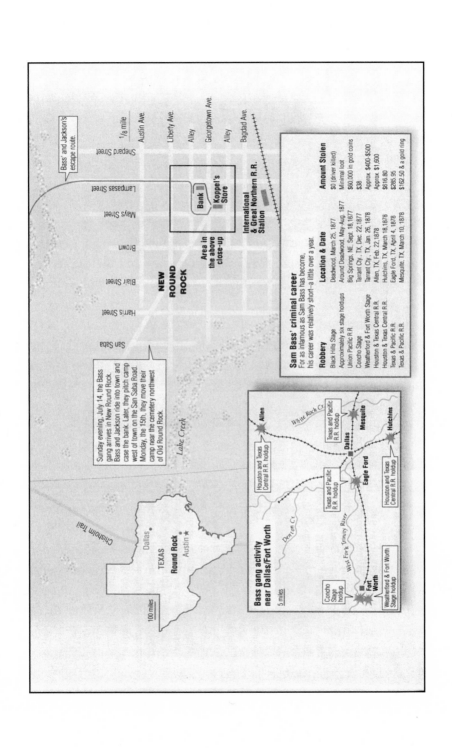

Bass and Jackson's escape route.

Austin Ave.

Liberty Ave.

Alley

Georgetown Ave.

Alley

Bagdad Ave.

⅛ mile

Shepard Street

Lampasas Street

Mays Street

Brown

Blair Street

Harris Street

San Saba

NEW ROUND ROCK

Bank

Koppel's Store

Area in the above close-up

International & Great Northern R.R. Station

Sunday evening, July 14, the Bass gang arrives in New Round Rock. Bass and Jackson ride into town and case the bank. Later, they pitch camp west of town on the San Saba Road. Monday, the 15th, they move their camp near the cemetery northwest of Old Round Rock.

Lake Creek

Chisholm Trail

Dallas

TEXAS

Round Rock

Austin ★

100 miles

Sam Bass' criminal career

For as infamous as Sam Bass has become, his career was relatively short—a little over a year.

Robbery	Location & Date	Amount Stolen
Black Hills Stage	Deadwood, March 25, 1877	$0 (driver killed)
Approximately six stage holdups	Around Deadwood, May-Aug. 1877	Minimal loot
Union Pacific R.R.	Big Springs, NE. Sept. 18, 1877	$60,000 in gold coins
Concho Stage	Tarrant Cty. TX, Dec. 22, 1877	$38
Weatherford & Fort Worth Stage	Tarrant Cty. TX, Jan. 26, 1878	Approx $400-$500
Houston & Texas Central R.R.	Allen, TX, Feb. 22, 1878	Approx $1,600
Houston & Texas Central R.R.	Hutchins, TX, March 18, 1878	$616.80
Texas & Pacific R.R.	Eagle Ford, TX, April 4, 1878	$285.95
Texas & Pacific R.R.	Mesquite, TX, March 10, 1878	$162.50 & a gold ring

Bass gang activity near Dallas/Fort Worth

5 miles

Allen

White Rock Cr.

Mesquite

Texas and Pacific R.R. holdup

Hutchins

Houston and Texas Central R.R. holdup

Dallas

Texas and Pacific R.R. holdup

Eagle Ford

Houston and Texas Central R.R. holdup

West Fork Trinity River

Denton Cr.

West Fork Trinity River

Concho Stage holdup

Fort Worth

Weatherford & Fort Worth Stage holdup

ENCOMIUM: BAD DAY AT ROUND ROCK

Bob Boze Bell and Rick Miller

July 19, 1878

Sam Bass has a bold plan. He and his outlaw band will case the bank in Round Rock, Texas, one more time and then strike tomorrow (Saturday) when the surrounding farmers make their weekly deposits.

The air is hot and muggy as three of the gang, including Bass, rein up in an alley behind the bank, tie off, and walk around to the main street (Georgetown Ave.) for one more look around. A fourth outlaw, Jim Murphy, has stopped at a store on the way into town, supposedly to quiz locals about the presence of lawmen. He is actually an informant and has warned the Rangers of the gang's plans.

It's about 4:00 p.m. as Bass, Seaborn Barnes, and Frank Jackson walk west along the north sidewalk, making mental notes as they survey the town. Two of the men carry saddlebags. Hoping to avoid suspicion, they cross the street and approach Koppel's store to buy tobacco.

Two local lawmen, "Caige" Grimes and Maurice Moore, spot what they believe to be concealed weapons on the Bass boys and start following the trio (although officials had received advance warning from gang-member Murphy, it is unclear whether these two lawmen suspected the trio of being members of the Bass Gang). Walking into Koppel's, Bass and company step to the counter and engage the clerk. Seconds later, Deputy Grimes walks in and puts his hand on Sam Bass (feeling for the weapon), asking at the same time if he is armed. The outlaw actually says "Yes," and the three bandits spin and fire as one. Hit five times, Grimes staggers to the door, calling out "Boys, don't."

Standing in the doorway, Deputy Moore takes a bullet in the chest but jerks his pistol and fires into the smoke. As the shooting continues, he staggers backwards out of the hornet's nest.

Sam Bass grimaces in pain as he and his men scramble for the street (Sam lost the middle and ring fingers of his right hand in the exchange with Moore).

Texas Ranger Dick Ware is in the barbershop when he hears the shooting and runs into the street to join the fight. He ducks behind a hitching post and fires at the fleeing outlaws as they cross George-town. The outlaws fire back, hitting the hitching post and sending splinters flying.

At Highsmith's livery stable, the owner and two Rangers run through the stalls to head off the outlaws as they come down the alley.

Barnes, Jackson, and the wounded Bass enter the alley and make a beeline for their horses. A saloon keeper fires at the fleeing bandits from his rear doorway and the outlaws slow their advance, warily eyeballing every window and door. When the gang approaches the rear of the stable, the Rangers hidden there open fire (Highsmith's rifle jammed), just as Ranger Ware and two others enter the alley behind the outlaws. Now Bass and company are in a crossfire, but in spite of the zinging bullets, Barnes and Jackson reach their horses unscathed and get ready to mount.

Concealed in the back of the stable, Ranger George Herold steps out and points his Winchester at Sam Bass, ordering him to surrender. A mere fifteen feet away, Bass clicks his empty pistol (in his good hand) at Herold and tries to mount his horse. Herold cuts loose with his rifle and Bass is hit near the spine, the bullet exiting thru his cartridge belt and disintegrating. "Oh, Lord!" Bass cries as he sags and crashes against the stable fence.

From the west end of the alley, Ranger Dick Ware peeks out and draws a bead on Seaborn Barnes, who is forking his horse. Ware fires and Barnes is hit just behind the left ear, the bullet exiting his right eye. Barnes topples from his horse, dead.

Hit twice and in pain, Bass retrieves Barnes' saddlebag and remounts with Jackson's help. The two then spur their steeds and gallup north out of town. Incredibly, Jackson has escaped without a scratch.

Even more incredible, the Rangers can't find enough good horses for a decent posse. (They're standing in a stable, but for some reason there's only "one plug" on the premises. One of the Rangers commandeers Barnes' horse.) After a feeble attempt pursuing Bass and Jackson, the makeshift posse gives up and returns. Shortly, Jim Murphy shows up and identifies Seaborn Barnes. (Seaborn had been shot in the legs in a previous shootout and Murphy correctly identified the scars.) The townspeople suspect him of being one of the robbers, but Murphy confesses his informant role and the Rangers save him from harm.

Too weak to ride, Sam Bass was found the next day under a tree about three miles north of town. He was brought back to Round Rock in a wagon, and doctors examined his wounds, pronouncing them fatal. A stenographer was brought in to write down any confession, but while the young outlaw admitted his involvement in the Union Pacific robbery, he was mum about any of his recent Texas crimes, saying, "It is agin my profession to blow on my pals." He also informed the Ranger commander, "If I killed Grimes it was the first man I ever killed." At 3:55 p.m., Saturday, July 21, Bass uttered his now famous last words: "let me go . . . the world is bobbing around." It was Sam's 27th birthday.

Deputy Grimes' widow was given one of the outlaws' horses and $250 from the railroad. Deputy Moore survived his chest wound only to die in another gunfight in 1887.

The Texas Rangers continued to search high and low for Frank Jackson, but he escaped justice. Some say he lived out his days on a cattle ranch in New Mexico.

Jim Murphy had infiltrated the Sam Bass gang to get his father and brother cleared for their alleged involvement in aiding and abetting the gang. Forever labeled a rat, Murphy—according to legend—committed suicide in June 1879. Bass biographer Rick Miller claims, however, that Murphy "inadvertently swallowed" a wash containing "toxic belladonna," concluding "there is no evidence, as was claimed, that he committed suicide out of remorse or fear."

THE TEXAS RANGERS REVISITED: OLD THEMES AND NEW VIEWPOINTS

Harold J. Weiss, Jr.

... there is glamor in the names
Of the men who made the Rangers, as the record still proclaims:
The lifter left the cattle and the outlaw hid his gat
When they thought about the rider in the tall—white—hat.[1]

Such verse conjures up timeless images of Rangers battling desperadoes in furious gun battles. The Rangers as heroic figures can be seen as Cossacks on horseback, Mounties without uniforms, six-shooter Sir Galahads who knew no fear and persevered as guardians of law and order. In their relentless pursuit of lawbreakers, these fearless Rangers "rode the border and the outlaw rode for life."[2]

Continuity in historical analysis has two important elements: enduring traits in a time continuum, and the imprint of such longstanding characteristics on the public. From events in their early history the Texas Rangers gained a reputation as a mounted body of officers capable of pursuing their foes in Indian country or along the Mexican border; were identified with a particular weapon—the six-shooter—that contributed to their image as fighters who neither gave nor asked for quarter; and were an irregular force with no uniforms, some privately supplied equipment and provisions, and a noticeable lack of military discipline. This rough-and-ready image, which first appeared in the fight for Texan independence and the Mexican War, left its imprint on the imagination of those writers who have recorded the exploits of outlaws and lawmen.

Although tradition played an important part in Ranger affairs, different eras in Texas history produced different types of Rangers. Through the decades of settlement, revolution, and statehood; the period of the Civil War and Reconstruction; the growth of agriculture and industry; the rise of urban Texas; and American involvement in two world wars, the operations of the Texas Rangers can be divided into three distinct periods:

1. 1823–1874: the heyday of the Rangers as citizen soldiers. Within this time frame ranging companies and other volunteer units engaged in a military struggle with Indian tribes and Mexicans for control of the land.

2. 1874–1935: the age of the Rangers as old-time professional lawmen. In 1874, to protect the frontier and suppress lawless segments of the population, the legislature created a Special Force of Rangers under Capt. L. H. McNelly and the Frontier Battalion, commanded by Maj. John B. Jones. By the beginning of the twentieth century, the Frontier Battalion had evolved into a complex organizational structure with a chain of command and career-minded officers who carried out administrative duties and investigative work, from tracking criminals to collecting and analyzing evidence. Such processes were the hallmarks of the old-style professional peace officers throughout the American West.

3. 1935–present: the period of the Rangers as new-style modern police. In 1935 the Rangers became part of the modern state police movement in the United States when they were transferred along with the Highway Patrol to the newly created Department of Public Safety. The move reinforced professionalism, as political patronage

decreased and bureaus were created for communications, education, intelligence, and identification and records.[3]

Each generation must use its experiences to reinterpret—some might say reinvent—the actions of the Texas Rangers in the field. The historiographical map of the Ranger companies is covered with accounts that chronicle dates and events, narrate the adventures of intrepid Rangers, or criticize the same body of men for using force beyond the line of duty. The highlights of this historical literature are twofold. First, there is the professional stature of Walter Prescott Webb. Although it did not stress a central thesis as did his other works, Webb's monumental study of the Rangers brought together a vast array of factual information and attracted public attention to the exploits of nineteenth-century Ranger captains. J. Frank Dobie called this classic work the "beginning, middle, and end of the subject."[4] Yet before his untimely death Webb realized that his Ranger book needed to address more fully events in the twentieth century, as did his articles for the Michigan *State Trooper,* and that a fresh approach to the conflict between Anglos and Hispanics would contribute to a more balanced view of law enforcement in modern Texas.[5]

This interplay between the Rangers and Mexican Americans, another major theme in the historical literature on Ranger operations, has resulted in endless controversy. Too often the story of the border conflicts has been framed in dichotomous relationships. For some, the Rangers have become heroic figures who saved Texans from foreign invasion and rampant crime. As one Ranger captain said graphically, "Hell, . . . whenever there's a mean ass, they call on us."[6] For others, though, the image of the Rangers is just the opposite: from iron-fisted range riders with the "sensitivity of a rattlesnake" to the derogatory verse *"Rinche, pinche, Cara de chinche'* (Mean ranger, face of a bug)."[7] Such opposing viewpoints, with each side emotionally defending its position, do not create an atmosphere that encourages asking new questions and seeking new answers in order to understand the complex world of modern law enforcement.[8] Viewing the Rangers in white hat-black hat terms will freeze their historiography in time, with more ties to local interests than regional and national concerns.

Citizen soldiers were an age-old instrument of British military policy that became embedded in American culture. Non-Texan rangers engaged the enemy on the battlefields of eighteenth-century America. While the Native Americans in Texas were encountering the northward expansion of New Spain, ranger units fought in the woodlands and valleys east of the Mississippi River in the French and Indian War and the American Revolution. At that time rangers, like those under Robert Rogers in both wars, gained fame as a "flying army" of sharpshooters who could either fight alongside other soldiers or carry out guerrilla operations. In addition, the use of rangers in the late 1700s coincided with the use of light infantry to protect the flanks of an army and the recognition by the military of the battlefield abilities of buckskin-garbed frontiersmen who held rifled long guns and knew how to fight Indian-style. Thus, before Anglo-Americans settled in Texas, ranger-frontiersmen had a distinctive role as soldiers in irregular warfare: unmilitary dress with the firepower of a special weapon.[9]

To play this role before and after their formal organization in 1835, the Texas Rangers needed an implacable foe. They found not one, but several: the unyielding Mexicans and the indomitable Apaches, Tonkawas, Comanches, and other Indian tribes. In this multifaceted struggle through the movement for independence and early statehood, Texians were repeatedly mustered in and out of ranging companies. A recent critic of the Rangers maintained that they were "born out of vigilantism" because they "developed out of private ranger companies."[10] More to the point is the fact that in the days of Stephen F. Austin the Rangers began as citizens acting as occasional soldiers. In the 1820s Mexican law called for the training and use of the militia and allowed Austin to handle local governmental matters. Austin, who first placed the Rangers under a militia officer, and other militia representatives realized that mounted Rangers could patrol the Indian frontier until other military units could take the field.[11] Although the existence of the Rangers in pre-Civil War Texas was sporadic and no career-minded captains arose from the ranks, a few officers left their marks on Ranger traditions of martial skills. These included John C. "Jack" Hays and his cohorts Michael Chevallie, John S. "Rip" Ford, Richard A. Gillespie, Benjamin "Ben" McCulloch, and Samuel H. Walker.

The concepts of rangers and citizen soldiers have become umbrella terms for a variety of roles and occupations on both sides of the Atlantic. Rangers can be defined simply as wanderers, or as officials involved in the care of parks and forests; military raiding parties; or armed groups who range over a region for its protection. From Scotland and the royal parks of England to the colony of Georgia to frontier Texas, and with a mixture of Celtic culture, English traditions, and modern attitudes, rangers took part in search-and-destroy missions and won public acclaim. A recent historian described the first Rangers in Texas as men who "fought under no flag, wore no uniform, and in practice observed no prescribed length of service. One would even have to stretch the definition of the term to call them militia, for militia mustered at regular intervals for drill."[12] Yet by the time of the settlement of Anglo Texas, volunteer rangers in western states with an Indian frontier did align themselves with organized militia units, which could be called into federal service.[13] Although the exact relationship between Ranger companies and militia units in antebellum Texas remains unclear, one Texian made an important point: "every settler was a minuteman . . . ready to start at a moment's warning."[14] To stand and fight for family and community was the essence of the citizen soldier. "The Texas Ranger," according to one expert, "was none other than the *ordinary citizen soldier.*"[15]

The steadfast attitudes in favor of citizen soldiers in American society in the eighteenth and early nineteenth centuries made the rise of the Rangers in Anglo Texas inevitable. Two points about the first Rangers are clear: in the 1820s small groups of from ten to thirty Rangers were periodically formed to protect property and settlements from Amerindians, and in November 1835, during the Texas Revolution, three companies of fifty-six men were organized, with John J. Tumlinson as one of the company captains and Maj. Robert M. "Three-Legged Willie" Williamson directing their operations. Ranger activities reached their zenith in antebellum Texas in the 1840s. Armed with rifles and revolvers, mustered in more organized bodies in small numbers or by the hundreds, used as scouts and spies, ordered to fight in defensive lines or attack in hit-and-run style or make frontal assaults on enemy positions, Rangers under the command of "Devil Jack" Hays gained a reputation for initiative and bravery as mounted gunmen in their battles with Comanches and as state volunteers under the American flag in the Mexican War. In retrospect, the exploits of Hays's volunteer soldiers played an important role in reinforcing the traditional American dislike of large standing armies and their professional codes.[16]

The intermittent use of the Texas Rangers as either a state force or as troops taken into federal service continued for the next two decades. Ranger leaders like "Old Rip" Ford and James H. Callahan stood out in violent encounters with Comanches and Mexicans in the 1850s. Two significant developments, which have been underplayed in Texan chronicles, were the actions of Henry McCulloch, veteran Ranger and Confederate officer, in handling the Indian frontier and the activities of draft dodgers, deserters, and bushwhackers in Texas during the Civil War;[17] and Gov. Edmund J. Davis's creation not only of the state police to enforce Reconstruction, but also of organized companies of Rangers—the "governor's police"—to pursue Indians and outlaws and recover stolen cattle and horses in the 1870s.[18] Thus, the Texas Rangers continued their sporadic existence, remained distinct from professional soldiers, and began to adapt to changes in the period between 1823 and 1874.

Scores of minor skirmishes and major battles since the era of New Spain took place between European settlers and the Indian tribes in Texas. One can argue that battle-hardened Anglos, Hispanics, and Amerindians fought each other on equal terms. What, then, allowed the Native Americans to win battles but lose the war?' For one thing, the feared Comanches came up against superior firepower in Hays's Rangers, with their five-shot Paterson Colts. After battles at Walker's Creek and other places, more Comanches than Rangers lay dead on the field.[19] Another important factor was the inability of the Indian tribes to unite in order to plan strategy and build villages that could withstand a prolonged siege. Flacco, the Apache leader, fought with distinction alongside Hays, and in 1858 a combination of Rangers under Ford and reservation Indians under Shapley P. Ross took the offensive and won a significant victory by destroying Iron Jacket's Comanche village in a six-hour running fight on the north bank of the Canadian River.[20] Primitive Indian arms could not stand up against state and federal troops allied with other Indians.

Most historians agree that the pivotal event in the making of the early Ranger mystique was the Mexican War. For decades the search for a decisive victory in a bloody battle dominated the relations between Mexico and Texas. Then in 1846 came the North American Invasion, as it is called south of the border. The role of the Rangers in this conflict can be viewed in three different ways. First, the Texans under Hays became effective soldiers whose mobile tactics allowed them to carry out varied assignments, from scouting missions to leading a charge against an enemy stronghold to protecting supply lines by engaging Mexican guerrillas. Second, a Ranger image recognized throughout the United States developed from these assignments. Into Mexico rode Hays's Rangers. Out of Mexico came a mounted irregular body of Rangers armed with revolvers and knives and celebrated in song and story for their rough-and-ready appearance and their fearlessness. Finally, the most controversial aspects of the role of the Rangers in this war resulted from their contacts with Mexican civilians away from the battlefields. That the Rangers took clothing, chickens, pigs, and whiskey can be seen either as plundering a helpless people or as foraging in the accepted military tradition. That they killed civilians for taking horses, throwing stones, stealing handkerchiefs, or knifing a Ranger in the streets can be viewed either as unnecessarily harsh retaliation or as following the rules of an uncivilized war. In a guerrilla war both sides can be accused of using terrorism, of believing in war for war's sake. At the end of the fighting, however, the Rangers stood tall. Santa Anna was leaving the country with an American military escort. Although the Rangers talked about shooting their old nemesis, they lined the road instead and watched his carriage disappear. For the Rangers the bloodshed had come to an end.[21]

Since the mid-1800s Texas and the United States had undergone vast changes. For America the Industrial Revolution and involvement in two world wars had brought the country into the modern age. For Texas a wave of new settlers pushed settlements into the Panhandle and West Texas and diminished the importance of the Mexican American population. Railroads crisscrossed the state and the search for oil and gas became part of the new industrialism. In urban America the war against crime and disorder led to changes in big-city police departments, the creation of new agencies like the FBI, and the spread of the state police movement from Texas and Massachusetts.[22]

With the creation of McNelly's Rangers and the Frontier Battalion in 1874 under Gov. Richard Coke, the Rangers continued to engage Indian tribes in combat and guard the border against forays by Mexican nationals, but increasingly their duties turned to arresting those Texans suspected of breaking the law. The rate at which the Rangers changed from citizen soldiers to professional lawmen accelerated as each Ranger officer (an important term in future legal disputes) was given "all the powers of a peace officer" and had the "duty to execute all criminal process directed to him, and make arrests under capias [writ] properly issued, of any and all parties charged with offense against the laws of this State."[23] Armed with this authority, Rangers would arrest those who committed arson, embezzlement, and murder; those who stole horses and cattle; and those who tried to get away with such crimes by fleeing to another state.[24]

After the 1870s, the Texas Rangers had to mesh two interrelated but somewhat discordant factors: organizational structure and charismatic leaders. The former provided the operational network for the Rangers to act as police; the latter produced heroic images that kept the Rangers in the public limelight. In their role as organized police, the Rangers had to answer for themselves a question common to law enforcement work throughout the American West: in fighting crime, were they justified in bending the rules limiting the use of intimidation and violence? Whenever they answered in the affirmative, the lines between the Rangers and the outlaws they pursued became blurred. But those Rangers who tried to carry out their duties with a minimum of gunplay deserve the highest praise. A peace officer in this frame of mind was "truly the one who tamed the west."[25]

Although the number and size of Ranger companies varied from decade to decade between 1874 and 1935, stability remained a hallmark of the organization and operations of the Frontier Battalion. Initially this force consisted of six companies with seventy-five men each (reduced to forty within a few months to handle budgetary problems). By the 1890s four companies remained, with sometimes less than a dozen Rangers left with each captain to patrol the countryside, investigate crimes, and arrest felons from the Panhandle to South Texas. Dressed in broad-brimmed hats, "round-a-bout" vest-like jackets, and possibly wearing a shield-type badge or one with the more popular wagon-wheel, five-pointed star design, the privates in the companies of the Frontier Battalion reported to their sergeants and captains, and the officers, in turn, kept open lines of communication with headquarters in Austin.[26]

In 1901 and 1919, Texan state authorities made important modifications to this organizational structure. By 1901 a legal dispute arose over whether commissioned officers, and not the rank and file of the companies in the field, were peace officers who could make arrests. Some Rangers faced charges of false arrest. To solve this problem the governor's office and the legislature changed the name of the Frontier Battalion to the Ranger Force and stipulated that all Rangers be given all the powers necessary to make arrests and execute criminal processes. The number of companies and their manpower, however, remained basically the same. The demise of the Frontier Battalion, in name at least, did not result from a fiery gun battle, but from words spoken from a judge's bench.[27]

By the beginning of the twentieth century the Frontier Battalion or the Ranger Force had evolved into a complex organization. The most important characteristic of the old-time Ranger captain was the ability to recognize the centralizing forces connecting field offices to the main headquarters and at the same time handle the decentralized aspects of the organizational structure. In the chain of command, power flowed from the governor to the adjutant general and his staff, including the battalion quartermaster, to the officer in command of a company in the field to the Ranger in charge of a subcompany stationed at various locations. At the top of this pyramid one adjutant general, John A. Hulen, kept track of Rangers and their companies by using numbered and colored pins on a Texas map, and Battalion Quartermaster W. H. Owen criticized one captain for making the central office wait for his reports "all the time."[28] At the bottom of the pyramid Capt. William J. "Bill" McDonald acknowledged his instructions by ending some of his letters with the phrase "Yours to command."[29] Initially, Major Jones gave personal leadership and discipline to this organization in the 1870s. But the high-water mark of operational effectiveness came with the career-minded "Four Great Captains" by the early 1900s: McDonald, James A. Brooks, John R. Hughes, and John H. Rogers. The old-time Rangers became organizational Rangers.[30]

For a police agency to perform in a professional manner, it must achieve administrative efficiency. Captains and other commissioned and noncommissioned officers in the Frontier Battalion or the Ranger force carried out administrative duties that ranged from the selection of recruits and the dismissal of Rangers to maintaining company stations and obtaining supplies and equipment, assigning personnel to details to scout and investigate crimes, and handling citizen complaints and making reports to superiors. At one point George W. Arrington, the "iron-handed" captain of the Panhandle, even submitted to central headquarters monthly weather reports, with twice-daily citations such as "Clear & Cold Wind S."[31] A more important responsibility, however, was the hiring and firing of personnel. A century ago, men who joined the Rangers could ride, shoot, scout, track criminals, act like detectives, speak Spanish, and control mobs. In 1901 Adj. Gen. Thomas Scurry instructed company commanders to "enlist only such men as are courageous, discreet, honest, of temperate habits and respectable families."[32] Yet Rangers were discharged for desertion, drunkenness, insubordination, lack of judgment in the use of firearms, being in league with outlaws, and what one captain called "low down ungentlemanly things."[33] After some new enlistments this same captain was able to "boast of having a sober company and one that is not gambling and drinking all the time.'"[34]

Besides a command structure and centralized administrative work, three other factors characterized the old-time professional Rangers between 1874 and 1935: their use of deadly force; their ability to track criminals and collect and analyze evidence; and their need to adapt to technological change and relate to other lawmen, local, state, and national. Recently a Texas historian tried to find a new approach to the study of the history of the Rangers. He stressed the use of force and made the point that the "Rangers did not always get their man." This writer went on to show that outlaw Tom Ross escaped from a shoot-out with Rangers and other peace officers and that Ross even got the drop on Captain Rogers in another episode.[35] Although such events were humiliating to the Rangers, the important point is that the use of coercion is not the distinguishing feature of a police officer; it is only a tool to consider in pursuit of a legitimate goal.

The reality of the Rangers in the late nineteenth and early twentieth centuries lay between the images of the good guys in white hats and *"Los Diablos Tejanos"* (the Texas devils) in black hats. On the plus side, a few Rangers scattered over vast distances, carried out hundreds of scouting expeditions, arrested thousands of lawbreakers, and guarded jails and courts on numerous occasions. More dramatic were the cases that brought fame and renown to the Ranger organization. In 1876, during the bloody Sutton-Taylor feud, Lt. Lee Hall and his Rangers surrounded a house during a wedding celebration, arrested seven of the Sutton faction without bloodshed, and then stood guard in the courtroom with their Winchesters ready.[36] The next year, during the Horrell-Higgins feud, Sgt. N. O. Reynolds and his men got the drop on the Horrell brothers and talked them into surrendering without firing a shot.[37] Then came encounters with well-known bandits and gunmen: the arrest more than once of John King Fisher (who knew, as did Mexican prisoners, that any attempt at rescue or escape would bring instant death); the manhunt for and shooting of Sam Bass; Lt. John B. Armstrong's role, with other lawmen, in the capture of John Wesley Hardin (he knocked Hardin unconscious with his six-shooter); and the part played by ex-Ranger Frank Hamer in the slayings of Clyde Barrow and Bonnie Parker in 1934.[38] Such intrepid Rangers had one thing in common: they did their duty to the best of their ability in difficult times.

Yet some of these same Rangers had blots on their records. A few were removed from their posts; others learned from their experiences and became better Rangers. From the time that William G. Tobin carried out his orders in an incompetent manner in pre-Civil War Texas to a pick-pocket's theft of cash and a diamond pin from McDonald in 1910, Rangers failed to solve cases and make arrests and some allowed their prisoners to escape.[39] Even famed Sgt. Ira Aten suffered a "loss of face" when a fugitive he was watching escaped while Aten was drinking a cup of coffee.[40] Furthermore, Major Jones had to remove about fifteen Rangers from the service when they sided with an ex-Ranger in the Mason County War.[41] Most humiliating to the old-time Rangers, however, was the surrender of Lt. John B. Tays and his entire command to armed Hispanics from both sides of the border in the El Paso Salt War in 1877.[42]

By the late 1800s the most controversial aspect of the law enforcement work of the Frontier Battalion was its use of weapons—revolvers, rifles, and shotguns—in investigating crimes and maintaining order. The Rangers as peace officers could legally make arrests with or without warrants, and could use "all reasonable means" to do so. Justifiable homicides could also be committed by peace officers in Texas in preventing arson, burglary, castration, disfiguring, maiming, murder, rape, robbery, or theft at night. In addition, in Texas and other states in the nineteenth century, judges changed the English common-law tradition, which required one to retreat before defending oneself, to the American legal doctrine of self-defense, by which one could stand one's ground and fight. Thus, Texans and their police forces had ample legal authority to use violent means.[43]

Yet the Texas Rangers were not extraordinary gunfighters in the Old West. Only one prominent old-time Ranger—Captain Hughes—had the honor of being named to the roster of the most deadly gunfighters of all time.[44] One of the more bizarre gun battles took place between two feuding one-time Rangers, G. A. "Bud" Frazer and James B. "Deacon" Miller. In two shoot-outs between them, the steel breastplate that Miller wore for protection saved his life. Then in 1896 Miller found Frazer in a saloon and killed him with a blast from a shotgun.[45] In retrospect, the reputation of the horseback Rangers as gunmen rested not only on their involvement in gunfights, but also upon their proven marksmanship, their use of their weapons to intimidate opponents, and the fanciful stories woven around their exploits.

Particularly troublesome for the Rangers as lawmen after 1874 were their role of guarding the Rio Grande border and their use of force against Mexican Americans in southern Texas. Cultural, ethnic, and religious differences between Anglos and Hispanics persisted in the decades after the Mexican War. From Sam Houston's "Grand Plan" to conquer Mexico in 1860 with thousands of Rangers, Indians, and Mexicans to the 1915 Plan of San Diego for an uprising of people of Spanish descent on both sides of the border to retake the Southwest, American expansionism and Mexican territorial beliefs came into conflict with each other and kept some individuals dreaming of conquest.[46] In this charged atmosphere, people found reasons to cross the border for nefarious purposes whenever necessary. As late as 1917 Mexican raiders crossed the Rio Grande, attacked the L. C. Brite ranch near Marfa, looted stores, and killed several individuals. In addition, Rangers (like Captain McNelly) and federal troops found it necessary to invade Mexico in warlike manner.[47] In the tug-of-war along the border, which involved cattle rustling, gunplay, liquor smuggling, and violations of American neutrality laws, some participants, such as Juan "Cheno" Cortina and Gregorio Cortez, have been seen by Anglos as bandits and murderers and by Texas Mexicans as revolutionaries and Robin Hood heroes.[48] The Rangers in South Texas gained notoriety for executing their Hispanic prisoners. The companies under the "Four Great Captains" at the turn of the twentieth century did not follow such a policy. On the other hand Capts. H. L. Ransom and J. M. Fox shot a number of Mexican prisoners on the spot during World War I.[49] Such treatment of those of Spanish descent tarnished the Rangers' heroic reputation.

Important in the Rangers' transition from soldiering to policing was the rise of the professional police movement in this country, with its stress on careerism, the science of detection, and the use of technology derived from industrial America. The Rangers as mounted state police or, as one Ranger wrote, "mounted constables," were using modern techniques of police work by the early 1900s.[50] Long before the advent of computerized information systems, a list of fugitives, sometimes called "Bible II" and published by the state from reports received from county sheriffs, with colorful descriptions of thousands of criminals, allowed the Ranger organization to apprehend wanted men in a more efficient manner and integrate their activities more fully with those of local peace officers.[51] Equally important to the professionalization of the Rangers was their participation in the movement to prevent crime and improve the techniques of criminal investigation. From the 1877 sweep through Kimble County by several companies to arrest lawbreakers, to the 1889–1890 use of undercover agents and dental information by Aten and Hughes and the 1905 use of hand-prints by McDonald, Rangers acted aggressively to deter crime.[52] In addition, the adoption of new technologies, such as repeating handguns and rifles, trains and cars, telegraph and telephone lines, and typewriters, improved investigative methods in a changing so-ciety.[53] The Rangers had become more professional since the Jones-McNelly era.

Through the early decades of the 1900s two problems brought grief to individual Rangers and forced organizational changes: the interrelationship between Rangers and politics, and the troubles along the border between 1910 and 1920. The tactic of direct ac-tion and the practice of *la ley de fuga* used by McNelly's force in the 1870s along the Rio Grande were resurrected in grand style in the second decade of the twentieth century. On the one hand, a few Rangers made a gallant effort to cope with outlaw bands, Mexi-can revolutionaries seeking arms and public support, wartime spies and draft-dodgers, liquor smugglers, and a gringo-hating genera-tion along the border. On the other hand, as one historian wrote, "instead of meeting these challenges, of acquitting themselves he-roically in such critical times, the Rangers fashioned a dismal re-cord of murder and injustice."[54] In 1919 Rep. J. T. Canales initiated a legislative inquiry that heard testimony about intimidations, pistol whippings, and cold-blooded killings during Ranger operations. A reorganization of the Rangers resulted from the investigation. Four companies remained, each with seventeen Rangers including the captains. The legislation also created a headquarters company with six men under a senior captain. Although it helped to restore pub-lic confidence, the new law failed to address the issue of political influence and patronage in Ranger affairs. The next generation of political leaders could follow the policies of those, like Gov. James E. Ferguson and James B. Wells of Cameron County, who had ham-pered Ranger attempts to administer evenhanded justice.[55]

The new-style Texas Rangers developed for several reasons. Most important was the fact that the governors between 1911 and 1935 did not follow a consistent policy for the selection, upkeep, and deployment of the Rangers. The appointment of hundreds of Special Rangers cheapened the badge, and the corrupt "Ferguson Rangers," like Capt. James Robbins who took bribes and embezzled funds, further tarnished the reputation of the organization.[56] Other Rangers, however, especially in the era of Governors Dan Moody and Ross S. Sterling, carried out their duties with distinction, from the closing of vice dens in the oil boom towns by veteran Capt. William L. "Will" Wright to the capture of the Cisco bank robbers in 1927 by a posse led by Capt. Tom Hickman.[57] Yet Wright called for less politics in Ranger affairs and Hickman talked about combining the force with other Texas lawmen and using experts in fingerprints and ballistics.[58] Such reform movements to reduce political patronage and modernize police operations have been common in police work in this country since the time of Theodore Roosevelt.

The year 1935 was crucial in the history of the Texas Rangers. A time of questioning had come to an end. Using the Griffenhagen study of Texas law enforcement and the work of Dallas attorney Albert S. Johnson, Gov. James V. Allred and the state legislature created a Department of Public Safety, which included the Rangers, the Highway Patrol, and a Headquarters Division, to act as a modern center for the science of detection. Special Rangers had their numbers reduced and their powers limited. And the appointment of former Ranger Manuel T. "Lone Wolf" Gonzaullas to head the Bureau of Intelligence eased the transition of the rest of the Rangers into the DPS and the field of criminalistics. Texas had joined the list of states that had developed and modernized their police forces and organized central crime labs.[59]

The new-style Rangers resembled their pre-1935 counterparts in two ways: they maintained law and order in disputes between labor and management, and they investigated criminal cases that required working with other lawmen in Texas and across the nation. Like state police elsewhere, Rangers have been sent to keep the peace in violent confrontations between labor and management. In these difficult situations the actions of the Rangers have received mixed reviews. In some strikes, like the dispute between cowboys and ranch owners in the Panhandle in the late 1800s, the arrival of the Rangers aided the cause of management. In other violent encounters, such as the railroad strikes of 1922, the entire Ranger force was insufficient to handle the affair and the military had to be called in. In the strike by Texas-Mexican workers in Starr County in the late 1960s, Capt. A. Y. Allee and his Rangers kept order, but their use of force in making arrests and their methods of handling the mass media and the union movement among Mexican Americans resurrected the image of the brutal, Hispanic-hating Rangers.[60] One can argue that the use of the Rangers in such labor-management confrontations has had adverse effects on their ability to collect information and solve criminal cases.

For more than a century both the old- and new-style Texas Rangers have had to work with numerous officials on the local, state, and national levels of government: army officers, county sheriffs, district attorneys, federal marshals, judges, mayors, and town police forces. Their formal and informal collaborative arrangements have ranged from the exchange of information about the modus operandi of Texan criminals to conducting joint manhunts to working out arrangements for the detention of prisoners and the presentation of evidence in the courtroom. From the time that a Ranger subcompany set up tents in San Saba County to assist local officials in solving murder cases in the late 1800s to the involvement of the DPS in disaster relief after Hurricane Carla in 1961, Rangers and other public authorities in the state stood shoulder to shoulder in maintaining law and order. Relations between the Rangers and law enforcement officers of the national government and other states have taken two basic forms: the exchange of information and collaboration in the pursuit of outlaws, particularly with federal marshals in Oklahoma and U.S. Army units in South Texas, and the extradition of fugitives between the states and with foreign countries. Such interaction has highlighted the cooperation and conflict in American intergovernmental relations.[61]

In recent decades the Texas Ranger Service continued to investigate felonious crimes, apprehend fugitives, and suppress riots and insurrections. Under DPS directors such as Homer Garrison Jr. and Wilson E. "Pat" Speir, appropriations increased; computerized equipment modernized information systems; and regional centers appeared in the organizational charts. Rangers were older, more experienced, and better trained and educated than their predecessors.[62] This was especially important in an era of procedural justice in which strict rules governed the admissibility of evidence in American courtrooms.

In the chronicles of the American Southwest the Texas Rangers ride into history in a dual role: as Texans and as Rangers. As Texans, some married and had children; others used their literary talents to write poetry and newspaper stories; and still others carried their Bibles with their guns. As Rangers, different labels can be attached to their actions in the field: intrepid heroes, brutal lawmen, organized peace officers, and professional state police. To look into the complex world of the Texas Rangers one must go beyond the good-evil syndrome embedded in Ranger historiography. The dichotomous views of some writers of Ranger roles—heroes or devils for the military deployment as citizen soldiers against Amerindians and Mexican nationals, white hats or black hats for their actions as peace officers against desperadoes and Robin Hood bandits—cannot withstand the scrutiny of historical research. Yet the image of the Rangers will not really change until old stories are told in new terms. An army officer once wrote about Captain McDonald, "It is said here [in Brownsville] he is so brave he would not hesitate to 'charge hell with one bucket of water.'"[63] Maybe Jack Hays would have done that as a citizen-soldier Ranger, but McDonald was a police officer. And as a cop, he would have followed procedures: investigate and call for more Rangers and more buckets.[64]

NOTES

1. William B. Ruggles, *Trails of Texas* (San Antonio: The Naylor Co., 1972), 17.

2. Ibid.

3. For a comprehensive survey of the Rangers in the nineteenth century, see Walter Prescott Webb, *The Texas Rangers: A Century of Frontier Defense* (Boston: Houghton Mifflin Co., 1935). For an historical sketch of the twentieth-century Rangers and their heroic deeds, see two works by Ben Procter: *Just One Riot: Episodes of Texas Rangers* in the *20th Century* (Austin: Eakin Press, 1991), and "The Texas Rangers: An Overview," in *The Texas Heritage*, ed. Ben Procter and Archie P. McDonald (St. Louis: Forum Press, 1980), 119–131. For a look at the Rangers and other peace officers in the West, see Frank R. Prassel, *The Western Peace Officer: A Legacy of Law and Order* (Norman: University of Oklahoma Press, 1972), and Harold J. Weiss Jr., "Western Lawmen: Image and Reality," *Journal of the West* 24 (Jan. 1985), 23–32.

4. J. Frank Dobie, *Guide to Life and Literature of the Southwest* (1943; rev. ed., Dallas: Southern Methodist University Press, 1981), 60.

5. Llerena B. Friend, "W. P. Webb's Texas Rangers," *Southwestern Historical Quarterly* 74 (Jan. 1971): 293–323 (cited hereafter as *SHQ*). See also Stephen Stagner, "Epics, Science, and the Lost Frontier: Texas Historical Writing, 1836–1936," *Western Historical Quarterly* 13 (Apr. 1981): 165–181. Webb enjoyed writing a second book on the Rangers—*The Story of the Texas Rangers* (2nd ed.; Austin: Encino Press, 1971)—without the deadening facts and scholarly notes of his other work. For Webb's professional career, see Necah Stewart Furman, *Walter Prescott Webb: His Life and Impact* (Albuquerque: University of New Mexico Press, 1976).

6. Procter, *Just One Riot*, 16.

7. The rattlesnake quotation is from W. Eugene Hollon, *Frontier Violence: Another Look* (New York: Oxford University Press, 1974), 42. For the Texas-Mexican taunt, see Archie P. McDonald, comp., *The Texas Experiment* (College Station: Texas A&M University Press for the Texas Committee for the Humanities, 1986), 80.

8. An analysis of dichotomous relationships is in David Hackett Fischer, *Historians' Fallacies: Toward a Logic of Historical Thought* (New York: Harper and Row, Publishers, 1970), 9–12.

9. Don Higginbotham, *Daniel Morgan: Revolutionary Rifleman* (Chapel Hill: University of North Carolina Press, 1961), 121 (quotation). For an introduction to the varied use of the rangers in the revolutionary war, see Mark Mayo Boatner III, *Encyclopedia of the American Revolution* (New York: David McKay Co., 1966), 149, 153, 586, 664, 909, 934–936, 945–946, 1009–1010.

10. Alfredo Mirande, *Gringo Justice* (Notre Dame, IN: University of Notre Dame Press, 1987), 67 (2nd quotation), 68 (1st quotation).

11. The Austin Papers, ed. Eugene C. Barker, *Annual Report of the American Historical Association for the Year 1919* (Washington, D.C.: Government Printing Office, 1924), II [I], Pt. 1, 678–679; and two works by Eugene C. Barker, *The Life of Stephen F. Austin: Founder of Texas, 1793–1836* (1925; repr., New York: Da Capo Press, 1968), 98–108, 162–167, and *Mexico and Texas, 1821–1835* (1928; repr., New York: Russell and Russell, 1965), 21–23. Also see Mark E. Nackman, "The Making of the Texan Citizen Soldier, 1835–1860," *SHQ* 78 (Jan. 1975): 231–253; and Allan R. Purcell, "The History of the Texas Militia, 1835–1903" (Ph.D. diss., University of Texas at Austin, 1981), 62–106. For a succinct account of the field operations of the first Rangers, see D. E. Kilgore, *A Ranger Legacy: 150 Years of Service to Texas* (Austin: Madrona Press, 1973).

12. Stephen Hardin, *The Texas Rangers* (London: Osprey Publishing, 1991), 4.

13. Jim Dan Hill, *The Minute Man in Peace and War: A History of the National Guard* (Harrisburg, PA: The Stackpole Co., 1964), 11, 14–15.

14. Nackman, "The Making of the Texan Citizen Soldier, 1835–1860," 231. For the relationships between the militia, Rangers, and regular troops in antebellum Texas, see Purcell, "The History of the Texas Militia, 1835–1903," 75–100.

15. Nackman, "The Making of the Texan Citizen Soldier, 1835–1860," 46 (quotation). For stimulating accounts of American military attitudes, Celtic culture, and the southern heritage to the Texas Rangers, see Marcus Cunliffe, *Soldiers and Civilians: The Martial Spirit in America, 1775–1865* (Boston: Little, Brown and Co., 1968); Hardin, *The Texas Rangers*, 3–4; and Grady McWhiney, *Cracker Culture: Celtic Ways in the Old South* (Tuscaloosa: University of Alabama Press, 1988).

16. Hardin, *The Texas Rangers*, 3–20.

17. David Paul Smith, *Frontier Defense in the Civil War: Texas' Rangers and Rebels* (College Station: Texas A&M University Press, 1992).

18. John L. Davis, *The Texas Rangers: Images and Incidents* (1975; rev. ed., San Antonio: University of Texas Institute of Texan Cultures, 1991), 46 (quotation); Bern Keating, *An Illustrated History of the Texas Rangers* (New York: Promontory Press, 1980), 93–97. For a study of the state police and Reconstruction, see Ann Patton Baenziger, "The Texas State Police during Reconstruction: A Reexamination," *SHQ* 72 (Apr. 1969): 470–491. For a scholarly work that shows the mix of Rangers, volunteers, militia, and other troops in early Anglo Texas, see John H. Jenkins and Kenneth Kesselus, *Edward Burleson: Texas Frontier Leader* (Austin: Jenkins Publishing Co., 1990).

19. James K. Greer, *Colonel Jack Hays: Texas Frontier Leader and California Builder* (New York: E. P. Dutton and Co., 1952), 22–125; Dorman H. Winfrey, "John Coffee Hays," in *Rangers of Texas,* ed. Roger N. Conger, et al. (Waco: Texian Press, 1969), 5–25.

20. Thomas W. Dunlay, *Wolves for the Blue Soldiers: Indian Scouts and Auxiliaries with the United States Army, 1860–90* (Lincoln: University of Nebraska Press, 1982), 20–23; W. J. Hughes, *Rebellious Ranger: Rip Ford and the Old Southwest* (Norman: University of Oklahoma Press, 1964), 129–159; Harold B. Simpson, "John Salmon (Rip) Ford," in *Rangers of Texas,* 95–99.

21. For the secondary literature on the Rangers in the Mexican War, see Henry W. Barton, "The United States Cavalry and the Texas Rangers," *SHQ* 63 (Apr. 1960): 495–510; Greer, *Colonel Jack Hays,* 126–216; Hughes, *Rebellious Ranger,* 22–56; Stephen B. Oates, "Los Diablos Tejanos!" *American West* 2 (Summer, 1965): 41–50; Webb, *The Texas Rangers,* 91–124; Harold J. Weiss Jr., "The Bloody Texans in the Mexican War: The Reasons Why," *Westerners Brand Book* (New York Posse) 16, no. 1 (1969): 1–5, 21–22; and Frederick Wilkins, *The Highly Irregular Irregulars: Texas Rangers in the Mexican War* (Austin: Eakin Press, 1990).

22. The most recent histories of Texas with up-to-date information on the Texas Rangers include the following: Robert A. Calvert and Arnoldo De Leon, *The History of Texas* (Arlington Heights, Ill.: Harlan Davidson, 1990), and David G. McComb, *Texas: A Modern History* (Austin: University of Texas Press, 1989). For an older study, see T. R. Fehrenbach, *Lone Star: A History of Texas and the Texans* (New York: American Legacy Press, 1983).

23. H. P. N. Gammel, comp., *The Laws of Texas,* 1822–1897 (10 vols.; Austin: Gammel Book Co., 1898), 8:91.

24. An informative study of criminal violence in Texas in the nineteenth century has yet to be written. For a recent look at Texan violence with emphasis on gunfighters and the struggle between settlers and the Amerindians, see Bill O'Neal, "Violence in Texas History," in *Texas: A Sesquicentennial Celebration,* ed. Donald W. Whisenhunt (Austin: Eakin Press, 1984), 353–369. For two older views of violence in Texas and the Southwest see W. C. Holden, "Law and Lawlessness on the Texas Frontier, 1875–1890," *SHQ* 44 (Oct., 1940), 188–203, and C. C. Rister, "Outlaws and Vigilantes of the Southern Plains, 1865–1885," *Mississippi Valley Historical Review* 19 (Mar. 1933): 537–554. Interpretive frameworks to study Texas crime and violence will be found in Richard Maxwell Brown, "Western Violence: Structure, Values, Myth," *Western Historical Quarterly* 24 (Feb. 1993): 5–20, and Gary L. Roberts, "Violence and the Frontier Tradition," in *Kansas and the West: Bicentennial Essays in Honor of Nyle H. Miller,* ed. Forrest R. Blackburn, et al. (Topeka: Kansas State Historical Society, 1976), 96–111.

25. Dennis Brennan, "Who Really Tamed America's Wild West?" *The Lion* 54 (May 1972): 8.

26. Webb, The *Texas Rangers*, 307–342; Webb, *The Story of the Texas Rangers*, 116 (quotation).

27. Harold J. Weiss, Jr., " 'Yours to Command': Captain William J. 'Bill' McDonald and the Panhandle Rangers of Texas" (Ph.D. diss., Indiana University at Bloomington, 1980), 147–156.

28. For Hulen's method, see *Austin Statesman*, July 14, 1900. For Owen's quotation, see Owen to Captain William J. "Bill" McDonald, Aug. 7, 1896, *Letter Press Book*, Ranger Records, Records of the Adjutant General of the State of Texas (Archives Division, Texas State Library, Austin; cited hereafter as AGR).

29. See the complimentary closing in the letter from McDonald to Adj. Gen. William H. Mabry, Feb. 19, 1891, Gen. Corr., AGR.

30. For sketches of the careers of the "Four Great Captains" see William W. Sterling, *Trails and Trials of a Texas Ranger* (Norman: University of Oklahoma Press, 1963), 305–362, 363 (quotation), 364–396. For a revisionist account of the career of Captain McDonald, see Weiss, "'Yours to Command.'" For the modernization of American society in this era, see Robert H. Wiebe, *The Search for Order, 1877–1920* (New York: Hill and Wang, 1967).

31. Webb, *The Texas Rangers,* 422 (description of Arrington); "Weather Report, Month Ending Feb. 29, 1880. Co. C," Ranger Records, AGR.

32. "General Order No. 62, July 3, 1901, typed transcript of message, Ranger Correspondence, Walter Prescott Webb Papers, Center for American History, University of Texas, Austin; cited hereafter as CAH.

33. McDonald to Captain E. M. Phelps, Oct. 6, 1900, Gen. Corr., AGR.

34. McDonald to Mabry, Sept. 30, 1891, ibid.

35. James I. Fenton, "Tom Ross: Ranger Nemesis," *Quarterly* of the National Association and Center for Outlaw and Lawman History 14 (Summer, 1990): 4 (quotation), 19–21.

36. Hughes, *Rebellious Ranger,* 38 *("Los Diablos Tejanos")*; Dora Neill Raymond, *Captain Lee Hall of Texas* (Norman: University of Oklahoma Press, 1940), 69–78. For a history of the Sutton-Taylor feud, see C. L. Sonnichsen, *I'll Die Before I'll Run: The Story of the Great Feuds of Texas* (New York: Harper and Bros., 1951), 19–87.

37. James B. Gillett, Six *Years with the Texas Rangers, 1875 to 1881,* ed. M. M. Quaife (New Haven: Yale University Press, 1925), 69–80. A sketch of the Horrell-Higgins feud is in Sonnichsen, *I'll Die Before I'll Run,* 97–118.

38. For the events in the lives of these bandits and gunmen, see O. C. Fisher, with J. C. Dykes, *King Fisher: His Life and Times* (Norman: Univer-

sity of Oklahoma Press, 1966); H. Gordon Frost and John H. Jenkins, *"I'm Frank Hamer": The Life of a Texas Peace Officer* (Austin: Pemberton Press, 1968); Wayne Gard, *Sam Bass* (Lincoln: University of Nebraska Press, 1969); Chuck Parsons, *The Capture of John Wesley Hardin* (College Station: Creative Publishing Co., 1978); and Webb, *The Texas Rangers*, 297–304 (Armstrong), 519–546 (Hamer).

39. The analysis of Tobin's actions is in Hughes, *Rebellious Ranger*, 167–170. For the episode with McDonald, see the summation of a newspaper story from Wichita [Falls] *Daily Times*, n. d., Card File Index 144, newspaper collection of Wichita Falls *Times*, WPA Historical Survey Project (CAH). According to an account in another newspaper, McDonald apprehended but then lost the pickpocket after the thief had passed the valuables to a confederate. *Austin Statesman*, Oct. 15, 18, 1910. For an example of a Ranger losing a prisoner, see Gillett, *Six Years with the Texas Rangers*, 192–193.

40. Harold Preece, *Lone Star Man: Ira Aten, Last of the Old Texas Rangers* (New York: Hastings House, 1960), 117–121, 122 (quotation), 123–125.

41. Gillett, *Six Years with the Texas Rangers*, 46–52.

42. Webb, *The Texas Rangers*, 345–367.

43. Richard Maxwell Brown, *No Duty to Retreat: Violence and Values in American History and Society* (New York: Oxford University Press, 1991); William M. Ravkind, "Comments: Justifiable Homicide in Texas," *Southwestern Law Journal* 13 (1959): 508–524; George W. Stumberg, "Defense of Person and Property under Texas Criminal Law," *Texas Law Review* 21 (1942–43): 17–35; John P. White, *The Code of Criminal Procedure of the State of Texas, Adopted at the Regular Session of the Twenty-fourth Legislature, 1895 . . .* ([Austin]: Gammel Book Co., 1900), 159 (quotation).

44. Bill O'Neal, *Encyclopedia of Western Gunfighters* (Norman: University of Oklahoma Press, 1979), 4–6, 160–163.

45. Ibid., 113–114, 230–233. See also Glenn Shirley, *Shotgun for Hire: The Story of "Deacon" Jim Miller, Killer of Pat Garrett* (Norman: University of Oklahoma Press, 1970), and C. L. Sonnichsen, *Ten Texas Feuds* (Albuquerque: University of New Mexico Press, 1971), 200–209.

46. James A. Sandos, *Rebellion in the Borderlands: Anarchism and the Plan of San Diego, 1904–1923* (Norman: University of Oklahoma Press; 1992); William M. Hager, "The Plan of San Diego: Unrest on the Texas Border in 1915," *Arizona and the West* 5 (Winter 1963): 327–336; Webb, *The Texas Rangers*, 197–216 (Houston's "Grand Plan"). For an introduction to the course of empire and the cultural conflict between Americans and Mexicans, see Arnoldo De León, *They Called Them Greasers: Anglo Attitudes toward Mexicans in Texas, 1821–1900* (Austin: University of Texas Press, 1983), and Reginald Horsman, *Race and Manifest Destiny: The Origins of American Racial Anglo-*

Saxonism (Cambridge: Harvard University Press, 1981). Of the numerous accounts about life along the Mexican-American border, see Linda B. Hall and Don M. Coerver, *Revolution on the Border: The United States and Mexico, 1910–1920* (Albuquerque: University of New Mexico Press, 1990), and Oscar J. Martinez, *Troublesome Border* (Tucson: University of Arizona Press, 1988). See also Matt S. Meier and Feliciano Rivera, *Dictionary of Mexican American History* (Westport, CT: Greenwood Press, 1981).

47. James R. Ward, "The Texas Rangers, 1919–1935: A Study in Law Enforcement" (Ph.D. diss., Texas Christian University, 1972), 1–3; Webb, *Texas Rangers,* 255–280; Michael G. Webster, "Intrigue on the Rio Grande: The *Rio Bravo* Affair, 1875," *SHQ* 74 (Oct. 1970): 149–164.

48. Mirande, *Gringo Justice,* 50–99. See also John B. McClung, "Texas Rangers along the Rio Grande, 1910–1919" (Ph.D. diss., Texas Christian University, 1981); Americo Paredes, *"With His Pistol in His Hand": A Border Ballad and Its Hero* (Austin: University of Texas Press, 1958); and Ward, "The Texas Rangers, 1919–1935," 98–103.

49. For information about Captains Fox and Ransom, see Ward, "The Texas Rangers, 1919–1935," 9–11, 15.

50. The quote is taken from Gillett, *Six Years with the Texas Rangers,* 19.

51. Erik Rigler, "Frontier Justice in the Days Before NCIC," *FBI Law Enforcement Bulletin* 54 (July 1985): 16–18, 19 (quotation), 20–22.

52. Helen F. Bonner, "Major John B. Jones: The Defender of the Texas Frontier" (M.A. thesis, University of Texas at Austin, 1950), 51–55 (Kimble County); Jack Martin, *Border Boss: Captain John R. Hughes—Texas Ranger* (1942; repr., Austin: State House Press, 1990), 66–75, 85–100; Webb, *The Texas Rangers,* 328–333 (Kimble County); Weiss, " 'Yours to Command,'" 169–176.

53. The use of science and technology in police work affected law enforcement agencies throughout the western United States. Weiss, "Western Lawmen," 25. For information about Ranger weapons, see two articles by Charles Askins: "The Texas Ranger and His Guns," *American Rifleman* 130 (Nov. 1982): 44–45, 78–79, and "The Texas Ranger and His Guns," Part II, ibid. (Dec. 1982), 28–29, 75. See also Charles Askins, *Texans, Guns and History* (New York: Winchester Press, 1970).

54. Procter, *Just One Riot,* 4.

55. Ibid., 3–7; Evan Anders, *Boss Rule in South Texas: The Progressive Era* (Austin: University of Texas Press, 1982), 9–10, 37–38, 227–228, 252–254.

56. Procter, "The Texas Rangers," 1–3; Ward, "The Texas Rangers, 1919–1935," 223 (quotation).

57. Ward, "The Texas Rangers, 1919–1935," 145–209.

58. Ibid., 229–230; Stephen W. Schuster IV, "The Modernization of the Texas Rangers, 1930–1936" (M.A. thesis. Texas Christian University, 1964), 38–39.

59. Duayne J. Dillon, "A History of Criminalistics in the United States, 1850–1950" (Ph.D. diss., University of California at Berkeley, 1977), 156–162; Brownson Malsch, *Captain M. T. Lone Wolf Gonzaullas: The Only Texas Ranger Captain of Spanish Descent* (Austin: Shoal Creek Publishers, 1980), 119–150; Schuster, "The Modernization of the Texas Rangers, 1930–1936," 34–66.

60. David Montejano, *Anglos and Mexicans in the Making of Texas, 1836–1986* (Austin: University of Texas Press, 1987), 87–88 (cowboy strike); Ward, "The Texas Rangers, 1919–1935," 76–81 (railroad strikes). For the troubles in the Rio Grande Valley in the 1960s, see Ben H. Procter, "The Modern Texas Rangers: A Law-Enforcement Dilemma in the Rio Grande Valley," in *Reflections of Western Historians*, ed. John A. Carroll with James R. Kluger (Tucson: University of Arizona Press, 1969), 215–231, and Julian Samora, et al., *Gunpowder Justice: A Reassessment of the Texas Rangers* (Notre Dame, IN: University of Notre Dame Press, 1979), 89–156.

61. For a work with some emphasis on the theory and practice of American intergovernmental relations and the Rangers, see Weiss, "'Yours to Command.'"

62. Procter, "The Texas Rangers," 124–130; Erick T. Rigler, "A Descriptive Study of the Texas Ranger: Historical Overtones on Minority Attitudes" (M.A. thesis, Sam Houston State University, 1971), 20–24, 30–34.

63. *Message from the President of the United States, Transmitting a Report from the Secretary of War, Together with Several Documents, Including a Letter of General Nettleton, and Memoranda as to Precedents for the Summary Discharge or Mustering Out of Regiments or Companies,* 59th Cong., 2nd Sess., S. Doc. 155, Pt. 1 (Ser. 5078), 65.

64. Numerous topics for original research in Ranger history remain to be addressed. These include traditional subjects, such as Ranger captains and heroic deeds, and the fields of class, gender, and race of the new western historians. A list of unexplored topics for research in Ranger history would include the following: American intergovernmental relations and the operations of the Rangers; beliefs and actions of the Christian Rangers, as, for example, Captain Rogers and Thalis T. Cook; a comparative study of the Texas Rangers and other notable police forces (the Arizona Rangers, Canadian Mounties, and Mexican Rurales); the image of the Rangers in novels and other media; the impact of criminalistics on the new-style Rangers since the 1930s; labor-management strife and the Rangers since 1874; law enforcement, the Rangers, and black Texans; the life-styles and thought patterns of the wives of the

Rangers; literate Rangers who excelled in the use of the written word; the origins of the organizational Rangers, from Captain Jones to Battalion Quartermaster L. P. Sieker; recreational pursuits of the Rangers in camp; and the work of the Rangers in World Wars I and II. For examples of publications that are useful to such research, see Chuck Parsons, *"Pidge," A Texas Ranger from Virginia: The Life and Letters of Lieutenant T. C. Robinson, Washington County Volunteer Militia Company "A"* (Wolfe City, Tex.: Henington Publishing Co., 1985), and Mrs. D. W. Roberts, *A Woman's Reminiscences of Six Years in Camp with the Texas Rangers* (1914; repr., Austin: State House Press, 1987).

2

"VALOR, WISDOM, AND EXPERIENCE": EARLY TEXAS RANGERS AND THE NATURE OF FRONTIER LEADERSHIP

Stephen L. Hardin

purred by Napoleonic notions of glory, Luther Giddings followed General Zachary Taylor into Mexico in 1846. As an officer in the First Regiment of Ohio Volunteers, he was no spit-
and-polish regular. The Ohioan nonetheless shared a number of
assumptions with West Pointers. Giddings believed, for example,
that a soldier identified himself by wearing an assigned uniform;
a soldier observed a code that demanded obedience to superiors;
a soldier belonged to a fellowship of arms, and members of that
exclusive fraternity—even the enemy—deserved respect and professional courtesy. Finally, Giddings held that a soldier was an agent
of the state, protecting his nation's interest, at his country's beck and
call. Although he had not read the Prussian military theorist Carl
von Clausewitz, Giddings would have endorsed his oft-misquoted
dictum, "War is the continuation of political intercourse with the
intermixing of other means."

Then, at Camargo, Giddings encountered fighting men who
challenged most of his preconceptions. To categorize these outrageous partisans he sought analogies from history:

The character of the Texas Ranger is now well known by both friend and foe. As a mounted soldier he has had no counterpart in any age or country. Neither Cavalier nor Cossack, Mameluke nor Moss-trooper are like him; and yet, in some respects, he resembles them all. Chivalrous, bold and impetuous in action, he is yet wary and calculating, always impatient of restraint, and sometimes unscrupulous and unmerciful. He is ununiformed, and undrilled, and performs his active duties thoroughly, but with little regard to order or system.

Giddings did not know what to make of these merciless Texans. They had already established a reputation as *Los Diablos Tejanos,* devils who viewed war as an opportunity for personal vengeance. He admitted their brute efficiency in a "chaparral skirmish," but was reluctant to accept them as real "soldiers." It was no accident that Giddings compared these unrestrained primitives to Cossacks, those savage denizens of the steppes. Indeed, to Giddings and others of Taylor's Army of Observation, Texas Rangers seemed conspicuous by their "loose discipline" and their indulgence in "madcap revels." In brief, provincials who knew little of the sanctioned customs of civilized war. They were mistaken. Rangers understood the protocol: they simply rejected it.

A system that tyrannized their ancestors had conditioned Anglo-Celtic Texans to cast off some three hundred years of Western military culture. The seventeenth century witnessed the rise of nation-states and war became, in John Dryden's phrase, "the trade of kings." In such a form of government, armies founded on strict discipline, centralized administration, and trained troops were inherent. The professional soldier, formerly a "free-lance" who sold his services to the highest bidder, enrolled in the service of the state. This new system demanded discipline and obedience to lawful superiors. It drew sharp distinctions between the "lawful bearer of arms" and the rebel, freebooter, and brigand.

By the eighteenth century, wealth generated by trade financed standing soldiers and the regiment became the pre-eminent unit of military establishments. In war, regulars were instruments of policy; in peacetime, they often became toys for bored monarchs who paraded them around palace grounds for the amusement of visiting dignitaries.

Increasingly, garrisons withdrew from the populace. As English historian John Keegan observed: "[Regiments] had been founded to isolate society's disruptive elements for society's good, though that had been forgotten. They ended by isolating themselves from society altogether, differentiated by their own rules, rituals and disciplines." A recruit who took the king's shilling expected to do his bidding. Many civilians began to see regulars as bullyboys who had turned against their own people for royal silver.

That apprehension was keen during revolts against the monarchy. At the battle of Culloden, during the Jacobite Rebellion of 1745–1746, British redcoats killed some one thousand Highlanders in combat and captured a thousand more. The British regulars slaughtered most of their prisoners out of hand. After all, as civilians, the rebels were no part of the regimental order and could hardly expect the honorable treatment normally accorded professionals. During the subsequent Highland Clearances, many of the defeated Scots fled to the southern colonies of North America, bringing with them their contempt for the English redcoats or, for that matter, any royal authority.

The American War for Independence only intensified that animosity. Between 1760 and 1775, a tide of popular resistance rose against Parliament's taxation plans. The use of British regulars to suppress protesters at Golden Hill, and later during the Boston Massacre, convinced Americans that redcoats were simply royal thugs. Major John Pitcairn's command to the "minute men" assembled on Lexington Common—"Disperse, ye damned rebels"—indicated that a replay of Culloden was in the offing. Indeed, atrocities committed at Paoli in 1777, where redcoats bayoneted scores of Americans as they tried to surrender, demonstrated the British contempt for those who challenged the king's authority.

Following the Revolutionary War, Americans codified a mistrust of regulars into their constitution, demonstrating a preference for "well-regulated militia." Most civilians believed a standing army incompatible with republican institutions. Nevertheless, the treasured American vision of a civilian militia proved chimerical as militia units were almost never "well regulated." Their parochial temper clashed with centralized authority, rendering unity of command impossible.

This problem was especially apparent during the War of 1812 when New York militiamen declined to cross state borders to invade Canada. At Bladensburg in 1814, militia units broke and ran at the first glimpse of a red coat; the British subsequently captured Washington D.C. and torched its public buildings. In the South, militia units did conduct a successful campaign against the "Redstick" faction of the Creek tribe. There, however, a desire to avenge the 1813 Fort Mims massacre strongly motivated volunteers under the dynamic authority of Andrew Jackson. Even so, he had to shoot six of them for desertion before the rest abandoned the assumption that they could return home whenever they pleased.

Jackson's victory at New Orleans appeared to validate the superiority of rustic vigor over the affected and effete. "Their system it is true, is not to be found in Vauban's, Steuben's or Scott's military tactics," declared a congressman of the stalwarts at Chalmette, "but it nevertheless proved to be quite effective." Even "Old Hickory" explained that the British, fresh from victory against Napoleon's marshals in Spain, expected scant opposition from "men whose officers even were not in uniform, who were ignorant of the rules of dress, and who had never been caned into discipline."

Among southerners of the 1820s and 1830s, ingrained resentment of the military establishment ran deep. This abhorrence for regulars went hand-in-glove with a growing grass roots political movement that sought to advance the "common man" over those privilege and education had favored. One of the few bills Tennessee Congressman David Crockett ever introduced called for the abolishment of the US Military Academy, which he blasted as a government boondoggle for the "sons of the rich and influential" who were "too nice to work." In the Old Southwest, frontiersmen fearing Indian raids soon learned that Washington, and even state capitals, were too far away to provide protection. By grim necessity community defense grew intensely personal. Every backwoodsman became a "lawful bearer of arms."

Southerners relied on a time-honored agent: the ranger. During the 1600s, Scots termed "ranger" any armed man who *ranged* a tract of countryside against raids by hostile clans. The practice migrated to the American colonies where as early as 1739 James Oglethorpe raised a Georgia unit, the Troop of Highland Rangers. Later, settlers employed the term for gunmen hired to patrol the woods against Indian attack. In times of immediate crisis, the militiamen mustered but they looked to the local ranger to organize and lead them. He was the professional.

Along with other trappings of Celtic culture, southern immigrants to Mexican Texas brought their ranger traditions and disdain for professional soldiers. In 1823, *empresario* Stephen F. Austin employed ten men he termed "rangers" to patrol his colony against Indian raids. In the beginning, since these irregular partisans were defending their families, settlers expected each man to arrive for duty well mounted and well armed from his own pocket. They wore no uniform, fought under no flag, expressed little esprit de corps. Except for paid captains, the troopers responded only in times of crisis and took their leave the instant they deemed the threat concluded.

Texians asked no man's permission to take up arms; they simply disregarded the prerogative of the state and defended their settlements. The antithesis of the regimental ideal, these civilian volunteers regarded war not as a "continuation of political intercourse" but as a matter of survival.

During the revolt against Antonio López de Santa Anna's centralist regime, Texian officials formalized ranger organization, but only slightly. On 24 November 1835, the interim Texas government approved an ordinance providing for a corps of mounted gunmen. Gone were the casual enlistments of the past. Privates signed on for a full year and earned $1.25 per day for "pay, rations, clothing, and horse service." While rangers saw some action against Mexican centralists, their primary mission remained fending off Indian incursions. As Bastrop resident John Holland Jenkins recalled, "The Indians were growing more and more troublesome, and Captain John Tumlinson raised a minute company of the few men and boys left at home. These held themselves in readiness for protecting . . . homes and families."

Even when notables such as Stephen F. Austin, William B. Travis, and Sam Houston declared the need for regulars, the traditional scorn for professional soldiers went unchecked. Robert Morris of the New Orleans Greys spurned a regular commission. He informed Houston that none of his men would "enter into any service connected with the Regular Army, the name of which is a perfect Bugbear to them." The revolutionary rhetoric sought to awaken "the principles of 1776" and portrayed Santa Anna as a despot in the George III mould and his minions as Mexican redcoats. Indeed, to stress the comparison, many revolutionaries labeled the centralists "bluecoats." The overwhelming majority of Texian fighting men were civilian volunteers and contentiously egalitarian. An 1835 broadside proclaimed their contempt for Mexican regulars: "Rise up, then, with one accord, and shoulder your rifles, march to the field of battle, and teach the hirelings of a tyrant that they can not battle successfully with citizen freemen." Reporting the death of his brother John at the Alamo, a vengeful Benjamin Briggs Goodrich jeered Santa Anna. "We will meet him and teach the unprincipled scoundrel that freemen can never be conquered by the hirling [sic] soldiery of a military despot."

Following victory at San Jacinto, Texians envisioned their infant republic stretching westward toward the Pacific but harsh realities frustrated dreams of empire. The Texas government was bankrupt. It possessed a bantam regular army, which was expensive to uniform, arm, and deploy. Furthermore, regulars proved useless against Indians. In 1840, the approach of Comanche braves at Plum Creek unmanned General Felix Huston of the regular army. Although the nominal commander of the Texian force, he offered tactical command to ranger captains Edward Burleson and Matthew Caldwell. Veteran frontiersman James Wilson Nichols recorded the general's rationalization to the pair:

Gentlemen, those are the first wild Indians I evar saw and not being accustom to savage ware fare and both of you are, I think it would be doing you and your men especially great injustace for me to ta[ke the] command . . . Now give me a deciplined civ[ilis] ed command and a deciplined enemy to fight [and] I would redily take command.

Sadly, for General Huston and his fastidious regulars, Texas suffered a genuine scarcity of "deciplined" Comanches. The times required an inexpensive partisan force that mustered in minutes, supplied its own mounts, provided for itself in the field, and required no fancy uniform: in brief, rangers.

The inherited animosity against professionals remained at the core of the ranger ethic. Volunteers defending hearth and home thought themselves on higher moral ground than brass-buttoned hirelings. As ranger Nelson Lee explained: "Discipline, in the common acceptation of the term, was not regarded as essential." Ranger Samuel C. Reid's description of Texans preparing for campaign ridiculed the pretention of the professional military.

No mock show of the pomp and pageantry of war was seen—no tap of spirit-stirring drum, or note of piercing fife—no trumpet-call, or bugle sound, was heard on the border side. But there was wiping of rifles and moulding of bullets— cleaning of pistols and grinding of knives—packing of wallets and saddling of steeds; in short, every step of preparation made, amid the encouraging smiles of mothers, wives, and sisters, . . . giving evidence that the frontier men knew full well the importance of the duty which they had to perform; and every movement which they made was an earnest that that duty would be gallantly done.

Commanding those who rejected conventional authority required a leader who shared his men's egalitarian values. A ranger captain was merely first among equals, but then that was the source of his power. Texans followed a man not because he had gone to an academy or perused treatises, but because he had proven his worth in the field. Edward Burleson, roughhewn and barely literate, would never have qualified as an "officer and gentleman" in the regular army. Jack Hays always minimized his contribution, quipping, "Any of us can command Texans. All they ask is to be shown the road to the enemy's camp." Yet, Nelson Lee and other rangers admired men like Burleson for their "valor, wisdom, and experience."

Once a captain earned the respect and confidence of his men, he had no need to "pull rank." Lee described Hays's command style: "Hays called us together, as was his custom always under circumstances of peculiar peril, and addressed us. After setting forth the imminent dangers that evidently surrounded us, he stated the course he had resolved to adopt, if it met our approbation, which it did, unanimously." Sam Reid attested that off duty Hays was a "pleasant companion, and the men familiarly call him Jack," although he also observed, "there is that about the man which prevents one from taking the slightest liberty with him."

Even when under the command of tested captains—perhaps especially then—Texans were capable of astounding brutality. Contemporary observers noted their viciousness. Giddings denounced them as "unscrupulous" and "unmerciful." While numerous incidents illustrate those traits, two are remarkable. The first occurred before the battle of Plum Creek. A lone Comanche brave galloped toward the Texan line, pulled up before it, and challenged the whites to send out their champion for single combat. The warrior ethic of the Plains Indians promoted a competition among braves. By performing feats of brazen physical courage, a young man attained status within his tribe and the respect of his enemies. These adversaries, however, did not share that ethic. One of them leveled his rifle and casually blasted the Indian off his pony.

Then, there is the account of Jack Hays's 1846 duel with a Mexican colonel. Outside Monterry, an enemy lancer regiment surprised a ranger company. Hays realized his command must take up a defensive position but that required time and he intended to buy it. He ordered his men to withdraw and then, according to James "Buck" Barry: "[Our colonel] rode out front with his sabre in his hand and challenged the colonel of lancers to meet him halfway between the lines to fight a sabre fight." Doffing his helmet, the enemy officer graciously bowed in acceptance. The actions of his commander perplexed Barry who recalled, "Hays knew no more about sabre fighting than I did." The lancer colonel's horse "seemed to dance rather than prance," as the two antagonists advanced like cavaliers of old. At the final moment Hays jerked to the right, ditched the blade, and, Comanche style, swung under his horse's neck. Too late, the Mexican discerned that "Devil Jack" had swapped cold steel for a hot pistol. The Paterson Colt chambered five shots, but at that distance, Hays required only one. The slug took the gallant Mexican squarely in the chest and a corpse toppled from the charger.

Like Giddings, modern critics find such churlish actions, well, unsporting. Yet, surely, that was the point. For Texas Rangers, war was not a sport. They viewed the battlefield as a killing ground not a stage to display bravado. Unlike the proud Mexican colonel, rangers disdained codes of conduct established by the same "gentlemen" who had hoisted the red flag of no quarter at the Alamo, who had perpetrated the massacres of Fannin's and Dawson's men, and the infamous Black Bean episode during the Mier Expedition. Warfare in Texas was a savage, dirty pursuit, unrestrained by codes of civilized behavior.

While tales of Indian raids abounded, one is sufficient to suggest their horror. About 1850 a Comanche war party swept into present-day Llano County and left behind a token of their loathing. The Indians murdered a white infant and impaled his head on a pole for his surviving family to find. The memory of such occasions branded the Texan psyche and landscape. When travelling State Highway Sixteen between Llano and San Saba, one should pause a moment to reflect on the origins of Babyhead Cemetery.

Rangers who frequently witnessed such outrages experienced a psychological transformation. They silently vowed to be as hard and unforgiving as the land itself. "Texans," Nelson Lee asserted, "had no other alternative than to return blow for blow, and to demand blood for blood." Terror became a weapon.

The traditional hostility toward professional soldiers died hard. When the republic joined the union, Texans assumed that federal troopers would shoulder the burden of frontier defense. US regulars, however, were no more competent than the republic's. "This fact the Indians soon learned," bemoaned "Buck" Barry, "and they soon became so active that the people began to call for someone who could cope with them." Bowing to pressure, the regulars requested assistance. State rangers attached themselves to federal units—but not to their regulations. Later, during the War Between the States, home guard units and rangers patrolled the frontier and resisted Confederate authority as much as they had any other.

Giddings was correct. The early rangers had much in common with Cossacks. The name "Cossack," by the way, derives from a Turkic word translated as *freeman*. Both Cossacks and rangers fought as free men and, as such, both cast aside western military culture. The early ranger was no dupe of the state; he did not fight for procedures, policies, or pay. His motivation stood over the hearth cooking game he had bagged, napped in the crib he had constructed, grew on land he had planted. Because his imperatives were so personal, he readily slaughtered any who threatened them. As the consummate individualist, he did not aspire to be part of a unit or belong to any establishment.

Yet, what began as a temporary defense of farm and family ended as a sanctioned institution. By 1876, marauding tribes no longer harried the frontier and leaders of acumen and foresight understood that rangers must convert from Indian fighters to lawmen. Many chafed in their new role: "We hardly knew whether we were Rangers, or court officers," one old-timer groused. Of course, court officers *were* what they had become. That was, perhaps, the supreme irony. In a bid to remain relevant, the ranger became the object of his grandfather's greatest scorn—a disinterested professional, an agent of the state, and the "legal bearer of arms."

Editors' Note—For the debate about when and how the first ranging companies took the field against Indian tribes in Texas in the 1820s, see Allen Hatley, *The Indian Wars in Stephen F. Austin's Texas Colony, 1822–1835* (Austin: Eakin Press, 2001); and D. E. Kilgore, *A Ranger Legacy: 150 Years of Service to Texas* (Austin: Madrona Press, 1973). See also Frederick Wilkins, *The Legend Begins: The Texas Rangers, 1823–1845* (Austin: State House Press, 1996).

FURTHER READING

Barry, James Buckner. *A Texas Ranger and Frontiersman: The Days of Buck Barry in Texas.* The Southwest Press, Dallas, 1932.

Bauer, K. Jack. *The Mexican War, 1846–1848.* Macmillan Publishing Co. Inc., New York, 1974.

Giddings, Luther. *Sketches of the Campaign in Northern Mexico by an Officer of the First Ohio Volunteers.* G. P. Putnam and Company, New York, 1853.

Hardin, Stephen L. *The Texas Rangers.* Osprey Publishing Limited, Oxford, 1991.

Jenkins, John Holland. *Recollections of Early Texas; The Memoirs of John Holland Jenkins.* University of Texas Press, Austin, 1958.

Keegan, John. *A History of Warfare.* Alfred A Knopf, 1993.

Lee, Nelson. *Three Years Among the Comanches: The Narrative of Nelson Lee, The Texas Ranger, Containing a Detailed Account of his Captivity Among the Indians, His Singular Escape Through the Instrumentality of his Watch, and Fully Illustrating Indian Life as It Is on the Warpath and in Camp.* Boker, Taylor, Albany, 1859.

McWhiney, Grady. *Cracker Culture: Celtic Ways in the Old South.* University of Alabama Press, Tuscaloosa, 1988.

Nichols, James Wilson. *Now You Hear My Horn: The Journal of James Wilson Nichols, 1820–1887*. University of Texas Press, Austin, 1967.

Reid, Samuel Chester, Jr. *The Scouting Expeditions of McCulloch's Texas Rangers*. G. B. Zieber and Co., Philadelphia, 1847.

Remini, Robert V. *Andrew Jackson and the Course of American Empire, 1797–1821*. Harper & Row, New York, 1977.

Webb, Walter Prescott. *The Texas Rangers: A Century of Frontier Defense*. Houghton Mifflin Company, Boston, 1935.

Wilkins, Frederick. *The Legend Begins: The Texas Rangers, 1823–1845*. State House Press, Austin, 1996.

3

THE GREAT COMANCHE RAID OF 1840

Donaly E. Brice

The Great Comanche Raid of 1840 was the boldest and most concerted Indian depredation in the history of Texas. It embodied two of the bloodiest Indian battles Texas has ever witnessed. More significantly, it represented a turning point in Texas history, marking the end of the Indian threat to frontier expansion, the decline in Mexico's ability to exploit Indians as agents in its schemes to re-conquer Texas, and the rise of Texans' military prowess in defending their frontiers. After a brief review of relations between Texans and Indians preceding the raid, the paper will explore the Great Comanche Raid in each of its facets.

To understand the reasons for this destructive raid upon the settlers of the Texas frontier it is necessary to look back to the early years of the Republic of Texas. During the first administration of Sam Houston, practically no Indian trouble existed because of Houston's understanding and benevolent action toward the Indians. Houston realized that to establish a stable government, it was necessary to make and keep peace with the Indians and the Mexicans. Not all of the leaders of Texas, however, shared Houston's views. Many believed that the Indians and Mexicans should be dealt with more harshly. Such were the feelings of Houston's successor, Mirabeau B. Lamar. In his inaugural address to the Congress of the

Republic of Texas in 1838 Lamar let it be known that the settlers on the Texas frontier were continually exposed to "predatory aggression" and "barbarous warfare" being waged by hostile Indians and Mexican banditti.

He argued that the benevolent policies extended by Houston's administration had only acted as incentives to various tribes to "persevere in their barbarities." Lamar felt that the time had come for a war of extermination against the Indian which would "admit to no compromise, and have no termination except in their total extinction, or total expulsion."[1]

Lamar was only partially correct in his accusations against the Indians. Few tribes would attack without provocation or without reason. The majority of the Native Americans in Texas never posed a major problem so long as they were not molested. Whether or not the Indian problem was as serious as perceived, the aggressive action taken against the Indians by the Lamar administration was the basic foundation for the Great Comanche Raid in 1840.

Lamar's anti-Indian policy was first initiated against the Cherokees, who, under the leadership of Chief Bowles, had emigrated from the United States into Texas about 1824 and settled in East Texas along the Angelina, Neches and Trinity rivers. The land upon which the Cherokees resided was very beautiful and was desired by the many settlers moving into Texas. In 1839 the Texas government received information that the Cherokees, along with other tribes, were involved in an alliance with the Centralist party in Mexico. This Mexican-Indian alliance was devised for the purpose of waging war on the settlers of Texas—either to kill them or drive them from the territory. Until Mexico could send a force large enough to retake Texas, the alliance was designed to keep the Texans from establishing a strong foothold.

Reports of these intrigues, although greatly exaggerated by Lamar and others among the anti-Indian faction, provided the excuse they needed to expel the Cherokees. In July 1839 the Cherokees were defeated by the Texas Army at the Battle of the Neches and were forcibly removed from Texas.[2] The tribe never again presented a threat, whether real or imagined, to the settlers of Texas. With the expulsion of the Cherokees and their associated tribes, additional lands were opened to the flow of Anglo settlement into the new Republic, Indian depredations in the more settled areas of the Republic became almost nonexistent. The major Indian threat was removed to the frontier areas, where settlers were daily threatened by such tribes as the Comanche and Kiowa.

In the pages to follow the ranging companies headed by Edward Burleson, Matthew Caldwell, Benjamin McCulloch, John Moore, John Tumlinson, and others hold an honored place in the Texas Ranger Valhalla. These Ranger leaders made their mark in the battles at Plum Creek and the upper Colorado River against the formidable foes of the Comancheria empire. In the former struggle Burleson had the assistance of his Indian auxiliary: the Tonkawas under Chief Placido. In the latter engagement Lipan Apache scouts under Chief Castro aided Moore in his destruction of a Comanche village. Future Rangers John Coffee Hays and Henry McCulloch also played a role at Plum Creek.

Of all the Indian tribes within the boundaries of the Republic of Texas, the Comanches presented the most serious threat to the settlers. Regardless of numerous treaties negotiated between the Comanches and the Texans, the Brazos and Colorado river valleys continued to be plagued by Indian forays. By 1839 many felt that the western line of the frontier would actually begin to recede eastward unless something was done about the Indian problem. In one letter to the Secretary of War, Albert Sidney Johnston, the writer stated that he was totally "convinced that speedy relief must be had, or depopulation will necessarily soon ensue."[3]

On January 10, 1840, Colonel Henry W. Karnes, commandant of the military post at San Antonio, notified the Secretary of War that three Comanche chiefs and one Mexican captive had visited the city the day before to discuss the possibility of negotiating a peace agreement with the Texans. The chiefs assured Col. Karnes that their people had "refused to treat with the Cherokees, who solicited them with large presents to enter with them in a war against the Republic." They also acknowledged that the Mexican Centralists had sent emissaries to their tribes attempting to "stir up a general war with" the Texans, but these offers, too, had been rejected. The chiefs informed Karnes that a representative had been chosen by their nation at a general council to discuss peace terms with the white men. Karnes refused negotiations without the release of all their white captives and restoration of all stolen property; besides giving guarantees that future depredators on the frontier would be delivered up for punishment.[4] Karnes was informed that these stipulations would be agreeable and was told that they would return to San Antonio in twenty or thirty days with other Comanche chiefs, as well as their white captives, to begin peace negotiations. After being presented with gifts, which was the general custom, the Indians left the city.[5]

Distrust of the Comanches and previously broken treaties prompted the Secretary of War to instruct Colonel William S. Fisher, Commander of the First Regiment of Infantry, to proceed immediately with three companies to San Antonio in order to seize the Indians as hostages if they failed to bring in their white prisoners as previously agreed upon. If the Comanches failed to fulfill their promise, they were to be held as hostages by the Texans until all the white captives were returned. Two commissioners, Adjutant General Hugh McLeod and Colonel William G. Cooke, were chosen to carry out the negotiations with the Indians.[6]

On the morning of March 19 two Comanche scouts arrived in San Antonio and informed the commissioners of the approaching Indians. Shortly afterwards, a party of sixty-five Indians, including men, women and children, entered the city. With them was only one white captive, a fifteen-year-old girl named Matilda Lockhart. Following the Indians' arrival, the twelve principal chiefs were led into the Council House where negotiations were to be held. Indians, not involved in the peace talks inside the Council House, remained outside in the courthouse yard."[7]

Since the Indians had promised to bring in all their white captives, the Texans were somewhat surprised that only one prisoner was returned. In questioning Matilda Lockhart the commissioners were told that there were other white captives at the Comanches' principal camp and that she had seen them several days before. She told the commissioners that they had planned to bring in the captives one at a time in hopes of receiving more ransom from the Americans.

As the council talks began, Colonel Fisher's troops were ordered into the vicinity of the council room. The Indians were questioned as to the whereabouts of the other captives. Chief Muck-war-rah told the commissioners, "We have brought in the only one we had; the others are with other tribes." Not believing this statement, Fisher told the chiefs that they had not upheld their promise to bring in all their captives. The women, children and others with their party would be allowed to leave in peace and go back to get the other white captives. Until then the chiefs in the Council House were to remain as hostages.[8]

At this time one company of troops was marched into the council room and another one to the rear of the building. Guards were posted at the doors in the council room and troops were lined across the room. The Indians were told that the soldiers were their guards and that they would not be harmed if they did not resist. The chiefs, realizing their situation, strung their bows and presented their knives in preparation for a fight. When one of the chiefs ran for the door and stabbed the sentinel, he was ordered shot. As the chief fell dead, others attacked the soldiers, who were ordered to fire. In a matter of seconds, all twelve Comanche chiefs lay dead.[9]

Hearing the gunfire and the noise from within the Council House, the Indians in the courthouse yard realized what was happening and fled in all directions. Soldiers, firing into the crowds of people, killed both Indians and whites. The company of troops under Captain William D. Redd, stationed in the rear of the Council House, was attacked by the Indians. Many of the Indians took refuge in various structures in the town.[10]

In the short but fierce battle, out of a total of sixty-five Indians, sixty-four were either killed or taken prisoner. Thirty chiefs and warriors, three women and two children were killed. Seven Texans were killed and eight were wounded.[11]

The Texans entered a twelve-day truce with the Indians in which they would be able to exchange the Indians captured at the Council House fight for the white prisoners at the Comanche village. One Comanche woman was released and allowed to return to her camp to take the news of the Indians' defeat and prepare for an exchange of prisoners. On April 3 Chief Piava arrived in San Antonio and announced that the Comanches had brought in white captives for exchange. Talks resumed on April 4. Although the consultation "almost reached blows" at times because of the tension and harsh feelings, a total of seven captives were finally returned to the Texans.[12]

The Comanches remained in the vicinity of San Antonio for the rest of the spring and part of the summer while recovering from the severe defeat which had been dealt them at the Council House Fight. Small parties of Comanches continued stealing livestock, burning houses and attacking individual settlers. However, the death of twelve of their chiefs was a serious blow to the Comanches, and they finally retired to Comancheria among the hills above San Antonio and Austin to make preparations to strike back at the Texans.

Late in May of 1840 the Texas government received word out of Matamoros that General Valentin Canalizo, the commandant of the Centralist forces on the northern frontier of Mexico, was once again attempting to incite the Indians to wage war upon the white settlers. Hoping to take advantage of the tense relations between the Anglos and the Indians following the expulsion of the Cherokees from East Texas and the slaughter of the Comanche chiefs at the Council House in San Antonio, General Canalizo once again sent emissaries into Texas to visit the Indians, primarily the Comanches. When news was confirmed that an Indian raid was imminent, the Secretary of War, Branch T. Archer, called for the formation of additional militia companies to repel the Indians. The attack never came, and after several weeks the volunteers dispersed and returned to their homes. It is almost certain that Mexican spies had been stationed in Texas to observe the movements of the Texans and that the anticipated raid was delayed because of the precautionary measures taken by the Texans. Shortly after the dispersal of the volunteers, the Comanches began their great raid.[13] The Comanche raid, which caught the Texans unaware, caused the deaths of many settlers and the destruction of much property.

To understand how the Indians were able to make a surprise attack on Victoria and Linnville, so far from their villages, it is necessary to have some knowledge about the geography of the region at that time.

At the time of this raid the country between the Guadalupe and San Marcos, on the west, and the Colorado on the east, above a line drawn from Gonzales to La Grange, was a wilderness, while below that line it was thinly settled. Between Gonzales and Austin, on Plum Creek, were two recent settlers, Isom J. Goode and John A. Neill. From Gonzales to within a few miles of La Grange there was not a settler. There was not one between Gonzales and Bastrop, nor one between Austin and San Antonio. A road from Gonzales to Austin, then in the first year of its existence, had been opened in July 1839.[14]

With little effort, then, the war party of Indians was able to move down through South Central Texas virtually unnoticed. Seething over their losses at the Council House Fight, the Comanches had been agitated by Mexican agents to make war on the Texans. During the night of August 4 a war party of approximately 600 Comanche and Kiowa Indians, accompanied by a few Mexicans, descended from the Hill Country above San Antonio, San Marcos and Austin and began their march to the coast in an effort to avenge the deaths of their chiefs.[15]

The first Texan encounter with the Indians occurred on August 5 in the Hallettsville area. A physician named Joel Ponton and a man named Tucker Foley, en route from Columbus to Gonzales, came upon a group of Indians from the main war party. Immediately upon seeing the Indians, the two men turned their horses and attempted to outrun the Comanches to a creek three miles behind them. Ponton was soon overtaken. However, the Indians seemed more interested in capturing the faster horse ridden by Foley. As the Indians overtook Ponton they attempted to make a passing attack on his life. Having received several wounds, Ponton fell from his horse and pretended to be dead. After the Indians disappeared, he crawled into a thicket and some tall grass and hid there. Following a three-mile chase, Foley reached Ponton Creek, where he tried to hide in the water but was soon discovered and captured. The Indians then returned to where Ponton had been left for dead. Unable to locate him, the Indians made Foley call for his companion, who, of course, refused to answer. The Comanches then tortured Foley by cutting off the soles of his feet and forcing him to walk some distance. The Indians then shot and scalped him.[16] During the night Ponton made his way to his home in the Lavaca settlement and related the attack made upon himself and Foley. Immediately, Captain Adam Zumwalt and thirty-six men set out for the scene of the attack. Foley's body was buried and the men began their pursuit of the Indians.[17] On that same day a mail carrier from Austin arrived in Gonzales and reported the discovery of a large, fresh Indian trail crossing Plum Creek and leading southward. A group of twenty-four men was then assembled where they hoped to locate the Indian trail.[18] Early on the morning of August 7 the trail was located. During the morning, Zumwalt's men from the Lavaca settlement joined Ben McCulloch's force and the combined ranging companies began following the trail. About midday the forces, consisting of sixty men, met a third ranger group of sixty-five men from Victoria and Cuero under the command of Captain John Tumlinson.[19] With the combined force, numbering 125, the men continued their pursuit. After combining forces with Tumlinson, they learned that the Indians had attacked the town of Victoria. Only after the Indians had retired for the night were Tumlinson's men able to slip away and go for help from neighboring settlements.[20]

At 4:00 p.m. on August 6 the Comanche war party made its sudden appearance on the northern outskirts of Victoria, sweeping down from the direction of Spring Creek. The citizens were caught completely unprepared, since they had not been informed of any hostile Indians in the vicinity.[21] When the Indians first appeared, the citizens of the town thought that they were a group of Lipans, a tribe that was friendly toward the settlers and that frequently visited Victoria to trade with the white residents.[22] It was not until the war party had surrounded the town and begun riding in toward the citizens and yelling loudly that the people realized what was happening. No concentration of defense could be made because the Indians were everywhere around the edges of the town. Few arms could be obtained on such short notice, but the people were able to prevent the Comanches from entering the populated sections of town. One group of citizens made an unprepared charge upon the Indians, which resulted in the deaths of William McMin Nuner, a Doctor Arthur Gray, and the wounding of several other men. In many parts of the town the Indians were repulsed and were forced to remain on the outskirts.[23]

During this raid on Victoria many of the Indians collected and drove away all the cattle and horses they could find. Several Mexican traders who were visiting Victoria at the time had over 500 head of horses staked on the prairie surrounding the town. The Comanches took all these horses as well as many others found running loose.[24] A large number of horses owned by "Scotch" Southerland and recently brought to Victoria were also captured by the Indians, bringing their total capture count to approximately 1500 horses and mules.[25]

Late in the afternoon, the Comanches retired to Spring Creek, three miles from Victoria. While near Spring Creek the Indians killed a settler named Varlan Richeson and two black men, and they captured a black girl. During the night, a group of men commanded by Captain John Tumlinson left the town in search of reinforcements. These men passed near the Indians' camp on their way to the Cuero settlement in De Witt County.[26]

When making raids on the settlers, it was the usual custom of the Comanches to gather their plunder and then retire to their homes before the Texans were able to assemble a force to attack them. However, contrary to custom, the Indians once again surrounded and attacked Victoria on the morning of August 7. A party of men returning from Jackson County encountered the Indians about a mile from Victoria. Pinckney Caldwell and a Mexican man were killed by the Indians, while the other two men in the party, Joseph Rodgers and Jesse O. Wheeler, rushed into the town with the enemy close behind. The Indians succeeded in burning one house and robbing several others near the edge of town, but, after meeting strong resistance from the citizens of the town they decided to move in the direction of the lower settlements, herding up livestock as they proceeded toward the coast.[27]

The Indians continued down the country to near Nine Mile Point, where they captured Mrs. Cyrus Crosby and her child.[28] The Comanches then began moving eastward in the direction of Linnville. Nine miles from Victoria the Indians attacked the Van Norman ranch and from there proceeded to the Clausel ranch, located nine miles from Linnville. The Indians wounded Clausel, burned his house and stole many of his cattle and horses.[29]

On the night of August 7 the Indians established their camp along Placedo Creek, on the Benavides ranch, twelve miles from Linnville. While there they killed a wagoner named Stephens. Another man, a Frenchman, escaped from the Indians by hiding in the thick foliage and moss of a large oak tree.[30]

During the night William G. Ewing, a merchant traveling from Linnville to Victoria, noticed Stephens' empty wagon and a great number of campfires along the creek. Thinking the camp to be that of Mexican traders bound for Linnville, Ewing passed near there and proceeded to Victoria, where he learned of the Indian raid. The man became very distraught when he learned how close he had been to the Indians' camp.[31] On the morning of August 8 the Indians again moved in the direction of Linnville, Along the way Mrs. Crosby's small child, being hungry and tired, began to cry. The mother was unable to quiet the child, and one of the Indians "snatched the babe from her, cast it upon the ground and speared it before her eyes."[32]

Shortly after Mrs. Crosby's child was killed, the Indians made their appearance at about 8:00 a.m. on the Victoria road. Several of the citizens of Linnville discovered the Indians about two miles from town.[33] Being unaware of any large Indian war party in the area, the citizens supposed the Indians to be Mexican traders bringing in a large herd of horses to sell or trade. The citizens of Linnville did not become aware of the impending danger until the Indians approached the town, riding at nearly full speed, and in the shape of a half moon for the purpose of surrounding the town.[34]

As the Comanches launched their savage assault upon the coastal town of Linnville, the bewildered inhabitants, many of whom were without guns or any form of defense, began to retreat and tried to reach safety on boats anchored in the bay. Many found refuge on the steamer *Mustang,* which was lying offshore. The Comanches pursued the fleeing inhabitants into the water. In attempting to reach safety Major Hugh O. Watts, the customs collector for the port of Linnville, was killed, and his wife and a black woman and child were captured.[35]

As the inhabitants watched from their boats, the Comanches burned, looted, and destroyed the town. Judge John Hays became "exasperated" at the sight and, in frustration, grabbed a gun and leaped into the bay. The water was three or four feet deep, and he waded to the shore, where he shouted at the Indians and threatened them to come within range of his gun. The Indians, thinking this man to be "bad medicine," cautiously avoided him. After much persuasion from his friends, the judge returned to the boat. Everyone, including the judge, was surprised when his gun was examined and found to be unloaded.[36]

The Indians spent the entire day in the town plundering and burning its many stores and houses. Feather beds were dragged from many of the houses and tied to the tails of the horses. Holes were cut in the ticking, and the Indians would yell in amusement as the feathers went flying. The Indians also seemed to find great enjoyment in tying lengthy bolts of cloth to their horses' tails and racing through the burning town. The inhabitants watched helplessly from their boats as almost all the buildings in Linnville were burned and destroyed. Large numbers of cattle were herded into pens, where they were burned or cut to pieces by the Comanches. Almost everything of value was either taken or destroyed by the Indians.[37]

Linnville had been established as an important shipping point of the Gulf Coast, and consequently many warehouses in the town were filled with all kinds of merchandise. In one warehouse owned by John J. Linn the Indians found several cases of hats and umbrellas. The Indians, wearing the hats and waving the umbrellas, went racing up and down the streets between the burning buildings.[38] Included in the diversity of plunder taken by the Indians were fine clothes, ribbons and bolts of cloth. Walter Prescott Webb described the scene in vivid terms:

The warriors put on the coats, the chiefs the tall hats, and they plaited the bright ribbons and calicoes from the warehouses into their horses' manes and tails, making gay streamers as the riders dashed about in the stiff sea breeze of the coast.[39]

The Indians began to retire late in the afternoon, carrying with them several hundred horses and mules loaded with the plunder taken from the stores and warehouses of Linnville. With the town in flames, they withdrew across a nearby bayou and established their camp for the night. There they planned to begin their return trip with their immense plunder to their homeland in the Hill Country to the northwest.

While Linnville was being burned, other Texans were making preparations to intercept the Indians. Captain Tumlinson and his ranging company of 125 men left Victoria and moved eastward on the Texana road. They established a camp about midnight at the Casa Blanca water hole and later sent a messenger to Texana for reinforcements. At about eleven the next morning the Indian war party was discovered on the west bank of Garcitas Creek, near its junction with Arenosa Creek. Tumlinson's right flankers, being more than a mile away from the main force and unaware of the Indians, were cut off and unable to rejoin Tumlinson's volunteers. The Texans began to advance upon the Indians in parallel divisions. The Gonzales and Lavaca companies occupied the right nearest the Indians, while the Victoria and Cuero companies were to the left about twenty paces. The Indians, "sporting huge helmets of buffalo or elk-horns—armed with glistening shields, with bows and quivers, with guns and lances, and mounted on fleet chargers," began to prepare for the Texans' advance.[40] When they got close to the Indians, Tumlinson's volunteers dismounted in the open prairie. The Indians began to encircle the Texans in their customary manner of warfare. While a portion of the war party occupied Tumlinson's men, the rest of the Indians ran with their pack animals and plunder to safety. The Indians, who greatly outnumbered the Texans, seemed to be more concerned with the safety of their booty than with killing the Texans. A short skirmish ensued in which one man, Benjamin Mordecai of Victoria, was killed. After losing several warriors the Indians began a hasty retreat, with Tumlinson's men in close pursuit.[41]

On August 10 Tumlinson was joined by Ranger Captain Clarke L. Owen and forty men from Texana. Owen reported having a minor skirmish with the Indians the day before. In this fight one man was lost. Having extra horses that were stolen from Victoria and

Linnville, the Indians were able to change mounts in order to gain distance on the Texans who had no fresh mounts.[42]

While the Indians were among the lower settlements and were plundering and devastating the countryside, word of the attacks upon Victoria and Linnville was being spread to Gonzales, Seguin, Austin, Bastrop and La Grange. The alarm was sounded for volunteers to congregate and intercept the Indians before they were able to return to their familiar haunts in the Texas Hill Country. When it was ascertained that the Indians were retreating on their downward trail, the Texans then realized that they would need to intercept the Comanches in the area of Plum Creek, in present-day Caldwell County.[43] Messengers were sent out to all points urging volunteers to rendezvous at Isham Good's cabin on the Gonzales–Austin road near Plum Creek.[44]

By the early morning of August 12, the number of volunteers at Good's Crossing on Plum Creek had steadily grown. The combined forces, numbering approximately 200, awaited the approaching Comanches. The ensuing battle began as a series of skirmishes as the Indians attempted to avoid the Texans' advances and concentrate more on securing their plunder and getting to the safety of their homes in the nearby hills. The Indians pressed onward in a north-westerly direction, all the while skirmishing with the Texans for about five miles across the prairie. With the Texan forces continuing to draw closer to the main body of the war party, the Comanches halted their retreat at a place later known as Kelley Springs.[45] The Indians took up a position in a large grove of live oaks and awaited the Texans' attack The volunteers advanced to within 200 yards of the Indians and then dismounted. Orders were given for the Texans to arrange themselves in a "hollow square" formation. While the Texans formed their lines, about twenty or thirty Comanche warriors and chiefs began encircling the volunteers, firing at them from a distance of sixty to eighty yards.[46]

As the warriors circled the Texans, others of the tribe used the time to drive all their horses and pack animals to safety. The Indians continued to charge the Texans for about thirty minutes. In the midst of the fighting one of the chiefs, who had been charging very close to the Texans' position, was shot from his horse. The loss of this individual demoralized the other warriors. A number of warriors removed the dead chief's body from the battlefield and carried it to the grove of oaks where a large concentration of Indians was located. The Indians began a loud wailing over the loss of their chief. Seizing this moment to attack with a basic ranger strategy proposed and led by Ranger Captain Matthew Caldwell, the Texans mounted and charged the Indians.[47]

Unable to withstand the Texans' assault, the main portion of the war party was dispersed. The Indians broke into small parties and began a hasty retreat, fighting along the way.[48] The small groups of Indians ran toward the hills above San Marcos, while the volunteers pursued them for approximately twelve to fifteen miles. The pursuit was ended between the present-day towns of San Marcos and Kyle.[49]

During the wild confusion of retreat, the Comanches endeavored to kill their captives taken in the raids upon Victoria and Linnville. As the Indians began their retreat, Mrs. Crosby, who had been captured near Victoria, dismounted and made an effort to escape into a thicket. She was killed by a Comanche warrior who shot two arrows which "passed clear through her."[50] A woman named Watts, whose husband had been killed in the attack on Linnville, was also shot with an arrow. Fortunately for her, the arrow was partially deflected by one of the stays in the corset which she wore. Mrs. Watts recovered from her painful wound and later married Dr. J. R. Fretwell and spent the remainder of her life in Port Lavaca.[51]

Following the Battle of Plum Creek the Texans gathered up the immense spoils left on the battlefield by the Comanches. Identified articles were returned to their owners, but much of the plunder could not be identified and was divided among the men who participated in the battle.[52]

After returning to the battlefield where the fight had begun, the Texans were joined by volunteer forces which had arrived too late to take an active part in the battle. Colonel John H. Moore had come from Fayette County with a group of men. Captain Tumlinson, Adam Zumwalt and Clarke L. Owen, having pursued the Indians all the way from Victoria and Linnville, arrived at Plum Creek with about 125 volunteers.[53]

The Comanches lost over eighty of their chiefs and warriors in the fight with the Texans at Plum Creek. Colonel Edward Burleson initially reported that more than sixty Indians were killed. But during the day, as more parties of volunteers returned with additional reports, it became evident that more than eighty Indians had been killed. Eight or ten bodies of dead Comanches were found in the San Marcos River; several bodies were located as far away as the San Antonio Road. It is probable that, after returning to their camp, many other Indians died from wounds inflicted during the fight. For many years afterwards, bones of the Comanches were found along their path of retreat.[54]

Texan losses were slight. Major General Felix Huston, who commanded the volunteers, reported that his losses were "one killed and seven wounded—one mortally."[55]

The destruction of the formidable Comanche-Kiowa aggregation at Plum Creek was a severe blow to the Indians, one from which they would never fully recover. After this fight, the Indians never again posed a major threat to the Central Texas area, nor did they ever again penetrate into or below the settled portions of Texas. In spite of their crushing defeat, the Indians continued minor depredations, making the frontier region unsafe for settlement. Many Texans believed that the Indians had not been punished severely enough for their devastating foray into the lower settlements. The Texans agreed that an additional show of force was needed to show that they would no longer tolerate the hostility of belligerent tribes in Texas. In October 1840 Ranger Colonel John H. Moore, along with approximately 90 volunteers, set out from Austin to penetrate deep into Indian territory and launch an offensive against the Comanches.

After about three weeks on the trail Chief Castro and his Lipan scouts reported to Colonel Moore that a large Indian trail had been discovered along the Red Fork of the Colorado River. On October 23 the scouts discovered the Comanche village along the south bank of the river near present-day Colorado City. Undetected by the Comanches, the Texans positioned themselves during the night, and at daylight on October 24, Moore ordered his men to attack the village.[56]

The volunteers were within 200 yards of the village before they were detected. The Comanches were taken by complete surprise and fled to the river, "which was in the shape of a half moon encircling the village." As the troops charged into the village, they fired on the retreating and confused Indians. Many of the Indians were killed before reaching the river. A large number were killed or drowned as they ran into the water. Those who succeeded in crossing the river had their retreat cut off on the prairie by a company of men led by Lieutenant Clarke L. Owen.

The entire assault on the Comanche village lasted only about thirty minutes. "The bodies of men, women and children were to be seen on every hand, wounded, dying and dead." Approximately 128 Indians were killed. The Texans captured 34 prisoners and recovered two Mexican boys who had been taken captives by the Comanches three months earlier. All the Indians' property was either captured or destroyed by the Texans. Among the spoils taken by the Texans were goods recognized as those stolen by the Indians in their raid on Linnville.[57]

Moore's expedition to the regions of the upper Colorado brought triumphant results. The Comanches, who had previously raided into the lower settlements, were totally destroyed—either at the Battle of Plum Creek or in the fight on the Colorado. After these defeats, the Comanches were never able to fully recover, and thus, they moved northward out of the Central Texas area. These engagements may have represented the most severe punishment ever inflicted upon the Comanches in Texas. With these two battles the Texans felt that the raids on Victoria and Linnville had been avenged.

The failure of the Comanche Raid of 1840 produced several significant results. The defeat of the Comanches thwarted the Mexican effort to employ the Indians in Texas as allies. Also evolving from this series of events was the development of cavalry tactics, the use of repeating firearms, a display of vigorous spirit in Indian fighting and the gaining of experience by future leaders in warfare. These features became part of the arsenal used by Texas Rangers during the latter nineteenth century and into the twentieth century.

After the Battle of Plum Creek, much of the booty recaptured from the Indians was divided among the participants in the fight. One man, James N. Smith, received a beautiful beaded shot bag with Roman cross designs on it. An examination of the contents of the bag revealed a letter written from a Mexican to one of the Indian chiefs. In the letter the Mexican stated that "they would meet each other at Corpus Christi or Lynvill [sic]."[58]

During their raid, the Comanches very cautiously avoided a fight. As noted, they seemed to be more interested in the plunder taken than they were in murder and revenge. The Indians' principal interest in their horses and pack animals tends to indicate that there was a need for the goods, possibly to be used in a larger and more formidable raid on the frontier settlements. Immediately after attacking Victoria, the Indians gathered up the large number of horses on the prairies. Again at Linnville the Comanches were more interested in the goods found in the stores and warehouses than they were in murdering the townspeople.[59]

Burdened with immense plunder, the Comanches began a slow retreat northward. Although a group of Texans under Ranger Captain John Tumlinson attempted to engage the Indians in battle, the Comanches showed a disposition to avoid fighting. They were more interested in getting their horses and plunder to the safety of the Hill Country. The Indians would encircle the Texans and skirmish with them while their plunder was pushed onward.[60]

When the Comanches were confronted by the Texas volunteers at Plum Creek, they once again tried to avoid a battle. The Indians immediately formed a line between their plunder and the Texans. As a number of Comanche warriors engaged the Texans in minor skirmishing, the major portion of the war party, along with captives, plunder, and horses, continued across the prairie. It was only after the Texans charged that the Indians were forced to fight.[61] Many of the volunteers could not understand why the Indians refused to fight. One Texan stated: "It has always been a mystery to me why the Indians became so terribly demoralized in this battle. It was fought on the open prairie, and they could see that they greatly outnumbered us. It is rather strange that they did not make a stand."[62]

Following the Battle of Plum Creek, Major General Huston reported that a Mr. Sutherland "had information from a Mexican, that the expedition was gotten up at Matamoros, and was to be composed of six hundred Indians and forty Mexicans; and this is confirmed by the fact that new Mexican blankets and other articles usually given as presents to the Indians, were found amongst the plunder."[63]

After the Great Comanche Raid the only major depredation made by the Comanches was carried out against the Mexicans in the states of Coahuila and Nuevo Leon, the latter suffering most severely. It is believed that this raid into Mexico resulted from the failure of the Mexicans to send promised support to the Comanches in their raids on Victoria and Linnville.[64]

Colonel Reuben M. Potter, who resided in Matamoros at the time of the Great Comanche Raid, stated that "there are many circumstances connected with the raids on Victoria and Linnville which support the claim that Mexican authorities instigated them and promised co-operation in carrying them out."[65]

Huston's victory at Plum Creek and Moore's victory on the upper Colorado utterly crushed the fighting power of the Comanches in Central Texas. These overwhelming victories also frustrated Canalizo's plans for retaking Texas with the help of Indian allies.

The Comanches' defeat helped to ease the constant threat of the most powerful and most feared Indian tribe in Central Texas. Believing that the Texans were invincible, the Comanches never again attempted to molest the Central Texas settlers to any great extent after 1840. Since the most powerful Indian tribe involved in the Mexican plot had been defeated, the whole scheme was abandoned.

It is significant that, with the defeat of the Comanches, there came the development of new tactics in frontier warfare against the Indians. Until the Great Comanche Raid, it was highly irregular for the Texans to charge a large body of Indians. The usual procedure for the volunteer soldiers was to dismount and await the Indians' charge or attack. These tactics were employed by Tumlinson's men as they followed the Comanches toward Plum Creek, but were changed by Huston as the battle progressed.[66]

The Battle of Plum Creek began with the Texans employing the traditional tactics of Indian fighting. Major General Huston's plan of action called for his men to dismount and form a hollow square with one side open. When it was realized that this form of fighting was ineffective, upon the advice of Ranger Matthew Caldwell, Huston ordered a general charge. Firing as they charged, the men advanced on the Indians. "The Indians did not stand the charge, and fled at all points."[67]

In Moore's fight on the upper Colorado, cavalry tactics were also used effectively. Moore's volunteers charged directly into the Indian village, firing their guns from horseback. As the enemy fled, Lieutenant Clarke Owen's men, acting as a cavalry unit, pursued the Indians and cut off their retreat. These men also fired from horseback. In this fight Ranger Captain Micah Andrews tested one of Colt's repeating rifles and reported that he was able to fire the Colt rifle ten times while his companions were able to fire their rifles only twice.[68]

The Battle of Plum Creek and the fight on the upper Colorado marked the beginning of a new era of frontier warfare. Mounted charges, firing from horseback, and the use of repeating firearms all helped to establish cavalry as a potent weapon against the Plains Indians.[69]

With the defeat of the Comanches, a new spirit was exhibited by the Texans. There was more determination and enthusiasm in the men's actions. Huston reported at Plum Creek that "nothing could exceed the animation of the men." It was also reported that Burleson exhibited "cool, deliberate and prompt courage and conduct." The other leaders had also "acted with the utmost courage and firmness."[70]

Until the Great Comanche Raid this new and exhilarating spirit displayed by the Texans was not present. Before 1840 the Texans showed little enthusiasm in Indian fighting. In previous Indian fights the Texans were usually hampered by negligence, incompetence, and failure. At Plum Creek, however, no mistakes were made, although Huston would have failed to deliver such a crushing blow to the Comanches had it not been for the advice of older and more experienced Indian fighters like Rangers Matthew Caldwell, Edward Burleson and Ben McCulloch. Moore's expedition into Comanche territory was a successful achievement. His appropriate orders and the troops' swift and accurate performance resulted in a total defeat for the Comanches. These battles helped to develop experienced Indian fighters and produce competent leaders who would later take an active part in the Mexican War and the Civil War.

The Great Comanche Raid of 1840 ended in disaster for the Indians. The Comanches, considered to be the fiercest of all Indians in Texas, were utterly crushed and never recovered from their defeat. The Great Comanche Raid was the last major threat to the settlers in the South Central Texas area, although minor skirmishes and depredations continued in the region for some years afterwards. The Comanche defeat introduced "an important epoch in Texas history, and indeed most of our historians regard it as the turning point in affairs with the Indians."[71]

Since Indian problems had hindered the settlement of the Texas frontier for many years, the defeat of the Indians in the Great Comanche Raid helped to accelerate the westward movement. Had it not been for the Great Comanche Raid, the Battle of Plum Creek and Moore's victory on the Colorado, the westward settlement of the Texas frontier would probably have been drastically retarded in the 19th century. The defeat of the hostile Comanches aided greatly in making the uninhabitable frontier of Texas a safe place for the settlers to build homes and raise families.

NOTES

1. For a more complete study of these events see Donaly E. Brice, *The Great Comanche Raid: Boldest Indian Attack of the Texas Republic* (Austin: Eakin Press, 1987). Hubert Howe Bancroft, *A History of the North Mexican States and Texas* (San Francisco: The History Company, Publishers, 1889), 2:315.

2. Walter P. Webb, *The Texas Rangers: A Century of Frontier Defense* (Austin: University of Texas Press, 1935), 47–54.

3. William Preston Johnston, *The Life of Albert Sidney Johnston* (New York: D. Appleton and Company, Inc., 1879), 115.

4. H. W. Karnes to Albert S. Johnston, January 10, 1840, Records Relating to Indian Affairs (RG 005), Doc. 74, Archives and Information Services Division, Texas State Library and Archives Commission (hereafter cited as ARIS/TSLAC).

5. Ibid.

6. A. S. Johnston to Lt. Col. Wm. S. Fisher, January 30, 1840, Records Relating to Indian Affairs (RG 005), Doc. 77, ARIS/TSLAC.

7. Rena Maverick Green, ed., *Memoirs of Mary A. Maverick* (San Antonio: Alamo Printing Company, 1921), 31.

8. Johnston, *Life of Albert S. Johnston,* 117.

9. John Henry Brown, *Indian Wars and Pioneers of Texas* (Austin: L. E. Daniell, n.d.), 77; Report from Col. Hugh McLeod to M. B. Lamar, March 20, 1840, Texas Congress, *Journal of the House of Representatives of the Republic of Texas,* 5th [Texas] Congress, lst Session, Appendix, 136–139.

10. Brown, *Indian Wars and Pioneers,* 77.

11. Report from Col. Hugh McLeod to M. B. Lamar, March 20 1840, *Journal of the House,* 5th (Texas] Congress, 1st Session, Appendix, 138.

12. Mildred P. Mayhall, *Indian Wars of Texas* (Waco: The Texian Press, 1965), 25–29; Letter from Capt. George T. Howard to Lt. CoL Wm. S. Fisher, April 6, 1840, "Memoirs of John Salmon Ford," ms, 2:227–228b.

13. Sam Houston Dixon, *Romance and Tragedy of Texas History* (Houston: Texas Historical Publishing Company, 1924), 1:266.

14. L. E. Daniell, *Texas: The Country and Its Men* (Austin: L. E. Daniell, n.d.), 49.

15. The number of Indians participating in the Great Comanche Raid seems to vary according to different reports. According to the *Austin City Gazette* of August 12, 1840, the Comanche raiding party consisted of approximately 500 Indians; a later *City Gazette* on August 19 stated that the party consisted of only 200 Indians; John Linn, a citizen of Victoria, reported that there were 600 Indians involved in the raid on Victoria. John J. Linn, *Reminiscences of Fifty Years in Texas* (New York: Sadler and Company, 1883), 338; Ben McCulloch, who was a major participant in the defeat of the Comanches at Plum Creek, stated that there were close to 1000 Indians. This estimate is probably too high since it varies drastically with the other reports. Victor M. Rose, *The Life and Services of General Ben McCulloch* (Philadelphia: Pictorial Bureau of the Press, 1888), 55.

16. John Holmes Jenkins, ed., *Recollections of Early Texas: The Memoirs of John Holland Jenkins* (Austin: University of Texas Press, 1958), 60–62.

17. Brown, *Indian Wars and Pioneers,* 79.

18. Ibid.

19. *Austin City Gazette,* September 2, 1840.

20. Ibid.

21. *The Texas Sentinel,* [Austin, Texas], September 19, 1840.

22. Linn, *Reminiscences,* 338–339.

23. *The Texas Sentinel,* September 19, 1840.

24. Linn, *Reminiscences,* 338–339.

25. Brown, *Indian Wars and Pioneers,* 79–80.

26. Linn, *Reminiscences,* 339.

27. Ibid.

28. Brown, *Indian Wars and Pioneers,* 80; Mrs. Cyrus Crosby, nee Nancy Darst, was born April 1, 1816, in Missouri. She was the daughter of Jacob C. and Elizabeth Bryan Darst. In January 1831 she arrived in the Green DeWitt Colony along with her father, her stepmother Margaret Hughes Darst, and her half-brother David S. H. Darst. Jacob C. Darst was one of the "Immortal Thirty-Two" from Gonzales who went to the aid of the Alamo and fell with its defenders on March 6, 1836. *J. W. Franks vs R. D. Hancock,* Texas Supreme Court Case Records (RG 201), Case File M7406, ARIS/TSLAC; "Darst" family file, Gonzales County Archives, Gonzales County Courthouse, Gonzales, Texas; *Memorial and Genealogical Record of Southwest Texas* (Chicago: Good-

speed Bros., Publishers, 1894), 82. Nancy Darst was married to Cyrus Crosby in Matagorda County on November 11, 1838. Matagorda County Marriage Records, Book A, 8, County Clerk's Office, Matagorda County Courthouse, Bay City, Texas.

29. John S. Ford, "Memoirs," ms, 2:233.

30. Brown, *Indian Wars and Pioneers*, 80.

31. Linn, *Reminiscences,* 340-341.

32. *Franks* vs *Hancock,* Texas Supreme Court Records (RG 201), File M7406, ARIS/TSLAC).

33. Linnville was located three and one-half miles northeast of Port Lavaca on Lavaca Bay. The town had been established in 1831 by John J. Linn. The site of the town was in Victoria County, but in 1846 the area became a part of Calhoun County. Walter P. Webb, et al., eds., *The Handbook of Texas* (Austin: The Texas State Historical Association, 1952), 2:60; Calhoun County Deed Records, Vol. C, 577, County Clerk's Office, Calhoun County Courthouse, Port Lavaca, Texas. After its destruction by the Comanches in 1840, the town was rebuilt and flourished for a few years until its importance as a seaport gave way to a deeper and more favorable harbor at Port Lavaca. Having lost its significance as a seaport the town eventually died out, never to be rebuilt.

34. *Austin City Gazette,* August 26, 1840.

35. Ford, "Memoirs," ms. 2:233; "David Brown Moves to Texas," Recollections of Cordelia Brown Harwood as told by Della Paxton Jones, Gonzales *Inquirer,* June 4, 1953; Gilbert Onderdonk, *Stories of Early Texas Life,* ms, 2–5, Gilbert Onderdonk Papers, Center for American History, University of Texas, Austin.

36. Linn, *Reminiscences,* 341.

37. *Austin City Gazette,* August 26, 1840.

38. Linn, *Reminiscences,* 341–342.

39. Webb, *The Texas Rangers,* 59.

40. *Austin City Gazette,* September 2, 1840.

41. Ibid.

42. Brown, *Indian Wars and Pioneers*, 80.

43. Ibid., 80–81.

44. Z. N. Morrell, *Flowers and Fruits in the Wilderness: Or Forty-six Years in Texas and Two Winters in Honduras* (Boston: Gould and Lincoln, 1872), 128.

45. A. A. Ross, M.D. to R. M. Farrar, May 28, 1932. Letter in possession of Donaly E. Brice, Lockhart, Texas.

46. Brown, *Indian Wars and Pioneers,* 81–82.

47. Brown, *Indian Wars and Pioneers,* 82.

48. *Journal of the House,* 5th [Texas] Congress, 1st Session, Appendix, 142.

49. Jenkins, *Recollections of Early Texas,* 65; Brown, *Indian Wars and Pioneers,* 82.

50. Brazos [pseud.], *The Life of Robert Hall* (Austin: Ben C. Jones and Company, Printers, 1898), 50–51.

51. Ibid.

52. *Austin City Gazette,* August 19, 1840; Jenkins, *Recollections of Early Texas,* 67–68; Brazos, *Life of Robert Hall,* 53.

53. Brown, *Indian Wars and Pioneers,* 82.

54. *Journal of the House,* 5th [Texas] Congress, 1st Session, Appendix, 142–144; *Austin City Gazette,* August 19, 1840; Brazos, *Life of Robert Hall,* 52.

55. Maj. Gen. Felix Huston's Report of Plum Creek Battle, August 12, 1840, Doc. 1966, A. J. Houston Papers, ARIS/TSLAC.

56. Col. John H. Moore's official report to the Secretary of War, *Telegraph and Texas Register* [Houston, Texas], November 18, 1840.

57. Moore's official report, *Telegraph and Texas Register,* November 18, 1840; Brown, *Indian Wars and Pioneers,* 84.

58. James N. Smith, "Autobiography," 3:218, ms, Center for American History, University of Texas, Austin.

59. Linn, *Reminiscences,* 339, 341–342.

60. Brown, *Indian Wars and Pioneers,* 80; Rose, *Life of Ben McCulloch,* 55–56.

61. Jenkins, *Recollections of Early Texas,* 64.

62. Brazos, *Life of Robert Hall,* 51.

63. *Journal of the House,* 5th [Texas] Congress, 1st Session, Appendix, 144.

64. Dixon, *Romance and Tragedy,* 268-269.

65. Ibid., 269.

66. *Austin City Gazette,* September 2, 1840; Brown, *Indian Wars and Pioneers,* 80.

67. *Journal of the House,* 5th [Texas] Congress, 1st Session, Appendix, 141–142.

68. Moore's official report, *Telegraph and Texas Register,* November 18, 1840.

69. *San Antonio Light* [San Antonio, Texas], January 15, 1966.

70. *Journal of the House,* 5th [Texas] Congress, 1st Session, Appendix, 142.

71. James T. DeShields, *Border Wars of Texas* (Tioga, Texas: Herald Company, 1912), 320.

★ 4 ★

THE DEADLY COLTS ON WALKER'S CREEK

Stephen L. Moore

The key Indian agent in Texas from the U.S., Pierce Butler, had more resources and thus more negotiating power than Sam Houston's appointed agents. He found the Indians receptive when he called for a meeting of all Plains Indians to be held at Cache Creek of the Red River in December 1843. Butler arrived with an escort of 30 U.S. dragoons and a large store of gifts.[1]

Butler spent 18 days with the Comanches and their associate tribes speaking of peace. He advised his superiors that the Indians would eventually need help in surviving as game became more scarce for hunting and the better farmlands were taken over by the Anglo Texas settlers, Butler took great interest in documenting the demographics of the Indian tribes he met with. In his report of January 31, 1844, Butler counted 1,500 people in the two main Wichita towns on the upper Trinity River. He found that another 500 or 600 lived in two Wichita communities near the Wichita mountains. Chief Jose Maria's Caddos had largely moved to the upper Trinity River, while some remained on the Brazos. Butler estimated the total population of southern Comanche tribes at 15,000 people, spread widely from Texas to the plains.[2]

The efforts of the Texas commissioners continued into the spring of 1844. Sam Houston built a permanent peace council house on Tawakoni Creek—complete with an apartment for his visits—and stocked it with corn. The most significant council occurred in April 1844, when some 500 Indians appeared at Tawakoni Creek's council house. The group consisted primarily of Delawares, Shawnees, Wichitas and Caddos. Texas commissioners James C. Neill, Leonard H. Williams, Benjamin Sloat and Thomas G. Western distributed goods and spoke of peace with the two prominent Indian speakers, St. Louis of the Delawares and Caddo Chief Bintah.[3]

Caddo chiefs Red Bear and Jose Maria made speeches, as did Chief Kechikaroqua, who spoke for the upper Trinity River Tawakoni Wichitas. The key point of discussion during April and May was the creation of a boundary line to run from the old Waco town north to the Red River, splitting the upper and lower Cross Timbers. The proposed line would pass just west of Bird's Fort, the westernmost Texas settlement. Chief Kechikaroqua insisted that President Houston should be present for the negotiations before he would agree to any such measure. The Caddos accused the Wichitas of stealing and raiding, further breaking down negotiations during late May.[4]

Sam Houston sent John Connor and Louis Sanchez to the Penateka camp on the upper Colorado River in May 1844, to discuss the proposed boundary line. In spite of talks that promised hope of an agreement, Connor and Sanchez's efforts stalled when dangerous news arrived in June. Captain Jack Hays' rangers had fought a battle with Comanches and the uneasiness in the wake of this fight would cause peace talks to halt until the fall.[5]

The newly seated Eighth Congress of the Republic of Texas passed a joint resolution on December 19, 1843, to cover the wages and "liabilities that have been created for the support" of Captain Hays' rangers during the year. The sum of $6,450 was dispensed to Hays for distribution to the men and the merchants who had supplied his company.[6]

When Jack Hays left Seguin on New Year's Eve 1843, he rode on horseback for the temporary Texas capital at Washington-on-the-Brazos. He was accompanied by congressman Frank Paschal, congressman George Howard, William Cooke and Antonio Menchaca. This party arrived on January 4 and was invited to chat with President Houston.[7]

Hays informed Houston that four companies of Cherokees from the United States had visited General Woll at San Fernando, across the Rio Grande. He had received the intelligence from Mexican traders, who indicated that Manuel Flores may have instigated the action.[8]

Sam Houston listened to the veteran Texas Rangers' ideas on how to maintain order on the southwestern prairies and pledged to work on legislation with his Congress. The friendship of the Texas president with Hays' father no doubt continued to work in his favor, as the Eighth Texas Congress passed an act for the protection of the southwestern and western frontiers on January 23, 1844. John C. Hays was authorized to raise a "company of mounted gunmen," and he was specifically designated as its commander. He was allowed a lieutenant and 40 privates. Hays was to be paid $75 per month, his lieutenant $50, and his privates $30 per month.

Hays' rangers were to be organized by February 1, 1844, or as soon thereafter as possible. Their original enlistment was to be for a period of four months, with payments to them made every two months. President Houston reserved the right to extend the service period of Hays' company in an emergency. Each ranger was to furnish his own arms, horse and equipment. As captain, Jack Hays was paid $75 a month. Lieutenant Ben McCulloch was paid $50 a month and each ranger was paid $30 a month. Their company was directed to "range on the western and southwestern frontier, from the county of Bexar to the county of Refugio, and westward, as the public interest may require."[9]

Captain Hays was not able to muster in his new company by February 1, but by February 25, he had 20 men. He was compelled to leave San Antonio during the month to scout between Gonzales and La Grange, sometime around February 20. He was accompanied by three trusted friends—William Cooke, George Howard and Frank

Paschal. They encountered four or five Mexican marauders along a stream called Peach Creek. They managed to capture a horse but lost the bandits in the creek bottom. The *Telegraph and Texas Register* also reveals that Captain Ben McCulloch was out after Mexicans in the same area with a volunteer company from Gonzales.

Hays and company returned to San Antonio a few days later, where he organized his new ranging company. Ben McCulloch was elected his lieutenant and 25 privates were on board by that time. During March and April, other rangers would join his company and finally bring his strength up to the designated 40 privates. Among those enlisting for service were congressman Frank Paschal and Sam Walker, who had only recently escaped from a Mexican prison. Walker, who had arrived in Texas in early 1842, had first served under Captain Jesse Billingsley during the Woll campaign and subsequently under Jack Hays. Walker stayed with the Mier Expedition after Captain Hays departed in December 1842, and was captured. Walker remained a prisoner through July 1843, when he managed to escape to the coast with others and secure passage on a ship back to New Orleans. He departed Louisiana in January 1844, and soon reached San Antonio as Captain Hays was forming a new ranger company. After his rough treatment in Mexico, Sam Walker had little desire to take any prisoners when he fought.

Other notable veterans whom Hays enlisted during March and April include Kit Acklin, Pasqual Buquor, Mike Chevallie, James Dunn, Matt Jett, William Jett, Griff Jones, Rufus Perry, Joe Tivey, Josiah Taylor and Rufus Taylor.

Hays made another trip to Houston to visit with President Houston around the first days of March 1844. Texas Revolution veteran John W. Lockhart was present at the hotel when Hays checked in and signed the register book. Lockhart was surprised that the "small, boyish-looking youngster, with not a particle of beard on his face," could be the famed Texas Ranger who was so often written about in the weekly newspapers. To his surprise, he found that the youthful-appearing frontiersman was indeed "the 'Captain Jack'" he had heard about and Lockhart noted that Hays stayed in town only long enough to conduct his visit with the government before departing quickly for San Antonio.[10]

Hays' company left San Antonio again by mid-March to pursue a group of Texas outlaws who had raided ranches near San Antonio and headed north towards the Colorado River with nearly 2,000 head of cattle. A new rumor that General Woll was marching on San Antonio again almost started a panic, but spies soon put down the rumor and calm returned. News that Hays was forming a new ranging company compelled some Mexican-born San Antonians to leave for the Rio Grande.[11]

Jack Hays rode out with his men to gain intelligence on the Woll rumor but soon found it to be of no concern. San Antonio merchant John Twohig was among the citizens joining Hays for this quick ride, but he accidentally shot himself in the process.[12]

In 1844 it was reported that the Mexican Army was again approaching San Antonio. One night while saddling my horse to go out, quietly and without creating any excitement with Col. Jack Hays and others to ascertain if the enemy was approaching, I received a severe wound in the right leg caused by the discharge of my own pistol while putting it in the holster which was then hanging on the pummel of my saddle. I was standing by the side of my horse. This wound was for a while considered fatal and I suffered much from it for over a year.

Twohig's wound would prevent him from riding with the rangers again in 1844, but Hays was able to assemble the most able company ever under his charge during this period. His men were armed with the five-shot Colt revolvers. Although Colts had been used by Hays, Sam Walker, and several others on occasion on the Texas frontiers, 1844 was the first year that the rangers were fully equipped with Colts. Ranger Sam Walker wrote to the Colt factory on November 30, 1846, saying, "the pistols which you made for the Texas Navy have been in use by the Rangers for three years." Walker by that point had been in enough combat with the rangers to say that the rangers' "confidence in them is unbounded, so much so that they are willing to engage four times their number." Another account by Texas Navy commander Edwin Ward Moore agrees that Colt revolvers reached the hands of the rangers from the Navy around the early part of 1844.[13]

Around June 1, 1844, Captain Hays and 15 rangers left camp near San Antonio and rode north to the area between the Pedernales and the Llano rivers. In a report written to Secretary of War George W. Hill two weeks later, Captain Hays said that his rangers were attempting to "ascertain what tribe of Indians was committing so many depredations."[14]

After scouring the northern country between the Pedernales and Llano, Hays turned for San Antonio. He wished to go no further "on account of the negotiations that were going on." Although he had seen "sufficient signs of Indians to have induced me to proceed farther up the country," Hays had orders to go no further and he prudently turned for home.[15]

His rangers recrossed the Pedernales River and made camp on June 8 at a stream later identified by Hays as Walker's Creek. This place was said to be four miles east of the Pinto Trace—the old Indian trail from Nacogdoches to the southwest—at a point equidistant from Austin, Gonzales and San Antonio. Modern maps show five creeks known as Walker, and accounts of this Hays expedition differ widely as to the location of this body of water. In his report, Jack Hays wrote that his men made camp "about fifty miles above Seguin." John Caperton, who prepared a biography of Jack Hays in 1879, wrote that this encounter with Comanches occurred "within about 35 or 40 miles of San Antonio, at a place called Cista's [Sisters] Creek." One source puts the ranger camp at a point on Sisters Creek, two miles above where it empties into the Guadalupe.[16]

The rangers dismounted their horses, unsaddling or loosening the cinches. Hays had a four-man patrol, well back protecting the rear, which soon galloped in to alert him that they were being followed. Two men, Kit Acklin and Alexander Coleman, had been collecting honey from a bee tree when Coleman spotted approaching Comanches from his elevated vantage point. "I immediately ordered my men to saddle, and prepare to fight," wrote Hays, "for I could have no doubt but that their intentions were hostile."[17]

His veteran rangers each carried a rifle and two of the new Colt five-shooters. They rode cautiously and soon spotted the Comanches who had been trailing their rear guard. Later evidence would show that this force of about 60 Indians included Yamparika Comanches, Kiowas and a few Shoshones.[18]

These Comanches only turned and rode away at a slow pace, indicating that they were not scared by the presence of the 16 rangers. They drifted back toward some woods, where Hays presumed many Comanches might be waiting. Experience taught the rangers not to charge them. "Hays was too old an 'Indian fighter' to be caught by such traps and made no efforts at pursuit," the Clarksville *Northern Standard* reported on July 24.[19]

The Comanches slowly circled, trying to draw the rangers into charging upon them, as they edged closer to the woods. Hays wrote that the Comanches used "every art and strategy to throw me off my guard, and induce me to give chase to them. They, however, did not succeed in their design." The Indians shouted insults at the Texans in Spanish and Hays reportedly shouted his own insults at Yellow Wolf, one of the Comanche leaders.[20]

Hays kept his men at a walk and moved up the side of the stream. Their ploy having failed, the Comanches galloped into the woods and vanished, but soon a considerable body of them was seen to be forming along the crest of a slight hill. The rangers halted, counting 60 to 70 Comanches riding back and forth waving their lances and shields and shouting challenges, dashing down the slope a few paces before wheeling back into line.[21]

This game went on for a time as the Indians tried to goad the rangers into firing at long range for which their padded shields would stop the balls. Once the rangers fired, the Comanches thought they could rush down the slope, showering them with arrows and engaging them at close range with their lances. Hays wisely held his ground and kept his men riding at a walk towards the hill.[22]

The rangers were visible to the Indians as they rode forward up the gentle slope, but as they came to the steeper base of the hill they were out of sight of the Comanches for a few critical moments. A few curious Indians rode down the hill to see where the Texans had gone. In that moment, Hays had led his men in a gallop around the hill for a charge up the slope to attack the surprised Comanches on their flank. The rangers fired their rifles into the massed Indians, killing a number of them. Rufe Perry stated that the rangers "went around to the other side of the brush and come in on them. About sixty of the red devils come out of the brush onto the prairie when we opened fire on them."[23]

The melee moved down the slope onto the level ground, and in a matter of minutes the Comanches rallied into formation and turned to charge the heavily outnumbered rangers. Jack Hays, knowing that his men had fired the last of their loaded rifles, shouted as the Indians closed in, "Drop your rifles, men."[24]

Hays and his small company of rangers were unwittingly changing the course of frontier fighting this day, trusting in their little-used five-shooter Colts. The Comanches had maneuvered the rangers out into the open and caused them to empty their rifles. Outnumbering the Texans some four to one, they must have felt some security against only the little pistols and knives carried by the rangers. Suddenly, however, Hays' men opened fire with their Colts and continued firing round after round. Comanches tumbled from their saddles. Hays wrote that the "five-shooting pistols did good execution. Had it not been for them, I doubt what the consequences would have been. I cannot recommend these arms too highly."[25]

Although the Comanches fled after the first severe round of Colt fire, the rangers pursued them and created several more close-action encounters. The fight was a moving one which was "desperate[ly] contested by both parties," according to Hays. In between moments of close action, the rangers were able to change cylinders on their pistols. Hays related that is was not until "after the third round from the five-shooters" that the Comanches gave way and fled. Even after that point, when the rangers' pursuit came too close to them, the Indians turned and made "desperate charges and efforts to defeat me."[26]

During these counter-charges, the Colt pistols took their toll on the Comanches. The rangers, however, suffered their own casualties in the counterattacks. During one Comanche assault, Sam Walker and Ad Gillespie were caught ahead of the other rangers. Walker shot an Indian who was riding in to spear him but as his back was turned another Comanche drove a lance into the Ranger. As the Indian jerked his lance out of Walker, John Carlin shot him through the head and assisted Walker into a thicket. In the wild action of the Comanches that suddenly surrounded them, the Texans fought bravely. Ad Gillespie was shot through with an arrow that knocked him from his horse.[27]

Captain Hays and his other men drove their attackers back while his wounded men were helped away. During this intense action, James Lee was also severely wounded by arrows and Andrew Erskine was less severely wounded in the thigh with an arrow. Another ranger, Peter Fohr, was killed outright. Despite his wound, Gillespie even managed to reload his rifle.[28]

Hays considered that his men had fought "with a courage that is rarely displayed" during this close contact portion of the fight when his rangers charged into the ranks of their opponents. In addition to Comanches, this force was found by Hays to contain a few Waco Indians and some Mexicans. By the time the fight had stretched out over three miles, there were still at least 20 Comanches able to fight, double the number of effective rangers. Hays could see a chief yelling at his warriors, trying to garner their courage for a final attack. Doubting that his rangers could survive another serious charge, he asked if anyone had a charged rifle. Gillespie nodded, dismounted and rested his Yager rifle on a large boulder. "Shoot that damned chief!" Hays cried. Gillespie's rifle blasted and a distance away the Comanche chief was knocked from his saddle in mid-war cry.[29]

This was enough for the surviving Comanches. The rest of them broke away, each trying to escape without an attempt to haul off their own dead and wounded. Any injured Indians who escaped this day did so on their own. The rangers had one dead, many wounded, and many horses killed or wounded. They were too tired to pursue. Hays felt his men had killed "twenty on the ground, and wounding, to the lowest estimate, twenty or thirty more" with their .36 caliber Colt pistols.[30]

Hays camped on the field while preparing his injured men and horses for the ride back to San Antonio. The second day after the battle four Comanches rode up, almost stumbling into the rangers' camp. They were apparently trying to locate some of their own wounded men, thinking the Texans had long cleared the scene. "I immediately ordered six men to give chase to them," wrote Hays, "thinking at the same time that they had embodied, and presumed to give me another fight." This time it was not a trap and the rangers pursued the four Comanches for a mile. They managed to kill three of them and the fourth escaped.[31]

In two days of fighting with their new Colt pistols, Hays' rangers had killed 23 Indians and Mexicans and had seriously wounded another 30. Their own 16-man force had suffered four rangers wounded and one killed.

The rangers returned to San Antonio, taking care of their own wounded, and arrived about June 15, 1844. Peter Fohr, the ranger killed in battle the previous week, left a will which he had created in San Antonio on September 2, 1843. It was presented for probate on June 15 by his attorney, Thomas Addicks.[32]

One day after reaching San Antonio, Captain Hays wrote a report of the Walker's Creek engagement on June 16. He ran into Mary Maverick on June 20 and told her about the big fight with the Comanches. He credited the escape of his men to Ad Gillespie killing the Comanche chief. "We were right glad they fled," Hays stated. "We were nearly used with the fatigue of a long day's march that day and the exertions on the battlefield, and we were almost out of ammunition. The Indians made a magnificent fight under the circumstances."[33]

A new colonizer who reached San Antonio in early July and heard of Hays' fight wrote, "This great victory was greatly due to the use of Colt's revolvers that the Texians used for the first time in this engagement, to the great astonishment of the Indians, who fought bravely."[34]

Among the names given as participating in the Walker's Creek fight are: Captain Hays, Sam Walker, Kit Acklin, Alexander Coleman, Rufe Perry, John Carlin, James Lee, Peter Fohr, Andrew Erskine, Ad Gillespie, Pitkin Taylor, Josiah Taylor, James Dunn and Mike Chevallie. Other names listed by early Indian wars historian A. J. Sowell as being present for Walker's Creek were his uncle Tom Galbreath, Creed Taylor, Sam Luckie, George Jackson, George Neill. None of these men appear to have served with Hays during this time, as they do not appear on any of his muster rolls. The accounts given by Sowell mix details of earlier Jack Hays Indian fights with the 1844 Walker's Creek battle, thus explaining his confusion over which rangers fought in which battle.[35]

Hays' fight at Walker's Creek was also known to some as the "Pedernales Fight" or "Hays' Big Fight." Sources differ as to the precise location of the fight. Hays may very well have dubbed the creek Walker's Creek, a name that might not have stayed with the stream. The battle did receive public notice. The *Houston Morning Star* ran a long account in its June 29, 1844, issue. Most of the writers of that period, however, failed to see the significance the five-shooter Colt pistol had played in Hays' rangers taking on such a superior frontier force with such success.

In time, however, historians would realize that in the 15 minutes of most intense gun action involving Hays' rangers and their Colt pistols the history of the West had been forever changed. "Up to this time, these daring Indians had always supposed themselves superior to us, man to man, on horse," ranger Sam Walker later wrote.

"The result of this engagement was such as to intimidate them and enable us to treat with them."[36]

The Walker's Creek Comanche battle fought by Hays, Walker and company was even later depicted as an engraving on the cylinder of about 100 presentation model pistols produced by Samuel Colt's company in 1847. Colt called his new .44 caliber, six-shot revolver the Walker Colt in honor of Sam Walker, who had met with Colt in New York to help improve designs on his new pistol. Colt had suggested to Walker in a letter dated November 27, 1846, that Walker and Jack Hays should look to Colt's Patent Arms as their supplier for repeating pistols. Walker quickly wrote back, confirming his confidence in the Colt brand: "The pistols which you made for the Texas Navy have been in use by the Rangers for three years, and I can say with confidence that it is the only good improvement that I have seen. The Texans who have learned their value by practical experience, their confidence in them is unbounded, so much so that they are willing to engage four times their number."[37]

Using Walker's suggestions, Colt would create the new 4.5-pound Walker Colt with a heavy nine-inch barrel to improve the accuracy over his earlier Colt Paterson five-shooter model which the Texas Rangers had used. Sam Walker had received a pair of the new Walker Colts by October 5, 1847. Four days later, he died in combat during the Mexican War at the pueblo of Humantla, still clutching one of the new Walker Colts in his hand.[38]

The 100 presentation models of the Walker Colt which depicted the 1844 Texas Ranger victory over the Comanches at Walker's Creek became collector's items. Sam Colt sent one pair to General Zachary Taylor and another pair to Jack Hays.

NOTES

1. Gary Clayton Anderson, *The Conquest of Texas: Ethnic Cleansing in the Promised Land, 1820–1875* (Norman: University of Oklahoma Press, 2005), 207.

2. Ibid., 207.

3. Ibid., 208.

4. Ibid., 209.

5. Ibid., 209.

6. (Karl) Hans Peter Marius Nielsen Gammel, *The Laws of Texas, 1822–1897* (Austin: Gammel Book Company, 1898), 2: 915.

7. Frederick Wilkins, *The Legend Begins: The Texas Rangers, 1823–1845* (Austin: State House Press, 1996), 174; James Kimmins Greer, *Texas Ranger: Jack Hays in the Frontier Southwest* (College Station: Texas A&M University Press, 1993), 94.

8. Greer, *Texas Ranger,* 94.

9. Gammel, *The Laws of Texas,* 2: 943–44.

10. Greer, *Texas Ranger,* 104–105.

11. Wilkins, *The Legend Begins,* 177.

12. John Twohig PE, R 242, F 649.

13. Wilkins, *The Legend Begins,* 177.

14. Hays to Secretary of War and Marine G. W. Hill, "Report of the Battle of Walker's Creek," June 16, 1844; contained in *Journals of the House of Representatives of the Ninth Congress of the Republic of Texas,* 32–33. Hereafter cited as Hays, "Report of the Battle of Walker's Creek."

I5. Ibid.

16. Ibid.; *Handbook of Texas Online,* s. v. "Walker's Creek, battle of," http://www.tshaonline.org/handbook/online articles/WW/btw2.html (accessed March 2, 2008); Greer, *Texas Ranger,* 96; John C. Caperton, "Sketch of Colonel John C. Hays, The Texas Rangers, Incidents in Texas and Mexico, Etc." Typescript, Bancroft Library, University of California, Berkeley, page 20.

17. Hays, "Report of the Battle of Walker's Creek"; Wilkins, *The Legend Begins,* 178; Greer, *Texas Ranger,* 96.

18. Anderson, *The Conquest of Texas,* 206.

19. Wilkins, *The Legend Begins,* 178; Mike Cox, *The Texas Rangers: Wearing the Cinco Peso* (New York: Forge, 2008), 90–91.

20. Hays, "Report of the Battle of Walker's Creek"; Greer, *Texas Ranger,* 106.

21. Wilkins, *The Legend Begins,* 178.

22. Ibid., 178–79.

23. Ibid., 179; "Biography of Cicero Rufus Perry, 1822–1898. Captain, Texas Rangers." Special collections of Daughters of the Republic of Texas Library, San Antonio, Tex.

24. Thomas W. Knowles, *They Rode for the Lone Star: The Saga of the Texas Rangers. The Birth of Texas—The Civil War* (Dallas: Taylor Publishing Company, 1999), 100.

25. Hays, "Report of the Battle of Walker's Creek"; Wilkins, *The Legend Begins,* 179.

26. Hays, "Report of the Battle of Walker's Creek."

27. Greer, *Texas Ranger,* 98.

28. Wilkins, *The Legend Begins,* 179–80; A. J. Sowell, *Texas Indian Fighters: Early Settlers and Indian Fighters of Southwest Texas* (1900; repr., Austin: State House Press, 1986), 809.

29. Hays, "Report of the Battle of Walker's Creek"; Wilkins, *The Legend Begins,* 180; Caperton, "Sketch of Colonel John C. Hays," 22; Knowles, *They Rode for the Lone Star,* 100.

30. Anderson, *The Conquest of Texas,* 206.

31. Hays, "Report of the Battle of Walker's Creek."

32. John C. Hays PD, R 160, F 421-28.

33. Rena Maverick Green, ed., *Memoirs of Mary A. Maverick. Arranged by Mary A. Maverick and Her Son George Madison Maverick* (San Antonio: Alamo Printing Co., 1921; repr., Lincoln: University of Nebraska Press, 1989), 77.

34. Sowell, *Texas Indian Fighters,* 132.

35. Ibid., 21-23, 809.

36. Cox, *The Texas Rangers,* 92.

37. Knowles, *They Rode for the Lone Star,* 131–33.

38. Ibid., 133–34.

★ 5 ★

LOS DIABLOS TEJANOS!

Stephen B. Oates

In the sweltering twilight of May 22, 1846, a company of sun-burned, grim-faced Texas Rangers, the advance unit of a newly organized Texas regiment, rode into Fort Brown, the farthest southern outpost of Anglo-American civilization in Texas and combat headquarters of General Zachary "Old Rough and Ready" Taylor, commander of the Army of the Rio Grande. The war with Mexico over the disputed Texas boundary and ultimate control of the American Southwest had begun less than a month before, but Taylor's troops had already won two decisive victories over a de-moralized Mexican army and sent it in headlong retreat for Mon-terrey, some one hundred fifty miles southwest of Fort Brown. The possibilities of crushing this army and ending the war in northern Mexico were bright indeed, and Taylor was already moving his vet-erans across the placid waters of the Rio Grande when the Texans, who had seen no action yet, halted on the weed-infested parade grounds and reported to the general. Taylor promptly sent them along to scout the hostile lands ahead of his advancing columns. As the Rangers splashed across the river into a Mexican sunset, they broke into their celebrated "Texas Yell." At last—at long last—they could shoot Mexicans legitimately and shoot to kill.

It was not long before the rest of the Texas regiment, under the overall command of a convivial, boy-faced colonel named John C.

"Jack" Hays, joined this advanced company near Matamoros. Taylor no doubt expected a great deal from Hays's outfit. The Rangers were veteran Indian fighters, known for their extraordinary courage and endurance. As individual fighters they were virtually incomparable: almost no one could fire a six-shooter with more accuracy; almost no one could move quicker and use a bowie knife with more skill in close-quarter combat. But as soldiers who had to respect rank and order, these Rangers were beyond hope; they soon proved themselves so wild and tempestuous in camp, so uncontrollable in battle, that even Taylor, as spirited and independent as any man, came to regard them as barbarians, as "licentious vandals." For no sooner had they arrived in Mexico than they began to commit distasteful acts of violence: they raided villages and pillaged farms. They hanged unarmed Mexican civilians. On one occasion Taylor lost his temper altogether and threatened to jail the lot of them. The occasion was a Fourth of July celebration near Matamoros in which the Texans stole two horse-buckets of whiskey to wash down a meal of Mexican pigs and chickens which they had killed "accidentally" while firing salutes to honor the day.

What could Taylor do with such men? He could not put all seven hundred of them in the Roundhouse no matter how much he might like to because the Rangers would be indispensable as scouts once the entire army was underway. As one of their own put it, "the Rangers were not only the eyes and ears of General Taylor's army, but its right and left arms as well." Nevertheless, the general had to do something, for on August 2 he received a report that the Rangers were at it again. While encamped at Matamoros they attended theaters, jingling spurs on their boots, rifles in their hands, Colt revolvers in their holsters, and pistols and bowie knives tucked in their belts. They not only frightened the citizenry but also picked fights with regulars in the United States Army and shot down signs in the middle of town.

What, Taylor kept asking, made these men do such things? Was it simply inherent in their nature? Were they criminals? Were they mad? Or had it something to do with that wild frontier beyond the Rio Grande whence they came, that land whose revolution some ten years before had finally started this war which Taylor was committed to win? For Texas in 1846 was indeed a hard, cruel frontier, whose soil was thin and dry, whose commerce was slight, whose Indians were most belligerent and, if Tonkawas, were man-eaters— a land where pioneers, if they lived at all, lived by their own cunning and granite will. The Rangers themselves came from the fringe areas of frontier Texas, from the thickly wooded and red-hilled districts in the east, from the twisted mesquite country in the west, and the sweltering brush regions in the far south. They came from a land whose civilization was divided into little remote pockets of settlers who had gathered together out of a common fear—a fear of coming violence, a fear of the unknown. Such isolated communities had only a trace of civil organization, almost no law, and one over-riding justice: revenge. Yes, vengeance was the moving spirit—a spirit of passion—by which men enforced their rights in frontier Texas. Avenge the horses which renegade Indians had stolen by moonlight; avenge those stout, red-necked women whom Comanche bands had roped and dragged through prickly pear until they were mangled beyond recognition as human; avenge the insults which a neighbor had shouted in moments of cold fury; avenge the friend who had died in the metallic blaze of some stranger's guns; and now, for the Texas Rangers fighting with Taylor, avenge the fathers and brothers, uncles and cousins whom the Mexicans had slain at the Alamo, at Goliad, and on the plain of San Jacinto. Yes, if Taylor was looking for an answer, this was it: this persisting compulsion to avenge atrocities committed upon their people now moved the Texans to commit atrocities themselves—to hang Mexican civilians, to gun down peon farmers in the moving sand south of the river, to open fire with savage pleasure on little brown boys running barefoot through the streets of Matamoros.

Somehow though, Taylor must discipline them or President Polk, who did not like the general for political reasons, might reprimand him in public for waging an uncivilized war. The trouble was that the Rangers were beyond discipline, and Taylor knew it. It was impossible to control hard-boiled frontiersmen who liked to drink and to swear and who were in Mexico to settle a score and were not to be bothered by rules and regulations in going about it. Except perhaps for their commander, Colonel Hays, who was mild mannered when he was not in battle, their officers had the same attitude. Veteran Indian fighters such as Ben McCulloch and Samuel Walker had become officers not because they could give orders or could click their heels but because they could outfight anyone in their commands.

Because of their attitude about fighting, Taylor had considerable misgivings in sending them to scout the region east of Monterrey when the army, after nearly a month of final battle preparations, at last resumed the march for the Mexican stronghold. On this scout the Texans lived up to his expectations, not only as the eyes and ears of his main column, but also as "licentious" vandals who committed further outrages. A glaring example was the time they caught a poor wretch trying to steal one of their horses and decided to show Mexicans in that area how Texans administered justice. They tied, gagged, and shot him dead, leaving the corpse in the blowing sand as they mounted and rode away to the west.

Moving through light and darkness, they overtook Taylor near Monterrey on September 17. It was here that their vandalism gave way to something far more annoying: a persistent refusal to follow orders. When McCulloch's Rangers, followed by Taylor himself and his immediate staff, made a reconnaissance the next day, the Texans kept pointing at a black fort halfway between the American camp and the city. Taylor warned them not to try anything, but the Rangers ignored him, let out an ear-splitting yell, and charged the fort without order or organization. "Like boys at play," said a regular who watched them,

> those fearless horsemen in a spirit of boastful rivalry, vied with
> each other in approaching the very edge of danger. Riding singly

and rapidly, they swept around the plains under the walls, each one in a wider and more perilous circle than his predecessor. Their proximity occasionally provoked the enemy's fire, but the Mexicans might as well have attempted to bring down skimming swallows as those racing dare-devils.

This remarkable exhibition opened the three-day battle for Monterrey. In it the Texans again demonstrated their daring and cheerful disregard for discipline. With pistols blazing, they led one wing of Taylor's army against three forts protecting the southwestern end of town; McCulloch's company, with a terrible cry, captured the Bishop's Palace almost single-handed. Then, before Taylor's main column could get into position on the other end of town, the Rangers ignored their orders to stay where they were and charged the city's inner defenses. Followed by light infantry, the Texans ran through a blanket of rain, shooting at blurred figures at windows and on rooftops, tunneling through adobe walls with pick and crowbar, sprinting through the watery streets to overwhelm artillery emplacements and to cut the gunners' throats. At last the Texans reached the heart of the city, only to receive an angry note from General Taylor to withdraw so that his artillery could shell the city before the main attack began. Outraged, the Texans sent back a note that they had carried the lower half of the city by themselves and that they would not budge. In a few moments the bombardment commenced with the Texans still in the target area, but as if by a miracle none of them was hurt. They soon received another message to hold their positions while the commanding general and the Mexicans had a talk. By nightfall an understanding had been reached, and the Mexicans began to evacuate. Not long after, on October 2, 1846, the Rangers, whose six months' enlistments were over, set out for Texas in pairs and groups; Colonel Hays and staff were the last to go in mid-October; and regulars who watched them leave praised them for their extraordinary courage against overwhelming odds.

General Taylor, too, grudgingly commended them for gallant action, even if they had disobeyed orders, and watched them ride off with unmitigated relief: the prospect of having nearly seven hundred idle Texans in Monterrey now that the fighting was over was a foreboding thought, even for Old Rough and Ready.

Taylor, however, had not seen the last of the Rangers. Captain McCulloch and twenty-seven of his most pugnacious Texans returned to Mexico when they heard that Santa Anna himself was leading an army over the desert with a ringing promise to drive the *gringos* from Mexico or to perish in the attempt. Taylor received the Texans cordially enough, putting them to work as scouts and couriers. On February 16, while the American army entrenched at Agua Nueva, the general sent the Texans across the desert to scout Santa Anna's position at Encarnacion, about thirty-five miles south of Monterrey. Beneath a sliver of moon, the Rangers slipped inside enemy lines and came finally to a low ridge overlooking the Mexican army, encamped on a vast plain. It was a chilling sight: tents and huts as far as the Texans could see, and thousands of men and wagons moving about in the flickering shadows of orange watch fires. In a few moments three of the Rangers slid down the ridge and crawled from fire to fire counting bedrolls and cannon and occasionally knifing a careless sentinel; at last they rejoined the others on the ridge, then all the Texans rode under the noses of Mexican pickets and raced back to report. Santa Anna, they concluded, had over twenty thousand men and a far superior field position for the forthcoming battle. Knowing then that he was heavily outnumbered, Taylor ordered a withdrawal from his exposed position at Agua Nueva to an almost impregnable one behind the Angostura Pass near Buena Vista where he could not be flanked. That afternoon, with blare of trumpet and tuck of drum, Santa Anna's legions attacked, but Taylor's army turned back assault after assault and at last forced the Mexicans to withdraw. Had the Rangers not been there to scout for him, Taylor might have engaged the Mexicans at Agua Nueva and gone down to defeat.

As it was Taylor had won a brilliant victory, a victory that ended the war in northern Mexico and made him enormously popular in the public eye. He would have thanked the Texas Rangers for their good work had they not got drunk after the battle and picked a fight with an entire regiment of regulars, starting a riot that required several hundred military police and a troupe of cavalry to bring under control. Satisfied then that the regulars now had sufficient respect for their fighting abilities, the Texans set out for home. After they had gone, General Taylor requested that no more Rangers come to help. The Texans, however, were not yet through fighting. When Winfield Scott invaded the Valley of Mexico in the spring of 1847, Jack Hays recruited a second regiment of Rangers and sailed down to join him. The new regiment, five hundred strong, had the task of clearing out all guerrilla fighters in the front and in the rear of Scott's advancing columns. They were under orders from the commander himself—who understood Ranger temperament better than Taylor did—to spread terror and take no prisoners, in short, to fight without quarter.

When the Texans disembarked at Veracruz that September, they heard disappointing news from the valley: Scott had already captured Mexico City; Santa Anna had fled into the mountains with the remnants of his bleeding army, and a makeshift government at Queretaro, some one hundred fifty miles northwest of Mexico City, was about to sue for peace, which meant that the war was virtually over and which depressed the Rangers enormously. That afternoon, still quite depressed, they rode over to Vergara, a few miles outside of Veracruz, to pitch camp. As they tried in vain to set up tents in the shifting sand and blowing wind, a band of infantrymen under a white flag came into camp with a barrel. This barrel, the infantrymen explained, was full of the best whiskey available in Veracruz: it was a peace offering from their regiment—the 9th Massachusetts Infantry—which was encamped there and which had heard about the Texans' propensity to fight their own countrymen if Mexicans were not available. The Texans thanked them with an air of supreme condescension and, after they had gone, proceeded to get pleasantly drunk. As they drank on into the evening, occasionally taking a potshot at flying birds or thrown rocks and sticks, one Ranger suggested that they go into Veracruz for the women of ill repute and for a good fight or two. And they might have done it, too, had not Adjutant Rip Ford, who did not drink, suggested a guerrilla hunt instead. There was a guerrilla band operating some thirty miles away, the adjutant had heard, which could easily be found and whipped. It was high time, he declared, for them to "sustain the reputation of Texas Rangers and not lie around in idleness." The Rangers quickly agreed, and they hurried away to get their guns and prepare to ride.

It was dark when the Ranger column moved out of camp. After an all-night ride which sobered them considerably, the horsemen entered a sweltering jungle with parasitical vines that had to be chopped away with bowie knives before they could advance. The Rangers at last reached a waterhole at the edge of a rolling prairie and stopped to rest. Suddenly, Adjutant Ford shouted something, then leaped on his horse and galloped away with his pistol blazing. Barely visible on a rise several hundred yards away was a party of guerrillas moving at a killing pace. Mounting on the run, the rest of the Rangers followed the adjutant, shooting recklessly, yelling, spurring their horses faster and faster. On they rode, the guerrillas alternately disappearing and reappearing in the tall grass and ravines, with Ford, not far behind now, trying desperately to draw a bead on the last rider; then came the other Rangers who fired their revolvers and fired again.

Over the prairie and through the woods the wild riders raced. At last the guerrillas' horses gave out and they had to take shelter at a ranch. From its buildings they fired at the yipping Texans who galloped past at full speed while returning the fire, then rode back and dismounted to fight the Mexicans hand-to-hand.

The fighting was over now except for a fisticuff two Rangers were having over a dead Mexican's sombrero. After that was over and all the loot had been fairly divided, the Texans headed toward Vergara at a gallop, fearing that a larger enemy force might soon come to overwhelm them. The ride back soon became a race, for "two things are considered uncomfortable by mounted men of pluck," Adjutant Ford mused, "to be in the rear in a charge, or behind in a retreat."

The next day, October 17, Colonel Hays, who had been in Veracruz during the past week, rode into camp with encouraging news: all the American troops in the Veracruz vicinity were finally going into action. Their orders were to proceed to Puebla, to "disinfest" the valley of Mexican bandits and irregulars, and then to join General Scott in Mexico City. On November 2, 1847, with Adjutant Ford and his newly organized spy company leading the way, the Texas Rangers set out for Puebla, followed by the 9th Massachusetts Infantry, then by regular cavalry and artillery. The column crawled through the Mexican sand and dust, thirsty and tired, still following the Rangers. The column forded rivers that were treacherous with quicksand and shifting mud, hacked its way through humid jungles of vine and bush, and finally reached Puebla on a warm, sticky afternoon in late November. On the plain outside of town there was a brief engagement between the Texans and a regiment of Mexican Lancers, brilliant in their glittering armor and snapping colors, who had ridden over from Izucar de Matamoros some miles away. The Rangers' charged them fiercely, and the Lancers, outfought and outflanked, soon fled.

That evening the Texans celebrated their victory by putting on a show for the local inhabitants. They rode recklessly about the town plaza, two and four and six abreast, jumping off and back on their mounts and picking hats and bandannas off the ground. Then, bored with that, they got up a great *fiesta*. A regular officer who saw the Texans celebrate recalled in later years that

> they certainly were an odd-looking set of fellows, and it seems to be their aim to dress as outlandishly as possible. Bobtailed coats and "long-tailed blues," low and high-crowned hats, some slouched and others Panama, with a sprinkling of black leather caps, constituting their uniforms; and a thorough coating of dust over all, and covering their huge beards gave them a savage appearance . . . Each man carried a rifle, a pair of . . . Colt's revolvers; a hundred of them

could discharge a thousand shots in two minutes, and with what precision the Mexican alone could tell.

The Mexican soldier could tell all right: he had stood up to these Texans that afternoon and had been soundly whipped. He had found out that they were uncanny marksmen who could pick a man off at full gallop over one hundred twenty-five yards away, while he had to shoot one of them at least five times to kill him. The Mexican would not of course admit that he was an extremely poor shot, that his cartridges contained twice as much powder as was necessary, and that this caused his musket to kick bruisingly, which in turn spoiled his aim. Nor would he admit that he feared the recoil of his weapon so much that he often closed his eyes and flinched while firing. No, the explanation lay with the Rangers themselves who were super-men knowing neither fear nor death. But worst of all, the Texans had six-shooters. "The untutored greaser," according to a veteran of the afternoon's action, had a "holy awe and superstition . . . in regard for the 'revolver.' They understood the term to mean a turning around and about—a circulator; and were led to believe the ball would revolve in all directions after its victims, run around trees and turn corners, go into houses and climb stairs, and hunt up folks generally." Consequently, Mexican officers had found it next to impossible to keep their men in line when the Rangers, firing their terrible revolvers and crying the "Texas 'Yell,'" came flying down on them.

That yell was another thing. It was awful to hear, even more terrifying in sound than the celebrated "Rebel Yell" of the Civil War. The Texas Yell consisted of a series of wildcat screeches followed by a bloodcurdling yip-yip—"such yells," said one Ranger, "exploded on the air" and "have been heard distinctly three miles off across a prairie, above the din of musketry and artillery."

This hideous yell, the revolver with its ubiquitous bullets, the enormous horses, the tall, bearded supermen from beyond the Rio Grande who defied Mexican *escopetas*—no wonder Mexicans at Puebla viewed the Texans' disturbances that evening with profound human terror. And no wonder, too, that when the Americans set out for the capital the next day, villages along the way turned out to watch the Texans ride by. And no wonder, finally, that citizens in Mexico City were frightened to death when on December 6 Colonel Hays led his Rangers into the heart of the city well ahead of the main column. "*Los Diablos Tejanos!*" "*Los Diablos Tejanos!*" cried the Mexicans as they crowded along the streets to get a look at the "Texas Devils."

The Rangers had been in town scarcely an hour when they began making trouble. While they waited on the Grand Plaza to get their camp assignments, a Mexican came along with a basket of candy; a Ranger leaned over from his horse and took a handful, but refused to pay. The nervous old man shrieked at him, but the Ranger only laughed, so the Mexican hurled a large stone at the Texan's head. Almost instantly there was a resounding roar as a pistol appeared in the Ranger's hand, and the Mexican leaped back as if from a powerful blow, dying before he struck the ground. "There must have been ten thousand people on the Grand Plaza," another Texan recalled. "They were desperately frightened; a stampede occurred. Men ran over each other. Some were knocked into the filthy sewers, all were frantically endeavoring to increase the distance between themselves and *Los Tejanos Sangrientes*—the bloody Texans."

Los Diablos Tejanos, What made them so vicious? They came to Mexico for revenge, they said, but revenge soon became a pretext for acts which transcend human understanding.

There was a hatred in Mexico City, a growing hatred of those *Diablos Tejanos* who brawled in Mexico's saloons and beat up her men and made violent love to her women. Finally, as the weeks passed and the number of outrages increased, the Mexicans had taken enough: one moonless night a large band of them caught a lone Texan in the streets and stabbed him until "his heart was visible, and its pulsations were plainly perceptible." When the Texans saw his slashed body the next day, they "burst into tears" and swore to avenge this ugly deed. That night, beneath a cloudy sky, some twenty-five of them walked deliberately into that "cutthroat" section where the slaying had occurred and murdered from fifty to eighty Mexicans, including young toughs called *leperos,* women and small boys.

This was of course too much for everyone: Mexicans over the city, no matter their age or sex, threatened a war of reprisal against the Texas Devils and sent a delegation to General Scott with a demand for retribution. If the Texans were not properly punished, the delegation warned, then the Mexicans would rise up and "seek satisfaction."

After they had gone, General Scott called the Ranger captains to his headquarters. The general was in an ugly mood; he would not, he declared, "be disgraced, nor shall the army of my country be, by such outrages." What, he growled, made them behave as they did? Did they wish to start this most unhappy war all over again, just when the Americans were about to consummate a treaty with Mexico which would permit them all to go home? Did the Texans not want to go home, did they want to stay here and fight? One captain suggested that that indeed was what was wrong: they all needed a good fight. Nothing else would assuage their pugnacity, their "incorrigible meanness," as one of their own had put it. Well, if it was a fight they wanted, perhaps the general could oblige them. He had in mind one of the most blood-thirsty bands of *guerrilleros* in Mexico, that of Padre Jarauta, which was hiding out somewhere in the valley east of Mexico City. Over the months this elusive band had ravaged American trains coming from Veracruz, had ambushed cavalry detachments and burned outposts. And it would give the Rangers a severe test.

The Ranger captains agreed to the operations at once and left. They were anxious to get in the saddle and prove themselves against the infamous *guerrilleros;* first, however, the Texans must find them, and that in itself was a formidable task.

The Padre's *guerrilleros* were clandestine marauders, but it was no secret that they lived freely among the *peons* and *leperos* in the villages all across the great valley, gorging themselves and dancing in fiestas lasting for days. They made the law in that region and the law was the bullet; they fancied themselves indomitable fighters and dressed in resplendent costumes that kept in awe the pauper youths who idolized them, who lied and stole for them. To the youths they were not men but gods, these *guerrilleros,* in their great sombreros, their velvet jackets so elaborately embroidered by their special senoritas, their skin-tight trousers that were slit open at the sides and fastened by dazzling gold buttons, and the tiny silver bells on their boots that tinkled as they walked, and those huge spurs, and their swords, and the *escopetas* in their hands and their lassos swung over their shoulders, which they could use with deadly dexterity in close-quarter combat. Yes, they were fighters without equals they said, and the poor who sheltered them and kept their secrets, the youths who worshiped and the senoritas who loved them, knew in their hearts that no one, not even the Texas Devils starting down the valley, could ever really defeat them.

Yet, the Texans, riding in a two-column front behind Hays, the Lone Star flag and the Stars and Stripes whipping about in the wind overhead, were coming now with every intention of defeating these *guerrilleros* once and for all. Riding by night and resting by day, the Rangers searched the whole valley for Padre Jarauta; they skirmished with his detachments at Otumba, Tehuacan, and Tulancingo, but could never find the Padre himself with his main column, said to be four hundred fifty strong. Finally, one evening in mid-February 1848, the Rangers were given a clue: a young senorita at a Tulancingo saloon remarked in a moment of intoxication that Zacualtipan was the Padre's secret headquarters. Moments later the Rangers, reinforced by a detachment of United States dragoons, mounted in the streets and moved at a gallop into the Mexico night. They reached the outskirts of Zacualtipan just as the February sun was coming up over the mountain peaks. They charged down the early morning streets, taking the *guerrilleros* almost completely by surprise. While the main force under Colonel Hays stormed the plaza, a dozen other Rangers leaped from their horses to engage a large body of partially dressed Mexicans who had gathered in an open lot. The Texans fought deftly with revolver and bowie knife in a fast moving hand-to-hand fight that lasted about fifteen minutes before the Mexicans broke and fled over the walls and away into the mountains beyond. The Texans then ran up the street to the plaza where a crazy, confused battle was raging: yelling like animals, Americans and Mexicans were wrestling and slashing at one another with long knives, were firing into each others' faces and stomachs at point-blank range. The killing finally ended at mid-afternoon with the *guerrilleros* following their Padre down the valley in head-long flight; and Adjutant Ford who saw the smoking streets littered with corpses recorded that at least one hundred fifty "Mexicans had ceased to feast on *tortillas*" that day.

It was a brilliant victory, even if the Padre had gotten away alive, and the Texans celebrated it that night, singing and dancing in the streets in spite of the stench of dead bodies in the air. The next morning they headed back toward Mexico City convinced that with this victory their service in Mexico had only begun, that on the day they caught this Padre again or caught any other Mexican bandit army they would fight a battle which Mexico would never forget.

As it turned out, Zacualtipan was the last battle for the Texas Rangers in Mexico. When they reached the capital, they learned that an armistice had been signed and that the Americans were evacuating; the Texans' orders were to ride to Veracruz where transports were waiting to take them home. It was a tragic turn of events, and the Rangers were extremely bitter about it.

On March 18, 1848, the Texas Rangers rode out of Mexico City with heavy hearts and headed for Veracruz. Some ten days later they reached Jalapa, where they heard news that cheered them considerably: General Santa Anna would pass through Jalapa on his way out of the country into exile. The men became quite excited; they would kill Santa Anna; they would. . . . But Colonel Hays warned them that they could do nothing to Santa Anna now, for the war was over and the fallen emperor was, according to the colonel's reports, traveling under a safe conduct pass from General Scott himself. Hays made them promise to pitch camp nearby and to stay there, then left them under Adjutant Ford and rode over to an estate some miles away where Santa Anna was expected to take supper; the colonel, Ford was told, wanted to have "a few words" with his old enemy.

Hays had been gone barely an hour when the Rangers became quite uncontrollable. The entire regiment was "in a white heat," Ford recalled; "revenge was the ruling passion of the hour" as the Texans started crying for Santa Anna's head.

Adjutant Ford did not know what to do. Colonel Hays was probably the only man who could dissuade the Rangers from their plan to murder Santa Anna when he passed over the road near their camp. It was not that Ford had had a change of heart about Santa Anna. The adjutant would have liked to get a shot at the Mexican himself, but under the circumstances he had to think of the consequences. For should the Rangers gun down Santa Anna when he was leaving the country under a safe conduct pass, they would all get into serious trouble. This Ford told them; he pleaded and reasoned with them and somehow—he would wonder how for years after—managed to convince them that if they did kill Santa Anna they would all go to prison. Grudgingly, they agreed not to harm him if Ford would at least let them get a look at the general as he passed. Ford consented.

Grumbling about their missed opportunities and bad luck, the Rangers aligned themselves on each side of the road and waited. Presently, Santa Anna whose "face blanched a little at the sight of his enemies of long standing" approached in an open carriage, followed by a Mexican guard of honor brightly dressed in plume and sash. As the carriage passed by, the Texans glared at the Mexican leader with cold hatred, looking as if they wanted more than anything to be turned loose on him or at least to shake their fists at him. Santa Anna seemed to sense their hatred. "He sat erect," a Texan observed, "not a muscle of his face moved; if his hour had come he seemed resolved to meet it as a soldier should." But the Texans did nothing, nothing at all; and after the carriage had disappeared in the trees, they filed back to camp more bitter now than before.

The next day the Rangers joined Colonel Hays at Jalapa and rode on to Veracruz, where on April 29, 1848, all of them except the colonel and Adjutant Ford were mustered out of service in a sad and solemn ceremony. A few days later, they boarded troop transports and sailed north for Texas, no doubt spending the humid days at sea reminiscing about the war and their part in it and how much more they could have done had it lasted longer. According to their officers, according to Texans back home, some already gathering at Port Lavaca to give them a rousing welcome reception, according to contemporary writers already assiduously at work recording their deeds of derring-do, the Rangers had done all that was humanly possible: they had helped whip a nation given to political coercion and persecution, to all those passions of despotism which so violated their Anglo-American heritage of freedom and the natural rights of man. Yes, in the short two years the war had lasted, the Texans had "waged hostilities upon a scale they deemed legitimate" and had proven themselves "good citizens and meritorious soldiers."

Yet what about the outrages they perpetrated on the Mexican people?

Said Adjutant Ford: "It was sometimes difficult to restrain these men, whose feelings had been lacerated by domestic bereavements and who were standing face to face with the people whose troops had committed" such "bloody deeds" as massacring Texan prisoners at Goliad and in the ill-starred Santa Fe and Mier expeditions. If the Rangers themselves had indulged in a few excesses, it was because they were an intensely proud band of fighting men who wanted revenge—even if revenge became a cloak for pillage and murder, the Rangers were still honorable—"good citizens and meritorious soldiers"—who had a "high grade of patriotism for Texas."

So the Rangers have been presented to posterity. No writer has dared to challenge this traditional image, to take them to task for their vainglory and unpredictable violence. Even the venerable Walter P. Webb, whose *Texas Rangers* has clearly become a classic study, refuses to say much about their worst crimes—their propensity to hang and stab civilian men and ransack their homes, to kill women and children under the pretext of revenge for a slain comrade, to fight their own countrymen when Mexicans were not available. The same is true of virtually every other study of these men—they may be scolded occasionally for a minor misdemeanor, such as stealing pigs and whiskey, but their demonic deeds either are entirely ignored or played down or explained away as the inevitable results of their militant patriotism. There is apparently no other explanation. The Texas Rangers were not sadists. *Surely* they were not that. *Surely,* as pioneer volunteers representing a democratic nation, they had killed for something beyond a mere love of violence. *Surely* as frontiersmen imbued with the republican principles of tolerance and Christian love—for they all, according to Ford, knew the historic meanings of their own Revolution and read the Bible—surely then they had been moved to kill civilians by something other than an indigenous racial hatred of Mexicans. *Surely,* unlike the citizen soldiers of Revolutionary France, the Texas Rangers had not succumbed to that intoxicating passion of killing just to kill.

It is difficult indeed to consider the possibility that these heroes of the Republic, whose courage and fighting prowess we still revere, regarded war as the barbarian hordes of Genghis Khan—that war was one occupation in which man could strip himself of all compassion, all diplomacy, and fight with uninhibited fury, as the violent nature of his soul dictated.

Editors' Note—The best summary of the role played by the Texians in the warfare with Mexico will be found in Charles D. Spurlin, *Texas Volunteers in the Mexican War* (Austin: Eakin Press, 1998). Up-to-date biographies of participants include Thomas W. Cutrer, *Ben McCulloch and the Frontier Military Tradition* (Chapel Hill: University of North Carolina Press, 1993); and Richard B. McCaslin, *Fighting Stock: John S. "Rip" Ford of Texas* (Fort Worth:

Texas Christian University Press, 2011). For a trenchant analysis of Americans and Mexicans in the war, see David A. Clary, *Eagles and Empire: The United States, Mexico, and the Struggle for a Continent* (New York: Bantam Books, 2009).

NOTES

In preparing *"Los Diablos Tejanos!"* I made extensive use of the Texas Governors' Letters File preserved in the archives of the Texas State Library in Austin, letters dating from 1816 to 1860. I also examined the correspondence of Zachary Taylor in the *House Executive Documents, No. 60*, 30 Cong., 1 sess. Taylor's letters abound with complaints and descriptions of Texan atrocities from the time his army occupied Matamoros until it drove Santa Anna across the desert in the battle of Buena Vista. Those letters of July 7 and October 1, 1846, and June 8 and June 16, 1847, are especially useful because they describe in vivid detail the Texans' vicious character and independence. Taylor concluded that they were too "licentious" to be good rank-and-file soldiers.

Winfield Scott's prodigious correspondence is also in the *House Executive Documents,* and several of his letters pertain to Ranger activities—especially their killings—in Mexico City and in the vast valley where the *guerrilleros* rode. These, Taylor's letters, and all of the official papers and records of the Rangers themselves, collected in Records Group No. 94 in the National Archives, constitute the official documents on which I based a large part of my story.

The most helpful sources were, however, the diaries and memoirs of the Rangers themselves. Rip Ford's Memoirs, located in the archives of the University of Texas in Austin, contain an intimate account—over one hundred pages—of the Rangers from the time they arrived in Veracruz until they left two years later. Ford recounts the operations outside of Jalapa, the ride to Mexico City, the Mexico City atrocities, and the expeditions against the *guerrilleros* in lively—and at times unbiased—detail. It is my opinion, as well as that of the late J. Frank Dobie and Walter Prescott Webb, that Ford's reminiscences are among the best on the Southwest. In fact, much of what I had to say about the Rangers are Ford's own observations.

Another splendid reminiscence is S. C. Reid, Jr., *The Scouting Expeditions of McCulloch's Texas Rangers* (Philadelphia, 1848) which recounts in considerable detail the Rangers' part in the Monterrey campaign. J. J. Oswandel's *Notes on the Mexican War, 1846-47-48* (Philadelphia, 1885) is full of anecdotes and contains a vivid description of the *guerrilleros,* as does Ephraim M. Daggett's sketch, "Adventure With Guerrillas," in Isaac George's *Heroes and Incidents of the Mexican War* (Greensburg, Pennsylvania, 1903).

Several members of the regular army wrote memoirs too and in them recorded their own impressions of these Texans. John R. Kenly's *Memoirs of a Maryland Volunteer, War With Mexico* (Philadelphia, 1873) has a long passage on the Rangers' part in the street fighting in Monterrey; so does Luther Giddings' *Sketches of the Campaign in Northern Mexico* (New York, 1853). T. W. Ridell's reminiscences, printed in the *Pioneer* (San Jose, California) of February 15, 1901, contain a few well-turned phrases about the Texans' part in the Buena Vista operations. Albert G. Brackett's *General Lane's Brigade in Central Mexico* (Cincinnati, 1854) has a rare sketch of Colonel Hays and his men when they landed at Veracruz and encamped at Jalapa. Brackett also describes the Rangers' disturbances in Puebla and their unforgettable entry into Mexico City. Colonel Ebenezer Dumont's letters, published in the *Indiana Register* and quoted in the *Democratic, Telegraph and Texas Register* (Columbia, Texas), February 24, 1848, describe Scott's wrath when he learned about the Texans' outrages in Mexico City; Dumont also sketches the Texans' entry into the capital, as do various correspondents for contemporary newspapers—such as the New Orleans *Delta* and New Orleans *Picayune*—some of whose pieces have been reprinted in *Jack Hays, the Intrepid Ranger* (Bandera, Texas, n.d.).

In addition to these sources, I examined a dozen or more secondary accounts of the war and of the Rangers' part in it and benefited immeasurably from the perceptions contained in them. The most helpful was, of course, Walter Prescott Webb's *The Texas Rangers*, which does not, however, recount the more violent acts the Rangers committed.

★ 6 ★

THE CALLAHAN EXPEDITION

Michael L. Collins

In the summer of 1855, Lipan Apaches, reportedly aided by Seminoles, conducted some of their most daring raids yet. They crossed into Texas and struck settlements as far north as the Blanco and Guadalupe rivers, taking horses, cattle, and scalps along the way. News of these depredations stirred the governor of Texas, Elisha M. Pease, to action. Aware that Texas frontiersmen were frustrated with the inadequate defense afforded by the few federal garrisons scattered along the border, Pease authorized the formation of a company of Rangers to protect the frontier and punish the marauders. Pease apparently feared that, should he fail to respond decisively to the situation, Texas minutemen might take matters into their own hands and march off to Mexico.[1]

Ironically, Pease turned to one such impulsive Texas leader, James Hughes Callahan. A native of Georgia, Callahan had come to Texas during the revolution of 1836, a twenty-four-year-old volunteer in the Georgia Battalion of the Texian army assigned to Colonel James Fannin's command. Following the battle at Coleto Creek, he had been spared execution by his Mexican captors, probably because they considered him useful as a skilled mechanic. As a prisoner, he was assigned to a labor detail in Victoria. Although fortunate to survive, he never forgot that Palm Sunday in 1836 when many of his fellow prisoners were brutally massacred at Goliad. Although he

120

had not stood with Houston on the plain of San Jacinto one month later, he had no doubt gloried at the news of Santa Anna's defeat and capture. In the ensuing months, the republic rewarded Callahan for his service with a commendation and a tract of land near Sequin in Caldwell County. A farmer and store owner there, he served with distinction as a citizen-soldier during the campaigns between 1840 and 1842, when volunteer companies of Rangers doggedly pursued both Comanche raiders and Mexican cavalry from the frontier line then extending along the San Antonio River. During this critical time, he learned the art of unconventional warfare from such notable Ranger captains as Ben McCulloch and El Diablo, Captain Jack Hays. Then in the autumn of 1842, he participated in General Alexander Somervell's expedition to the Mexican border. Although no evidence exists that he fought at Mier with Captain William S. Fisher and his recalcitrant volunteers, many of the men mustered into service with him were killed there. Others were later executed by Mexicans at Salado, while many more were marched off to central Mexico and imprisoned for two years in the dank dungeons of Perote Castle. Surely, like other Texans of the times, Callahan brooded over this humiliating defeat and for years seethed in anger about the barbaric treatment of the survivors of the ill-fated Mier expedition.[2]

Unsurprisingly, Callahan quickly stepped forward in response to Governor Pease's call to protect the frontier and punish the marauders. In addition to the stridently anti-Mexican feelings he held as a veteran of the border wars, he had lost several cattle to raiders during a recent foray along the Blanco, an assault he considered to be a personal affront demanding revenge. A seasoned soldier and veteran of border wars and well respected by the frontiersmen of the region, Callahan was a logical choice to lead a company of Indian fighters.[3]

On July 5, 1855, Governor Pease ordered Callahan to muster into service a company of mounted riflemen for a punitive expedition. Specifically, he instructed Callahan to recruit able-bodied men who could supply their own horses, weapons, and ammunition and who would enlist for three months. The governor informed Callahan that, with no appropriated funds to support such a venture, all volunteers must agree to "rely upon the justice of the Legislature to reimburse them later." Pease thus commissioned Callahan to track down and engage the Indian raiders, or in his words, "to follow them up and chastise them wherever they may be found." Although the governor made no mention of the Rio Grande border, his directive was clear.[4]

The forty-year-old Callahan needed no further instructions; he understood his mission. During the ensuing weeks, he had little trouble enlisting volunteers. Texans needed no encouragement or inducement to take up arms in defense of their families and friends, not against the Lipan, Kickapoo, and Seminole Indians or anyone else. Moreover, if reports out of Austin and San Antonio could be believed, any volunteers who rallied to Callahan's side were almost certain to track the Indian marauders onto Mexican soil. Most Texans welcomed the opportunity to cross into Mexico again and possibly engage enemy forces in battle. Besides, the aging president of the Republic of Mexico was said to be on the brink of being toppled from power in a Liberal revolution that summer. Many Texans realized that this was perhaps one last chance to strike a blow against the much hated "butcher of the Alamo," Antonio Lopez de Santa Anna. Nothing could have been more motivating.[5]

At San Antonio on July 20, 1855, Captain Callahan mustered into service a company of eighty-eight Rangers. Most were seasoned Indian fighters, some of them veterans of the late war with Mexico still intent upon avenging the past, others inexperienced farm boys eager for a fight with the enemies of their fathers, a few of them soldiers of fortune and filibusters fiercely determined to make a name for themselves. In certain ways, the expeditionary force resembled a mob more than a military unit. According to later allegations of the Mexican government, some of these adventurers may have been driven by the most mercenary of motives—bounties offered for the recovery of runaway slaves who had found refuge south of the Rio Grande.[6]

No one knows for sure, but evidence does strongly suggest that one of the primary goals of Callahan's expedition was the retrieval of fugitive slaves. As General Persifor Smith wrote later that year, "[A] report was current that a party was organizing to go into Mexico and take negroes that had run away from Texas, and horses that had been stolen, and I presume that the party of Capt. Callahan was the one alluded to." Smith concluded, "If so, their design was covered by the persuit [sic] of a trail of Lipans escaping with their booty."[7]

In an August 15 letter to Lieutenant Edward Burleson, Jr., of San Marcos, Callahan explained his plans to reward volunteers with more than just the hope of recompense from a parsimonious state legislature. "I want every man to understand that if he goes with me to the Devil's River or any place I wish to go and if anything is taken . . . it belongs to those that go and will be divided accordingly," he affirmed. Further clarifying his intentions, he vowed, "I wish you to inform the men under your command that if any property is taken from the Indians by any of the scout it belongs to the men that take it." He concluded that if "those in camp receive no share in such . . . this will induce the boys to go on scouts." Again, on August 31, from his camp at Enchanted Rock near Fredericksburg, he hinted that more was on his mind than simply punishing Indian marauders. "Some of the boys have found out the arrangements . . . but . . . I think it the best move to keep the matter as secret as possible for I am bound to go to the Rio Grande if nothing happens."[8]

Is it possible that the "arrangements" to which Callahan alluded might simply have been a reference to his distribution of the spoils of the expedition to his recruits? Did he merely wish to keep from others his intention to cross into Mexico? Or could the correspondence suggest a veiled reference to the bounties slave owners paid for fugitive slaves? The matter of Callahan's primary mission remains a mystery.

Regardless of the motives of the men who made up this expedition, one thing seems certain. The so-called Indian problem on the southwestern borders of Texas had become inexorably linked to the ongoing boundary troubles along the Rio Grande, troubles that had continued to kindle the burning embers of mistrust between the United States and Mexico. By 1852, scattered bands of renegade Seminoles and Lipan Apaches, in league with Mescalero Apaches, Kickapoos, and others, had established safe harbor on the Mexican side of the river, south of Eagle Pass near the spurs of the Sierra Madre Mountains. And from these enclaves, the displaced natives had conducted raids with impunity as far north as the Colorado River, each year retiring with their booty to the safety of their sanctuaries south of the Rio Bravo. Moreover, these marauders had reportedly received not merely encouragement but also bounties from Mexican scalp buyers, horse traders, cattle rustlers, and even Mexican officials who had tacitly sanctioned the forays to plunder Texan settlements along the frontier. All the while, Mexican magistrates had privately insisted that such Indian villages below the Bravo had served the peoples of northern Mexico as an effective buffer against depredations conducted by Comanches living in Texas. Indians on both sides of the border, therefore, had emerged as surrogate warriors in the continuing struggles between the United States and Mexico.[9]

No figure along that frontier was as widely hated by whites as the renegade Seminole chieftain Coacoochee, better known as "Wild Cat." A disciple of legendary Florida warrior Osceola, Wild Cat had earned his reputation as a fierce and formidable foe, even before he first set foot on Texas soil. During the Second Seminole War in Florida between 1835 and 1838, he had bedeviled the U.S. Army with his evasive tactics, which included attacking U.S. dragoons before vanishing into the malarial swamps of the Everglades. His acumen during the war and his refusal to be humbled by treaty makers raised Wild Cat's stature as a defiant warrior worthy of respect. Only grudgingly did he leave the wetlands of Florida to resettle in the recently established Seminole reserve near Fort Gibson, Indian Territory, in 1841. After squabbling with Cherokee leaders over conflicting land claims in that region, he accompanied Indian agent Pierce M. Butler on a trek across Texas in 1845, hoping to negotiate a peace pact with the Comanches. Following the trek, the proud Seminole chieftain returned to the borders of Arkansas convinced of two things: the swift-riding Comanches who ruled the plains of West Texas could not be trusted, and neither they nor Anglo-Texans would ever welcome the Seminoles into the sprawling empire of bison and grass that lay beyond the line of settlements west of Austin and San Antonio.[10]

After the U.S.-Mexican War, Wild Cat actively encouraged the Kickapoo, Lipan, and others to join him in establishing a safe haven south of the Rio Grande. In an alarming letter to Governor Bell on October 20, 1850, U.S. Indian agent Marcus Duval warned that the renegade chieftain was inspiring hundreds of slaves to escape bondage and unite with the Seminoles in Coahuila, below Piedras Negras, near the town of San Fernando, where they would enjoy the protection of the Mexican government. Duval cautioned Governor Bell that Wild Cat was determined to "keep up a constant excitement on your border" and that he was "not likely to be kept still except by force or fear." Then he urged that "speedy action is necessary for the interest of the Government of Texas." Indian agent John H. Rollins concurred in a letter to Governor Bell ten days later. Condemning Wild Cat as a dangerous master of deceit and duplicity, he charged that the Seminole chieftain had lied to his own people and to fugitive slaves, persuading them that Texas leaders had first promised them a homeland, then betrayed them by withdrawing the offer of sanctuary. "Indeed it is the intrigue of the times," Rollins insisted, "when a single chief boldly enters upon the execution of a plan that unless speedily frustrated must end in a general war with possibly all of the Indian tribes."[11]

Swift action, however, was not forthcoming. Federal agents remained reticent to engage Wild Cat, federal garrisons of troops along the Rio Grande border being too few in number and located too far apart. Moreover, Governor Bell's successors, James W. Henderson and Elisha M. Pease, failed to address the threat that lay less than sixty miles beyond the waters of the Bravo. In those days, therefore, the only thing lower than the morale of Texas frontiersmen was the state appropriation to defend their borders from marauding Indian raiders and Mexican robadors. Professor Webb stated it best when he wrote that during these years the state partisan Rangers became "little more than a historical expression."[12]

The result should have been predictable. Buoyed by a success measured in the swelling numbers of renegades and runaway slaves who came to his side, an emboldened Wild Cat—soon commissioned a colonel in the Mexican army—built alliances with the Kickapoo, Lipan, and Mescalero. Consequently, he grew more confident in his conduct of raids against Comanches and Anglo-Texans, whom he hated with equal intensity. Captain Abner Doubleday remembered that, during his time at Fort Duncan, situated on the north bank of the Bravo near Eagle Pass, Wild Cat acted brazenly, going so far as to threaten any American bluecoat who challenged him and his renegades. "They sent us word that [if we pursued them across the river] they would hang up the right arm of everyone of us in the square of the neighboring town of San Fernando in Mexico."[13]

Jane Cazneau, who met Wild Cat on several occasions, wrote that he looked more noble than savage, although she also insisted that the native chieftain was unusually vain. Frontiersman William Banta agreed, offering a colorful portrait of the charismatic Seminole leader, whom he met on many occasions. Towering over six feet tall, Wild Cat wore his raven black hair in braids that hung down his back, with several silver decorative plates dangling loosely from the tresses. At the bottom of the plait descended a handful of silver bells that jingled when he walked. Below a thick silver headband adorned with assorted bird feathers rose a furrowed forehead, accented by heavy black eyebrows and eyes peering "like an eagle." With buckskin leggings and a blue beaded tunic draped over his broad shoulders, he covered his long frame with a brightly colored Mexican blanket. A silver cross swayed from his neck, although he professed a greater love for jewelry than any faith in the "Jesus road." From his hip hung a long silver-plated tomahawk that could also be used as a smoking pipe. With two wives normally at his side, he carried himself with a regal bearing. "He was very communicative, polite, and firm in conversation," Banta recalled of the renegade leader, a fierce, determined, and fearless warrior.[14]

By 1855, Texas frontiersmen were well acquainted with Wild Cat and his threats against Anglo settlers. On September 18, when Callahan's company left Bandera Pass some thirty miles northwest of San Antonio, few if any of the Texans had reservations about their mission. In fact, some of the Rangers were filibusters who had recently fomented insurrection south of the Rio Grande, including William Robertson "Big" Henry, a native Virginian purported to be Callahan's second-in-command. A physical giant as determined as the menacing Seminole chieftain, Henry was an adventurer in every sense of the word. A colorful, boisterous combustible with an ego to match his large frame, Henry had first come to Texas during the Mexican War as a sergeant in the U.S. Army. Following that conflict, he settled down in San Antonio and became a respectable and popular, though somewhat controversial, figure among his fellow citizens. Soon after the war, he married Consolation Arocha, who later bore him three children. In 1854, he successfully campaigned for the post of city marshal. One historian has described Henry as "supremely confident and even fearless," while admitting that "his boldness often bordered on folly." A well-known contemporary, Ranger William A. "Big Foot" Wallace—himself a seasoned veteran of border wars with Mexico—commented that Henry "had rather exalted notions, and was difficult to control. He was brave and possessed merit, but had the . . . [reputation] of interferring [sic] with his superior officers."

To be sure, no one who knew Big Henry should have been surprised when they learned that the moody, impulsive, and sometimes insubordinate dreamer had raised a party of some twenty soldiers of fortune for his own personal invasion of Mexico in the spring and summer of 1855. Or that he reportedly offered his services to the Mexican insurgent, General Carvajal, leader of the secessionist movement in northern Mexico. Or that he published a proclamation in various newspapers urging Texans to "take matters into their own hands and correct the evils on the frontier" and to wage a "war to the death against Santa Anna and his government."

Henry assured Governor Pease just weeks before crossing the border with Captain Callahan that he was "engaged . . . in an honorable cause . . . assisting a down trodden people to cast off the Yoke of Tyranny" and to "overturn the despotic sway" of Santa Anna. To Henry, who seemed part patriot and part privateer, both mercenary and agent of "manifest destiny," surely a man given to grandiose schemes and designs, this expedition was more than a cause. It was a crusade. But who would have expected anything less from such an incendiary who was the great-grandson of Revolutionary War leader Patrick Henry?[15]

On September 25, 1855, Callahan's Rangers reached Encina on the Leona River, less than thirty miles from the border settlement of Eagle Pass. Before their arrival on the border, the expedition had been beset by delays as well as by dissension and disobedience within the ranks. Heavy rains had turned the plains into a quagmire, slowing the company's progress to no more than six or seven miles a day. To make matters worse, flooding conditions had pushed both the Frio and Nueces rivers beyond their banks, making it difficult for Callahan to safely ford the swollen streams. Then, after sloshing across the South Texas prairies for a week, tempers flared as a dispute erupted among the officers over the issue of command. Fear of desertions combined with disagreements over even the most petty of issues eventually led the force to divide into three columns—one commanded by the charismatic Callahan, a second by the headstrong Henry, and a third by the less experienced Nat Benton of Seguin (nephew of U.S. Senator Thomas Hart "Old Bullion" Benton), whose force of some thirty volunteers had caught up with Callahan only days earlier.[16]

All three parties advanced toward the Rio Grande. On September 29, the Texans reached the flooded river, which stretched out before them some three hundred yards in width. Upon surveying the scene, they could see that the currents were too swift for a crossing. Because of recent rains, the river rushed by with tremendous force, the currents discouraging even the boldest among the Texans. The parties had little choice but to encamp on the bluffs overlooking the Bravo some four miles above Eagle Pass, opposite Piedras Negras. The expeditionary force waited for four days before the waters finally subsided enough to cross. The Texans transported their horses and provisions across the river by boats reportedly seized at gunpoint by the impatient Captain Henry. Only a handful of men remained on the Texas side to guard the pack train. By October 3, a hundred well-armed, confident, and restless Mounted Rangers had arrived on the south banks of the river, prepared for any contingency or conflict in arms. Or so they thought.[17]

Divided in their loyalties and in their choice of leaders, they nevertheless stood united by their determination to fight Indian raiders, Mexican regulars, or anyone else. The Mounted Rangers moved beyond the sand hills that hugged the river banks. For more than twenty miles, they rode westward, through mesquite and chaparral thickets that strangled the trail to San Fernando. Callahan had been informed that ahead lay a party of Lipan Apaches and Seminoles, reportedly under the leadership of Wild Cat, who was also said to command a band of "Seminole Negroes" (men of mixed African and Native descent). As the Rangers approached Escondido Creek later that afternoon, a fusillade of gunfire erupted from a distant timberline. A force of Mexican troops and Indian scouts had been concealed there. Then some seven hundred of the enemy swarmed out of the thickets. Callahan halted his troops and ordered them to form a skirmish line; the captain rode to the front of his command shouting encouragement over the din of confusion. Incredibly, he ordered them to charge. As the Texans hurled themselves forward, their foes greeted them with a thunderous volley.[18]

Texas frontiersman and chronicler A. J. Sowell recorded that a "desperate fight" ensued. "Pistols, rifles, and shotguns rang out on every side, mingled with the yell of the Texans, the war whoop of the Indians, and the loud imprecations of the Mexicans," he reported. During the furious charge and exchange of gunfire, at least one Mexican officer and several of his men fell on the field, while four Texans tumbled from their saddles mortally wounded, among them young Willis Jones, the son of William Jones, the judge of Val Verde County. According to Sowell, six Rangers, including Captain Nat Benton and his son Eustis, suffered serious wounds.

By the time Callahan's Mounted Rangers had galloped through enemy lines, another column of Mexican infantry, numbering perhaps two hundred, appeared from a nearby tree line. Recognizing the danger, the captain ordered his men to retreat swiftly to a ravine some three hundred yards away, where they dismounted and made a stand. Several of the riflemen who had their horses shot from under them scrambled for the cover of an irrigation canal.[19]

The Rangers then witnessed perhaps the most heroic single act of the battle. Wesley Harris of Seguin and several of his comrades noticed that young Eustis Benton had fallen from his horse and lay exposed on the prairie. Without hesitation, they rode back onto the field of fire to retrieve his seemingly lifeless body. When they reached him, they discovered that although the ball had pierced the young Ranger's skull and remained lodged somewhere behind his eye, he was still breathing.[20]

Harris and his fellow horsemen also recovered the body of Willis Jones. But the other dead were by necessity left on the field. While the thick smoke and smell of gunpowder still hung in the air, both sides disengaged from the fight. Then night fell. Callahan and one of his subordinates later claimed that the Rangers had killed at least sixty *rurales* (rural mounted police) and Indians during the chaotic exchange that day. General Emilio Langberg, the military commander of the state of Coahuila, refuted that claim, reporting the loss of only four dead and three wounded. He also insisted that no Indians had participated in the skirmish, although according to Texan William Kyle, an eyewitness to the event, the four-hour battle was "one of the hardest Indian fights ever fought." No one knows for sure, but it is probable that Wild Cat was among the Texans' enemy that day, wearing the blue and red jacket of the Mexican cavalry. Regardless, as Callahan's company retreated hastily toward Piedras Negras, the Mexican troops withdrew and regrouped near San Fernando.[21]

That night, the Texans were still on Mexican soil, establishing a defensive perimeter and preparing for the possibility of another attack. But no second ambush awaited them so the next morning they cautiously fell back to Piedras Negras, then a settlement of approximately 1,500 inhabitants. Sometime before sunset on October 4, Callahan and his Rangers occupied the outskirts of the town, a collection mostly of modest adobe dwellings and mud-chinked jacales (primitive wooden structures with thatched roofs). According to J. S. McDowell, a member of the expedition, shortly after dawn the next day Callahan "demanded to the Alcalde to surrender the town. . . . In case of refusal he proposed sacking it forthwith." As McDowell recollected, "[A] deputation of Piedras Negras citizens came down. They accepted the terms of an unconditional surrender. We then marched in regular order . . . and halted in front of the Alcalde's house, attached to which was a rude stone fort, which we made our headquarters." At that point, the local magistrate, "a short fleshy man, waddled out, nervously waving a hastily improvised flag on a short stick. With many smiles and gracious bows he gave up his keys and authority to our leader. He also promised to have all the arms and munitions delivered immediately at the guard house." McDowell recalled that this arsenal "constituted quite a military museum." Callahan could now boast that he had occupied the town and that he had done so without facing even token opposition.[22]

One critically important fragment of evidence suggests that, after taking the border town, Callahan and others may have been planning an even larger campaign into the interior of Mexico. After apparently returning from Piedras Negras to San Antonio on October 7, William Kyle noted that "we have Piedras Negras in possession" and "have plenty of artillery" to wage an offensive campaign south of the border. (This may have been the same William Jefferson Kyle who was a prominent Fort Bend County sugar plantation owner and slaveholder.) Moreover, he estimated that as many as five or six hundred more men could be raised for an invasion force. "Old Rip is here and will go without fail," he announced in reference to the presence of the grizzled John Ford. The famed Ranger captain and newspaper publisher was known to favor the annexation of Mexico or at the very least the establishment of a buffer Republic of the Sierra Madre. "I will be back in Mexico in less than fifteen days," Kyle boldly predicted.[23]

Meanwhile, in Piedras Negras, with a small garrison of U.S. regulars across the river looking on from Fort Duncan, and with many of the town's residents fleeing with their belongings in carts and wagons down the road to San Fernando, Captain Callahan had every reason to reassure his men that their position was secure. But that soon changed. Within hours of seizing the town armory, Callahan got word that a large force of Mexican cavalry, perhaps numbering more than one thousand, was rapidly advancing on Piedras Negras. Some accounts contended that, upon hearing this news, a handful of Texans deserted and fled across the Rio Bravo, fearful that they would face certain death if they remained. With fewer than one hundred volunteers, the knowledge that U.S. troopers at Fort Duncan under the command of Captain Sidney Burbank remained under strict orders *not* to cross the river, and a swollen Rio Grande at his back, Callahan concluded that only extreme measures might spare the remainder of his men from annihilation or, at best, from capture. Determined that his command would not suffer a fate similar to that of Travis at the Alamo or Fannin at Goliad, he ordered his Rangers to set fire to the prairie and the jacales scattered along the western edge of town. If nothing else, he hoped, putting the torch to fields and thatched hovels between himself and the enemy would provide precious time needed to evacuate his command by ferry across the river.[24]

That decision would have devastating consequences. No sooner had the Texans torched the perimeter of the town than the wind-whipped flames quickly spread, leaping from one hut to another until a raging inferno had engulfed dozens of dwellings. Entire families fled in terror, scurrying through the chaos to some point of safety. As Callahan had planned, the Mexican federales and their Indian allies, who were closing in on the town, had no choice but to fall back from the blaze that separated them from the Texans. "Dense volumes of smoke were seen issuing from every house," wrote a correspondent for the New Orleans *Picayune,* who described the scene from the Texas side of the river. "In the twinkling of an eye the entire village was in flames, except a few houses around the plaza where the Texans intended to make a stand. They were now surrounded by a wall of flame, and the Mexican commander, [Colonel] Manschaca . . . withdrew his eight hundred men without firing a shot." The reporter recounted that "as night drew on . . . the flames of the village, built almost entirely of wood and straw, mounted into the heavens, illuminated the river and surrounding country with the brightness of day—the explosions of powder in the burning buildings, the . . . [gun]fire from the Texans upon spies and scouts from the enemy's camp, the shouting of the 'filibusteros' as they darted about, as it seemed from this side, amidst the very flames" made for "a mixture of sights and sounds never to be forgotten."[25]

Across the river at Fort Duncan, an exasperated Captain Burbank—who had not even been aware of Callahan's crossing days earlier—observed the horrible scene. "The Texans commenced firing the town and in a few minutes nearly every house in the place was in flames," he later reported to U.S. Adjutant General Samuel Cooper. Burbank also stated that, although Callahan sent a courier across the Bravo with a message requesting protection and assistance for his Rangers, Burbank flatly refused to render aid. Even two additional dispatches apparently failed to persuade Burbank to commit his forces in support of Callahan's men.[26]

Still, as Callahan ordered a retreat back across the river, Burbank hastened a battery of small artillery pieces to the riverbank to help cover the Rangers' movement. As it turned out, the cannon were not needed. Through the billowing, black smoke, which covered their escape, the Texans crossed the river in skiffs. According to one eyewitness, they left approximately thirty of their horses on the Mexican side of the river—horses Callahan later reported as "captured." To a man the company retired safely to the north bank with their wounded, including young Eustis Benton, who would miraculously recover from his head wound. But they did not depart until they had sacked the town and reduced it to cinders and ashes.[27]

J. S. McDowell denied that widespread pillaging and looting occurred that "night of sorrows." He insisted, "If any property was plundered and appropriated for private use by our men, except for forage and to appease hunger, such was an exception and not the rule." Yet another eyewitness, Jesse Sumpter of Eagle Pass, told a different story. "Callahan's party commenced hauling their plunder off the bank of the river which consisted of a large quantity of corn, beans, flour, and produce." He admitted that "there were a good many men riding about the town of Eagle Pass [later that night] and everyone that I saw had . . . jewelry displayed about his neck and breast, such as gold necklaces, chains, ear-rings, finger-rings, watches and other articles . . . which they seemed to take delight in displaying." Sumpter also noted that "one of Callahan's men rode up to my house. He seemed to have more of the jewelry than any of the others. . . . He was riding on a silver-mounted Mexican saddle, and the owner, Prado, happened to be in my house. When he saw his saddle, he knew it and pointed it out to me as being his. He told me he valued it at $100. While he was talking to me," Sumpter recalled, "he cried like a child, for he had lost everything he had except what he had on." If the Texans had not succeeded in holding Piedras Negras, they had apparently managed to take much of it with them.[28]

What Callahan's Rangers did not carry away, they destroyed. General Langberg summarized the carnage soon thereafter. "Piedras Negras offers now a scene of devastation," he reported. "A multitude of innocent families are without shelter—homeless and ruined." General Persifor Smith admitted to Governor Pease the following week that many of the residents of Piedras Negras were left in "utter destitution" and reduced to "seeking food on this side of the river to save themselves from starving." Captain Burbank concurred, writing to the adjutant general that the Mexicans who had fled their town before it was set ablaze were "in a state of great destitution." He even recommended that, given the emergency of the situation, the U.S. government "hastily" dispatch provisions to the scene to alleviate the suffering. Otherwise, he feared reprisal from the people of the border in response to the entire affair, which he termed "embarrassing." The razing of an entire border town—and in the presence of the U.S. garrison at Fort Duncan—had an incendiary effect upon U.S.-Mexican relations, just as Burbank predicted. Already smoldering in suspicion, intrigue, and even open animosity, the border situation would only grow worse. As Langberg summarized the entire affair, "[T]he shame of this barbarous and unjustifiable act shall be as lasting as the remembrance of the occurance [sic]."[29]

The incident was over, but not forgotten—or forgiven. By almost any measure, all that Callahan's reckless incursion had accomplished was to stir up old embers of hatred, fear, and mistrust along the border. The Callahan expedition rekindled and ignited anew the fires of discord and anger on both sides of the river. Predictably, Texans and their spokesmen in Austin as well as allies in Washington rallied to the defense of Callahan. Just one week after the sacking of Piedras Negras, Governor Pease wrote General Smith that the captain "was justified in pursueing [sic] the Indians across the

Rio Grande . . . when they had been committing depredations upon our citizens." Moreover, he stated, "if this leads to a border warfare between the Citizens of this State and the Mexicans and Indians no one will regret it more than myself, but the fault lies with the United States Government, whose neglect to furnish protection to our settlements . . . rendered it necessary." Pease further exonerated Callahan in an address to the Texas State Legislature on November 5. Again he defended the captain's decision to burn the village in view of the recent raids against Texan settlements conducted by Indians allegedly based below the Bravo. After all, he charged, Mexican officials in Coahuila had "made common cause" with the Indian raiders and had even harbored them.

A public meeting of citizens in San Antonio also applauded Callahan's actions, the rowdy assemblage going so far as to pass a resolution commending the Ranger for his courageous determination to punish those who plundered the frontier. Likewise, newspapers such as the *Texas State Gazette, The Texas State Times,* and the San Antonio *Herald* strongly supported military action, agreeing with Pease that Texans had the right to defend their property and their persons from the onslaught of *los barbaros Indios* (the barbaric Indians) who enjoyed sanctuary south of the border.[30]

U.S. Secretary of State William L. Marcy, in a series of dispatches to Mexico's minister to the United States, Juan N. Almonte, also supported Callahan's actions. He agreed that the Texans' expedition would never have occurred had local authorities in Coahuila suppressed the Lipan raiders living within their boundaries. More specifically, he reminded Almonte that the Mexican government had not fulfilled its treaty obligations to maintain order and peace along the border and that such negligence was also a clear violation of article 33 of an 1831 accord between the two nations. He further insisted that, according to accounts that had crossed his desk, "the Rangers were invited across the Rio Bravo . . . by a Mexican officer, who, it is presumed they believed to be competent for the purpose." Even if no such formal invitation had been issued to Callahan, he reasoned, the border crossing was still "justifiable by the law of nations." He then accused unnamed Mexicans living in and near Piedras Negras of "treacherously" leading the Texans into an ambush near Escondido Creek. As for the burning of the town and the conduct of both the Texans and Captain Burbank's regulars who assisted in their retreat, Marcy dismissed the events of that October night as "laudable" acts of self-defense. Moreover, he concluded that both the Rangers and troopers from Fort Duncan deserved "praise and not reproach."[31]

U.S. minister to Mexico James Gadsden offered similar arguments. Writing to the minister of foreign affairs of Mexico, Miguel M. Arrioja, on November 29, 1855, the American diplomat who had recently negotiated the purchase of the Gila River region for the United States, went so far as to define the Ranger company as a "regular organized military Corps in the service, and acting under the orders of the Executive of Texas." He claimed that Callahan's company had only been dispatched to the border "for the purpose of protecting the lives of its citizens from the scalping-knife and the tomahawk" and their property "from the plundering instincts of Savages instigated and known to be in the service of Mexico." He even stated that the "humane expedition" of Texans acted under the "higher law of self-preservation," which transcended the terms of any treaty or international convention.[32]

Not surprisingly, Mexican authorities disputed such claims. Learning at his station in Washington of a violation of his country's sovereignty by a company of Texas Rangers, Juan Almonte vehemently protested the border intrusion. Writing to Secretary Marcy on January 14, 1856, Almonte expressed outrage at what he repeatedly termed an "invasion" of Mexico by Callahan's company. He accused both Governor Pease and Captain Burbank of "connivance" in planning and implementing the expedition. Denying that any Mexican official had authorized the Texans to cross the border and insisting that there had been "atrocities committed by the aggressors," he demanded a formal investigation into the behavior and acts of "the fillibuster [*sic*] company of Captain Callahan." He likewise called for a military inquiry into the actions—or inaction— of the federal troops at Fort Duncan. More specifically, he singled out "the fitlibuster [*sic*] Captain Henry," questioning his role in the incursion and thus reinforcing his complaints to Marcy earlier in the year that the unpredictable Henry had raised mercenaries and engaged in mischief within the borders of Mexico. Lastly, on behalf of his government, Almonte requested that the "wicked men" who had participated in the expedition as well as the sponsoring governments of Texas and the United States be held responsible for the resulting damages and that the inhabitants of Piedras Negras be "properly indemnified."[33]

Perhaps Mexican officials did not realistically expect that any reparations would be paid to the residents of Piedras Negras. Indeed, none was forthcoming. Nor did these officials expect that leaders in Austin or Washington would ever admit that there might have been more to the military expedition than simply the punishment of Indian raiders. But for many years, rumors and reports persisted that at least some of the Texans had enlisted in what they understood to be a mission to recover runaway slaves from south of the border. And that these volunteers fully expected to be paid handsome bounties for any returned fugitives. The truth shall probably remain buried with Callahan and Henry.[34]

To Anglo-Texans, Callahan and his men were freedom fighters, brave defenders of the borders, indeed patriots. To people of Mexican heritage—on both sides of the river—the Texas devils were nothing more than filibusters, soldiers of fortune, and privateers, not heroic Rangers but riders from hell.

NOTES

1. Elisha M. Pease to James H. Callahan, July 5, 1855, Elisha M. Pease Papers, Texas State Library and Archives, Austin (hereafter cited as EPP); *Annual Report of the Commissioner of Indian Affairs,* 1851, 41–43, 254–56, 259.

2. Linn, *Reminiscences of Fifty Years in Texas,* 185; James T. DeShields, *Border Wars of Texas* (Austin: State House Press, 1993), 324; Wilbarger, *Indian Depredations in Texas,* 376; Homer Thrall, *A Pictorial History of Texas: From the Earliest Visits of European Adventurers, to A.D. 1879* (St. Louis: N. D. Thompson & Co., 1879), 520–21; John H. Jenkins III, ed., *The Papers of the Texas Revolution, 1835–1836* (Austin: Presidial Press, 1973), 7:86; John Henry Brown, *Indian Wars and Pioneers of Texas* (Austin: State House Press, 1988), 84, 601–602.

3. Pease to Callahan, July 5, 1855; Pease to Callahan, July 25, 1855; and Callahan to Pease, August 10, 1855, EPP. See also extracted from the governor's papers in the Texas State Library and Archives, Pease to Citizens of Bexar County, July 25, 1855, and W. E. Jones to Pease, September 22, 1855, in Winfrey, *Texas Indian Papers, 1846–1859,* 3:228–29, 243–46.

4. Pease to Callahan, July 5, 1855; and Pease to Callahan, July 25, 1855, EPP; Anderson, *Conquest of Texas,* 268–69.

5. Callahan to Edward Burleson, Jr., August 15, 1855; Callahan to Pease, August 18, 1855; and Callahan to Burleson, August 31, 1855, Edward Burleson, Jr., Papers, Center for American History, University of Texas, Austin (hereafter cited as EBP).

6. Callahan's muster roll may be found in Ranger Muster Rolls, Texas State Library and Archives, Austin; Amelia Barr, *All the Days of My Life: An Autobiography* (New York: D. Appleton, 1913), 217–18.

7. Manning, *Diplomatic Correspondence of the United States,* 9:192–93. A poignant inquiry into the fugitive slave question may be found in Ronnie C. Tyler, "The Callahan Expedition of 1855: Indians or Negroes?" *Southwestern Historical Quarterly* 70 (April 1967): 574–85; J. D. B. Stillman, *Wanderings in the Southwest in 1855,* ed. Ron Tyler (Spokane, Wash.: Arthur H. Clark Co., 1990), 119–20.

8. Callahan to Burleson, August 15, 1855; and Callahan to Burleson, August 18, 1855, EBP.

9. Marcus Duval to Bell, October 20, 1850, PHBP.

10. Doubleday, *My Life in the Old Army,* 349–50; see also Olmsted, *Journey through Texas,* 314–55; Montgomery, *Eagle Pass,* 137–41.

11. Duval to Bell, October 20, 1850; and John H. Rollins to Bell, October 30, 1850, PHBP; *Annual Report of the Commissioner of Indian Affairs,* 1851, 42–44, 253–59.

12. Webb, *Texas Rangers: A Century of Frontier Defense,* 127–36.

13. Doubleday, *My Life in the Old Army,* 179, 349–50; see also Jesse Sumpter, *Paso del Aguila: A Chronicle of Frontier Days on the Texas Border as Recorded in the Memoirs of Jesse Sumpter,* comp. by Harry Warren (Austin:

Encino Press, 1969), 4, 61–70 (hereafter cited as Sumpter, *Memoirs); Reports of the Committee of Investigation,* 409–11.

14. William Banta and J. W. Caldwell, Jr., *Twenty-Seven Years on the Texas Frontier* (Council Hill, Okla.: L. G. Park, 1933), 54–58, 77–86; Montgomery, *Eagle Pass,* 73–77.

15. William R. Henry to Pease, September 2, 1855, EPP; Elton Cude, *The Wild and Free Dukedom of Bexar* (San Antonio: Munguia Printers, 1978), 43–44; Ernest C. Shearer, "The Callahan Expedition, 1855," *Southwestern Historical Quarterly* 54 (April 1951): 432–34; Manning, *Diplomatic Correspondence of the United States,* 9:782–89; Stillman, *Wanderings in the Southwest in 1855,* 119–20. The *Texas State Gazette* (Austin), August 11, 1855, and the *San Antonio Herald,* August 14, 1855, carried reports of Henry's boasts of his incursions into Mexico that spring and summer.

16. Sowell, *Early Settlers and Indian Fighters,* 248, 527, 530–32; Winfrey, *Texas Indian Papers, 1846–1859,* 3:243–47; Shearer, "Callahan Expedition, 1855," 435–37.

17. Sowell, *Early Settlers and Indian Fighters,* 530–32; Shearer, "Callahan Expedition," 437–39.

18. Sowell, *Early Settlers and Indian Fighters,* 531–33.

19. Ibid.; William Kyle to Burleson, October 7, 1855, EBP; John Henry Brown, *History of Texas from 1685 to 1892,* 2 vols. (St. Louis: L. E. Daniell, 1893), 2:369–71.

20. Sowell, *Early Settlers and Indian Fighters,* 527, 533–35; Brown, *History of Texas,* 2: 369–71.

21. Kyle to Burleson, October 7, 1855, EBP; Brown, *History of Texas,* 2:369–71; Sowell, *Early Settlers and Indian Fighters,* 248, 532–34; Callahan's handwritten notes regarding those killed and wounded at Escondido Creek may be found on his company's muster roll in Ranger Muster Rolls, Texas State Library and Archives, Austin.

22. McDowell's eyewitness account of the burning of Piedras Negras may be found in the New Orleans *Picayune,* January 8, 1893; Shearer, "Callahan Expedition," 438–42; Winfrey, *Texas Indian Papers, 1846–1859,* 3:253–57.

23. Kyle to Burleson, October 7, 1855, EBP; see also Winfrey, *Texas Indian Papers, 1846–1859,* 3:253–54.

24. Sowell, *Early Settlers and Indian Fighters,* 533–34.

25. New Orleans *Picayune,* January 8, 1893.

26. Sidney Burbank to Samuel Cooper, October 4, 1855; and Burbank to Cooper, October 8, 1855, Ranger Correspondence, Texas State Library and Archives, Austin (hereafter cited as RC).

27. Burbank to Cooper, October 8, 1855, RC; Sumpter, *Memoirs,* 63–68.

28. New Orleans *Picayune,* January 8, 1893; Sumpter, *Memoirs,* 68.

29. Manning, *Diplomatic Correspondence of the United States,* 9:193; Shearer, "Callahan Expedition," 442–43; Langberg's letter was published in the *Texas State Times* (Austin), November 17, 1855; *Reports of the Committee of Investigation,* 192–93; Burbank to Cooper, October 8, 1855, RC.

30. Winfrey, *Texas Indian Papers, 1846–1859,* 3:253–57; Governor Elisha M. Pease, "Address to the Texas State Legislature," November 5, 1855, EPP; *Texas State Gazette* (Austin), October 20, 1855; *San Antonio Herald,* October 16, 1855; W. R. Henry to Santiago Vidaurri, August 12, 1856, Santiago Vidaurri Papers, Center for American History, University of Texas, Austin (hereafter cited as SVP).

31. Manning, *Diplomatic Correspondence of the United States,* 9:197–200.

32. Ibid., 9:788–789, 800–802.

33. Ibid., 9:816–17.

34. *Reports of the Committee of Investigation,* 192–93; see also, *Preliminary Report of J. Hubley Ashton, Agent of the United States, before the United States and Mexican Claims Commission, to the Secretary of State,* November 23, 1876, in 44th Cong., 2nd sess., 1876, S. Exec. Doc. 31, serial 1720, 18–67.

"RIP" FORD'S INDIAN FIGHT ON THE CANADIAN

W. J. Hughes

Throughout the year 1856, settlers on the northwest frontier of Texas found it possible to till their fields and graze their herds with comparatively little interference from Indian attack. So tranquil appeared the situation that the War Department began a series of transfers of the Regular Army contingents from the northwest garrisons, dispatching them to Utah, Kansas, and other territories where graver problems seemed to threaten.

Into the defensive void thus created the Comanche horsemen swept during 1857, and the reeking casualty lists and tolls of vanished or destroyed property again began to mount. The whites fought back desperately, but so futilely that the entire year witnessed not one successful punitive expedition against the painted marauders.[1] Frontier people, for several years irritated at the federal government's policy of placing part of the Penateka (Honey Eater) Comanches and the remnants of other tribes on two northwest reservations, now were vociferously angry, as incidents seemed to implicate the reservation Indians in collusion with the hostile bands.[2] The harassed settlers called on Governor Elisha M. Pease for more protection; he, in turn, called on the military.

Responsibility for protecting the region lay with Brevet Major General David E. Twiggs, commanding the Department of Texas (the Eighth Military Department). In a plaintive letter to Adjutant General Lorenzo Thomas, in the summer of 1857, Twiggs pointed out the impotency of his departmental strength to meet the red challenge and passed on a suggestion from Colonel Albert Sidney Johnston of the Second Cavalry that the Comanches be sought out and attacked on the buffalo ranges. Twiggs also included a suggestion that troops other than his own must be found for such an operation.[3]

Receiving no encouraging reply, Twiggs wrote again, this time suggesting to Secretary of War John B. Floyd the propriety of congressional authorization for the creation of a regiment of Texas Mounted Volunteers, to be sworn into federal service. His suggestion included the recommendation that this force, if created, should be commanded by the indefatigable John S. "Rip" Ford, a Texan prominent not only in private and political affairs but also one proved in battle as Colonel Jack Hays' chief of scouts during the Mexican war and by two years of Ranger command along the turbulent Rio Grande border.[4] The general's suggestion concerning a volunteer regiment was embodied in a bill introduced into Congress, and Texans kept an anxious and hopeful ear cocked toward Washington.[5]

While an economy-minded Congress vacillated, the frontier situation injected itself as a popular issue into the state gubernatorial campaign of 1857, between Sam Houston and Hardin R. Runnels, a wealthy Red River planter behind whom the Democrats had rallied. With the Whig party destroyed by the Kansas-Nebraska Act which he, as senator, had steadfastly opposed, Houston campaigned as an independent. Apparently reluctant to commit himself to any positive stand against the Indians, he "was accused . . . of blaming the frontier settlers for the Indian outrages. . ."[6] Runnels, on the other hand was vehement in his demands for increased frontier security, and the resulting vote from the frontier districts was a considerable factor in his election.[7]

When Runnels assumed office it was apparent that there would be no immediate congressional action on the volunteer regiment bill, generally referred to in Texas as the Ranger Regiment Bill, but the frontier situation could not wait on legislative discussion. While congressmen debated in Washington, men, women and children died beneath Comanche lances in Basque, Erath, Brown, and other counties on the fringe of settlement, and the executive file of incoming correspondence bulged with petitions for aid bearing the signatures of the irate, fortunate survivors.[8] Accepting his election as a popular mandate to solve the Indian problem, Governor Runnels in his first annual message to the Texas legislature urged immediate action to relieve the frontier.[9] Appropriate legislation was difficult to achieve because the legislature too was economy minded and certain East Texas members were apathetic toward western frontier problems, but the diligent and persistent efforts of State Senator George B. Erath on behalf of his frontier constituents finally obtained success.[10] A bill entitled "An act for the better protection of the frontier" passed the legislature and went to Runnels, who hastily signed it on January 27, 1858.[11]

The act authorized the governor to call into state service an additional one hundred men and to place them, along with the Rangers already in the field, under a single commander whose rank would be that of Senior Captain. While the term of enlistment was designated as six months, the act provided that the men might be discharged sooner or continued longer in service, as circumstances might dictate to the commanding officer. To equip, pay, and subsist the command, the act appropriated the sum of $70,000 from the state treasury.[12]

Late in 1857, when the proposal to create a state force was being widely discussed in Austin, the *State Gazette* had editorially recommended appointment of John S. Ford to command the organization. The extent of the newspaper's influence on the governor cannot be determined, but the day following his approval of the bill,

Governor Runnels officially informed Ford of his appointment as Senior Captain.[13]

The appointment was most logical. Ford's operations on the Rio Grande frontier from 1849 to 1851 had established his prestige as a thoroughly able Indian fighter, and the knowledge of Comanches he had gained there and on his El Paso journey with Major Robert S. Neighbors could well be employed in any projected campaign. Haste, too, was important, for the War Department contemplated the transfer of the Second Cavalry from the northwest frontier.[14] Ford's home was in Austin, and he was currently in the city serving on a United States grand jury;[15] he was fully acquainted with the situation and could begin preparations without delay. An additional reason for his appointment suggests itself: good-naturedly forgiven for his temporary aberration in favor of Know-Nothingism, Ford had returned to the Democratic ranks and had worked earnestly for the party's candidates during the campaign of 1857.[16] Here, then, was an opportunity to repay a political favor by an appointment which would meet with general approbation.

In a laudatory editorial, Colonel John Marshall, editor of the *State Gazette,* applauded the governor's choice:

> "It is an excellent appointment. The Captain had been previously recommended to the President, by members of both branches of the Legislature, by the Supreme and Federal Courts, and by many private citizens, for a field of five in the new regiment expected to be created at the present Congress. He is an old Indian fighter, and we predict that he will rid the frontier of all annoyance in the first campaign. . ."[17]

Ford, however, was less assured than the optimistic editor. It was his understanding of the problem to be faced, as much as his natural modesty, which made him feel that "These expressions were complimentary, but were calculated to lead the public to expect a great deal,—perhaps too much, from the officer mentioned."[18]

On the day he made public Ford's appointment, Runnels informed the Senior Captain that he was "clothed in the full and complete command of all the State Troops now in the service and of all to be called out in contemplation of the law of January 28th [*sic*], 1858. . ." He ordered Ford to co-operate with officers of the Regular Army "if expedient, convenient, or practicable," and to co-operate with Indian agents.[19] He granted Ford authority to make contracts for supplies, and closed his letter by stressing the necessity for action and energy.[20]

It was with energetic action that Ford responded. In less than a month, recruiting, organization, and most supply procurement had been accomplished. Recruiting, although rapid, was deliberate, for "The intention was to get good men."

When a majority of the company had been recruited, Ford, in spite of his commission from the governor, called for an election of company officers, in accordance with the usual custom followed by volunteers. The results of the election placed Ford in a dual capacity: by his election to the captaincy he was company commander, and by virtue of Governor Runnels' commission he was, in effect, battalion commander. To fill the other commissioned offices, the men elected as first lieutenant Edward Burleson, Jr., son of a vice-president of the Republic of Texas, and as second lieutenant they chose William A. Pitts. Dr. Powhatan Jordan accompanied the expeditionary force as surgeon.

Ford was fortunate in the choice of his company officers. Ed Burleson had served under Ben McCulloch on the northwest frontier during the Mexican War, and had been with Ford, as a lieutenant, on the Rio Grande frontier. Ford relied heavily on Burleson's experience, naming him quartermaster and commissary, and assigning him to act in the capacity of paymaster. Pitts, too, had twice seen Ranger service, once with Henry E. McCulloch and, again, with James H. Callahan; in the interim he had clerked in a store, had served Guadalupe County as deputy assessor and collector, and at the time of his enlistment held the position of sergeant-at-arms to the Texas legislature, resigning to join the company at Ford's solicitation. English-born Robert Cotter, youthful and observant, was persuaded to resign his place as a clerk in George Hancock's Austin dry goods store and enlist. Although Ford appointed him orderly sergeant, Cotter functioned actually as battalion sergeant-major.[21]

In preparation for the forthcoming expedition, Ford found it necessary to devote some attention to Ranger organizations already in the field. Lieutenant James H. Tankersley scouted with his company in Comanche County, and to the eastward, in Bosque County, Lieutenant Allison Nelson was active with a command. Ford had confidence in both of these officers, particularly in Nelson, who had organized and led a company during the Mexican War, but decided to muster out of service a company commanded by Captain John S. Connor and a small detachment under Lieutenant T. C. Frost, both operating in the Pecan Bayou country northwest of Austin. Ford may have lacked confidence in the command capacity of the latter two officers; it is equally possible that their being commissioned by former governor Pease, a political foe of Ford's, may have influenced the Senior Captain's decision. To replace these units, Ford requested Captain Henry E. McCulloch to raise a company and join the main command on the frontier, a request to which McCulloch agreed.

To arm the company, Governor Runnels at first turned to General Twiggs for a supply of Colt revolvers, the favorite Ranger weapon, but Twiggs refused to comply on the ground that he had no authority to issue the arms unless the state troops were sworn into federal service.[22] Nevertheless, the state managed to procure such weapons for those who had no personal arms, and the command was to ride out armed after the usual Ranger fashion; most of the men, like Ford, carried two Navy Colts, and every man had at least one, as well as the familiar muzzle-loading rifle. The firepower of the force was estimated at 1500 rounds without reloading, a volume impressive enough to draw newspaper comment.[23]

Ford assured his Rangers of dry ammunition and blankets by having made to his specifications waterproof leather panniers, "cayaques", of a type the baggage mules could not dislodge, and as final items of equipment he added two light wagons for the accommodation of any possible sick or wounded.

In late February, the command being as nearly ready as time had permitted, Ford gave the order to break camp and move out. The Rangers were eager to be in the field, away from the restrictions of garrison life. Although his camp regulations were few in comparison with those of the Regular Army, "Old Rip" Ford enforced them completely and in a manner to command thorough respect. At no time in his long career did he observe with tolerance any breach of his discipline.[24]

At daybreak on a chilly February morning the Rangers marched. One can visualize the column of riders as it wound through the shallow passes and past the low hogbacks of the rolling hills north of the capital. Nondescript, casual men in nondescript, casual clothing, they wore their coats buttoned tightly against the clammy cold. Rangers wore no uniforms; instead, each individual dressed in the garments he felt would serve best during an arduous campaign. Broad-brimmed hats, pulled low over eyebrows, and high boots, into which trousers were tucked, gave a certain uniformity to the column, as did the cap-and-ball rifles, walnut butts protruding forward from rawhide boots beneath the left legs of the horsemen. Coat skirts bulged at almost every hip where rode the heavy six-shooters, additionally protected from dust and dew by voluminous rawhide holsters.

Screening the column, and within eyeshot of it, was dispersed a thin fringe of scouts, alert but not anxious since the route for the first few days lay through relatively peaceful country. Behind this human screen the horsemen moved at a swinging walk in double file. At their head rode their quiet captain, at whose elbow, like an adhesive shadow, bobbed his personal orderly, Francisco de la Garza Falcon, whose service with Ford on the Rio Grande had kept that officer alternating between fits of smouldering irritability and hilarious good humor.

In the wake of the fighting force trailed the phlegmatic baggage mules, urged along by their contract drivers. Closing the files, except for the dusty rearguard, the light wagons rattled and chattered in protest at the stony trail.

Ford and Pitts led the column up the Colorado to Pecan Bayou and the Chandler settlement, now Brownwood. There they halted until they were joined by Burleson, who had traveled by way of San Antonio to procure supplies not available in Austin. At this camp (Camp Adams), Ford left a non-commissioned officer and six or seven Rangers, upon petition of the settlers, who were alarmed lest the mustering out of Connor's and Frost's riders should leave the region unprotected.[25]

The main command now marched northward under Burleson, who had orders to establish a base camp on Hubbard's Creek, in what is today northern Stephens County. Ford had selected a camp site approximately twenty miles from each of the two Indian agencies and about equally distant from Fort Belknap. From such a location he could keep watch on the reservation Indians, particularly the Comanches, to learn if they were giving clandestine aid to the hostile bands.

To make certain that no Indians lurked in the rear of the command, Ford and Pitts, with a small detachment, followed the main body, reconnoitering the valleys of the Colorado, Pecan Bayou, and Jim Ned Creek. When they overtook Burleson, they learned that he had mistaken his orders, had marched several miles past the intended site, and had pitched the camp on the Clear Fork of the Brazos, just above its junction with Hubbard's Creek, about twelve miles above present-day Breckenridge. The location, however, met Ford's requirements: it was convenient to the reservations and to Fort Belknap, and it had a plentiful supply of wood, grass, and water. Ford approved the site and named it Camp Runnels.[26]

Ford felt that the command was too small to launch a campaign before McCulloch's company arrived. While he waited, he carried out a training program, consisting primarily of mounted drill and target practice, the latter exercise including firing both on foot and from horseback, at various gaits. Meanwhile, the detachments of Nelson and Tankersley arrived in camp and joined in the drill and in the scouting patrols that Ford regularly maintained between the reservations, patrols which convinced the Rangers of the duplicity of the Comanches on the Clear Fork reservation.[27]

February passed, March began to slip away, and Ford grew increasingly impatient for McCulloch's arrival. Finally, he received the disappointing news that McCulloch was not coming. Immediately Ford called on William Preston and William N. P. Marlin to raise small companies of twenty-five or thirty men, and both promptly complied.[28]

Ford believed that the command was still not numerous enough to guarantee success. However, an effort to raise twenty more men was frustrated by the selfishly motivated interference of J. R. Baylor, who in the preceding year had been dismissed from the post of Agent at the Comanche reservation. By mid-April of 1858 even the frontier had heard that the volunteer regiment bill had passed Congress and was awaiting presidential action. Baylor, like many others, hoped to raise a company for service, and wanted to be sure that sufficient men would be on the frontier to form his company, should the regiment be called out while Ford's command was away. If all the frontier fighting men went with the Rangers against the Comanches, Baylor's hopes might be in vain. Possibly the news also explains McCulloch's failure to come to Ford's support.[29]

According to the *State Gazette* of May 22, Baylor's hopes were in vain anyway. An item in that issue stated that Governor Runnels would appoint Ford, H. E. McCulloch, William G. Tobin, E. A. Palmer, E. R. Hord, A. Nelson, A. M. Truitt, E. A. Carroll, J. H. Rogers, and Sam Bogart "to command companies in the Texas Ranger Regiment."[30] One may speculate as to what would have happened along the frontier if a full regiment of veteran Rangers led by that hard-bitten corps of commanders, had ever been permitted to take the field.

While the Rangers drilled and scouted, Ford spent much time with Captain Shapley P. Ross, agent at the Brazos reservation where the Caddos, Tonkawas, and other tribal remnants were being trained in the white man's way. Ford hoped that volunteers from these tribes would provide him with a scouting and auxiliary force, and Major Robert S. Neighbors, Supervising Agent of the Texas Indians, came out from Waco to assist Agent Ross in recruiting such a group. Some initial delay occurred in the procurement of scouts. Casa Maria, the able Caddo leader, was reluctant to offer his tribe's participation because of a tripartite treaty among the Caddo, Creek, and Comanche nations, an agreement providing that if one member of the trio attacked another, the third member must be notified previously, else it would join against the aggressor. With Ross' permission, the Caddo chief sent notification to the Creeks. The Caddo courier returned in a few days with Creek acknowledgment of the message, and the way was clear to organize the Indian complement.[31]

The mounting war spirit on the reservation infected Agent Ross, and that doughty veteran of Indian campaigns under Jack Hays and Peter H. Bell indicated his willingness to lead the Indian contingent, should at least one hundred of his charges agree to go.[32] At his suggestion the chiefs scheduled a feast and war dance for April 9, after which Ross would know how many braves the war party would number. John Ford and several of his men rode in to observe the activities. The dance judging by the Senior Captain's description, must have been a memorable spectacle:

> "The war-dance was 'grand, gloomy, and peculiar.' Every participant had his own way in the matter; some sounded the fear-inspiring warwhoop; others crept along, cat-like, to pounce upon their astonished and demoralized foes; a squad would move up and attack an imaginary band of Comanches, and a shout of triumph would go up, loud enough to set a donkey's ears to ringing. Many sang in a style which would have crazed an old maiden school teacher. Every face had a daubing of rueful colors, intended to strike terror into the beholder. The sight of one was enough to

stampede a regiment of dudes, and a battalion of school-marms. The impression made upon a civilized spectator may be illustrated thusly: An immense paint pot, hundred of miles in depth and circumference, filled with colors of every conceivable hue and shade has been overturned, the contents have deluged the infernal regions; hell has taken an emetic, and cast up devils upon earth, and here they are."[33]

At the end of the dance, more than Ross' requisite one hundred signified their determination to march with the Rangers, thus assuring Ford of the agent's valuable experience. It was to be a fortunate development for the command, since business was to summon Lieutenant Burleson back to the settlements at the last minute, and the reluctance with which Ford granted his battle-tested subordinate leave of absence was somewhat tempered by the company of the veteran Ross.

By early April, Captain Ford already knew the location of the Comanche village he planned to surprise. His target was the Nokoni band, camped along the Canadian River near the Antelope Hills, the band to which frontiersmen attributed most of the winter's depredations. There was current in the settlements a tale that Ford had dispatched a spy to the camp, who returned bearing the Nokoni challenge to the Rangers to come after them.[34] By mid-April the Rangers were almost in condition to accept the challenge. Powder, cartridges, and percussion caps for six-shooters and rifles were packed for convenient transportation and distribution; Surgeon Jordan had overhauled and arranged his medical instruments and supplies; picket ropes for all animals had been issued to the men. No forage was packed; the mounts and baggage mules must subsist on grass. For the men Ford had apportioned rations—bacon, flour, and other essentials including extra amounts of coffee and sugar.[35] On the campaign bacon would give way to buffalo meat and bread would not be missed, but coffee, all the better for sweetening, was an item few Rangers ever patiently did without.

An unexpected addition to the equipment was an ambulance, provided by Captain William Ford, seventy-three-year-old father of the Ranger commander. In this vehicle the elder Ford had jolted into the middle of Camp Runnels' busy preparations, announcing his intention of attaching himself to the expedition. John Ford was glad to get the ambulance and approved his father's intention, since the old gentleman "possessed strong will—[was] a good rider, and capable of enduring considerable fatigue."[36]

By sundown on April 21 the last patrols were in and all preparations completed. Revielle and the order to saddle-up came in rapid succession on the following morning. With good-natured jibes at Lieutenant Marlin's company, which was to remain to guard the camp[37] and to patrol along the Clear Fork, the eager command tossed blankets and bedrolls into the wagons, gobbled a hasty breakfast, and formed into the marching column. Then, with 102 Rangers, his pack train and his vehicles at his back, "Old Rip" Ford rode north looking for trouble.[38]

For two days the company rode slowly, awaiting the arrival of the Indian auxiliaries. The Rangers camped on the night of June 24 at old Fort Belknap, on the main Brazos about twenty miles above its confluence with the Clear Fork. Another short march on the following day brought them to the Cottonwood Springs, approximately six miles below the present town of Olney. On April 26 Shapley Ross and 113 of his colorful wards joined the Rangers, and late in the afternoon, after the last stragglers had come up, Ford led the command onward.

Representatives of at least a half-dozen Indian nations accompanied the Texans. Casa Maria and Jim Pock Mark led the Caddo-Anadarko group; tough old Placido and his lieutenant, O'Quinn, marched with their cannibal Tonkawas; a mixed command of Shawnees and Delawares followed Jim Linney; Ah-qua-quash (Shot Arm) brought his Wacos, and the Tahuanacos were there under Nid-o-wats. To augment these warriors there came Caddo John, Jem Logan, Chul-e-quah, and the Indian linguist, Keechi, who had lived and hunted with the Comanches, and who may have been the spy sent to the Nokonis, if that story be true. To young Bob Cotter from his seat atop his mount, "Old Wooly," the massed command made "a very imposing scene—Indian and white man together hunting one common enemy, the wily Comanche, the terror of mothers and children on this frontier.[39]

Not all Placido's people had horses, but Ford attested that the Tonkawa footmen marched well, and the column was not delayed thereby. In the late afternoon of April 27 the force marched through the lush pastures and thick timber along the Little Wichita and pitched camp on its bank. Evidently it was a favorite camping spot; Sergeant Cotter counted 140 campfires twinkling in the dusk along the stream, and presumed that they belonged to a large party of Indians.[40]

At the Little Wichita encampment the Tonkawas decided upon a ceremonial rattlesnake feast, and soon accumulated a squirming pile of reptiles. Ford's irresponsible orderly, "Don Monkey", precipitated a crisis by innocently contributing a blacksnake to the menu. There was prompt Tonk reaction, and had not the captain quickly intervened "it appeared probable from the demonstrations of the incensed snake-eaters that . . . the Don would have come to grief."[41]

The march of April 29 took the command across the Big Wichita, at a point where Cotter thought the land good, although insufficiently timbered.[42] Captain Ford, however, saw the area otherwise. To him the locality of the crossing was "a dreary one. The sand, the apparent sterility of the soil, the abhorrent taste of the salty water, combined to produce a gloomy feeling. Some of us spoke of the Dead Sea, and Sodom and Gomorrah."[43]

On the afternoon of April 29, Ford reached the Red River and determined to camp on the north bank. After the main body of horsemen had trotted across, Lieutenant Tankersley, officer of the day and thus in charge of the rear-guard and baggage train, unloaded the wagons, distributed their burdens among his men, and urged the vehicles and baggage mules at a gallop through the quicksands of the treacherous stream, an accomplishment roundly cheered by the intent company.

The expeditionary force was now in the buffalo pastures, and consumed several days in traversing the thirty-odd westward miles to Otter Creek, at the base of the Wichita Mountains. The command moved slowly to permit hunting, and now buffalo meat replaced bacon in the rations. The many ravines were an impediment. Time after time it was necessary to unhitch the mules, unload the wagons, and lower the vehicles with ropes down the precipitous bluffs. Even so, Ford believed that he was moving with satisfactory speed, considering the circumstances.

The command spent two days at Otter Creek in hunting buffalo and feasting on the succulent meat which later called forth a panegyric from "Old Rip."[44] Between hunts the Rangers climbed to the crests of the mountains, returning laden with currants, strawberries, grapes, and other wild fruits which Sergeant Cotter found in profusion.[45] Then, the commissary replenished, Captain Ford led the mixed command north by west up the North Fork of Red River. Now the party moved with great caution, maintaining scouting squads out from fifteen to twenty miles in all directions from the column. For several days the battalion followed the river, passing en route a marker indicating Captain R. B. Marcy's route of 1852.[46] On May 7, having found no Indian sign, Ford swung the column to the right, away from the North Fork and its "gyp" waters, crossing on the next day to the upper course of the Washita, where scouts discovered the recent trail of a large warrior band, estimated on the basis of the remnants of their camp fires to number about four hundred.

Confident that he had struck a Comanche trail, Ford followed it cautiously for two days. On the evening of the second day, the reservation Indians brought in a Comanche arrowhead which they had extracted from a previously wounded buffalo they had killed. On the next morning, that of May 11, a hurrying scout brought news that a Comanche had been sighted killing buffalo, and that the direction in which his meat-laden horse had been led indicated the way to the Comanche camp.

Hastily, "Rip" Ford prepared to attack before a wandering enemy hunter should stumble across the battalion. Blankets and rations were lashed to the saddles; William Ford, a couple of Rangers, and the mule drivers (and probably "Don Monkey") were detailed to guard the pack train and vehicles, and at about two o'clock in the afternoon the Senior Captain led his combat force carefully in the direction shown by the scout.

As the afternoon waned, Ford brought the command to a halt on the Fort Smith-Santa Fe "bull-wagon" road, a short distance southeast of the gap through which the track emerged from the Antelope Hills.[47] In a valley to the north, distant Comanches were on the move. Immediately, at Ford's order, the Rangers and their allies disappeared into the ravines flanking the road. Dismounting, Ford and Ross moved to where the road topped the Washita-Canadian divide, and from that high point gazed speculatively at the enemy.[48]

The curious Rangers, eyeing their commanding officer, beheld a lithe, erect man of average stature, his broad hat pushed back to prevent its interference with his spy glass. From beneath his hatbrim, brunette hair curled above a high, clear forehead. Intent blue eyes peered over high, weathered cheek bones, past the bridge of an aquiline nose.[49] As he shifted his position to follow the movements of the hostiles, unconsciously he may have favored his right arm, weak from an old Comanche wound.[50] Past middle age by frontier standards, at forty-three he was already an old man to the youngsters who made up most of the Ranger ranks.

Perhaps a few youthful troopers may have realized vaguely that the officer they watched already was becoming a legendary figure. Each night, at home or in the field, he studied his Bible, in accordance with a youthful promise to his mother, and in his quietly humorous way he taught Sunday School classes for the young men of Austin;[51] yet he belonged to no church. Except to shout an order through the din of attack, he seldom raised his voice, although when he spoke it was bluntly, and very much to the point—on occasion, profanely so.[52] Among those who lived by the gun, he was a peer who "reckoned to be able to hit a man every time with a six-shooter at one hundred and twenty-five yards."[53] Of each officer in his command he had full knowledge as to capabilities and competency; moreover, almost every trooper in the ranks bore a nickname aptly bestowed by "Old Rip," and his own nickname had been applied as a retaliatory gesture by the Rangers of earlier commands.[54] He never slept, so his guards maintained.[55] The quiet confidence, born of jobs well done, that radiated from his bearing was reflected by the high morale in the ranks.

Meanwhile, oblivious of the intent eyes of his command, John Ford gazed northward into the heart of Comancheria, a battle plan taking shape behind the cool, blue stare.

The Comanches drifted out of sight. The Rangers and the painted auxiliaries mounted and reformed. The column moved slowly and quietly northward through lengthening shadows, concealed by the broken land. When late evening twilight had covered the Canadian and its tributary valleys, the invaders drew rein and made a dry camp. Guards rimmed the bivouac area, and Ford sent forward a squad of scouts to find Keechi, who had gone ahead to locate the Comanche camp.

The empty-handed return of the scouts caused Ford to alter his plan of attack. He had planned to move the command up near the Comanche village during the night. Just before dawn he would have the Indian allies stampede the Comanche horse herd and, in the confusion, the Ranger attack would smash into the encampment. Now, however the opportune time had passed. The column must move in daylight, and Ford could only hope to find and strike the Nokonis before they should discover him. The latter possibility probably did not alarm "Rip" Ford as he prowled his outpost perimeter; it was an occupational hazard of frontier command.

As daylight of May 12 began to lift over the Canadian, the officer of the day passed from one blanket-shrouded figure to another, waking the sleepers. The guard returned. Dusky faces blossomed with fresh war paint. Bronzed hands fixed white cloth badges to bizarre head-dresses, that friends might be distinguished from hostiles in the dusty tumult of battle. Red man and white methodically checked caps and loads. Ford called an order; Rangers swung into their saddles, and the swarthy auxiliaries scrambled onto their ponies. At a fast gallop the column left the hills for the quiet valley below.[56]

After a run of about six miles, action came swiftly at seven o'clock. Across the Ranger route appeared five Comanche lodges, around which Indian figures were in motion. The Texas yell and a variety of tribal warwhoops rent the still morning as the command descended upon the small camp. Two Comanche braves leaped for their ponies and galloped hard for the rising ground three miles north across the valley. The command thundered through the camp in pursuit, except for the Tonks who stayed to appropriate prisoners and horses and to demolish the camp.

As the galloping pursuers topped the rise, Ford saw spread before him the snowy lodges of a village of Tenawa Comanches, about three miles distant, on the north bank of the Canadian. In their haste to warn the camp, the two fleeing Comanches unintentionally betrayed a safe ford through the swampy banks and across the sandy channel of the Canadian. Ross and his Indian warriors, followed by the Rangers, splashed across at a run to firm ground on the north bank. There the Rangers pulled up, grinning at the drenched orderly sergeant who belatedly joined them; "Old Woolly" had stumbled on an unseen rock, catapulting Cotter head foremost into the shallow stream.[57]

Over the drum of hoofbeats and the ululation of battle cries, Ford shouted to Ross to take the reservation tribesmen forward and open the fight. Their advance would give the captain time to form the Ranger ranks, and would temporarily deceive the Comanches into thinking that they had only Indians, armed no better than themselves, to meet. Ross beckoned to his chiefs, and the painted partisans swung into position on the right front. "Rip" Ford surveyed his eager Rangers. "Steady, boys until I give the word," he called.[58]

Into the two hundred yards of open ground between Ross' Indians and the Comanche lodges, a single, armored figure rode to bar the way. Po-bish-e-quash-o (Iron Jacket) he was, head chief of the band, possessor of a powerful medicine which enable him to blow aside the arrows of his foes. An ancient coat of scaled mail, possibly looted by some long-dead ancestor from an unfortunate conquistador, covered him from throat to thigh. Riding assuredly before his hereditary enemies, he described small circles, then advanced briefly, swelling his cheeks and expelling his breath vigorously toward the reservation auxiliaries. He moved deliberately, confident of his invulnerability.

Abruptly his medicine failed. Most of his enemies carried firearms rather than bows and arrows. A ragged volley burst upon him, and his horse crashed to the ground. As he sprang clear and straightened to face his attackers, a second, crisper blast crumpled him forward, and a lagging shot finished him.[59] A wail of surprised anguish arose from the dead medicine man's followers, and "Rip" Ford seized the moment to hurl his Rangers against the camp of the bewildered foe.

Despairing of making a stand, the Tenawas broke and fled. Ford and Pitts, leading the right wing of the Ranger formation, stormed through the encampment in pursuit, while Nelson, supported by Tankersley and Preston, drove with the left wing to intercept the warriors running for the hills.

As the Comanches scattered, the Rangers dispersed to run them down; the battle became a series of mounted duels spread over eighteen square miles of broken ground, "and it appeared like every man picked his Indian and took after him, man to man."[60] "The din of battle . . . rolled back from the river—the groans of the dying, the cries of frightened women and children mingled with the reports of fire-arms, and the shouts of men as they rose from hill top, from thicket, and from ravine,"[61] and to Sergeant Cotter it seemed that "Capt. Ford . . . was everywhere, directing and controlling the movements of his men."[62]

As the mounts grew jaded and the Comanche warriors fell back out of range, the firing dwindled away and the Rangers and their allies turned back toward the village. When Ford and the irresponsible Pitts rejoined the main body, they found that Nelson and Ross had regrouped the Indians and the returning troopers.

Ford reined in beside Ross. "What time in the morning is it?" he asked.

Ross stared at the Senior Captain. "Morning, hell!" he blurted. "It's one o'clock."[63]

It was Ford's turn to stare. He had been totally unconscious of time during the six crowded hours of combat.

The sound of firing and the stream of fugitives had brought Nokoni Comanches hurrying from a large encampment several miles upstream. The appearance on the hills of these reinforcements swarming above the stricken village had caused Nelson, at Ross' suggestion, to call the command together. For a brief time the Rangers stood quietly, resting their winded horses, while their savage allies and the Comanches exchanged bitter badinage and mocking gestures across the valley. Then the reservation warriors rode out into the flat to challenge the newcomers, who swept from the hills to join battle. The Rangers witnessed a unique sight.

> A scene was now enacted beggaring description. It reminded one of
> the rude and chivalrous days of Knight-errantry. Shields and lances,
> and bows and head dresses—prancing steed and many minutias
> [sic] were not wanting to compile the resemblance. And when the
> combatants rushed at each other with defiant shouts, nothing save
> the piercing report of the rifle varied the affair from a battle field
> of the middle ages. A detachment of Rangers was advanced to
> reinforce the friendly Indians, and the Comanches quited the field,
> and the imposing pageant vanished from view like a mimic battle
> upon the stage.[64]

The second encounter did not develop according to plan. Ross' Indians had hoped to lure the Comanches into an ambush, but when Lieutenant Nelson led the Ranger left wing in a sweep around the base of a small hill to fall upon the unsuspecting hostiles, Placido's yelling Tonkawas sprung the trap prematurely and the Comanches rode for the hills. The Rangers followed as rapidly as they could upon their weary horses, but were unable to come to grips with the enemy. Furthermore, most of the reservation Indians had removed the white badges from their head-dresses, claiming that the insignia made them easy targets for the Comanches.[65] Since it was impossible to distinguish friendly from enemy warriors at long range, the Texans headed back after a run of a couple of miles. It was with great difficulty that Captain Ford persuaded the raging Pitts and the equally agitated old Placido to retire. "They wanted more blood."[66]

As the Rangers again plodded through the debris of Iron Jacket's shattered village, commenting on the piles of gorgeously beaded buffalo robes, the bales of dried meat, and the heaped containers of corn-meal, salt, and coffee obtained from the *Comancheros*,[67] Ford was astonished to notice that among the bodies of Comanche braves there were some which lacked hands and feet. The reason became clear when he again rejoined Ross. The missing extremities dangled from Tonkawa saddle bows; those wolfish people were planning a victory feast.

Between imprecations hurled upon them by a captive crone, the invaders learned that Buffalo Hump and a large band of his people were hunting about a dozen miles down the Canadian. Possibly in no hurry to renew an old acquaintanceship, and certainly apprehensive lest his camp might be exposed to attack, Captain Ford decided to retire to the supply train. Slowed by the winded horses and impeded by prisoners and the captured pony herd, the force did not reach the train until dusk.

That night as the Tonk allies squatted above their grisly banquet, "Old Rip" silently debated his further operations. A clash of angry voices suddenly sent him hurrying to the Tonkawa fires. There he found Ranger Billy Holzinger, pistol drawn, angrily tugging against the restraining hands of comrades and loudly berating O'Quinn, the astonished Tonkawa war chief. Sharp questioning exposed the difficulty. O'Quinn, as an authority on human flesh, had been asked by a Ranger what nationality the Tonk considered best eating. The gourmet had promptly recalled the flavor of "a big fat Dutchman he and his men killed on the Guadalupe river in 1849." Holzinger immediately hotly accused O'Quinn of making fun of his country-men. Some time later it dawned on the irate Holzinger that the raid to which O'Quinn referred was one which nearly resulted in the loss of his own scalp.[68]

With order restored by his firm commands, Captain Ford again returned to an analysis of his situation. He decided to strike out for Camp Runnels the next morning, since his mounts were too fatigued for further operations and his meat rations had been ex-hausted for several days.[69] There were further considerations:

Capt. Ross expressed the opinion that the friendly Indians were satisfied with what they had done, were quite elated at the number of horses captured, and thought, perhaps, it would be wise to let well enough alone. No one cognizant of the number of warriors the seven bands of the Comanches could bring into the field, and of the accessions they would receive from other tribes, was of the opinion the small force now bearding them on their hunting grounds would maintain themselves very long. They were already badly stirred up; there was no hope of getting another fight out of them; they were intensely on the alert. These were among the reasons, indeed the main reason, for the return to Camp Runnels.[70]

On the morning of May 13 the command broke camp and set out for the Clear Fork base. After what may have been the last camp on the homeward trail, at Cottonwood Springs, the Rangers sepa-rated from their Indian comrades. The tribesmen had sent word ahead to the Brazos agency of their coming, and the colorful wel-come, and praise for the trophies, horses, and captives, by those who had remained behind, reminded Ford of the "reception of Saul and David from the field of Sohoceh."[71]

From Cottonwood Springs the Ranger column rode due south, and on the evening of May 20, the Texans unsaddled their leg-weary mounts once more in the Camp Runnels compound, just less than a month after their departure.

Ford reported to Governor Runnels two days later, in a communication expressing his approval of the command. He praised the wise counsel and able co-operation of Shapley Prince Ross; he recommended to Runnels' attention the prompt, cheerful, and able conduct of Nelson, Tankersley, and Preston; finally he commended the men for "obedience, patience and perseverance," mentioning them as behaving under fire "in a gallant and soldier like manner," and expressing his belief "that they have fully vindicated their right to be recognized as Texas Rangers of the old stamp." Also he remembered his Indian allies: "They deserve well of Texas and are entitled to the gratitude of the frontier people."[72]

In his operations Ford had marched about five hundred miles over unfamiliar country, had fought almost continuously for seven hours, and had led the command back safely from the heart of a hostile land. The Rangers had lost one man, Robert Nickles of Nelson's company, and that loss might have been prevented had not Nickles become demoralized and attempted to outrun the Comanches.[73] A Waco Indian had been killed during the second fight. Ford officially reported two men killed and three wounded in the fighting on May 12, Ranger George W. Paschal, Jr., being the only white man injured. In contrast, Ford had counted more than seventy dead Comanches, although he felt sure the number must be higher, and had witnessed the wounding of a large number, but had no way of estimating how many. The command had seized eighteen women and children, among them a youngster said to be the son of Iron Jacket.[74] More than three hundred Comanche horses had been taken and most of them turned over to the reservation Indians. The expedition had possibly forestalled a major raid. A captured Mexican lad stated that the Comanches were drying and packing meat for use on a campaign against the settlers and reservation tribes. Both Ford and Cotter had seen the bales of dry meat in Iron Jacket's camp.[75]

On May 23 Captain Ford followed up his official report with a private letter to Runnels, in which he expressed the hope that "the fight will satisfy the people, vindicate you from the assaults of your enemies, and be of permanent advantage to the frontier." He emphasized that that portion of the frontier was "dreadfully exposed", referring to the depredations—in this instance, horse-stealing—which had occurred while his command was absent (and which, it appears, Marlin's command had been unable to prevent), and then wrote "I have reason to believe the Agency Comanches are the [guilty] parties, and if I fix it upon them I shall give them hell and trust to the people to sustain me." He added that the frontier people were "forting", and that some families had been "forted up" since the command had departed in April.[76]

However, as Ford's official report reveals, the true value of the expedition was more significant than a battle victory, regardless of how the latter might be applauded.

> This expedition had decided several questions—Indians can be pursued and caught in the Buffalo region—the country beyond Red River can be penetrated and held by white men, and the Comanches can be followed, overtaken, and beaten, provided the pursuers will be laborious, vigilant, and are willing to undergo privations.[77]

Within a fortnight, Ford's success was known to the national administration.[78] Apparently it helped to create the shift in military policy which both frontiersmen and frontier military commanders like Twiggs had so long and unsuccessfully urged.[79] The War Department changed from the defensive concept to one of attack. In the brief time yet to precede the Civil War, and in the long, red span of years between Appomattox and Wounded Knee, commanders were to take the trail into the heartland of the nomadic foe. Van

Dorn, Custer, Miles, Mackenzie, Crook—behind campaigners such as these the long blue files were to ride and strike and ride again, perhaps unconsciously seeking all the while to emulate an example set in the spring of 1858 by a hundred youthful Texans led by "Old Rip" Ford.

NOTES

1. John Salmon Ford, "Memoirs," IV, 679. MS, Eugene C. Barker Texas History Center of University of Texas Library, Austin (pagination follows that of typescript, Archives Division, Texas State Library, Austin). Hereinafter cited as Ford, "Memoirs." Rupert Norval Richardson, *The Comanche Barrier to South Plains Settlement: A Century and a Half of Savage Resistance to the Advancing White Frontier* (Glendale, Calif., 1933), 231.

2. Ernest Wallace and E. Adamson Hoebel, *The Comanches: Lords of the South Plains* (Norman, 1952), 301–302; Richardson, *Comanche Barrier,* 231–232.

3. Copy, Twiggs to Thomas, June 16, 1857, Governors' Letters File, Archives Division, Texas State Library, Austin. Hereinafter cited as Gov. Ltrs., T.S.L. This primarily is a file of letters received, but contains many communications received as enclosures.

4. Ford, "Memoirs," IV, 677. Muster rolls in the National Archives (Record Group 94) show Ford's Federal service as a Ranger as extending from August 23, 1849, to September 23, 1851.

5. Various letters to Runnels from Texans in Washington. Gov. Ltrs., T.S.L.

6. Anna Irene Sandbo, "Beginnings of the Secession Movement in Texas," *The Southwestern Historical Quarterly,* XVIII, 57.

7. The major causes of Houston's defeat possibly were his opposition to the Kansas-Nebraska bill and his association with the Know-Nothing movement.

8. Gov. Ltrs., T. S. L. Examples are those from Brown County, October, 1857; San Saba, Stephenville, and Meridian, November, 1857; and Stephenville, again, January, 1858.

9. Executive Record Book, Governor H. R. Runnels, 1857–1859, No. 277, Archives Division, Texas State Library, Austin. Hereinafter cited as Exec. Rec. Bk. These contain official copies of correspondence emitting from the executive office.

10. *State Gazette* (Austin), January 30, 1858, quoted in Ford, "Memoirs," IV, 680.

11. H. P. N. Gammel (comp.), *The Laws of Texas: 1822–1897* (10 vols.; Austin, 1898), IV, 949–950.

12. Gammel, *Laws of Texas,* IV, 949–950.

13. Runnels to Ford, January 28, 1858, Gov. Ltrs., T.S.L. The governor probably was most responsive to the views of the *State Gazette.* Its editor was one of the recognized leaders of the Democratic party in the state, and is credited with having obtained Runnels' election. W. S. Oldham, "Colonel John Marshall," *The Southwestern Historical Quarterly,* XX, 133 ff.

14. The transfer finally was effected by War Department General Order No. 8, dated April 15, 1858, copy in Gov. Ltrs., T. S. L.

15. Frank Brown, "Annals of Travis County and the City of Austin (From the Earliest Times to the Close of 1875)," Ch. XI, 44. Unpublished MS, University of Texas Library Archives, Austin (pagination follows that of typescript, Archives Division, Texas State Library, Austin). Hereinafter cited as Brown, "Annals."

16. Brown, "Annals," Ch. VIII, 14; Ford, "Memoirs," IV, 660.

17. *State Gazette* (Austin), January 30, 1858, quoted in Ford, "Memoirs," IV, 680.

18. Ford, "Memoirs," IV, 680–681.

19. At the time, Major Robert S. Neighbors held the position of Supervising Agent, Texas Indians, charged with the administration of the two Reserves. Resident agents were Captain Shapley Prince Ross, at the Brazos reservation, and a Colonel Leepers, at the Camp Cooper, or Clear Fork, Reserve. Leepers appears to have been a purely political appointee and, in Ford's opinion, a singularly inexperienced and incompetent official. Ford to Runnels (private), May 7, 1858, Gov. Ltrs., T.S.L.

20. Runnels to Ford, January 28, 1858, Gov. Ltrs., T.S.L.

21. Ford, "Memoirs," IV, 681, 744–45, 748–49.

22. Twiggs to Runnels, February 13, 1858, in reply to Runnels' request of February 10, Gov. Ltrs., T.S.L.

23. *Dallas Herald* item, republished in *State Gazette* (Austin), May 22, 1858, p. 2, c. 3.

24. Ford, "Memoirs," IV, 683; Robert Cotter to John Marshall, May 20, 1858, published in *State Gazette* (Austin), May 29, 1858; Charles L. Martin, "The Last of the Ranger Chieftains," *The Texas Magazine, IV* (January, 1898), 39–40. Hereinafter cited as Martin, "Last of the Ranger Chieftains."

25. Ford, "Memoirs," IV, 683. These were probably some of T. C. Frost's men, retained in service. Ford to Runnels, February 27, 1858, Gov. Ltrs., T.S.L.

26. Ford, "Memoirs," IV, 686.

27. Allison Nelson to Ford, April 20, 1858, Gov. Ltrs., T. S. L.

28. Ford, "Memoirs," IV, 686.

29. Ford to Runnels, April 26, 1858, Gov. Ltrs., T.S.L. McCulloch may have had other reasons. He may have belonged to a different faction of the Democratic party from Ford, or he may have felt that he, not Ford, should have been given the appointment. At any rate, in his letter to the governor from Camp Runnels on May 23, 1858, Ford says, in speaking of his wish to command the Ranger Regiment, "If not too late I shall run for Colonel. I suppose I should be the Runnels candidate as McCulloch has pulled against you, or at least it would be put up so, as they couple me with you in abuse. You know the arrangement between Captain McC. and myself and how signally he failed to comply. I am thankful, that I had a little success without his assistance."

30. *State Gazette* (Austin), May 22, 1858, p. 2, c. 6.

31. Ford, "Memoirs," IV, 686–687.

32. Ford to Runnels, April 7, 1858, Gov. Ltrs., T.S.L.

33. Quoted from Ford to T. Scott Anderson, Texas Secretary of State, in Ford, "Memoirs," IV, 688.

34. *Dallas Herald* item, republished in *State Gazette* (Austin), May 22, 1858, p. 2, c. 3.

35. A ration was the amount of provisions necessary to sustain one Ranger for one day.

36. Ford, ''Memoirs," IV, 689.

37. This detachment, consisting of about twenty-five men, was mustered into service by Ford at almost the last moment before the Rangers departed for Comanche country.

38. Ford to Runnels, May 22, 1858, Gov. Ltrs., T.S.L. The communication of this date was Ford's official report of the expedition. It was published in the *State Gazette* (Austin), May 29, 1858, p. 2, cc. 4–5.

39. Cotter to Marshall, May 20, 1858, also printed in *State Gazette,* May 29, 1858.

40. Cotter to Marshall, May 20, 1858, *Ibid.*

41. Ford, "Memoirs," IV, 689–690.

42. Cotter to Marshall, May 20, 1858, *State Gazette,* May 29, 1858.

43. Ford, "Memoirs," IV, 690.

44. Ford, "Memoirs," IV, 692.

45. Cotter to Marshall, May 20, 1858.

46. Ford to Runnels, May 22, 1858, Gov. Ltrs., T.S.L. Captains R. B. Marcy and G. B. McClellan had explored the Red River country for military purposes in 1852. The marker to which Ford referred may have been the cotton-

wood tree blazed by McClellan to indicate the location of the 100th meridian. See Randolph B. Marcy, *Exploration of the Red River of Louisiana, in the
Year 1852; House Executive Document 33rd Congress, 1st Session* (Washington: A.O.P. Nicholson, 1854), 19–20. Ford probably was familiar with Marcy's
report and map of the expedition, the latter erroneously placing the 100th
meridian more than a degree too far eastward. The map, however, shows the
Antelope Hills in correct relationship to the 100th meridian but Ford, if he
was aware of the discrepancy, made no mention of it. Ford was entering into
Indian Territory to fight, outside of the legal limit of Ranger authority. Possibly he did not know it; probably he did not care.

47. Ford to Runnels, May 22, 1858, Gov. Ltrs., T.S.L.

48. Ford to Runnels, May 22, 1858, Gov. Ltrs., T.S.L.

49. Martin, "Last of the Ranger Chieftains," 38.

50. In 1850, Ford had been scratched across the back of the right hand by
an arrow in a skirmish near the Rio Grande. A half-dozen years later the arm
had become almost totally paralyzed, the result, Ford suspected, of poison on
the arrowhead. He eventually recovered use of the arm but every year thereafter suffered from a skin eruption on the hand. Ford, "Memoirs," III, 545.

51. Brown, "Annals," Ch. XIII, 38. Brown had been in one of Ford's classes,
and had been a paper carrier for the *National Register* (Austin) and the *Texas
Democrat* (Austin) from 1847 to 1849, when Ford was editor of the newspapers.

52. Martin, "Last of the Ranger Chieftains," 40; Ford, "Memoirs," II, 395.

53. Frederic Remington, "How the Law Got into the Chaparral," *Harper's
New Monthly Magazine*, XCVI (December, 1896–May, 1897), p. 61. Remington quotes Ford directly from an interview which took place in San Antonio
a few years before Ford's death.

54. Martin, "Last of the Ranger Chieftains," 40. Martin was a lieutenant in
Ford's regiment early in the Civil War. There are several accounts, some amaz-
ingly pat, as to the source of Ford's nickname. In view of Ford's apparent mental attitude in the years immediately following the death of his young wife,
Louisa, in 1846, and his consequent carelessness about his personal safety, it
seems hardly surprising he should have earned the sobriquet, still not uncommon in rural areas. An indication of his attitude is given in Ford, "Memoirs,"
II, 395–396.

55. Martin, "Last of the Ranger Chieftains," 40.

56. Cotter to Marshall, May 20, 1858, *State Gazette, May* 28, 1858.

57. Ford, "Memoirs," IV, 696.

58. Cotter to Marshall, May 20, 1858, *State Gazette*, May 28, 1858.

59. Ford to Runnels, May 22, 1858, Gov. Ltrs., T.S.L.; Ford, "Memoirs," IV, 696; Remington, "How the Law Got into the Chaparral," 64. After the battle the Rangers removed Iron Jacket's coat of armor and divided it for souvenirs, according to Sergeant Cotter, who sent a scrap of it in a letter to the governor. Cotter to Runnels (n.d.), Gov. Ltrs., T.S.L.

60. Cotter to Marshall, May 20, 1858, *State Gazette,* May 28, 1858.

61. Ford to Runnels, May 22, 1858, Gov. Ltrs., T.S.L.

62. Cotter to Marshall, May 20, 1858, *State Gazette,* May 28, 1858.

63. Remington, "How the Law Got into the Chaparral," 60. Remington quotes Ford directly.

64. Ford to Runnels, May 22, 1858, Gov. Ltrs., T.S.L.

65. J. W. Wilbarger, *Indian Depredations in Texas* (Austin, 1935), 325.

66. Ford, "Memoirs," IV, 698.

67. *Comancheros* were traders, often from Santa Fe, who dealt with the Comanches for horses. Texans believed that such bargaining encouraged the horse-stealing raids into Texas, and were bitter against the traders. A party of Mexican *Comancheros* had left Iron Jacket's camp only two days before the Ranger attack. Ford to Runnels, June 2, 1858, Gov. Ltrs., T.S.L.

68. Ford, "Memoirs," IV, 528–529.

69. Ford to Runnels, May 22, 1858, Gov. Ltrs., T.S.L.

70. Ford, "Memoirs," IV, 699.

71. Ford, "Memoirs," IV, 702. Judging by the description, one suspects that Ford may have accompanied Ross and the Indians to the Brazos reservation.

72. Ford to Runnels, May 22, 1858, Gov. Ltrs., T.S.L.

73. Ford, "Memoirs," IV, 697.

74. Ford to Runnels, May 22, 1858, Gov. Ltrs., T.S.L.; Cotter to Marshall, May 20, 1858, *State Gazette,* May 28, 1858. Ford, "Memoirs," IV, 702. Ford does not say why he officially reported eighteen prisoners when he actually took sixty. Three, including the Mexican boy, escaped the night after the fight.

75. Ford to Runnels, May 22, 1858, Gov. Ltrs., T.S.L. Cotter to Marshall, May 20, 1858, *State Gazette,* May 28, 1858.

76. Ford to Runnels (private), May 23, 1858, Gov. Ltrs., T.S.L.

77. Ford to Runnels, May 22, 1858, Gov. Ltrs., T.S.L.

78. Runnels to the Texas Delegation in Congress, May 28, 1858, Gov. Ltrs., T.S.L.

79. Copy, Twiggs to Thomas, June 16, 1857, Gov. Ltrs., T.S.L.

PHOTO GALLERY

Rangers and Popular Images

But one thing seems clear to everyone who returns from field work: other people are other. They do not think the way we do. And if we want to understand their way of thinking, we should set out with the idea of capturing otherness.

—Robert Darnton, *The Great Cat Massacre and Other Episodes in French Cultural History.*

Some Lone Star scholars insist that Texas, with its heritage of slavery, segregation, and historic dependence upon cotton, is southern. Another group of historians argue that Texas is western, as evidenced by its cowboys, cattle drives, mountains, and desert. Still others say that the Lone Star State is unique, winning its independence from Mexico during the Texas Revolution and existing as an independent republic for ten years prior to joining the Union.

—Glen Sample Ely, *Where the West Begins: Debating Texas Identity.*

He must have courage equal to any, judgment better than most, and physical strength to outlast his men on the longest march or hardest ride.

—Walter Prescott Webb, *The Story of the Texas Rangers.*

In classic Ranger tradition, [Captain Barry] Caver made his own rules based upon the immediate situation, educated guesses, and simple instinct.

—Charles M. Robinson III, *The Men Who Wear the Star: The Story of the Texas Rangers.*

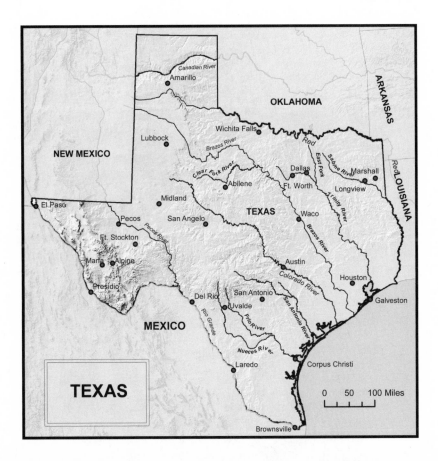

Lone Star Lawmen: The Second Century of the Texas Rangers by Robert Utley (2007). Map from p. xvi. By permission of Oxford University Press, Inc.

A Texas Ranger as a man-at-arms in the popular mind. The legendary fighter-Ranger sits on horseback in a majestic Wild West pose in the heyday of citizen soldiers in the antebellum era. After all is said and done, this sketch has become a paradigm of visual representation in Texan and western folklore. It resembles too much the way people envisioned mountain men in the frontier era of the American West. (*Harper's Weekly*, Vol. 5, 1861, p. 430.)

A lawman-Ranger in the popular mind. In the 1900s in novels by Zane Grey and Louis L'Amour, in pulp magazines like the *Texas Rangers*, and in comic books, such as *Texas Rangers in Action*, tales about the wild and woolly West captured the public's imagination. In action-oriented stories outnumbered lawman-Rangers made their stand against badmen of all creeds and colors. In the above illustration the artist gave his rendition of Texas Ranger Captain Bill McDonald as a riot buster. Yet "Captain Bill," whether in reality or fictionalized formats, was no model for the Lone Ranger. (Albert Bigelow Paine, *Captain Bill McDonald, Texas Ranger: A Story of Frontier Reform*, 1909, p. 211.)

Colonel Jack Hayes, from a Daguerreotype by Noeselle, New Orleans.—p. 108.

John Coffee "Jack" Hays (1817–1883): He had a boyish look and mild manners, which surprised those looking for a rugged Ranger leader. Hays and his men used revolvers, carried out horse charges, gave the Texas Yell, and built a Ranger tradition that captured the public's imagination. Jack Hays became the prototype for future Ranger officers. (Courtesy Texas State Library and Archives Commission.)

Captain McCulloch, from a Daguerreotype by J. McGuire, New Orleans.

Benjamin "Ben" McCulloch (1811–1862): He was more flamboyant and more taken with a military career than Jack Hays. McCulloch gained a reputation as an effective Indian fighter and as an able scout and spy for the army of General Zachary Taylor in the U.S.-Mexican War. He became a Confederate general and was killed in the action at the Battle of Pea Ridge in Arkansas. (Courtesy Texas State Library and Archives Commission.)

Captain Walker, from a Daguerreotype by J. McGuire,
New Orleans.—p. 188.

Samuel H. "Sam" Walker (1817–1847): With his piercing eyes and reddish
hair, he became one of the early icons of the Texas Rangers. Although he ably
served in ranging companies at different times and places, this Ranger image
was based mainly upon his celebrated role in the development of the Colt revolver. As a member of the regular US army, Walker lost his life in the struggle
with guerrillas in the U.S.-Mexican War. (Courtesy Texas State Library and
Archives Commission.)

William Alexander Anderson "Bigfoot" Wallace (1817–1899): Standing six feet two inches and weighing about 240 pounds, Wallace approached the physical appearance of the legendary citizen-soldier Ranger in the public's mind. Yet his impact on the formative years of the Rangers never equaled that of the more prominent Texans in his day. But the picturesque Wallace surpassed his fellow Rangers as a storyteller and folk hero. (Courtesy Texas State Library and Archives Commission.)

John B. Jones (1834–1881): In the Lone Star State he had a distinguished military career, as Confederate army officer, head of the Frontier Battalion of Rangers, and adjutant general of the state of Texas. Most important, Jones and Adjutant General William Steele in the 1870s developed policies and procedures that changed the scope and operations of the Texas Rangers—from an Indian-fighting force to horseback lawmen in search of outlaws and desperadoes. (Courtesy Texas State Library and Archives Commission.)

The best-known photograph of the Frontier Battalion of Texas Rangers, as they gathered in El Paso to stop a prizefight in early 1896. The first row shows the pyramid Ranger organization in the late 1800s (left to right): Adjutant General William H. Mabry (in a Napoleonic stance) and the "Four Great Captains," John Hughes (Co. D), James Brooks (Co. F), Bill McDonald (Co. B), and John Rogers (Co. E). To some McDonald's stance illustrates his showmanship qualities. One person missing in the photo was the battalion quartermaster who showed the field captains the ins and outs of running a company. (Courtesy Texas State Library and Archives Commission.)

The death photo of Rangers in Company D in the late 1800s. Bass Outlaw (eight from left) killed a fellow Ranger and was, in turn, gunned down by a local peace officer in 1894. In addition, Rangers who died in the line of duty included the following: Charles Fusselman (third from left) pursued cattle thieves and took a fatal bullet in the head in West Texas in 1890; and Captain Frank Jones (sitting) and other Rangers, including John W. "Wood" Saunders (fifth from left), tracked Hispanic outlaws, inadvertently crossed the Mexican border in West Texas, and engaged in a shootout in 1893. Jones was hit in the thigh and chest and killed. At one point in official reports about the gun battle, the Ranger captain said as he went down, "I am shot all to pieces." Other noteworthy Rangers in the above photo include Ira Aten (extreme left) and John R. Hughes (sixth from left). Hughes would succeed Jones as captain of Company D and become the best gunman in the Frontier Battalion. (Courtesy Texas State Library and Archives Commission.)

★ 8 ★

RANGERS, "RIP" FORD, AND THE CORTINA WAR

Richard B. McCaslin

The greatest border challenge for newly elected Texas Governor Sam Houston came on the Rio Grande, when Juan N. Cortina, a rancher and accused cattle rustler who was a folk hero to some local Tejanos, shot the Brownsville marshal and fled into Mexico. Cortina returned to occupy Brownsville with a small force in September 1859, intending to murder those who had secured an indictment against him. He and his followers did kill several people before Jose Maria de Jesus Carvajal, the commander of the garrison in Matamoros, convinced his cousin Cortina to stop. Cortina retired to Rancho del Carmen, his mother's ranch upriver, where he gathered more men by declaring that he would fight for the rights of Mexican Texans. The federal units at Brownsville and other posts along the lower Rio Grande had been removed due to the relative peace that had fallen over the region, as well as a general decline in the town after the creation of a free trade zone in northern Mexico, so Brownsville militia had to battle with Cortina's men. Cortina could not take Brownsville, but he controlled much of the surrounding countryside, and his ability to cross the Rio Grande repeatedly showed he had little to fear from either Texas militia or Mexican troops.[1]

To cope with Cortina, Maj. Samuel P. Heintzelman was sent with a small federal force. Hardin R. Runnels, who did not relinquish the

170

governor's office to Houston until December 1859, in turn commissioned William G. Tobin, a merchant from San Antonio, to recruit a Ranger company and go to Heintzelman's assistance. When it became apparent that Cortina had only a few hundred men, plans to send even more Army personnel were cut, which forced Heintzelman to rely more heavily on the Rangers. Unfortunately for him, when he arrived at Brownsville on December 5, he discovered that Tobin had not done well. One day after Tobin's Rangers rode into Brownsville, some of them participated in lynching one of Cortina's lieutenants who had been captured by militia from town. Fighting escalated with violent retributions on both sides, and casualties mounted. Cortina repulsed an attack by militia and took two cannons from them, killed four of Tobin's Rangers in an ambush, and then repelled an attack by Tobin two days later.[2]

Federal authorities might not have taken Cortina seriously, but Texas leaders did. When a rumor surfaced that he had burned Corpus Christi, Texas Senator Forbes Britton of that port stopped former ranger and Texas leader John S. Ford on an Austin street and demanded that he do something. Ford thought he had convinced Britton that the rumor was untrue when Runnels, the lame duck governor, happened upon them. Convinced by Britton that the danger was real, Runnels ordered Ford to rescue Corpus Christi. Whether Britton believed the rumor, or was just concerned about an impending election, always puzzled Ford, but he knew many Texans had expected him to be appointed to command. With a six-month commission and eight men, Ford rode to Goliad, where in November he received instructions from Runnels to lead a company of Rangers to the Rio Grande, not Corpus Christi, and take command of all state troops there. Ford lobbied for more support by explaining to the governor that Cortina was a much more dangerous enemy than the Comanches. Ford believed that Cortina's support came from his convincing Mexicans that slave-owning Texans stood alone, abandoned by the federal government, and that Americans who did not own slaves would help against Texas.

Warming to his subject, Ford wrote that there was "no doubt that an insolent foe has unfurled his banner within our limits and invites us to the combat. Shall we accept the challenge of the nation whose sons committed the massacres of the Alamo and of Goliad, who fled before us at San Antonio, San Jacinto, and many other fields? Can we allow foreign hordes to invade us, to murder and hang our citizens, and to escape unharmed, without tarnishing the honor of a good name gained by deeds of daring, by fortitude in adversity and in the endurance of privation? It seems to me there can be but one course for Texas. Expel the invaders let it cost what it may in blood and treasure."[3]

Ford assembled fifty-three men at Banquete, a day's ride west of Corpus Christi. Volunteers from that community had joined Tobin but returned home after his defeats. Now some responded to a new challenge from Ford: "Have you any desire to wipe off the reproach that has been cast upon Texas by her allowing a foreign flag to wave upon her soil with impunity? Come if you wish to fight!" They rode south with Ford, arriving in Brownsville on December 14 as cannon boomed in the distance. Mifflin Kenedy, who had mustered his militia to confront the newcomers only to discover it was his friend Ford, reported that Heintzelman had taken his soldiers and Tobin's Rangers upriver that morning, December 14, to engage Cortina. Ford and his riders rushed to the battlefield, thirteen miles from town, but arrived too late to participate in the main fight. Cortina had ambushed Heintzelman and in turn had been forced to retreat. After a rest, Ford and his Rangers joined in pursuing Cortina and his men, most of whom escaped when rain dampened the powder of the pursuers that night and made further effort useless. Ford, after taking command of all of the Rangers, returned with Heintzelman to Brownsville the next day.[4]

Heintzelman was not impressed with the Texans' first fight under his command. In fact, he angrily wrote in his journal, "We would undoubtedly have done better without the Rangers." Initially he did not know quite what to do with Ford, referring to him as doctor, captain, and even colonel in his journal as their first meeting approached. Having met him on the battlefield, he accepted the title of major, but even that was problematic. Runnels in his first orders to Ford appointed him as a major, but just one week later he instructed Ford to have his men and those in Tobin's company "immediately" choose who would serve as major in charge of both commands. Instead, Ford simply assumed the rank of major upon arriving in Brownsville and then delayed the election, apparently worried that he might lose to Tobin. Heintzelman dryly noted that "Capt. Tobin & Major Ford do not get along well together." His solution was to send them on separate patrols, with a third column composed of the only federal troopers he had: a company of the Second United States Cavalry under the command of Capt. George M. Stoneman. They found nothing, and thus when Heintzelman marched upriver again on December 21, 1859, with about 150 federals and almost 200 Rangers, he still had little confidence in the latter. Meanwhile, Ford had purchased Sharps carbines for some of his men, enhancing their firepower in anticipation of another fight.[5]

Cortina had settled near Rio Grande City, and Ford found his camp. He had been assigned to guard Heintzelman's flanks as he marched, and on December 26 his Texans located their quarry. Ford was told to slip around Cortina's left flank with three Ranger companies and occupy a position on the road from Rio Grande City to Roma by daylight on December 27. The main attacking force would advance into Rio Grande City at dawn. Unfortunately, Ford discovered that the brush was too thick for his march, that Cortina's pickets were posted to prevent a flanking movement, and that Cortina's force was much larger than anticipated. Ford stopped near Ringgold Barracks to wait for Heintzelman; when he arrived, Ford asked to lead an attack upon Cortina's left flank. Heintzelman agreed and assigned the remaining Rangers to Ford. Before sunrise on December 27, Ford drove in Cortina's pickets, repulsed a reconnaissance party, and then swung around Rio Grande City to attack Cortina's command post. There he found Mexicans arrayed in a defensive line. He assigned Tobin to attack their left, at a cemetery, while Ford led an assault on their right, across the road from Roma to Rio Grande City near the river itself. He left the center to Heintzelman's federal troops, who had artillery.[6]

Ford ran into trouble when he came under fire from two Mexican cannons as he crossed the road to Roma. He sent a detachment to silence the guns, which they did with small arms fire from the protection of a fence. Ford joined this group, intending to seize the guns, which were those Cortina had taken in November. While Ford's men drove the gunners from their pieces, a charge by some of Cortina's mounted men prevented a capture. The gunners returned, fired a blast of grapeshot that slightly wounded Ford and more than a dozen of his men, then withdrew with their guns. Tobin, repulsed at the cemetery, joined Ford just after the Mexican riders retired. Heintzelman, who could not tell exactly what was occurring because of a heavy fog, arrived and gave Ford permission to pursue the Mexicans, who had begun a slow retreat. Stoneman cleared the river bank of Cortina's stragglers, and when Cortina himself rallied some men about five miles down the road to Roma, Ford shattered his lines and finally captured a cannon. William R. Henry, the erstwhile filibusterer, fired the piece at the Mexicans as they resumed their retreat. Cortina and some of his followers avoided capture by crossing the Rio Grande, but others simply fled into the brush, abandoning the other gun to Ford. That night Stoneman with his company garrisoned Roma while the Rangers retraced their steps to Ringgold Barracks. There Ford's guests included Samuel J. Stewart, a justice of the peace and former sheriff in Rio Grande City whose execution by Cortina had been prevented by the arrival of the Texans and federals.[7]

The clash near Rio Grande City on December 27, 1859, also known as the Davis Ranch fight, reportedly cost Cortina at least sixty men dead and forced him to flee across the Rio Grande. It also convinced Heintzelman to support Ford over Tobin in the dispute about who would command the Rangers as major. He wrote in his ever-present journal: "1 hope [by] all means that Ford will be elected the Major. He is by all odds the better man. He controls his men &Tobin is controlled by his. I would rather have Ford with 50 than Tobin with all his men." Despite this, when Ford decided to hold the elections for major on New Year's Day in 1860, Tobin won. Heintzelman was told that many of the Rangers voted against Ford because he wanted to stop the rough behavior that Tobin tolerated. A significant number of Texans, led by Ford, subsequently decided not to serve under Tobin. Ford's former newspaper partner, Joseph Walker, who had been elected to lead Ford's company in the Davis Ranch fight, refused to stay, as did most of Ford's original recruits. Tobin ordered the malcontents to Brownsville to be mustered out, while he asked Houston, the newly inaugurated governor, to allow him to enlist replacements.[8]

Ford led Walker and many others to Brownsville, where to their delight they were hailed as heroes. They also found a pair of commissioners, Angel Navarro and Robert H. Taylor, sent by Houston to investigate matters along the Rio Grande. The two men had endured a hostile reception from local leaders, who decided the outsiders might actually sympathize with Cortina, but the atmosphere changed when it soon became apparent that Navarro and Taylor disliked Cortina and supported Ford over Tobin. The two had little choice about the latter decision—people in Brownsville told them that Tobin's men were undisciplined and dangerous, perhaps even more of a menace than Cortina in looting local settlers, and that Tobin had been repeatedly defeated by Cortina. Conversely, Ford required discipline, and he won. Within days of their arrival on the Rio Grande, Navarro and Taylor ordered Tobin to Brownsville to be discharged. At Heintzelman's request, the Rangers were reduced in number and reorganized as two companies with Ford as senior captain. He could not be a major because there was not a battalion of five companies to command, but he took charge of all of the Rangers, in cooperation with Heintzelman. To the great pleasure of many local leaders, Navarro and Taylor declared that Cortina was in fact a "thief, assassin, and a murderer" who had been allowed to do as he wanted for too many years because the Mexican majority followed him and the Anglo minority needed his influence. The result had been chaos, with Mexican officials supporting Cortina, and Ford and Heintzelman were to work together to restore order by eliminating him.[9]

Ford later claimed that his announced decision to resign was just a ruse to get out from under Tobin's control and move to Brownsville, where he expected Cortina would strike next, and he knew his company would follow him there. If so, his maneuver had worked brilliantly. Tobin and his troublesome recruits were vanquished, and friendlier faces now served with Ford. Matthew Nolan, who had been a bugler for the Army in the Mexican War and for Ford in both 1850 and 1858, now became his first lieutenant. John J. Dix Jr., who would be a lifelong friend, was one of Ford's second lieutenants. Walker and others went home, but Ford's second company was commanded by John Littleton, a Karnes County sheriff who had been wounded in fighting against Cortina in November. He decided to stay, and like Nolan would lead a company again under Ford during the Civil War. Ford christened his new command as the "Rio Grande Squadron." There were many veterans in the ranks and, with Ford as senior captain, much was expected of them when Cortina showed signs of staging an unexpected resurgence.[10]

In the aftermath of his victory at Davis Ranch in December 1859, Heintzelman had confidently declared that "Cortina's forces" were "entirely dispersed," and he told his subordinates "to keep out small parties to pick up any stragglers who may be disposed to be troublesome." Ford never harbored any such misconceptions about his opponent, and he warned Houston that Cortina was not finished as he could draw support from those in rebellion against President Benito Juarez in Mexico. When Houston sent a proclamation to Ford for Cortina and his men, promising amnesty if they would lay down their arms and return home, Ford delivered the missive but expected no positive result. He also did not trust the reassurances

of Gen. Guadalupe Garcia, who commanded the garrison at Matamoros (and had done so during the infamous James H. Callahan
incursion in 1855). Perhaps Ford understood better than other Anglos the larger context for the unrest along the Rio Grande because
he was again being offered a command by the ever-hopeful Jose
Maria de Jesus Carvajal, who saw in the travails of Juarez a chance
for personal glory. Ford declined to join Carvajal. Instead, he and
Littleton, along with many others, met repeatedly with Heintzelman to urge an attack on Cortina, even if they had to cross the Rio
Grande into Mexico to reach him. By early February Heintzelman
reluctantly agreed, and he ordered Ford into the field in tandem
with two companies of Army troopers.[11]

On February 1, 1860, Ford rode out of Brownsville with his
Rangers alongside United States cavalry under the command of
Stoneman and Lt. Manning M. Kimmel, whom Ford had first met
at Camp Radziminski during his unsuccessful try to secure Van
Dorn's cooperation against the Comanche in 1859. The combined
force moved slowly up the Rio Grande, searching for raiders. On
the second day Ford arrived at the ranch of Cortina's mother, Maria
E. G. Cavazos de Cortina, to whom he was formally introduced by
Savas Cavazos, Cortina's half brother by their mother's earlier marriage. Ford was impressed and deeply affected by her gentle manner, as well as her earnest plea to not harm her son, and he promised to protect her. The Americans scattered along the Texas side of
the river to prevent any crossings, which led to the first engagement
for the Rio Grande Squadron. Ford on February 4 sent a small party
of Rangers to establish a camp at a bend in the river opposite Bolsa
Ranch. They encountered about thirty of Cortina's men, and a fight
ensued that quickly escalated. Tobin with his command, riding to
muster out at Brownsville, joined the melee, while the steamboat
Ranchero, laden with specie and cargo worth $300,000, chugged
into range as well. Army gunners on the deck of the *Ranchero*
opened fire with the guns captured by Ford at Davis Ranch. A cou-

rier raced to get Ford, who arrived with additional Rangers several hours into the fight.[12]

Believing Cortina had several hundred men across the Rio Grande, Ford decided to attack. Tobin swam the river with ten mounted men to secure the far bank while the *Ranchero* ferried Ford and three dozen Rangers, including Littleton and Dix, across the border. Ford in his haste forgot to grab his guns from his saddle, but he led dismounted Rangers in a flank attack on Cortina's men firing from behind a fence. The Mexicans broke and ran, seeking shelter in the brush while Cortina himself served as a solitary rearguard. Only one Texan, Fountain B. Woodruff, was killed, and none were seriously wounded, while Cortina's losses were reported as twenty-nine killed and forty wounded. Bolsa Ranch was set ablaze, though not by Ford's order, and Tobin resumed his march for Brownsville shortly before midnight, when Stoneman and Kimmel arrived with their troopers.[13]

Ford and Stoneman, as the ranking captains on the field, consulted that night and decided to escort the *Ranchero* downriver. To do this effectively, Ford would ride down the Mexican side with Rangers, while Stoneman would parallel him on the Texas side, close enough to provide support if necessary. Informed of this, Heintzelman responded with admonitions not to venture too far into Mexico and to maintain strict discipline. Ford's original orders from Runnels in November 1859 had forbade him to cross the Rio Grande without permission from Mexican authorities, and when Heintzelman informed Garcia of Ford's plan and asked for his cooperation in catching Cortina, the Mexican general responded with a demand that Ford leave Mexico and reported that he had already sent troops to intercept the Rangers. Ford met the Matamoros militia at Las Palmas Ranch. A tense negotiation ensued, during which Ford became convinced that some of the Mexican troops he faced were Cortina's men. A clash was averted when the Matamoros authorities decided not to protest Ford's escort, while he, in obedience to an order from Heintzelman, agreed to let the Mexicans guard their side of the river for the remainder of the *Ranchero's* journey. Ford and Stoneman, with their men, returned peacefully to Brownsville on the Texas side of the Rio Grande.[14]

Ford reported to Houston that Cortina had been badly beaten at Bolsa Ranch, but he expected his opponent to recruit another force. Heintzelman within a week sent Ford to patrol again along the Rio Grande, but this time he told the Texans to stay on their side of the river. Rangers, when not being drilled by Ford, continued to patrol together with cavalry for the next six weeks. Ford also enforced strict discipline, forbidding alcohol in his camp and telling Houston that his men "gambled very little" because "they have had nothing to gamble for." The main casualty during this quiet interlude was Ford, who was badly injured when his horse stepped in a hole at full gallop and fell on him. He had to be carried to his quarters, blood dripping from his nose and mouth.[15]

Ford and his Rangers returned to Mexico in March 1860, when Garcia reported to Heintzelman that Cortina was camped at La Mesa, just a few miles from Ford's base at Agua Negra Ranch. Heintzelman conveyed the news to Ford just to alert him, but an idea grew. Ford secured permission from Carvajal, now appointed as the governor of Tamaulipas, for the Americans to cross the Rio Grande, and Heintzelman ordered Stoneman with two companies of cavalry to accompany Ford, who for once moved slowly. He claimed that he still suffered from the injuries sustained when his horse fell, but he also worried that Cortina might be setting a trap, perhaps with the assistance of Garcia. A reconnaissance indicated an ambush had indeed been set, and Stoneman agreed to an indirect march that brought the Americans close to the Mexican camp before they were detected. Ford's Rangers formed the right wing and Stoneman's cavalry became the left for a charge that enveloped a hastily formed defensive line. After the fight, it was discovered that the Americans had overwhelmed a Mexican militia unit, killing four or five men and even mortally wounding a woman. Ford and Stoneman quickly released all prisoners and restored captured property to its owners, or at least most of it.[16]

Later that morning a larger Mexican force approached. A Mexican officer asked for Ford, whom he addressed as colonel, to meet with his commander, who actually was a colonel and refused to speak with Stoneman, a captain. The Mexican colonel berated Ford and demanded an explanation for entering Mexico and firing on Mexican militia. Ford in turn asked why an ambush had been prepared on the main road, forcing the Americans to take another route to avoid being attacked themselves. The colonel, rather than answer, boasted that if the Americans had attacked him earlier that morning, they would have been defeated. When Ford angrily asked whether he would like to try his luck, the Mexican colonel declined. Further discussion revealed that mounted men driven from the field by Stoneman's troopers at La Mesa were indeed Cortina's, working with the militia. Irritated at this clear evidence that Mexican officials supported Cortina, the Americans, rather than obey the colonel's order to wait for further instructions from Matamoros, returned to their camp on the north side of the Rio Grande.[17]

Ford again led his Rangers in tandem with Stoneman's cavalry down the Mexican side of the Rio Grande in late March and found some of Cortina's men at Bolsa Ranch. One, Faustino, was an "old Mexican Indian" notorious for leading raids and killing at least six Americans. When he was captured by the Rangers, Ford simply declared that he did not wish to see him. He later wrote in his memoirs, "A shot was heard—the scene closed." Because this incident became the source for stories of many alleged killings by Ford's men, a few months after Ford's death in 1897 a former Ranger, Will Lambert, claimed responsibility for the execution. An Austin newspaperman in 1859, Lambert had been with Ford only a short time when he caught Faustino. Told by Ford that he did not wish to talk with the captive, Lambert marched Faustino into the brush and shot him, then told Ford that he had escaped. Ford responded quietly, "You'll do." Whether or not Ford condoned this act, he reported every atrocity committed by both sides to Heintzelman and was never called to task for excesses, though his report of Faustino's death omitted much of the detail provided years later by Lambert.[18]

While resting his horses at Bolsa Ranch, Ford was approached by a courier who delivered an order from Heintzelman to return to Texas. Ford and Stoneman grumbled; they had been hoping for orders to ride into Matamoros. Instead, acting on a tip from an informant, Ford led his Rangers and the cavalry to Cortina's ranch south of Matamoros. Hearing gunshots as they approached, the Americans assumed their advance had been attacked and raced into the settlement, only to find they had interrupted a Saint Joseph's Day celebration, during which it was customary to fire blanks. One Mexican was killed when he fled into the brush, loaded live rounds, and angrily began firing at the Rangers. That night another spy told Ford that Cortina had fled toward Monterrey, and the Rangers took up the pursuit. They missed their quarry again at a ranch forty miles away, and so Ford and Stoneman decided to return to his camp at Agua Negra Ranch in Texas, which they reached on the night of March 21, 1860.[19]

Ford could not resist one last strike, against Reynosa, whose residents sheltered some of Cortina's veterans and boasted they would not fall as easily as La Mesa. Ford and Stoneman laid plans by which the Rangers would cross the Rio Grande and occupy Reynosa. When firing began, as they expected it would, Stoneman would hurry across the river to support the endangered Texans. Ford smoothly occupied the smaller village of Reynosa Vieja at midnight on April 3–4, 1860, but Cortina's veterans escaped. Ford's Rangers consoled themselves by organizing a fandango, but at daylight Ford continued to Reynosa, where the alarm had been raised and several hundred defenders had gathered, thinking they were being attacked by bandits. The Rangers divided into three columns, led by Ford, Littleton, and Nolan, and entered the town, but despite their best efforts they could not goad the Mexicans into firing a first shot. Instead, once the defenders realized they were not being attacked by bandits, Ford was invited to meet with the town council at the courthouse. A tense meeting ended with Ford agreeing to return to Texas and send demands in writing for the surrender of Cortina's followers. The disappointed Texans were escorted to the ferry, and settled for the night near Edinburg, where Stoneman had waited anxiously for shots to be fired.[20]

Ford sent his written demand for Cortina's veterans to the Reynosa council, and they politely replied that they had no such men. Ford fumed and the council prepared to meet his attack, which they fully expected. Tension mounted as bullets from the Texas side of the Rio Grande wounded several Mexicans, and bullets from the Mexican side fell in the Ranger camp. The situation did not improve when Littleton and other Rangers, with Ford's approval, built a re-alistic-looking gun emplacement with bricks and placed a log on an oxcart inside of it, which looked to Reynosa residents like a cannon aimed at them. To complete their jest, the Texans filled a cow horn with gunpowder and grease, and then launched it with a boom to-ward the town by exploding powder in a small hole underneath it. The flaming missile convinced Mexicans they had been fired upon, and many of them stayed on guard through the night for the attack that would surely follow. In turn, Kimmel raced his troopers to the river crossing when he heard gunfire, which again proved to be a religious procession celebrating a saint's day.[21]

Lt. Col. Robert E. Lee arrived with more federal troops on April 7, 1860, less than twenty-four hours after the horn was launched. After talking with Ford, who had joined his column as it approached the river, Lee sent a note to assure Reynosa officials that he did not want a war, but he also admonished them not to support Cortina. They responded that they also did not wish to fight, that no Cor-tina followers were in their town, and that Ford should not have entered their town. Lee agreed on all counts. This brought an end to Ford's campaign, which was not unexpected. While Ford operated on the Rio Grande, Duff Green came to Austin on a fact-finding mission and reported to the James Buchanan administration that Texans were as guilty as Mexicans in creating havoc along the border. Heintzelman also decided that the Rangers were impediments to peace; after all, Ford had ignored his orders on several occasions. With Cortina apparently deep in Mexico, Army leaders did not need Ford. Finally, Houston, like Ford, had considered attacking Mexico to seize territory or to distract his fellow Americans from the impending sectional crisis, but he dropped this notion by late January 1860, when he appointed an agent to muster Ford's command out of service. Navarro urged Houston to establish a protectorate over northern Mexico, and Houston discussed the matter with Lee, but when the latter refused to take part in such a scheme, Houston ordered Ford to Goliad. Houston's agent, George McKnight, asked Lee if Ford could enter federal service, but Lee declined, and Ford led his command away from the Rio Grande without further protest. After all, he could not satisfactorily answer the governor's queries about atrocities committed by Tobin's men, and he had actually asked for a leave of absence in early March.[22]

Ford left the Rio Grande as a conquering hero among the Texans, and with warm praise from Army leaders as well. Before riding north, he and his Rio Grande Squadron enjoyed a banquet and dance in Brownsville that was attended by Lee and other officers, who perhaps appreciated a speech by Ford assuring everyone of his love for the Union. Lee certainly defended Ford when Garcia tried to complain about the Reynosa intrusion. Heintzelman had already heaped accolades upon Ford in his official report submitted in March; after all, Cortina had lost more than 150 men killed while American losses were only fifteen. Perhaps another eighty Mexicans also died during the conflict, but Cortina's surviving followers abandoned him and he had fled far south, away from the Rio Grande. In a letter to Houston formally declining to accept the Rangers into federal service, Lee repeated the praises of Heintzelman for Ford and Littleton. The attention lavished by the people of Brownsville on the Texans did not suit Heintzelman, however, and he left town without Lee and Ford on May 7, 1860. The two joined him on the road on May 10, and they rode together for three days until Ford left to rejoin his command at Goliad. There McKnight mustered out the Rangers and thought he had collected all of their state-issued weapons, but Ford was amused to encounter some of his men along the road to Austin still carrying their arms and laughing at how they had hoodwinked Houston's agent. Like his Rangers, Ford had not yet been paid, and he did not indicate later that he did anything to correct their theft. [23] After settling his accounts in Austin, Ford returned to Brownsville.

Editors' Note—In historical literature the life and times of Juan N. Cortina can be divided into several time periods:

First, by the early 1900s the image of Cortina in Texas and the nation came from the pens of Ranger "Rip" Ford, historian Walter Prescott Webb, and folklorist J. Frank Dobie. In his memoirs Ford showed ambiguous feelings about Cortina, seeing him as a border raider who stood tall in battle. All three writers, moreover, contributed to the negative image of Cortina: one who carried out a reign of terror.

Second, after World War II Charles W. Goldfinch tried to reinterpret Cortina's life and gave a more balanced view in his academic writings of the "Red Robber of the Rio Grande." Goldfinch tried to relate the violent events associated with Cortina with his need to stand against the oppression of Mexican Americans in South Texas. The views of Goldfinch will be expanded upon by the next generation of historians.

Third, in the late 1900s, especially during the Chicano Renaissance, Hispanic historians and sociologists argued that Cortina was a social bandit who reacted to the evils of a racist society. These writers utilized the concept of a social bandit as developed by Eric Hobsbawm. Among those who penned this version of Cortina, a few stand out: Albert Camarillo, Pedro Castillo, Arnoldo De Leon, David Montejano, and Carlos Larralde.

Fourth, by the turn of the twenty-first century coverage of the exploits of Cortina have appeared in numerous published and unpublished works: in books by Benjamin Johnson and Elliot Young; in unpublished formats by Manuel Callahan, James Douglas, and Michael Webster; and in pop culture stories by James Michener and Larry McMurtry. Varied interpretations evolved, including that of Douglas who argued Cortina fought oppressors to benefit himself. Jerry D. Thompson in his recent book, *Cortina: Defending the Mexican Name in Texas*, has arisen as the most authoritative voice on Cortina.

NOTES

1. Ford, *Rip Ford's Texas*, 260, 264–265; Brown, Annals of Travis County (Brown Papers, CAH), 19: 20; Ford, Memoirs (Ford Papers, CAH), 763. 870; Ford to Ed Burleson Jr., Aug. 11, 1859 [quotes] (Ed Burleson Jr. Papers, CAH); *Claims of Texas Against the United States*, 43; Hughes, *Rebellious Ranger*, 160–161; Amberson, et al., *I Would Rather Sleep in Texas*, 164–166; Collins, *Texas Devils*, 111–118; Chance, *Carvajal*, 169–170; Thompson, *Cortina*, 7, 22, 36–37, 40–47, 50–51.

2. Ford, *Rip Ford's Texas*, 265; Ford, Memoirs (Ford Papers, CAH), 662–·663, 734; William G. Tobin to Runnels, Nov. 27, 1859 (GR); Jerry D. Thompson, ed., *Fifty Miles and a Fight: Major Samuel Peter Heintzelman's Journal of Texas and the Cortina War* (Austin: Texas State Historical Association, 1998), 131–132; Corpus Christi *Ranchero*, Dec. 3, 1859; *Claims of Texas Against the United States*, 44, 48; United States Congress, *Troubles on the Texas Frontier*, House Ex. Docs. 81, 36th Cong., lst Sess. [Serial Set 1056], 5–7; Hughes, *Rebellious Ranger*, 16l–162; Collins, *Texas Devils*, 118–122, 124–126, 128–130, 133; Amberson et al., *I Would Rather Sleep in Texas*, 167–169; Webb, *Texas Rangers*, 182; Thompson, *Cortina*, 52–65, 68–72, 74, 77, 78; Cox, *Wearing the Cinco Peso*, 154, 155; *NH0T*, 3: 543.

3. Ford, *Rip Ford's Texas*, xxxiv, 265–266; Ford, Memoirs (Ford Papers, CAH), 769–771; Runnels to Ford, Nov. 17, 22, 1859, Ford to Runnels, Nov. 22, 1859 (GR); *Claims of Texas Against the United States*, 143–144; San Antonio *Express*, Jan. 19, 1890; Hughes, *Rebellious Ranger*, 161–162; Collins, *Texas Devils*, 125–124; Thompson, *Cortina*, 61–62. Ford tended to believe that Forbes Britton, in convincing Gov. Hardin R. Runnels to send Rangers to the Rio Grande in 1859, had shown himself to be a "first class actor." See John S. Ford, The Cortina War (DeShields Papers, DRT).

4. Ford, *Rip Ford's Texas*, 266–267; Ford, Memoirs (Ford Papers, CAH), 771–773, 870; Ford to Runnels, Dec. 16, 1859 (GR); San Antonio *Ledger & Texan*, Dec. 10, 1859; Corpus Christi *Ranchero*, Dec. 3 [quote], 24, 1859; *Difficulties on Southwestern Frontier*, 87–88; *Troubles on the Texas Frontier*, 7–8; Collins, *Texas Devils*, 131–132, 136–137; Martin L. Crimmins, ed., "Colonel

Robert E. Lee's Report on Indian Combats in Texas," *SWHQ* 39 (July 1935): 21 –32; Thompson, *Fifty Miles and a Fight*, 138, 140–141; Hughes, *Rebellious Ranger*, 162–163; Thompson, *Cortina*, 73–74.

5. Ford, *Rip Ford's Texas*, 268–269; Ford, Memoirs (Ford Papers, CAH), 774, 776, 777; Runnels to Ford, Nov. 17, 23 [1st quote], 1859 (GR); Ford to H. E. Woodhouse, Dec. 20, 1859 [receipt] (Texas Adjutant General, Pre–War Ranger Records, TSLA); Thompson, *Fifty Miles and a Fight*, 125, 140–142 [2nd quote], 143, 147–149; Crimmins, "Lee's Report," 25; Hughes, *Rebellious Ranger*,162, 164; Brackett, *United States Cavalry*, 202.

6. Ford, *Rip Ford's Texas*, 269–272; Ford, Memoirs (Ford Papers. CAH), 777–780; *Claims of Texas Against the United States*, 45; Hughes, *Rebellious Ranger*, 164–165; Thompson, *Cortina*, 77–80; Corpus Christi *Ranchero*, Jan. 7, 1860; Austin *Texas State Gazette*, Jan. 14, 1860.

7. Ford, *Rip Ford's Texas*, 274–275; Ford, Memoirs (Ford Papers, CAH), 782–785; Ford to Sam Houston, Dec. 29, 1859, Tobin to Houston, Jan. 30, 1860 (GR); Corpus Christi *Ranchero*, Jan. 7, 1860; Austin *Texas State Gazette*, Jan. 14, 1860; *Difficulties on Southwestern Frontier*, 96–98; *Troubles on the Texas Frontier*, 9, 72; Thompson, *Fifty Miles and a Fight*, 155; Hughes, *Rebellious Ranger*, 166–167; Collins, *Texas Devils*, 142–146; "Starr County Elected Officials," http://www.rootsweb.ancestry.com/-txstarr/elected.htm (accessed Dec. 28, 2008).

8. Ford, *Rip Ford's Texas*, 274–276; Ford, Memoirs (Ford Papers, CAH), 772–773, 784–785, 791; Tobin to Samuel P. Heintzelman, Jan. 2, 1860 (Texas Adjutant General, Pre-War Ranger Records, TSLA); Tobin to Houston, Jan. 2, 1860 (GR); Thompson, ed., *Fifty Miles and a Fight*, 142, 164; Hughes, *Rebellious Ranger*, 168; Collins, *Texas Devils*, 125, 135 n9, 162–164; Amberson, et al., *I Would Rather Sleep in Texas*, 169; Charles M. Robinson Ill, *The Men Who Wear the Star: The Story of the Texas Rangers* (New York: Random House, 2000), 130–132. A writer in the San Antonio *Ledger*, Jan. 14, 1860, opined that Ford's delay in holding the elections led to his defeat. Ford attributed his defeat to his strict discipline and the efforts of John D. Littleton, who understood that if William G. Tobin became a major, it would create a vacancy for a captain. Littleton was elected captain to succeed Tobin, but quickly switched sides and joined Ford, who later claimed that he always regarded both Tobin and Littleton as his friends. See Ford, The Cortina War (Manuscript, n.d., DeShields Papers, DRT).

9. Ford, *Rip Ford's Texas*, 276–279; Ford, Memoirs (Ford Papers, CAH), 791–793; San Antonio *Ledger*, Feb. 18, 1860; Corpus Christi *Ranchero*, Feb. 25, 1860; Angel Navarro and Robert H. Taylor to Tobin, Jan. 12, 1860, Taylor to Houston, Jan. 16, 1860, Heintzelman to Navarro and Taylor, Feb. 2, 1860, Navarro and Taylor to Ford, Feb. 2, 1860, Navarro and Taylor to Houston,

Feb. 4, 1860 (GR); *Claims of Texas Against the United States,* 45; Thompson, *Fifty Miles and a Fight,* 187; *Difficulties on Southwestern Frontier,* 118–119; Hughes, *Rebellious Ranger,* 168–170; Collins, *Texas Devils,* 164–167, 174–176; Thompson, *Cortina,* 87–90.

10. Ford, *Rip Ford's Texas,* 154, 242, 279–280, 353; Ford, Memoirs (Ford Papers, CAH), 521, 736, 790–794; Corpus Christi *Ranchero,* Dec. 3, 1859; *Difficulties on Southwestern Frontier,* 122; Hughes, *Rebellious Ranger,* 153, 167, 169–170; *NHOT,* 2:657; 4: 237–238.

11. Ford, *Rip Ford's Texas,* xxxii, 229, 241; Ford, Memoirs (Ford Papers. CAH), 662–663, 734; Heintzelman to Tobin, Jan. 2, 1860 [quotes] (Texas Adjutant General, Pre-War Ranger Records, TSLA); Houston to Ford, Dec. 30, 1859 (GR); Corpus Christi *Ranchero,* Jan. 7, 1860; Amelia W. Williams and Eugene C. Barker, eds., *The Writings of Sam Houston, 1813–1863,* 8 vols. (Austin: University of Texas Press, 1938–1943), 7: 390, 409; Thompson, *Fifty Miles and a Fight,* 174, 179, 182, 195; Shearer, "Carvajal Disturbances," 443; Hughes, *Rebellious Ranger,* 167; Thompson, *Cortina,* 81–82, 87; Amberson et al., *I Would Rather Sleep in Texas,* 161–162.

12. Ford, *Rip Ford's Texas,* 281–282, 245; Ford, Memoirs (Ford Papers, CAH), 739, 796, 807–808, 897–898; Hughes, *Rebellious Ranger,* 170–172: Corpus Christi *Ranchero,* Feb. 11, 18, 1860; Austin *Texas State Gazette,* May 26, 1860.

13. Ford, *Rip Ford's Texas,* 282–286; Ford, Memoirs (Ford Papers, CAH), 796–801, 813, 828, 830; Tobin to Houston, Feb. 6, 1860, Ford to Houston, Feb. 9, 1860 (GR); Ford to C. W. Thomas, Feb. 5, 1860 (Ford Papers, TSLA); Corpus Christi *Ranchero,* Feb. 11, 18, 1860; *Difficulties on Southwestern Frontier,* 110–111, 112–115, 119–120; *Claims of Texas Against the United States,* 45, 46; *Troubles on the Texas Frontier,* 10–11, 13, 63–70, 75, 96, 97; Thompson, *Cortina,* 83–84; Collins, *Texas Devils,*168–173; Amberson et al., *I Would Rather Sleep in Texas,* 171–172.

14. Ford, *Rip Ford's Texas,* 286–289; Ford, Memoirs (Ford Papers, CAH), 802, 806, 809–813; Thompson, *Fifty Miles and a Fight,* 188–189, 191; Runnels to Ford, Nov. 23, 1859 (GR); Ford to Heintzelman, Feb. 4, 1860 (Texas Adjutant General, Pre-War Ranger Records, TSLA); Heintzelman to Ford, Feb. 4, 1860 (Ford Papers, TSLA); Hughes, *Rebellious Ranger,* 172.

15. Ford, *Rip Ford's Texas,* 291; Ford, Memoirs (Ford Papers, CAH), 807–808, 818–819; Ford to Houston, Feb. 9, Mar. 25 [quotes], 1860, John J. Dix to Ford, Mar. 4, 1860, Arthur Pue to Ford, Mar. 10, 1860, Ford to Thomas, Mar. 11, 1860, Heintzelman to Ford, Mar. 14, 1862 (GR); Thompson, *Fifty Miles and a Fight,* 195; Hughes, *Rebellious Ranger,* 172–173.

16. Ford, *Rip Ford's Texas,* 290–293, 295; Ford, Memoirs (Ford Papers, CAH), 817–818, 819–822, 825; Heintzelman to Ford, Mar. 14, 1860, Ford

to Houston, Mar. 17, 1860 (GR); Ford to Thomas, Mar. 11, 1860 (Ford Papers, TSLA); Corpus Christi *Ranchero,* Mar. 24, 1860; *Troubles on the Texas Frontier,* 80, 81; *Rebellious Ranger,* 173–174; Collins, *Texas Devils,* 192–196; Chance, *Carvajal,* 172; Thompson, *Cortina,* 85.

17. Ford, *Rip Ford's Texas,* 293–295; Ford, Memoirs (Ford Papers, CAH), 822–825; Hughes, *Rebellious Ranger,* 175; Thompson, *Cortina,* 83–85, 87.

18. Ford, *Rip Ford's Texas,* 295–296; Ford, Memoirs (Ford Papers, CAH), 826–833, 834 [quote]: Will Lambert, "Col. John S. Ford," *The Southern Tribute* 1 (March 1898): 177–184 [quote on 181]; Ford to Heintzelman, Mar. 24, 1860 (Ford Papers, TSLA); *Troubles on the Texas Frontier,* 99; Hughes, *Rebellious Ranger,* 175–176; *NHOT,* 4:45–46; Lewis E. Daniell, *Personnel of the Texas State Government, with Sketches of Distinguished Texans* (Austin: City Printing Company, 1887), 196–197.

19. Ford, *Rip Ford's Texas,* xxxii, 296–298; Ford, Memoirs (Ford Papers, CAH), 835–839; Ford to Heintzelman, Mar. 24, 1860 (Ford Papers, TSLA); Hughes, *Rebellious Ranger,* 176–177; Thompson, *Cortina, 85;* Webb, *Texas Rangers,* 184–193.

20. Ford, *Rip Ford's Texas,* 299–303; Ford, Memoirs (Ford Papers, CAH), 825, 840–845; Hughes, *Rebellious Ranger,* 178–181; Collins, *Texas Devils,* 198–202; Thompson, *Cortina,* 85; Corpus Christi *Ranchero,* Apr. 14, 21, 1860; San Antonio *Ledger,* Apr. 28, 1860.

21. Ford, *Rip Ford's Texas,* 303–304; Ford, Memoirs (Ford Papers, CAH), 846–848; Hughes, *Rebellious Ranger,* 181–183; Thompson, *Cortina,* 86; San Antonio *Ledger,* Apr. 28, 1860.

22. Ford, *Rip Ford's Texas,* 305–308; Ford, Memoirs (Ford Papers, CAH), 848–851; Thompson, *Fifty Miles and a Fight,* 183–184, 214, 227–230; Williams and Barker, *Writings of Houston,* 7: 444, 490, 499–500, 523, 541– 545; Navarro to Houston, Jan, 11, 31, 1860; Ford to Houston, Mar. 2, 1860 (GR); *Troubles on the Texas Frontier,* 86–89, 100; *Claims of Texas Against the United States,* 47; Hughes, *Rebellious Ranger,* 179–180, 183–184; Thompson, *Cortina,* 92–93; James L. Haley, *Sam Houston* (Norman: University of Oklahoma Press, 2002), 366–367; Carl Coke Rister, *Robert E. Lee in Texas* (Norman: University of Oklahoma Press, 1946), 115, 121–123; Collins, *Texas Devils,* 176–178, 203–206; Webb, *Texas Rangers,* 203–207; NHOT, 4: 423; Brackett, *United States Cavalry,* 206–207. Albert G. Brackett, as the captain of a company of the 2nd United States Cavalry, was the officer sent by Robert E. Lee to speak with community leaders in Reynosa.

23. Ford, *Rip Ford's Texas,* 298, 307–308; Ford, Memoirs (Ford Papers, CAH), 851, 853; Robert E. Lee to Houston, Apr. 20, 1860 (GR); Thompson, *Fifty Miles and a Fight,* 244–247; Rister, *Lee in Texas,* 123–127; Hughes, *Rebellious Ranger,* 177, 184; Thompson, *Cortina,* 86.

★ 9 ★

HISPANIC TEXAS RANGERS CONTRIBUTE TO PEACE ON THE TEXAS FRONTIER, 1838 TO 1880

David E. Screws

In the last decades of the twentieth century, historian Rodolfo Acuna accused earlier writers of being apologists for the crude, and sometimes brutal, manners of the Texas Rangers during the days of the Texas frontier (Acuna 1981: 25). For most of the nineteenth century much of Texas was nothing more than a frontier, and the methods of enforcing peace and order on frontiers were often as violent as the crimes. Acuna also expressed the belief that all rangers were Anglos, "recruited gunslingers who burned with a hatred of Mexicans" who were sent to the border to "maintain a closed social structure that excluded Mexicans" (Acuna 1981: 27). Montejano believed that a Frontier Battalion was established to represent "the armed force of the Anglo-Texas order" (Montejano 1987: 33–36).

An examination of history reveals that many Hispanics served the Republic of Texas and the state of Texas as rangers. There is evidence as early as 1848 that they performed well and were highly respected by their Anglo counterparts. Several Anglo rangers, camped in Mexico in 1848 during the Mexican War, were discussing which race of people made the best ranger spies. One ranger agreed that Americans made good spies, but he conceded that "the Mexicans excel them" (Reid 1848: 114).

Who were these men and where did they range? Brownson Malsch's biography of Manuel Trazazas Gonzaullas, a twentieth-century ranger known as Lone Wolf Gonzaullas, concluded he was the only ranger of Spanish lineage to attain the rank of captain (Malsch 1980: 1). However, the records of the Texas Rangers contain the names of a number of captains of Spanish descent, beginning with Capt. Lewis Sanches, during the decade of the Texas Republic. Sanches led a ranger company of 12 Hispanics and 4 Anglos in August 1838. The following month his force grew to 21 Hispanics and 8 Anglos. In June and July of 1839, he mustered another company which included 25 Hispanic rangers (Muster and Pay Rolls 1838, 1839a). The latter company was raised to campaign against the Cherokee Indians (Wilkins 1996: 46).

Capt. Jose Gonzales commanded a company of 46 mounted volunteers from September 10, 1839, to November 21, 1839. The unit was listed as Militia of the Republic of Texas and included 27 Hispanics. Lt. Mauricio Carrasco was second in command (Muster and Pay Rolls 1839b). Joining the campaign to quell Indian disturbances in Central Texas, Capt. Antonio Perez mustered a ranger unit comprised of 15 Hispanics, including himself, and one Anglo. This unit ranged from January through most of May 1841 (Muster and Pay Rolls 1841a). Perez' unit, in conjunction with John C. Hays' company, took the field in April 1841 in pursuit of bandits operating against merchant routes between San Antonio and Laredo. There were no records of any engagements, but the bandits were warned of the approaching rangers and fled into Mexico (Wilkins 1996: 96).

In the 1870s, Company G of the Frontier Forces was formed to range the Texas border in Hidalgo and Starr counties, between Rio Grande City and Laredo. This predominantly Hispanic unit was commanded by Capt. C. G. Falcon, also of Spanish descent. The rolls included Alvino, Antonio, and Estefan Falcon, evidence that the surname applied to men of Spanish origin. Seven Anglos and more than 30 Hispanics served under Falcon from October 8, 1870, to December 31, 1870 (Muster and Pay Rolls 1870a; Ingmire 1982).

Capt. Gregorio Garcia, who commanded Companies D and N of the Frontier Forces, ranged the El Paso, Fort Quitman, and San Elizario areas in 1870 and 1871. Over a period of about nine months nearly 40 different men served in his command, all of Spanish descent (Muster and Pay Rolls 1870–1871a; Ingmire 1982). In 1878, Captain Garcia was still serving in the area during the El Paso Salt War, a conflict that arose over the mineral rights to salt extracted from several lakes near El Paso. A group of Anglo Texans had formed a company to produce the salt. However, their ownership was challenged by Antonio Borajo, a priest, and his ally, Don Luis Cardis. Charles Howard, a local politician, entered the fracas and murdered Cardis. The clamor for the arrest of Howard led to mob violence and the rangers were called upon to quell the disturbance. Captain Garcia's rangers held Charles Ellis' store while another ranger detachment under Lt. John B. Tays held ranger headquarters against a mob of angry locals. The mob wanted Charles Howard turned over to them for betraying them in deals which gave him control of the salt lakes, and the murder of Cardis. After two days of fighting, the rangers were driven from Ellis' store and joined Tays' men in ranger headquarters. The siege ended when the rangers surrendered after promises that all would be treated well. Howard was executed by the mob (Webb 1991: 347–359). Almost one year later, on October 5, 1879, Captain Garcia sent Pablo Mejia to Lt. George Baylor with a report of an Apache attack on some hay cutters. This action set in motion one of Baylor's forays into northern Mexico in pursuit of Apaches (Gillett 1925: 151).

Telesforo Montes only carried the rank of lieutenant, but he served as the highest ranking man in another ranger unit serving in the San Elizario area from May 1874 to April 1876. His name appeared on muster rolls as commanding officer of a detachment of

25 men with Spanish surnames and a single Anglo name (Muster and Pay Rolls 1874a).

The Benavides family of Laredo provided strong leadership along the lower Texas border during the Cortina wars and the American Civil War. Before the Civil War, Capt. Santos Benavides led a local militia in several significant skirmishes. John S. Ford described him as "a clever gentleman" (Ford 1963: 298).

Juan Nepomuceno Cortina, also called Cheno, perpetrated many of the disturbances along the Mexico-Texas border. According to Samora, Bernal, and Pena (1979: 35), "Mexicans rushed across the border to pledge their allegiance to the man whose name was legend in Matamoros." Cortina had his followers; however not every Mexican, or Mexican American, "rushed" to his aid. Capt. Santos Benavides and his company obviously wished the bandit would stay out of Texas. In addition to Benavides' predominantly Hispanic command no less than 26 more men with Spanish names enlisted in at least six different companies raised for the purpose of suppressing the violence attributed to Cheno Cortina. These companies were mixes of Hispanics and Anglos working in concert for peace along the border. Their muster dates ranged from October 1859 to February 1860 (Muster and Pay Rolls 1859, 1859–1860; Ingmire 1982[1]).

A letter from Capt. A. C. Hill to Governor Sam Houston, written in February 1860, illustrated the state of affairs on the border. Hill explained that Cortina was "up to his old trade" on both sides of the river. He asked Houston to overlook the fact that they had crossed the border to hunt down Cortina in Mexico. Hill explained that "not only the chief authorities of our federal forces here say it is right, but the chief authorities of Matamoros and their commanding officers say it was right." He added that "the citizens were anxious that" he "should range near the junctions of the roads" to catch Cortina, and some other thieves. A. C. Hill closed the letter with a list of the men serving in his company. Nine of the 20 men bore Spanish surnames (Hill 1860).

Bicente Olmos, riding with John S. Ford for four months in 1860 (Ingmire 1982), participated in the fight at La Bolsa Bend on the Rio Grande during the Cortina struggles. Robert H. Taylor and Angel Navarro, state-appointed commissioners in the region, had discharged a Maj. W. G. Tobin for hanging an innocent man, replacing him with Ford. Ford's company drove Cortina south of the river at La Bolsa. That battle secured a measure of peace on the border, and encouraged "Mexican-born citizens of the United States to return to their ranches on the American side" of the Rio Grande (Ford 1963: 278–287).

In April 1861 Captain Benavides marched his troops out of Laredo and attacked Cortina's men at Redmond's Ranch, inflicting defeat on the border bandit. "The victory of Captain Benavides had an excellent effect" on conditions along the Rio Grande (Ford 1963: 324).

In March 1864 Santos Benavides, bearing the rank of colonel in the Confederate Army, along with Captains Refugio and Cristoval Benavides and just over 70 soldiers, successfully defended Laredo from a force of about 200 federal troops. Refugio Benavides pursued the Union soldiers, who retreated down the river toward Rio Grande City (Ford 1963: 355–357).

Refugio Benavides' men saw action in several more places along the border. They were involved in a small scrape near Las Rucias Ranch on June 25, 1864, and routed federals near the port of Brownsville on July 30. Col. Daniel Showalter failed to put the balance of his force into action in support of Benavides at Brownsville, forcing him to remove his command from the field (Ford 1963: 362–366). In September 1864 Captain Benavides and Capt. W. H. D. Carrington threw their men at the center of a federal force of 900 at Palmito Ranch, inflicting heavy casualties and causing the federals to withdraw (Ford 1963: 374). After the war ended, Refugio Benavides' name surfaced once again in connection with the Texas Rangers. He appeared as the ranking officer, although now as a lieutenant, of a company of rangers operating out of Laredo. The unit served from mid-June to mid-December 1874 (Muster and Pay Rolls 1874b).

Jesus Sandoval, who rode with Capt. Leander H. McNelly's company out of Corpus Christi, is mentioned in several memoirs. Sandoval had crude methods of extracting information out of captured criminals, methods some historians use to illustrate Anglo rangers' "forceful dealings with Mexicans" (Samora et al. 1979: 52). Sandoval was a Mexican American, not an Anglo, dealing with Mexican bandits from south of the border.

With hard work and skill, Jesus Sandoval had built a successful ranching operation north of Brownsville, where he resided with his wife and daughter. Bandits struck the ranch while Sandoval was away on business, burning his home and raping his wife and daughter. His wife and daughter sought refuge in a convent in Matamoros, where they lived out their lives. The grieving Sandoval sought the only way he knew to avenge his loss. He enlisted in the Texas Rangers (Jennings 1930: 74–75). Records showed that he served McNelly from May 1, 1875, to January 20, 1877 (Ingmire 1982). The ranger company took an immediate liking to the new ranger. His services as a guide were invaluable. He knew all the cow trails along the Rio Grande, as well as all the river crossings. But Sandoval, constantly reminded of the fate of his family, "lived to kill bandits" (Durham 1969: 44). In one incident Sandoval was placed in charge of an "American" prisoner who was in possession of a stolen saddle. Sandoval repeatedly raised the man off the ground with a rope around his neck until the prisoner leaked the required information: 50 bandits and 300 head of stolen cattle were coming toward the border.

Just as the Mexican bandits attacked Anglo and Mexican ranches alike, Sandoval meted out equal treatment to Anglo and Mexican prisoners. In the situation described above, Sandoval executed the man after he had told him what he wanted to know (Durham 1969: 53–55).

Captain McNelly acquired so much respect for Sandoval that he overlooked his mistakes. In pursuit of Cortina south of the border, Sandoval led them to the wrong place, almost putting them in danger of meeting what appeared to be Mexican troops. McNelly and Sandoval were seen "caucusing," but McNelly was not scolding his guide. The pair were simply involved in a discussion to find the best way out of the predicament (Durham 1969: 108–109). The other privates also held Jesus in great esteem. Once, when Sandoval had been gone most of two days, he rode in with news of a raid in Nueces County. One private wrote, "Come to think of it, we'd missed the old man since he rode out yesterday morning" (Durham 1969: 93). Another wrote, "He was sinewy and strong, active as any man." His horsemanship was impeccable. "He could mount a pony without putting his hand on him," running alongside before springing into the saddle. In the saddle, he became a very graceful and daring rider (Jennings 1930: 74). The embittered man was known to sulk for hours, keeping to himself, but when the other rangers addressed him he would respond pleasantly. "He worshiped the rangers and was ready to go to any trouble to please them" (Jennings 1930: 78). In the words of the Anglos, Jesus "made a fine ranger" (Webb 1991: 242).

Many more Hispanics served as privates in numerous units throughout Texas in the 1800s. At least 15 of them served in the units of John Coffee Hays in the first half of the 1840s (Muster and Pay Rolls 1841b; Ingmire 1982). Nine additional units included the names of 11 more Hispanic rangers during the Republic of Texas era (Ingmire 1982).

Capt. Owen Shaw listed 25 Hispanics on his rolls, with ranging periods starting on January 11, 1852, to as late as February 17, 1853 (Ingmire 1982). Six of these men were serving in the unit at the Battle of San Roque on September 17, 1852. Ranging out of their station in Laredo, Shaw and his men attacked the Indians in the San Roque Arroyo, killing 9 and wounding 11. Only one managed to escape (Webb 1991: 143–144). After the small battle Shaw's company was proclaimed "one of the best ever called into service" (Webb 1991: 144).

In 1852 and 1853, Capt. G. K. Lewis mustered in a ranger company that contained 13 more Hispanics (Ingmire 1982). In addition to those already accounted for to this point, at least 10 ranger units contained the names of 29 Hispanics in the field from 1847 to 1861 (Ingmire 1982[2]). One of those units, that of Capt. W. C. Dalrymple which included Francisco Falcon, Tiophilo Martine, and Justa Sanches, was ordered north to Cooke County in 1860 to protect settlements from Indian raids (Webb 1991: 199).

Various companies of the Frontier Forces enlisted the efforts of large numbers of Hispanics to quell problems in the early 1870s. Company H, led by Capt. Bland Chamberlain, carried the names of 12 Hispanics (Muster and Pay Rolls 1870b, 1871; Ingmire 1982). Capt. John R. Kelso commanded a unit ranging out of Camp Wood, near Uvalde, in 1870 and 1871. Ten men with Spanish surnames were counted among his troops (Muster and Pay Rolls 1870–1871b; Ingmire 1982). Company C, the unit of Capt. Peter Kleid, enlisted the support of nine Hispanic men in 1870 (Ingmire 1982). Capt. Manuel Bau, and Company A, patrolled the Maverick County region, basing their operation in Eagle Pass, Texas, in 1872 and 1873. Bau's unit contained 17 Hispanics (Ingmire 1982). In the 1870s, at least 7 more ranger units listed a total of 15 Hispanics serving in their ranks, along with their Anglo counterparts (Ingmire 1982[3]).

In addition to Jesus Sandoval, McNelly had at least seven more Hispanics who enlisted for various periods beginning in July 1875 and mustering out as late as May 31, 1876 (Ingmire 1982). Capt. Neal Coldwell mustered in Company F of the Frontier Battalion in 1874 (Gillett 1925: 67). L. Sanchez rode with the company for one month in 1874 while S. Guajardo served for longer durations in 1874, 1875, and 1876 (Ingmire 1982). Another company with a Hispanic guide was involved in a fight with robbers near Fort Stockton on July 31, 1880. All of the thieves were killed (Roberts 1914: 112–114).

Hispanics, with the understanding that they were contributing to the peace of the Texas frontier, served in the Texas Rangers throughout the nineteenth century. These men were respected as peace officers by the corps of rangers and by the Anglo and Mexican American citizens they served to protect.

Records revealed that nearly 400 men with Spanish surnames served in the Texas Rangers between 1838 and 1880, at least 10 of them in the capacity of an officer. Some of the units were entirely made up of Hispanics, but most of them consisted of both Mexican American and Anglo rangers. These men were equals. They slept on the same hard ground each night, ate the same meager fare at their fires, and rode hard in the saddle for hours on end. They fought the same enemies, whether Mexican, Anglo, or Indian. Their efforts protected both Hispanics and Anglos, especially along the border, from theft and murder. Their often brutal methods attested to the harshness of the times.

These men with Spanish roots should be written about in histories with the same pride and respect afforded them by the writers of the several memoirs cited in this essay. If the image of the ranger is that of the "strong, courteous fighter for truth and justice" (Samora et al. 1979: 4), then let that image characterize the hundreds of Hispanics who helped forge a civilization out of the Texas frontier as Texas Rangers.

NOTES

1. Alphabetical listing of men in the companies of Captains A. C. Hill, John Donelson, G. Hampton, Henry Berry, W. G. Tobin, and Andrew Herron.

2. Alphabetical listing of men in the companies of Captains Henry E. McCulloch, John G. Walker, Levi English, W. N. P. Martin, Peter Tumlinson, Thomas Johnson, William Woods, W. C. Dalrymple, A. B. Burleson, and Thomas Harrison.

3. Alphabetical listing of men in companies of Captains Franklin Jones, John W. Sansom, George Haby, Daniel Herster, Robert Ballentyne, Theodore Tuschinsky, and Lt. J. B. Tays.

REFERENCES

Acuna, Rodolfo. 1981. *Occupied America, A History of Chicanos.* Harper and Row, New York.

Durham, George, as told to Clyde Wantland. 1969. *Taming the Nueces Strip, The Story of McNelly's Rangers.* Reprint. University of Texas Press, Austin.

Ford, John Salmon. 1963. *Rip Ford's Texas,* edited by Stephen B. Oates. University of Texas Press, Austin.

Gillett, James B. 1925. *Six Years with the Texas Rangers, 1875-1881.* Yale University Press, New Haven.

Hill, A. C. 1860. Letter from A. C. Hill to Governor Sam Houston, Feb. 9, 1860. Archives Division, Texas State Library, Austin.

Ingmire, Frances Terry, compiler. 1982. *Texas Ranger Service Records.* Vols. I–VI. Ingmire Publications, St. Louis.

Jennings, Napoleon Augustus. c. 1930. *A Texas Ranger.* Turner Company, Dallas.

Malsch, Brownson. 1980. *Lone Wolf, The Only Texas Ranger Captain of Spanish Descent.* Shoal Creek Publishers, Inc., Austin.

Montejano, David. 1987. *Anglos and Mexicans in the Making of Texas, 1836–1986.* University of Texas Press, Austin.

Muster and Pay Rolls

Rolls of numerous ranger companies listed under commanding officers' names. Archives Division, Texas State Library, Austin.

1838   August–September. Rolls of Capt. Lewis Sanches.

1839a   June–July. Rolls of Capt. Lewis Sanches.

1839b   September 10–November 21. Rolls of Capt. Jose Gonzales.

1841a   January 20–May 20. Rolls of Capt. Antonio Perez.

1841b   July–September. Rolls of Capt. John C. Hayes.

1859   November 10–December 20. Rolls of Capt. Henry Berry.

1859–   Dec. 30, 1859–Jan. 1, 1860. Rolls of Sgt. A. C. Hill.
1860

1870a   October 8–December 31. Rolls of Capt. C. G. Falcón

1870b   November 14–December 31. Rolls of Capt. Bland Chamberlain.

1870–   September 1, 1870–April 30, 1871. Rolls of Capt. Gregorio
1871a   Garcia.

1870–   September 1, 1870–September, 1871. Rolls of Capt. John R.
1871b   Kelso.

1871   January 1–February 28. Rolls of Capt. Bland Chamberlain.

1874a   May 27–November 27. Rolls of Lt. Telesforo Montes.

1874b   June 13–December 13. Rolls of Lt. Refugio Benavides.

Reid, Samuel C. Jr. 1848. *The Scouting Expeditions of McCulloch's Texas Rangers*. G. B. Zieber and Co., Philadelphia.

Roberts, Dan W. 1914. *Rangers and Sovereignty*. Wood Printing and Engraving Co., San Antonio.

Samora, Julian, Joe Bernal, and Albert Pena. 1979. *Gunpowder Justice, A Reassessment of the Texas Rangers*. University of Notre Dame Press, Notre Dame.

Webb, Walter Prescott. 1991. *The Texas Rangers, A Century of Frontier Defense*. Reprint. University of Texas Press, Austin.

Wilkins, Frederick. 1996. *The Legend Begins, The Texas Rangers, 1823–1845*. State House Press, Austin.

★ 10 ★

THE "BATTLE" AT PEASE RIVER AND THE QUESTION OF RELIABLE SOURCES IN THE RECAPTURE OF CYNTHIA ANN PARKER

Paul H. Carlson and Tom Crum

"I will venture to say that there have been more different erroneous stories written and printed about Cynthia Ann Parker than any person who ever lived in Texas," wrote Araminta McClellan Taulman, a member of the famous Quanah Parker family, to *Frontier Times* editor J. Marvin Hunter in 1929. She may have been right—especially about the December 19, 1860, "battle" along Mule Creek near Pease River and the taking of Naudah (Cynthia Ann Parker) from her Comanche family and friends. Because the Comanches at Mule Creek were caught by surprise, were running away, put up no resistance except when cornered, and all but a few of them were killed in the village, the "battle" perhaps more accurately should be considered a massacre, as several historians have called it.[1]

Eyewitness reports of the fight—or more properly, "massacre"—and the recapture of Parker are often suspect and unreliable. They contain conflicting information, fabrications, and errors of major significance. Some of the eyewitnesses changed their stories (including written accounts), an important diary of a participant in the incident was rewritten by persons unknown years later, and the original copy of at least one crucial document is missing and perhaps stolen. Even the location of the battle site remains in question. For historians trying to sift through the confusing record, use of such accounts has led to predictable results: too many books and articles, from the first ones written in the 1880s to the most recent ones written in the last few years, have been based on the fabrications, altered reports, and refashioned diaries.[2] Consequently, a major need exists to examine extant eyewitness reports and to judge their reliability as historical documents.

Lawrence Sullivan "Sul" Ross, who led the Texas Ranger attack at Mule Creek, by changing his narrative of events throughout the following decades, used his participation in the affair at Pease River for political gain, not an uncommon occurrence in nineteenth-century Texas. Other accounts of the fight—Charles Goodnight's recollections, the rewritten diary of Jonathan Baker (the diary was not rewritten by Baker, it must be added) and especially probably non-participant Benjamin Gholson's oral testimony—are also problematic. Over time the brief engagement along Mule Creek, at least in our collective consciousness of myths and folklore, has gone from being remembered as a revenge attack to a major battle, and one that destroyed Comanche hegemony in northwest Texas. How did it happen? How did a brief, crushing blow on mostly women in a tiny hunting camp become in many histories a major battle and something of a *cause célèbre*? And, how is it that many of us who write about the so-called battle cannot get the story straight?

Answers to the first two questions bear upon at least three developments. First, they concern Sul Ross's growing political ambitions in the 1870s and afterward. Ross entered Texas politics in the 1870s, becoming a state senator in 1880 and governor in 1887. Presumably for political reasons, he changed his accounts of the Pease River incident—the official report of which has Ross playing a secondary part—to give himself a more central role in the fight and the recapture of Cynthia Ann Parker. Second, they relate to Parker's highly dramatic and sentimental return to Anglo civilization. To the Anglo-Texas world, although not to Naudah, her capture from Comanches and reunion with the extended Parker family became a popular and happy success story, one that people repeated often. And, third, the answers connect to the emergence after 1875 of Cynthia Ann's son Quanah to a position of Comanche prominence. As Quanah gained stature, the fight along Mule Creek and the capture of his mother Naudah moved into the realms of myth, legend, and folklore.

Answers to the question of why historians cannot get the story straight are more complex. They have to do with what one considers reliable sources, with getting the facts right, with altered and missing documents, and with the large number of differing stories and puzzling eyewitness statements. To illustrate the conundrum, consider briefly two differing accounts. In one, Texas Ranger Hiram B. Rogers who, like Sul Ross, fought at Mule Creek in 1860. "I was in the Pease river fight," he recalled in 1928, "but I am not very proud of it. That was not a battle at all, but just a killing of [women]. One or two [men] and sixteen [women] were killed."[3] A quite opposite view appears in James T. DeShields's *Cynthia Ann Parker: The Story of Her Capture* (1886), one of the earliest histories of the incident at Pease River. Based on a Sul Ross interview, DeShields, a book dealer and political friend of Ross, concluded about the event: "So signal a victory had never before been gained over the fierce and war-like Comanches; . . . The great Comanche confederacy was forever broken. . . . The blow was a most decisive one."[4]

Additionally, the conflicting stories transformed the identity of one of the Comanche men who died in the attack. From a lesser leader whose name was not mentioned in the earliest eyewitness reports, the man became a minor chief, Mohee. Later, eyewitnesses and subsequent secondary accounts turned him into a warrior and band leader whose reputation after the Pease River incident grew until he had become a person of some consequence—Puttack or

Peta Nocona, the husband of Naudah (Cynthia Ann) and supposedly "the head chief of the Nokoni Cornanches."[5] Nocona's name,
however, cannot be found on any of the contemporary lists of Comanche chiefs, and, moreover, Horace Jones, a U.S. Army scout and
an acquaintance of the Comanche warrior, said, "Peta Nocona was
not one of the 'big men' among the Indians."[6]

Such telling and retelling of the incident has led to the question
of what constitutes reliable sources in the fight at Pease River and
the recapture of Cynthia Ann Parker. At least five different men,
for example, each claimed he had identified the captured woman as
Parker, or at least to have been the first to recognize her as a white
person. And, later, one of the alleged eyewitnesses stated that when
the handful of Texas Rangers and soldiers attacked it, the Indian
village contained five hundred to six hundred Comanches with between 150 and 200 of them warriors.[7]

The events leading to the attack, to the recapture of Cynthia
Ann Parker, and ultimately to the question of reliable sources began in November 1860. Late in the month, a band of Comanche
warriors struck farms, ranches, and outlying settlements in Parker,
Young, Jack, and Palo Pinto counties west of Fort Worth. The Indians stole horses and mules, burned the house of Henry Reilly,
carried off clothes and material possessions, and killed at least six
people, including five women. One of the women was a pregnant
Martha Sherman, whom the Indian men tortured and scalped. She
survived three days before dying.[8]

Immediately after the bloody raid, a group of citizens from
Young County, under the command of a Capt. W. J. Mosley, rode
in pursuit of the war party. The citizens followed the Comanche
trail to a temporary village on the Pease River but there discovered
Indian warriors were present in numbers too large to be attacked.
Mosley quickly led his men back to the settlements to await the organization of a larger force.[9]

Such a force soon gathered. It contained three units. Sul Ross,
who in September 1860 had been authorized by Governor Sam

Houston to raise a company of "mounted volunteers" for "service in the neighborhood of [Fort] Belknap," commanded forty Texas Rangers. Capt. J. J. "Jack" Cureton led some sixty-eight or seventy or ninety-two private citizens—militiamen—from Palo Pinto and neighboring counties. And, First Sergeant John W. Spangler, Company H, Second Cavalry, headed a contingent of twenty Federal troops sent by Ross's friend Nathan G. Evans from Camp Cooper on the Clear Fork of the Brazos River in present-day Throckmorton County.[10]

On December 14, 1860, in very cold weather, the punitive force left its rendezvous camp along Salt Creek in Young County north of Fort Belknap. Four days later advanced scouts discovered a small but fresh trail of Indians, and Ross pushed forward with Spangler's Federal troops and about half of his Rangers. Because of the weakened condition of their horses, Cureton's militiamen and the remaining Rangers, some of whom were on foot, could not keep up and fell to the rear.

Early on the morning of December 19, having found a small Comanche village, Ross struck with his depleted force. With fewer than twenty Texas Rangers and twenty Federal troops he charged through the tiny hunting camp along Mule Creek not far from its junction with the Pease River in modern-day Foard County. His official report, dated January 4, 1861, indicates that "the village [consisted] of eight or nine grass tents, which the Indians, fifteen in number, were just deserting." Ross's men, who suffered no injuries (not even minor ones) in the attack, killed, the report indicates, twelve of the Comanches and captured three: a woman who turned out to be Cynthia Ann Parker, her daughter Topsannah (Prairie Flower), and a young boy whom Ross brought to Waco and named Pease Ross. The men collected "about forty head of animals," and the whole episode lasted just over twenty minutes—thirty at the most.[11]

In the weeks afterward, as news spread that the captured woman proved to be Cynthia Ann Parker, the engagement attracted state-wide attention. A girl the Comanches had taken in 1836 when she was about nine years old, Cynthia Ann had grown to womanhood among the Comanches, married a warrior, and bore three children. Without her, perhaps the Pease River incident would have remained another little-noted, though deadly, encounter between Comanches trying to hold onto their land while making a desperate living by raiding and Americans trying to carve out a home for themselves in the region along the western edge of settlement in northwest Texas.

The successful attack brought fame to Sul Ross. Although only twenty-two-years-old at the time of the Pease River fight, Ross gained more from the "battle" than anyone else. Like many before him, he used his Indian fighting and Civil War experiences for political gain, and, indeed, one contemporary claimed it was the "Pease River fight and the capture of Cynthia Ann Parker that made Sul Ross governor of Texas."[12]

The Pease River command was not Ross's first. In 1858, Ross had led a band of Indian auxiliaries with Federal troops into Indian Territory (Oklahoma), and he took part as a Texas Ranger captain under Col. Middleton T. Johnson in an unsuccessful Indian campaign in the spring and summer of 1860. Many people in northwest Texas believed Ross responsible for the failed Johnson expedition, and some thought he ought to hang for the debacle, blaming the failure on his association with Indians of the Brazos Reservation, where his father, Shapley Prince Ross, served as Indian agent from 1855 to 1858.[13] The resentment continued after Ross received an appointment from Governor Houston to raise his own Ranger company (his second) for service in Young and surrounding counties. Indeed, on October 13, 1860, at a barbecue in Palo Pinto the resentment led eighty men in attendance to sign a resolution requesting Ross to resign his new commission and leave the frontier.[14]

Ross was not alone in receiving the wrath of frontiersmen. Citizens in Palo Pinto, Young, and neighboring counties likewise did not appreciate the United States soldiers, such as those at Camp Cooper and Fort Belknap, stationed in northwest Texas. Apparently, they believed the Federal troops did little to protect them from Kiowa and Comanche raids and had kept them from attacking the Brazos River reservations before government authorities in 1859 removed the Indians and closed the reserves. Meanwhile, in the aftermath of Abraham Lincoln's presidential election victory in early November 1860 and the Southern secessionist movement it spawned, resentment against the Federal troops worsened. Amid such personal and political hostility came the raid at Pease River and its subsequent reports, reminiscences, diary entries, and questionable eyewitness statements.[15]

Ross provided varying accounts of the incident over a thirty year period, and they serve as something of a portal for viewing the eyewitness discrepancies. A few hours after the December 19, 1860, attack, Ross and his command rode back down the Pease, where they met Jack Cureton's company and the remaining Texas Rangers coming up the opposite side of the river. Ross made a brief statement about the fight, and, according to Jonathan Baker, who was one of Cureton's men, he told them among other things, "he had overtaken a party of 15 Indians and had killed 12 of them and had taken 3 prisoners!"[16]

In a second report, one made near Fort Belknap on December 23, 1860, just four days after the event, Ross told a newspaper correspondent about the attack. The *Dallas Herald* published the Ross comments on January 2, 1861. The newspaper quotes Ross as stating that thirteen Indians were killed, and the *Herald's* correspondent also states: "The entire party of Indians was either killed or taken prisoner." The numbers are similar to those in Sgt. John Spangler's report, wherein Spangler states, "We saw in advance of us a band of Indians about twenty-five in number." Spangler also reported, "[w]e succeeded in killing fourteen and taking three prisoners."[17] As for the number of Comanches killed, both the Ross and Spangler accounts differ a bit from the notes of Jonathan Baker. In his diary, Baker writes that after two days of investigation "[w]e cannot find but seven Indians killed, four [women] and three [men]." He provided a plausible explanation for the differences in numbers when he made the following diary entry:

Some of the men who came in late say that they trailed some six or eight Indians who made their escape during the fight yesterday. So Capt. Ross was mistaken about killing all the Indians. I think probably he was honestly mistaken, being deceived by the report of Sergt. Spangler of the Dragoons who reported to him that he killed a party of seven that ran in a different direction from where Ross was engaged. We cannot find but one in this place killed, but we find the trail of six leaving the place, hence we hesitantly conclude that Spangler lied and let the Indians get away.[18]

Contrary to anything he may have told Ross at the scene, in his military report Spangler wrote, "I regret to state that some of the Indians made their escape."[19]

In his third account, dated January 4, 1861, Capt. Ross filed his official report of the fight to Governor Sam Houston. The account landed in the Adjutant General's Office in Austin, where it remained until after the turn of century when it disappeared. In the long report, Ross said the battle occurred on December 19, 1860, and stated that his men killed twelve Indians, took three prisoners, and captured "about forty" horses. Not one of his men were injured, he noted, but Lt. M. W. Somerville "came very near being killed by the chief, who had dismounted, evidently determined to sell his life as dearly as possible."[20]

Ross and Baker, of course, were not the only participants at Mule Creek to leave a personal account of the attack. Among the most significant of the other accounts, but among the least used by scholars, are the two official reports of Sgt. John Spangler. On December 24, 1860, Spangler wrote a two-page note to his superior officer Capt. Nathan G. Evans, stationed at Camp Cooper. Understandably, the Spangler account deviates a bit from the Ross report of January 4, 1861, for as others have noted, "in a battle every man has his own point of view, and some of them see things different, and some see things that other participants do not see at all."[21] In his report, Spangler confirmed some of Capt. Ross's information. He wrote, for example, that the Comanches were "about twenty-five in number." He noted that Ross with two of his lieutenants and "about ten of his men (state troops)" provided assistance, "the remaining portion of his command could not give us any [help] on account of [the] poor condition of their animals, they not being able to keep up with us." He said, after "a hotly contested engagement of about half an hour," we killed fourteen Indians, took three prisoners, and captured "all their animals numbering forty-five, also all their tents and camp equipage."[22] In January 1861, Spangler, having been asked by his superiors to clarify issues of the incident, sent a second report to Capt. Evans. In it, Spangler was more specific and verbose, but the details did not change. He said, for example, that some of the Texas Rangers were ill equipped and rode horses too poor to keep up with the Federal troops. He saw only about five or six Rangers in the fight, and noted that the Federal troops and not the Rangers captured the white woman who turned out to be Cynthia Ann Parker. He again claimed fourteen dead Comanches.[23]

Meanwhile, Ross's second account, the short one given to a *Dallas Herald* correspondent on December 23, 1860, provided a hint of the errors and misinformation to come. He states: "I thrashed them out with my own company," ignoring the role Spangler's Federal troops from Camp Cooper played. Ross also noted that the expedition was "in cooperation with Captain [Cureton's] gallant company of citizens from Palo Pinto and other counties." Again he did not mention the Federal troops, who were in the fight, but he did mention Cureton's militiamen, who were not participants. The *Herald* correspondent, however, in something of a postscript to the Ross report, noted that Spangler and the twenty troopers were engaged in the "fight" and that the Ross command had taken about forty horses at the Indian village.[24] In mentioning Cureton's command, was Ross trying to regain favor with the citizens of Palo Pinto County? It had only been a little over two months previous since they had signed a resolution seeking his resignation and removal from the frontier.

Also, in not mentioning Spangler's troops, was Ross attempting to lessen the roll of the regular soldiers because of the accelerating secession movement after Lincoln's election and the Texas frontiersmen's contempt for the Federal troops?

Elsewhere, Ross presented a different story. In his official report of January 4, 1861, to Governor Houston, Ross praised Spangler and the regulars. Of Spangler, he wrote, "a braver man never lived." Of the presence of the Federal troops, he said that "much credit is due Captain [Nathan G.] Evans from the people of Texas for his willingness at all times to co-operate with those who desire to chastise the guilty savage." He also praised Cureton's men, writing that they were "a gallant company of ninety-two citizens, with whom I was anxious to co-operate."[25] Despite the praise for Spangler and Evans, however, Ross would adopt the more self-serving tone evident in the December 1860 *Dallas Herald* and in later accounts of the battle.

By the next decade, the story of the Pease River incident was a very different one from contemporary reports, and Sul Ross was responsible for many of the changes. His reports and accounts remain the key to understanding the fight along Mule Creek. They explain how the incident at Pease River, at least in our collective memory, became a major battle. They suggest how misinformation and errors found their way into our histories, and they illustrate how the question of what constitutes reliable sources in the battle at Pease River and the recapture of Cynthia Ann Parker remains tricky.

The *Galveston News* on June 3 and *The Dallas Weekly Herald* on June 19, 1875, both printed a letter covering the Pease River battle that Ross had written about 1872. Sent to John Robinson and the *Galveston News* at the time it was written, the letter was not published until June 3, 1875. In it Ross wanted to "correct" a brief statement by one J. Eliot of Navarro County that had appeared in *The Texas Almanac for 1872*. The short Eliot narrative did not cite Sul Ross and his men for capturing Cynthia Ann Parker; however, as Federal troops and not the Rangers had taken Cynthia Ann, as Ross later admitted, Eliot's note was in fact correct in not crediting Ross.[26]

In the letter Ross claimed "we had complete possession of all their supplies and three hundred and fifty head of horses, killing many of them and completely scattering the others." When compared with the "about forty" horses reported by the *Dallas Herald's* correspondent and stated in the Ross report to Sam Houston and the forty-five described in Spangler's report, Ross's numbers in 1875 seem considerably exaggerated.[27] Ross also claimed in the letter that two of Cynthia Ann Parker's "sons by an Indian husband were killed in the battle." Presumably he meant Quanah and Pee-nah (variously Peanut or Pecos). And, significantly, in this 1870s version of the Pease River attack, which he called a "correct history," Ross wrote, "I came up with Mohee, the Comanche chief of that party of Indians, and after a short fight I killed him."[28]

Also in the letter, Ross for the first time used the date of December 18, 1860, for the battle, a minor error that nonetheless continues to be repeated. The problem with the mistake is that it is now literally etched in stone: The state of Texas in 1936 engraved the date on a granite historical marker erected near the battle site. It is also the date given in the articles on Cynthia Ann Parker and Peta Nocona in *The New Handbook of Texas*. Not only is the December 18 date inconsistent with Sul Ross's first three reports of the attack, but also it conflicts with a diary entry by Jonathan Hamilton Baker, the eyewitness account of guide Peter Robertson, the official reports Sgt. Spangler made on December 24, 1860 just five days after the fight—and January 16, 1861, and the December 1860 post returns of Camp Cooper, each of which states that the battle was on December 19.[29]

Clearly the letter altered the Ross story: Ross carried forward the December 18 error in each of his subsequent accounts. The number of horses taken, killed, or scattered, and the supposed death of Cynthia Ann Parker's sons represent other differences from his official report of 1861. And, moreover, in the letter Ross took a central role in the battle when he wrote that he himself killed the Comanche leader Mohee.[30] (In Ross's subsequent reports, the name of the chief was Peta Nocona.) Although the error in the date of the battle is understandable, one cannot easily dismiss the two other discrepancies. The change in the number of horses and mules, for example, from about 40 to 350 seems unreasonable.

The change in the name of the chief is also problematic and also addresses the question of reliable sources. In the 1870s Ross said he killed Mohee. But in her biography of Sul Ross, Judith Benner, citing an entry in the Ross Family Papers, argued that in the 1858 battle at Wichita Village in Indian Territory Mohee wounded Ross. Before the warrior could deliver the final, fatal blow, however, Lt. James P. Major, afterwards a Confederate general, killed Mohee. Both Benner and DeShields state that Mohee was an old acquaintance of Ross, who had known the Comanche warrior since childhood. If this information is correct, Ross claimed in the 1870s that he killed an Indian leader near the Pease River whom he had known since childhood, and who had two years before the Pease River battle died after wounding and attempting to kill Ross.[31]

Around 1884, in yet another account of the Pease River attack, Sul Ross told his story to James DeShields, an account DeShields published in 1886 in his biography of Cynthia Ann Parker. John W. Wilbarger, with DeShields's permission, published the DeShields-Ross interview with only minor variations in *Indian Depredations in Texas* (1889). About the same time, Elizabeth Ross Clarke, also, it seems, relying on DeShields's interview with Ross for information about the Pease River fight, wrote a long, unpublished narrative of Sul Ross. Until recently the story in DeShields and Wilbarger—particularly Wilbarger as it has been more accessible—was the Ross version that most people writing about the incident used.[32]

In the DeShields interview Ross said he, having sent the Federal troops under Sgt. John Spangler to "cut off [the Comanche] retreat," attacked the camp with forty Texas Rangers. Also, Ross claimed he fought with Peta Nocona, whom he called "a noted warrior of great repute," and he stated that Nocona, after being shot "walked to a small tree . . . and leaning against it, began to sing a wild, weird song"—presumably his death song. Likewise, he announced that while on horseback chasing Nocona, who had "a young girl about fifteen years of age mounted on his horse behind him . . . I fired my pistol striking the girl . . . near the heart, killing her instantly." In the interview he noted that Cynthia Ann Parker's sons, Quanah and Pee-nah, had escaped. Obviously, Ross was once again making changes or additions: including the number of Texas Rangers involved, the killing of the double-riding girl, the escape of Quanah and Pee-nah, and the fight with Peta Nocona.[33]

The important differences in Ross's 1870s and 1880s accounts from his accounts of 1860 and 1861 relate to the claim of killing a chief or leader, the number of Rangers involved in the fight, which Ross seems to have significantly exaggerated, and the claim that he, rather than Federal troops, captured Cynthia Ann Parker. In 1894, Ross would admit to Susan Parker St. John, Parker's first cousin, that Federal troops had in fact captured Cynthia Ann.[34] These changes are significant. They emerged as Ross's political ambitions rose, and as the Pease River incident gained notoriety through changes in public perceptions of it as a battle of some importance rather than a revenge massacre.

Ross was aware of the potential political benefit of the fight along Mule Creek and the recovery of Cynthia Ann Parker. In October 1880, when he was a candidate for the Texas Senate, Ross wrote a letter to his friend Victor Rose. At the time Rose was in the process of compiling a political sketch concerning some of Ross's exploits, including the capture of Parker, and Ross wanted his part in the "battle" at Pease River embellished. In the letter, Ross concluded, "I am satisfied the publication of this would swell my vote greatly."[35]

In his official report, as noted, Ross did not mention that he killed a chief or any warrior. But in the 1870s letter he wrote that he killed Mohee. Ten years later he claimed the dead chief was Peta Nocona. DeShields referred to Nocona as "indomitable and fearless" and an "implacable chief."[36] If killing a man can produce fame and notoriety, it follows that the greater the victim the greater the fame (as in the assassination of an American president), and in the political climate of nineteenth-century Texas, Ross stood to receive more attention, and to gain a larger measure of prestige, in having killed Peta Nocona, "a noted warrior of great repute" and the father of the great Quanah Parker, than to have killed Mohee or some other lesser chief.[37]

Clearly, a man died along Mule Creek in what has been described as a hand-to-hand fight, but the person was probably not a major chief nor was he likely Peta Nocona. Horace Jones, the government interpreter stationed at Camp Cooper in 1860 when Cynthia Ann Parker arrived there, said he saw Nocona a year or two after the battle and talked with him. As early as 1886, shortly after DeShields's book appeared claiming Ross fought Nocona, Quanah denied his father was at Mule Creek or was killed there. He repeated the denial in 1896, at the Texas State Fair in Dallas in 1909, and again in 1910.[38]

Charles Goodnight, the famous Texas Panhandle rancher, was also at the Pease River attack. He served as a civilian scout for Jack Cureton's militiamen and watched some of the fighting from a low hill. His tale adds further to the question of reliable sources.[39] Goodnight stated that he and seven or eight others were on the field before the fight ended, but not in time to take part in it. He saw enough of the engagement to state, "[t]he Rangers passed through the [women] and shot the men as they came to them. The Sergeant and his men fell in behind the [women]," he said, "and killed every one of them, almost in a pile . . . . To the credit of the old Texas Rangers," he concluded, "not one of them shot a [woman] that day. The Sergeant in charge of the military squad probably did not know them from [the men] and probably did not care."[40] Goodnight's desire to put a good light on the Texas Rangers produced additional contradictions. Goodnight, for example, stated that the Indian boy who was captured was riding double behind the chief. Accordingly, in an attempt to lighten his horse's load, the chief threw the boy off, and Ross then saved the youth.

The Ross versions differ on this point. Ross, in his 1861 official report, has the chief dismounting, "evidently determined to sell his life as dearly as possible." In the 1870s, he writes, he came up to Mohee and killed him. About 1884 he claimed a Comanche girl, not a boy, was riding double behind the chief and that he shot and killed her, and her dying fall from the horse dismounted the chief. Perhaps, we might speculate, in his desire to convey the idea that Texas Rangers killed no women, Goodnight substituted the boy for the girl, and because the boy was not killed, Goodnight had the chief pushing him off the horse, rather than Ross shooting him. [41]

Like Sul Ross and Charles Goodnight, Jonathan Baker left an account of his participation in the incident at Pease River. There are no questions concerning the authenticity of Jonathan Baker's original diary, but concerns exist about the typed copy of his diary. The typed version is, unfortunately, the version most often cited.[42] In 1932, Texas historian J. Evetts Haley secured the typed copy of the diary from Baker's daughter Elizabeth Baker in Seattle, Washington. Now located in the records of the Dolph Briscoe Center for American History at the University of Texas at Austin, it is a bit different from the earlier, handwritten version with its improved prose, corrected grammar, and material that was not part of the original diary. A person or persons unknown made the changes.[43] The errors in the typed diary begin with Baker's first name, given in the typed version as "James." In the account concerning the Pease River activities, the typed copy omits words and phrases that exist in the original diary, paraphrases other portions, and in one instance adds a lengthy, nearly preposterous entry that one can only conclude is fiction. Although he cited the typed copy as a reference in his book on Charles Goodnight, J. Evetts Haley recognized that at least a portion of the entry was erroneous.[44]

The most troubling and problematic accounts of the battle along Mule Creek and the recapture of Cynthia Ann Parker are the two interviews of Benjamin Franklin Gholson. Although in both of them Gholson claims to have been a member of Ross's Texas Ranger company and to have participated in the battle, these claims are questionable. The first of the accounts is contained in an interview he gave J. A. Rickard in August 1928, some sixty-seven years after the battle, when Gholson was eighty-six-years old. He provided the second account three years later in an interview with Felix Williams and Harvey Chelsey.[45] Gholson's accounts deviate substantially in several ways from other participants. Gholson, for example, claims that Peta Nocona and some of the warriors formed an oblong circle, and used their horses for breast works. None of the other first-hand accounts mentioned that the Indians formed such a circle. Gholson also claims that after a twelve-mile chase with eleven other Texas Rangers he counted seventy Indians sitting on their horses, and they were carrying thirty-two dead or wounded companions.[46] Gholson's figures regarding the number of Indians conflict with all other accounts. Moreover, it seems unlikely that the Rangers' horses could have held out for any chase close to twelve miles and back, for Sgt. Spangler, in his Christmas Eve, 1860, report noted that the Rangers' horses, as there was little or no grass along their line of march, were in an exhausted condition because the men had not been able to feed them scarcely anything but cottonwood bark for seven days. Ross in his 1875 *Dallas Weekly Herald* letter also commented on the broken-down condition of Ranger and civilian horses—for the same reasons Spangler noted: poor forage.[47]

Gholson also reported that on the return trip from the twelve-mile chase he and the other Texas Rangers brought in seven Indian scalps. If we are to accept his account, he and eleven other Rangers traveled twenty-four miles on jaded horses and chased 109 Indians for twelve of the miles, killing at least seven of them and wounding or killing at least another thirty-two, with the remaining seventy Comanches making their escape from twelve Rangers. Furthermore, Gholson claimed that when they left for home, the men held twenty-six Indian scalps, two of which were from women. One Indian had not been scalped, he stated.[48] Again, the Gholson figures regarding the number of Comanches killed substantially disagree with those of other participants.

Gholson's 1931 interview with Felix Williams and Harvey Chelsey is even more troublesome. In it Gholson states that there were between five hundred and six hundred Indians at the Mule Creek camp, with 150 to 200 of them being warriors. During the interview he reported a second time that Peta Nocona and the Comanches formed an oblong circle, using their horses for breastworks, but this time he stated that the Rangers and Federal troopers killed seventeen Indians in the circle, five in one volley.[49] In this interview, Gholson also said the men captured 370 horses, a number that, as we have seen, is sharply out of line with the accounts of all other participants except Ross's 1870s claim that they shot or scattered 350 horses. No other eyewitness uses such high figures. Perhaps Gholson, recalling events of some sixty-seven and more years in the past, was describing another Texas Ranger-Indian fight. Perhaps he was among the Texas Rangers whose horses had broken down, thus putting him several miles away. Or, perhaps he was not at the "battle" at Pease River and was fabricating the story, relying on the accounts of it that he had read. He repeats Ross's error of December 18 for the fight and he follows Ross's 1870s figure on the number of horses captured, although on two other occasions Ross had claimed "about forty." As his accounts are not reliable, was Gholson deliberately offering some good yarns and exaggerated tales to amuse himself and his interviewers?

Although he had probably read about the incident, Benjamin Gholson most likely was not present at the Pease River fight. On April 16, 1917, he filed an application for a pension for having participated in the Indian wars. On the first page of his application, he states that he served under the following commands: Capt. John Williams, October 1, 1858, to March 1859; Capt. J. M. Smith, March 1, 1860, to May 20, 1860; L. S. Ross, May 1860 to August 11, 1860; and S. L. Ross from September 20, 1860, to last of March 1861.[50] Thus, on his pension application Gholson transposed the initials before the name of Ross, names that existed directly above and below one another on the document. Was the transposition intentional or a mistake? The two units—L. S. and S. L.—represent Sul Ross's first and second companies, and the Pease River fight occurred during the time that Gholson claimed on his pension application that he was in the service of S. L. Ross's company—or Ross's second company. But, Gholson's name does not appear on the muster roll/payroll of Sul Ross's second company.[51]

On July 9, 1917, a few months after submitting the application, E. C. Tieman, Acting Commissioner of the Bureau of Pensions, sent a form to Gholson. The form, designed to prevent fraud in the pension process (among other things), contained a number of questions relating to Gholson's service. His responses, dated July 27, are revealing. In answer to the question "When did you enlist?" Gholson wrote, "Williams 2nd Co. Oct. 1st, 1858. Ross 1st Co. May 1860. Smith Co. March, 1860." He did not mention Ross's Second Company.[52] In answer to the question "When were you discharged?" Gholson wrote, "March, 1859, August 1860, May 1860." There is no mention of a discharge date of March 1861, the date mentioned by Gholson for his service under S. L. Ross. In answer to the question "The name of organizations in which you served?" Gholson wrote, "Williams 2nd Co., Ross' 1st Co. M. T. Johnson Reg., Smith's Co:[53]

In March 1860, Governor Sam Houston had authorized Col. Middleton T. Johnson to form a Texas Ranger command. Five companies initially formed. Capt. J. M. Smith raised the Waco company, which Ross joined. In May 1860, Smith received a promotion to lieutenant colonel of the entire command, and Ross won election to take Smith's position in the Waco company. Thereafter, the company became known as Ross's 1st Company.[54] Thus, Johnson's, Smith's, and Ross's 1st Company were all the same, and they disbanded in August of 1860. There is no roll for Capt. J. M. Smith's Company of Rangers for 1860 on file in the Archives of the Texas State Library. Clearly, there are questions concerning Benjamin F. Gholson's accounts of the attack at Pease River, and almost as clearly, it seems, he was not there. Unfortunately, many biographers and historians have relied on the Gholson reminiscences to write their version of the fight at Mule Creek.[55]

Finally, what happened to Sul Ross's official report of January 4, 1861? And why did it disappear? The original document, according to E. M. Phelps, assistant adjutant general of Texas, was on file in the adjutant general's office as late as February 1908. In fact, that month Phelps sent a copy of the Ross report to editors of the *San Antonio Express* in response to "a recently published interview with [a] Major Loeffler . . . who claims to have effected the capture of [Cynthia] Ann Parker and her baby, Quanah Parker, in the Indian fight on Pease river, December 19, 1860."[56] In his cover letter, Phelps wrote:

This claim on the part of Major [Loeffler], as shown by the original report of Capt. L. S. Ross, commanding company Texas rangers, to Gov. Sam Houston, made on January 4, 1861, not quite two weeks after the fight, has no foundation . . . the report showing that the capture, which Major Loeffler claims the credit for making, was made by Lieutenant [Tom] Killeher [Kelliher] of Ross' company. . . . In corroboration of the above a copy of the original report, now on file in the adjutant general's department, is printed.[57]

Sometime afterward the original report disappeared. J. Evetts Haley, while working on his biography of Charles Goodnight, probably looked for it in 1936 or before, and could not find it. As late as 1994, officials in the Texas State Library and Archives could not locate it. "I have searched Governor Houston's records for any reports on the Pease River incident from Sul Ross," wrote Laura K. Saegert, an archivist with the Archives Division of the Texas State Library, on July 1, 1994. "I also checked the Texas Ranger correspondence and the Adjutant General's correspondence and found no reports in those files at all."[58] Was it misfiled after Phelps sent a copy to the *Express?* Was it pilfered?

In addition to the problems with the reports and accounts of the Pease River incident, some questions remain as to the location of the battle. The 1936 Texas State Centennial marker is located approximately one-and-one-half miles from the junction of Mule

Creek and the Pease River. It is on land that once belonged to John Wesley, who was reputed to have been Foard County's earliest permanent Anglo settler.[59] In 1942, Rupert N. Richardson, one of the great historians of Texas, wrote that in 1923 he had visited the site with Wesley. Richardson's description of the site suggests that Wesley showed him the area where the state marker has been placed. Richardson described the site: "The scene of the fight was at a place where the creek and the river ran almost parallel. Chains of high sand hills run parallel with the streams, the chain between the creek and the river being especially pronounced."[60]

The Richardson picture carefully summarizes the battlefield as indicated by the state marker. It does not accurately represent the site according to reports of the participants. Sul Ross, for example, characterized the camp as being "located on a small stream winding around the base of a hill."[61] Charles Goodnight recounted the site as follows: "we came to where this creek entered the Pease. A short distance from the river a row of sand hills intersected the course of the creek, and just south of these the Indians were camped . . . from the creek to the foot of the first hills to the west was about a mile and a half of perfectly level ground."[62] The Ross and Goodnight descriptions place the Indian camp much closer to the junction of Mule Creek and Pease River than the state marker. Indeed, none of the area around the marker fits the Ross and Goodnight sketches. Approximately five hundred yards from its mouth, Mule Creek cuts a low ridge of sand hills. Here, in all probability, was the location of the Comanche camp, and where the attack started. Because it was principally a "running fight," or chase, the so-called battle spread over a wide area south of the Pease River. Thus, some shooting may have occurred in the vicinity of the marker, but it was not the place of the Indians' camp, or the site of the major part of the attack.

Whatever may have actually happened or wherever the killings took place, the December 19, 1860, "battle" along Mule Creek near the Pease River—the slaughter of mostly women that lasted just over twenty minutes—and the recapture of Cynthia Ann Parker represent events that have moved into the realms of myth, legend, and folklore. Regrettably, the altered stories, missing documents, and conflicting reports relative to the paired events have led to a tangled web of semi-truths and a whole set of histories based on unreliable knowledge.

NOTES

1. Araminta McClellan Taulman, "The Capture of Cynthia Ann Parker," *Frontier Times* 6 (May 1929): 311. For comments that the Pease River fight was a massacre, see Margaret Schmidt Hacker, *Cynthia Ann Parker: The Life and the Legend* (El Paso: Texas Western Press, 1990), 21; Gary Clayton Anderson, *The Conquest of Texas: Ethnic Cleansing in the Promised Land, 1820–1875* (Norman: University of Oklahoma Press, 2005), 332; and Bill Neeley, *The Last Comanche Chief: The Life and Times of Quanah Parker* (New York: John Wiley & Sons, Inc., 1995), 47–49.

2. See, for example, J. W. Wilbarger, *Indian Depredations in Texas* (1889; repr., Austin: Steck Company, 1935), 333–39; Robert H. Williams, "The Case for Peta Nocona," *Texana* 10, No. 1 (1972): 55–72; Roger N. Conger, "Lawrence Sullivan Ross," in Roger Conger, et al., *Rangers of Texas* (Waco: Texian Press, 1969), 124–27; and Jo Ella Powell Exley, *Frontier Blood: The Saga of the Parker Family* (College Station: Texas A&M University Press, 2001), 154–60.

3. Hiram B. Rogers to J. A. Rickard, August 1928, "Recollections of Ranger H. B. Rogers of the Capture of Cynthia Ann Parker" (interview transcript), filed with Recollections of B. F. Gholson at the Dolph Briscoe Center for American History, University of Texas at Austin (hereafter, Rogers, "Recollections").

4. James T. DeShields, *Cynthia Ann Parker: The Story of Her Capture* (1886; repr., Dallas: Chama Press, 1991), 44-45. See also Wilbarger, *Indian Depredations in Texas,* 338–39; Elizabeth Ross Clarke, "Life of Sul Ross," n.d., Ross Family Papers, Texas Collection, Baylor University, Waco, Texas; and John Henry Brown, *Indian Wars and Pioneers of Texas* (1893; repr., Austin: State House Press, 1988), 317. Wilbarger, with DeShields's permission, copied from the DeShields book, and it is likely that Clarke also borrowed heavily from DeShields.

5. Quote in Stanley Noyes, *Los Comanches: The Horse People, 1751–1845* (Albuquerque: University of New Mexico Press, 1993), 307. See also Neeley, *The Last Comanche Chief,* 1.

6. See Gerald Betty, *Comanche Society before the Reservation* (College Station: Texas A&M University Press, 2002), 4; Thomas W. Kavanagh, *Comanche Political History: An Ethnohistorical Perspective, 1706–1875* (Lincoln: University of Nebraska Press, 1996), 353. Second quote in Marion T. Brown's letter

to her father, Dec. 20, 1886, in *Marion T. Brown: Letters from Fort Sill, 1886–1887,* ed. C. Richard King (Austin: Encino Press, 1970), 36; Jack K. Selden, *Return: The Parker Story* (Palestine, Tex.: Clacton Press, 2006), 230; and Anderson, *The Conquest of Texas,* 332.

7. Benjamin F. Gholson to Felix Williams and Harvey Chelsey (interview), Aug. 26, 1931, in Rupert N. Richardson, ed., "The Death of Nocona and the Recovery of Cynthia Ann Parker," *Southwestern Historical Quarterly* 46 (July 1942): 17 (hereafter, Gholson, interview with Williams and Chelsey, 931). (Richardson and Walter Prescott Webb disagreed over the spelling of the names of Williams and Chelsey. See "Texas Collection," pp. 63–74 from that same issue of the *Quarterly.*) For other large numbers of Comanches, see Benjamin F. Gholson to J. A. Rickard, "Recollections of B. F. Gholson" (interview transcript) August 1928, Dolph Briscoe Center for American History, Benjamin F. Gholson Collection, The University of Texas at Austin (hereafter cited as Gholson, Recollections, 1928); DeShields, *Cynthia Ann Parker,* 45.

8. Joseph Carroll McConnell, *The West Texas Frontier* (Palo Pinto, Tex.: Texas Legal Bank & Book Co., 1939), 26–32; Elmer Kelton, *The Indian in Frontier News* (San Angelo: Talley Press, 1993), 59–61; Doyle Marshall, *A Cry Unheard* (Aledo, Tex.: Annetta Valley Farm Press, 1990), 29–35; Robert M. Utley, *Lone Star Justice: The First Century of the Texas Rangers* (New York: Oxford University Press, 2002), 121; Hatcher, *Cynthia Ann Parker,* 24; and Anderson, *The Conquest of Texas,* 332.

9. Lawrence Sullivan Ross to Governor Sam Houston, Dec. 8, 1860, Governor's Papers (Archives Division, Texas State Library, Austin). For the Mosley reference see McConnell, *The West Texas Frontier,* 33; and Jack Loftin, *Trails through Archer* (Austin: Nortex Press, 1979), 55.

10. Judith Ann Benner, *Sul Ross: Soldier, Statesman, Educator* (College Station: Texas A&M University Press, 1983), 47, 49, 50; Richardson, ed., "The Death of Nocona and the Recovery of Cynthia Ann Parker," 15–16; U. S. Department of War, Returns from United States Military Posts, 1800–1916, Camp Cooper, December 1860, Roll 253, M-617, RG 94 (microfilm: National Archives; hereafter cited as Post Returns, Camp Cooper). Quote in Amelia W. Williams and Eugene C. Barker (eds.), *The Writings of Sam Houston* (8 vols; Austin: University of Texas Press, 1938–43), 8: 139–140.

11. The description presented here follows the earliest accounts of the Pease River fight: "From the Frontier," *Dallas Herald,* Jan. 2, 1861; "Indian News," the *Galveston Civilian,* Jan. 15, 1861; and Capt. Sul Ross to Gov. Sam Houston, Jan. 4, 1861, as it appeared in "More About the Capture of Woman Prisoner," *San Antonio Express,* Feb. 23, 1908, and in "Cynthia Ann Parker Again," *The Beeville Bee,* Feb. 28, 1908 (hereafter Ross to Houston, Jan. 4, 1861). See also Peter Robertson, interview, c. 1920-21, in J. Marvin Hunter, ed., "The Cap-

ture of Cynthia Ann Parker," *Frontier Times* 16 (May 1939): 364–65 (hereafter, Robertson, interview with Hunter, c. 1920).

12. Cited in Benner, *Sul Ross*, 58.

13. See L. W. Kemp, "Ross, Shapley Prince," in Ron Tyler, Douglas E. Barnett, Roy R. Barkley, Penelope C. Anderson, and Mark F. Odintz (eds.). *The New Handbook of Texas* (6 vols.; Austin: Texas State Historical Association, 1996), 5: 690; Kenneth F. Neighbours, *Robert Simpson Neighbors and the Texas Frontier, 1836–1859* (Waco: Texian Press, 1975), 162; and F. Todd Smith, *From Dominance to Disappearance: The Indians of Texas and the Near Southwest, 1786–1859* (Lincoln: University of Nebraska Press, 2005), 219–220.

14. Jonathan Hamilton Baker, entry for Oct. 13, 1860, Diary of Jonathan Hamilton Baker (Private Collection, Tarrant County Historical Commission, Fort Worth; hereafter cited as handwritten diary.) See also Judith Ann Benner, "Ross, Lawrence Sullivan," in Ron Tyler, et al. (eds.), *The New Handbook of Texas*, 5: 688; Benner, *Sul Ross*, 38, 45.

15. See, for example, C. C. Reister, "Early Accounts of Indian Depredations," *West Texas Historical Association Year Book* 2 (1928): 18–21; Benner, *Sul Ross*, 36–37; Anderson, *The Conquest of Texas*, 321–317; and Tom Crum, 'The Folklorization of the Battle on Pease River," *West Texas Historical Association Year Book* 72 (1992): 70–71.

16. Baker, entry for Dec. 19, 1860, handwritten diary.

17. "From the Frontier," *Dallas Herald*, Jan. 2, 1861; First Sgt. John W. Spangler to Capt. Nathan G. Evans, Second Cavalry, Camp Cooper, Dec. 24, 1860, submitted with Evans to Maj. M. A. Nichols, Assistant Adjutant General, Department of Texas, Dec. 26, 1860, Letters Sent, Camp Cooper, E. 1, RG 393, Part V (National Archives).

18. Baker, entry for Dec. 20, 1860, handwritten diary.

19. Spangler to Evans, Dec. 24, 1860.

20. Ross to Houston, Jan. 4, 1861; "From the Frontier," *Dallas Herald*, Jan. 2, 1861.

21. Taulman, "The Capture of Cynthia Ann Parker," 312.

22. Spangler to Evans, Dec. 24, 1860.

23. John W. Spangler to Nathan G. Evans, Jan. 16, 1861, in "Spangler Report," *San Antonio Ledger*, Feb. 2, 1861 (hereafter Spangler to Evans, Jan. 16, 1861).

24. See "From the Frontier," *Dallas Herald*, Jan. 2, 1861. See also "Indian News," *Galveston Civilian*, Jan. 15, 1861; "The White Captive," *Galveston Civilian*, Feb. 55, 1861; and Ross to Houston, Jan. 4, 1861.

25. Ross to Houston, Jan. 4, 1861. The official report, which disappeared from the records of the Texas Adjutant General's Office sometime after 1908,

appeared, in the *San Antonio Express* on February 23, 1908 (p. 26) under the headline "More About the Capture of Woman Prisoner," and on February 28, 1908, in *The Beeville Bee* under the headline "Cynthia Ann Parker Again" (p. 1). The report also can be found in *Texas Extra: A Newspaper History of the Lone Star State,* comp. Eric C. Caren (Edison, NJ.: Castle Books, 1999), 103.

26. "The Parker Captives," *Galveston News,* June 3, 1875; "The Parker Captives," *The Dallas Weekly Herald,* June 19, 1875; J. Eliot, "Frontier Legends," *The Texas Almanac for 1872* (Galveston: Richardson, Belo & Co., 1872), 162. See also "The Parker Captives—General L. S. Ross," *The Dallas Weekly Herald,* June 19, 1875.

27. "From the Frontier," *Dallas Herald,* Jan. 2, 1861; Spangler to Evans, Dec. 24, 1860; Baker, entry for Dec. 19, 1860, handwritten diary, Rogers, "Recollections."

28. "The Parker Captives," *Galveston News,* June 3, 1875; "The Parker Captives," *The Dallas Weekly Herald,* June 19, 1875.

29. Margaret Schmidt Hacker, "Parker, Cynthia Ann," in Tyler, et al. (eds.), *The New Handbook of Texas,* 5:57–58; Robert H. Williams, "Peta Nocona," in Tyler, et al. (eds.), *The New Handbook of Texas,* 5:165; Baker, entry for Dec. 19, 1860, handwritten diary; Robertson, interview with Hunter, c. 1920; Spangler to Evans, Dec. 24, 1860; and Spangler to Evans, Jan. 16, 1861; Post Returns, Camp Cooper, December 1860. On the matter of the wrong date see also DeShields, *Cynthia Ann Parker,* 41; Hacker, *Cynthia Ann Parker,* 24; and Utley, *Lone Star Justice,* 122.

30. "From the Frontier," *Dallas Herald,* Jan. 2, 1861; Ross to Houston, Jan. 4, 1861; Wilbarger, *Indian Depredations in Texas,* 335; Clarke, "Life of Sul Ross," 57; "The Parker Captives," *Galveston News,* June 3, 1875; "The Parker Captives," *The Dallas Weekly Herald,* June 19, 1875.

31. Benner, *Sul Ross,* 29; Clarke, "Life of Sul Ross," 51; Wilbarger, *Indian Depredations in Texas,* 330; W. S. Nye, *Carbine and Lance* (Austin: Shelly and Richard Morrison, 1994), 80. See also William Y. Chalfant, *Without Quarter: The Wichita Expedition and the Fight on Crooked Creek* (Norman: University of Oklahoma Press, 1991), 41–44; and Kavanagh, *Comanche Political History,* 364, 375.

32. DeShields, *Cynthia Ann Parker,* 41–45; Wilbarger, *Indian Depredations in Texas,* 333–39; Clarke, "Life of Sul Ross." See also E. L. Connally, ed., "Capture of Cynthia Ann Parker," *Texana* 2 (1964): 74-77.

33. DeShields, *Cynthia Ann Parker,* 41-42, 44.

34. L. S. Ross to Susan Parker St. John, interview transcript, 1894, Joseph Taulman Papers, Dolph Briscoe Center for American History, The University of Texas at Austin.

35. Perry Wayne Shelton, *Personal Civil War Letters of General Lawrence Sullivan Ross with Other Letters* (Austin: Shelly and Richard Morrison, 1994), 80.

36. DeShields, *Cynthia Ann Parker,* 38, 44; Wilbarger, *Indian Depredations in Texas,* 334, 338. See also Clarke, "Life of Sul Ross," 58.

37. DeShields, *Cynthia Ann Parker,* 42; Wilbarger, *Indian Depredations in Texas,* 336. See also William Warren Sterling, *Trails and Trials of a Texas Ranger* (Norman: University of Oklahoma Press, 1968), 282.

38. See letter of Marion Brown to her father, Dec. 20, 1886, in *Marion T. Brown: Letters from Fort Sill,* ed. C. Richard King, 35; "Quanah Parker Sets History Straight," *The Semi-Weekly Farm News* (Dallas), Oct. 29, 1909; and Paul I. Wellman, "Cynthia Ann Parker," *Chronicles of Oklahoma* 12, No. 2 (1934): 163–70. For a thorough discussion of the whole issue, see Tom Crum, "Folklorization of the Battle on Pease River," *West Texas Historical Association Year Book* 72 (1996): 69–85. For a different view, see Williams, "The Case for Peta Nocona," 55–72.

39. J. Evetts Haley, ed., "Charles Goodnight's Indian Recollections," *Panhandle-Plains Historical Review* 1 (1928): 20-29; J. Evetts Haley, *Charles Goodnight: Cowman and Plainsman* (Norman: University of Oklahoma Press, 1955), 54-58.

40. Haley, *Charles Goodnight,* 55.

41. For Goodnight's version see Haley, *Charles Goodnight,* 55, 56; and Haley, ed., "Charles Goodnight's Indian Recollections," 21–27. For the Ross version see Ross to Houston, January 4, 1861; "The Parker Captives," *The Dallas Weekly Herald,* June 19, 1875; DeShields, *Cynthia Ann Parker,* 41–44; and Wilbarger, *Indian Depredations in Texas,* 336–37.

42. See, for example, Benner, *Sul Ross,* and Exley, *Frontier Blood.* Although J. Evetts Haley used the typed version when writing *Charles Goodnight,* he understood that it had problems.

43. Baker, handwritten diary. The second Baker diary is Diary of Jonathan [James] Hamilton Baker, 1858–1918 (typescript), The Dolph Briscoe Center for American History, University of Texas at Austin (hereafter cited as typescript diary).

44. Baker, typescript diary, 95; Haley, *Charles Goodnight,* 57–58.

45. Gholson, Recollections, 1928; Gholson interview with Williams and Chelsey, 1935, 16-21.

46. Gholson, Recollections, 1928. See also, Francis M. Peveler, "Reminiscences," Oct. 14, 1932, Notes to J. Evetts Haley, Nita Stewart Haley Memorial Library, J. Evetts Haley History Center, Midland, Texas.

47. Spangler to Evans, Dec. 24, 1860; "The Parker Captives," *The Dallas Weekly Herald*, June 19, 1875.

48. Gholson, Recollections, 1928.

49. Gholson, interview with Williams and Chelsey, 1931, 16–18.

50. Declaration for Survivor's Pension for B. F. Gholson—Indian Wars, United States Pension Office, Apr. 16, 1917 (Archives Division. Texas State Library, Austin. Hereafter cited as Gholson, Pension Application.). For a different view see Robert W. Stephens, *Texas Rangers Indian War Pensions* (Quanah, Tex.: Nortex Press, 1975), 33–34.

51. Muster Roll/Payroll, L. S. Ross Company, Texas Rangers, Nov. 17, 1860 (Archives Division, Texas State Library, Austin). See also B. F. Gholson, "Record of Service—Indian Wars," July 1, 1919, Adjutant General's Department, State of Texas, Austin; Payroll Records, Texas Rangers, L. S. Ross's Ranger Company, C. R. Johns, Comptroller of the State of Texas (Archives Division, Texas State Library, Austin).

52. Questionnaire relative to military service for B. F. Gholson, United States, Bureau of Pensions, Department of Interior, Washington, D. C., July 1 and July 9, 1917 (Archives Division. Texas State Library, Austin).

53. Ibid.

54. Benner, *Sul Ross,* 38–40.

55. See, for example, Benner, *Sul Ross;* Exley, *Frontier Blood;* Charles M. Robinson III, *The Men Who Wear the Star: The Story of the Texas Rangers* (New York: Random House, 2000); Frederick Wilkins, *Defending the Borders: The Texas Rangers, 1848–1861* (Austin: State House Press, 2001).

56. "More About the Capture of Cynthia Ann Parker," *San Antonio Express,* Feb. 23, 1908, and "Cynthia Ann Parker Again," *The Beeville Bee,* Feb. 28, 1908.

57. "More About the Capture of Cynthia Ann Parker," *San Antonio Express,* Feb. 23, 1908.

58. Laura K. Saegert to Judge Tom Crum, July 1, 1994 (original in possession of Tom Crum).

59. Williams, "The Case for Peta Nocona," 55.

60. Richardson, ed., "The Death of Nocona and the Recovery of Cynthia Ann Parker," 16.

61. DeShields, *Cynthia Ann Parker,* 62; Wilbarger, *Indian Depredations in Texas,* 336.

62. Haley, *Charles Goodnight,* 54.

★ 11 ★

CAPTURING THE GRAND MOGUL
(JOHN WESLEY HARDIN)

Leon Metz

As late as June 17, 1874, the Texas Rangers suspected John Wesley Hardin still considered Comanche home. Ranger W. J. Maltby wrote Major John B. Jones from Brownwood, and said the local people are still "severely threatened by the notorious outlaw John Hardin and a band of desperadoes that he has enlisted under his banner." Maltby believed Hardin was still in the county and "seeking the lives of the best citizens." For the next three years newspapers frequently reported Hardin activity in Texas when he actually was in Alabama and Florida.[1]

Hardin considered vanishing into Mexico as well as Great Britain, but a Hardin on the run needed funds. Joe Clements and Neill Bowen were in Kansas where their cattle remained unsold, awaiting a favorable market. A desperate John Wesley dispatched his younger brother Jefferson to Kansas with instructions to sell regardless of price. Jeff returned with five hundred dollars. Neill Bowen followed shortly thereafter, and he and Hardin settled accounts. Hardin said he had considerable money when he left the state.[2]

Brenham, Texas, City Marshal Harry Swain, a relative of Jane, took her and daughter Mollie to New Orleans by boat. Hardin rode horseback across the land route, traveling under the alias of Walker. From New Orleans he went to Cedar Keys, Florida, then on to Gainsville near the geographic center of the state. Hardin wrote Jane on September 8, 1874, complaining that he had problems paying his board, and it was good that he was living alone.

Nevertheless, he purchased Samuel H. Burnett's Gainsville Saloon. On opening day Bill McCulloch and Frank Harper, two Texas stockmen, strolled in. Everybody recognized each other although the cattlemen promised never to reveal Hardin's new identity or hiding place. By now John Wesley Hardin had become John H. Swain, adopting the last name of Jane's relatives.

As usual with Hardin, events happened fast. A city marshal named Wilson argued with black men in front of the saloon, and during the resultant struggle, Wilson deputized Hardin for assistance. Hardin knocked down one man and shot another. Those still on their feet went to jail.

Shortly afterwards, a black man named Eli attempted to rape a white woman, and was jailed. At midnight, several masked men, including Hardin, came calling. They burned the jail, cremating Eli.[3]

Hardin sold his saloon during early 1875. He, Jane and Mollie relocated a few miles south in Micanopy, Florida where the Hardin, alias Swain, family re-entered the saloon business. Due to a need to keep moving, in July 1875 the Hardins turned up at Jacksonville, remaining a year on the northeast coast of Florida, just south of the Georgia line. Hardin characterized Jacksonville as "a resort for people from the North who go down there to make money."[4] Jacksonville even then dominated the social and commercial world of Florida, its wide streets shaded by huge live oaks, its commercial houses thriving. Here Hardin contracted to furnish 150 head of beef to the butchering firm of Haddock & Company.

Haddock died before the steers arrived, and his company refused to accept the animals. This left little financial maneuvering for Hardin, so he forsook the saloon business and entered the butchering trade. Slaughtering cattle may not have enriched the family but between that and the gambling tables, Swain earned a satisfactory living. On August 3, 1875, his only son, John Wesley

Hardin, Jr. was born in the Hardin/Swain home at 127 Pine Street, Jacksonville, Florida.

Throughout his career John Wesley Hardin cultivated peace officers. Killing them was understandable, but he also recognized the value of having them as friends. In spite of his constant assertions that Hickok intended to murder him, Hardin and Hickok had a respectful relationship. The Cherokee County, Texas Sheriff Richard B. "Dick" Reagan befriended Hardin, the Gonzales County Sheriff William E. Jones had allowed, even encouraged, his jail break. Sheriff Jack Helm had allegedly been Hardin's friend until Hardin killed him, and Comanche County Sheriff John Carnes had shielded Hardin from lynch mobs.

The city marshal of Brenham, Harry Swain, was related to Hardin's wife, and thus did favors for Hardin. Gus Kenedy, a Jacksonville city policeman, became one of Hardin's closest Florida associates. Some of Hardin's Florida mail reached him through the Nassau County Sheriff, Malcolm McMillan, another relative of Jane Hardin through the Bowen side of the family. Sheriff Malcolm McMillan warned Hardin that Pinkerton operatives were asking questions.

On January 20, 1875, the Texas legislature, in a joint resolution, offered "a reward of four thousand dollars for the apprehension and delivery of the body of the notorious murderer, John Wesley Hardin, . . . [to the] jail house door of Travis County."[5] A general consensus among legislators regarding the number of men Hardin had slain placed the figure at twenty-seven. Some legislators believed four thousand dollars was too much for any desperado, regardless of reputation. On the other hand, since the resolution meant "dead or alive," a couple of representatives argued that neither Hardin "nor anyone else, should be shot down without trial." No doubt Hardin would have agreed.

Comanche Senator John D. Stephens pushed the resolution so vigorously that Hardin allegedly threatened his life, a threat supposedly routing the senator into concealment until Hardin's absence from the state had been confirmed. Anyway, the resolution passed sixty-nine to six, and the reward made John Wesley Hardin the highest-priced desperado in the annals of Texas.[6]

This kind of money would certainly entice Pinkerton operatives, just as it would beguile Texas Rangers. This kind of money meant Texans had grown weary of law breakers and would pay to see them dead or in jail. This kind of money explained why Hardin stayed constantly on the run. This kind of money had influence.

"I remained in Jacksonville until I was forced to leave by detectives," Hardin exclaimed. "I escaped before they could get papers from the governor."[7]

Hardin sent Jane, Mollie and John Jr. to Aufaula, Alabama. He and Jacksonville city policeman Gus Kenedy—who apparently quit his job so that he could ride with Hardin—planned to rendezvous with them in New Orleans. However, somewhere around the Georgia/Florida line, Hardin and Kenedy killed two alleged Pinkerton detectives during a shootout.[8]

As for why Pinkertons would pursue Hardin, one answer is that the Pinkertons were the largest, best known and most prestigious private investigative firm in the world. They sought Hardin for the reward. Various Pinkerton bounty hunters were "stringers" or part-timers, people ordinarily unlisted as regular employees.

Following the possible Pinkerton killings, John Wesley Hardin retired to Pollard, Alabama, three miles north of the Florida line. Here he joined Jane and the children. They considered fleeing to Tuxpan, Mexico, a coastal village between Tampico and Veracruz, but that scheme went awry because of the risk of yellow fever in New Orleans. The family therefore settled briefly at Pascagoula, Mississippi, on the Gulf Coast while Hardin commuted to Mobile, Alabama for gambling purposes.

An irony is that with Hardin on the run, his family paid the price. They did without, hid, lied in his behalf while he, a fugitive from justice, imprisoned them in a circle of grief while he caroused in the saloons and wagering houses.

During the 1876 presidential elections, Republican Rutherford B. Hayes fought an intense, bitter battle against Samuel J. Tilden. Strong sectional emotions flourished, and an election brawl started in a Mobile gambling establishment and boiled over into the streets. Hardin implied that he and Kenedy killed two men. They tossed their weapons into back yards and gave police their most innocent look when arrested in a coffee house. Kenedy and Hardin spent several days in jail before the State dismissed charges.[9]

The Alabama *Mobile Register* of May 3, 1877, said "Gus Kenedy and J. H. Swayne were arrested for disorderly conduct on Tuesday night last, and fined $5." The newspaper mentioned no deaths but did write that "Sergeant Ryan, of the police force, while in discharge of his duty, was shot in the arm by one of three parties whom he and Officer Spencer [ejected from] a house." A day later, the *Register* referred to "charges of malicious mischief" against Swain and Kenedy summarizing that part of their fine required them to be "kicked out of town." The police confiscated a deck of "swindling cards," their backs marked so that crooked dealers could easily determine the faces. Hardin might have been a legend in Texas, but in Alabama he was little more than a routine card shark.[10]

From his base in Pollard, Hardin and Shep Hardy, a forty-year-old married laborer from Florida, entered the logging business along the Styx River. The enterprise failed because Hardin could not chop wood and gamble at the same time. Hardin's letters to Jane in mid-1877, document a man spending more and more time away from his family. She and the children lived with her brother Brown Bowen as Hardin struggled to send her twenty dollars. Even confidence men had their bad days.[11]

The tenuous brother-in-law relationship between John Wesley Hardin and Brown Bowen continued to unravel. After killing Tom Haldeman in Texas, Bowen fled to Kansas in 1873 and thereafter appeared in Florida and Alabama where he may have had brothers and sisters, and certainly aunts and uncles. Bowen married Mary Catherine Mayo, a lady ten years his junior.[12] Although a son was born in 1876, the event failed to moderate the nature or reputation of Brown Bowen. Bowen was a multi-murderer, a rapist, a whiner, an individual of neither pluck nor manhood, a sly man of non-existent virtue who happened to be the brother of Jane Hardin. This reluctantly made him family to John Wesley Hardin. Hardin failed to realize the danger of just being near Brown Bowen. David Haldeman, the father of Tom Haldeman, relentlessly goaded Texas Governor Richard Hubbard into offering a reward of suitable significance for Bowen, that Bowen be forcibly returned to Texas and tried for murder. Haldeman even located Brown Bowen in Alabama, and demanded that the authorities do their duty. The elder Haldeman's undeviating campaign for justice would have far-reaching Hardin (and Bowen) consequences. That desire for vengeance triggered the first step in a protracted road back to Texas for both Bowen and Hardin.[13]

Over in Austin, the government had not forgotten Hardin although it was trying to disregard Bowen. The State put a $500 reward out for Brown Bowen, an interesting sum but still insufficient for much Texas Ranger or out-of-state heed. But Hardin had a bounty of $4,000 dead or alive, and once the State turned its attention toward him, there was no turning back. Governor Richard Hubbard might have weighed three hundred pounds, but those were relentless pounds when it came to apprehending the desperado. He made his wishes known to the red-headed, North Carolina-born J. Lee Hall who took command of the Special Forces of Texas Rangers from Leander McNelly in January 1877.

Hall promoted Sergeant John Barclay Armstrong to lieutenant, and the unit returned to DeWitt County where Armstrong made additional Sutton-Taylor Feud arrests. Of course, some of that ardor momentarily faded in May 1877, when in Goliad, he carelessly shot himself in the groin. Nevertheless, the ranger recovered quickly. In April 1877, Armstrong apprehended the number two desperado in Texas, King Fisher. Following that, Armstrong became obsessed with capturing John Wesley Hardin and pocketing the four thousand dollars.

In those more relaxed days before the turn of the century, state lines meant little to law officers in quest of wanted men with bounties on their head. The Texas Rangers habitually chased Texas outlaws into Mexico, New Mexico, Arizona and even California. The length and duration of the pursuit usually depended upon the amount of reward money involved. Many individuals became sheriffs, marshals and Texas Rangers because of this extra income, a pecuniary inducement to the job.

Rangers Hall and Armstrong suspected Hardin had his wife and children with him. They understood the exceptionally strong bonds of family, knowing that contact would undoubtedly be made between families still living in Texas and families who had fled.

Hall and Armstrong retained John Riley Duncan, better known as Jack Duncan. A Kentucky-born policeman, Duncan was a jovial, good-natured man with black hair and eyes. He worked as a city detective in Dallas, and was the best sleuth in the state, a man occasionally operating as a Pinkerton stringer.[14] In the spring of 1877, Governor Hubbard appointed Duncan as a special ranger assigned to Lieutenant John B. Armstrong. Their job involved tracking down and either capturing or killing John Wesley Hardin.[15]

The twenty-six-year-old Duncan, using the alias of Mr. Williams, slipped into Gonzales County disguised as a merchant. Mr. Williams approached Brown's father, Neill Bowen, and expressed an interest in renting a storehouse. The two men became friends long enough for Duncan to intercept a Pollard, Alabama, letter from Brown Bowen to his father. Brown closed by mentioning that his sister sent love to all. That sister could only be Jane Hardin, and where she was, there would John Wesley Hardin likely be.

In order to get out of Gonzales County without arousing suspicion that he was a spy, Duncan wired code words to Texas Ranger John B. Armstrong: "Come get your horse." Within a day or so, the rangers arrived and, playing along with the ruse, pretended to arrest Duncan. They released and congratulated him as soon as all were safely out of sight.

Hall was busy with other cases, so Armstrong acquired train tickets and requested that warrants be forwarded for (both) John Wesley Hardin and John Swain to Montgomery, Alabama. The lawmen reached Montgomery on June 20, 1877.

Duncan, falling back on his sleuth trade, moseyed over to Pollard as a transient, then south a mile or so to Whiting (locally known as Junction) where Hardin and Bowen lived. He casually inquired about a man named Swain, and learned that Swain had left for Pensacola, Florida to gamble. Subsequent inquiries led them to William D. Chipley, a superintendent of the Pensacola Railroad who lived in Pensacola and disliked both Brown Bowen and John Swain.

According to the *Pensacola Gazette*, an altercation between Chipley and Bowen occurred at the Pensacola station and hotel. An intoxicated Bowen chased a black man around the terminal and through the hotel dining room. The black man escaped as Superintendent Chipley passed by while going to his office. Bowen cornered Chipley, screaming "Why didn't you stop that nigger for me?" An astonished Chipley responded, "I have nothing to do with your nigger." An angry Bowen then pointed a cocked six-shooter at Chipley who jammed his hand between the firing pin and the frame. He jerked the gun from Bowen's hand and beat him over the head with it. The confrontation ended with Bowen swearing he would kill Chipley.

An odd aspect of this affair is that another newspaper, the *Atlanta Constitution* published essentially the same story, only it named Swain as the offending thug. Judging from his background, Bowen was the more logical assailant. Hardin certainly had his prejudices, but Bowen was the more cruel and vindictive.[16]

After conversing by wire with Duncan and Armstrong, Chipley steamed north by train to meet them in Whiting. Since Armstrong still awaited Texas warrants for Hardin and Swain, Chipley brought a Pensacola judge as well as the Escambia County, Florida, Sheriff William H. Hutchinson. The sheriff was a twenty-seven-year-old

Alabaman, a Confederate veteran, a former logger now in his first term as a lawman.

The Pensacola authorities sought assurances that the Texas Rangers would also arrest Brown Bowen. Armstrong affirmed that, so everybody headed south to Pensacola from Whiting. In Florida, the lawmen learned that Brown Bowen had left (or perhaps was never with) the Hardin party. Hardin himself planned a return to Pollard on the afternoon train. Since everyone agreed that the best opportunity, and least dangerous time, to make an apprehension would be in the railroad car, Sheriff Hutchinson deputized several residents. He stationed deputies around the depot in case Hardin/Swain should elude officers on board. The date was August 23, 1877.

As anticipated, John Wesley Hardin and his gambling associates Shep Hardy, Neal Campbell and twenty-one-year-old Jim Mann, entered the smoking car where Hardin sat alongside the aisle relaxing with his pipe. Armstrong positioned himself in the express car next to the smoker as Sheriff Hutchinson and a deputy nonchalantly strolled through, throwing off drunks and undesirables while mentally evaluating Hardin and his friends. Up front, the engineer had been told to move out when someone yanked the bell cord according to a pre-arranged code.

Exactly what happened next depends upon who recalled the incident. The agreed-upon facts seem to be these: Hardin was leaning back with both arms raised overhead and clutching the back of the seat as if stretching. Sheriff Hutchinson and the muscular Florida Deputy A. J. Perdue re-entered the car from behind Hardin and grabbed him. Perhaps a better description would be that both men tumbled upon him. A wild cursing, screaming, kicking, struggle followed.

Armstrong (carrying a revolver and still suffering from his self-inflicted groin wound) limped down the aisle toward the bundle of fiercely grappling men. He ignored the uproar, paused over the melee, hesitated while waiting for an opening, and swung the heavy six-shooter, bringing it to rest with a resounding whack upon Hardin's head. The alias Mr. Swain slumped senseless. In fact, he lay unconscious so long that Armstrong feared he had killed him. The officers slapped on the leg irons, but could not find the handcuffs. So they bound Hardin with rope, and lashed him to his seat.

As passengers stampeded from the car, Jim Mann, sitting opposite Hardin, probably thought he and the others were beset upon by madmen. He jumped up and fired a wild round or two, but was slain by deputy Martin Sullivan.[17] Mann was not wanted for anything, and would have been released had he not panicked. Someone yanked the bell cord, and the train lurched forward as one of the lawmen found a six-shooter dangling inside Hardin's trousers, a suspender strap through the trigger guard. It was a fine hiding place, but not much could be said for it regarding a fast draw. Had Hardin been able to reach it, chances are he would have shot only himself. He stated in a letter to Jane that "I had no show [opportunity] to get my pistol," and "Jane I expect that it is a good thing they caught me the way they did for they had 40 men withe the Shariffe and Deputie of pensicolia. So you see I would have been a corps."[18] Hardin signed the letter "J. H. Swain."

The train stopped within a short distance, and Armstrong explained to Sheriff Hutchinson and Deputy Perdue the true identity of John Swain. He paid them $500 for their assistance. Hutchinson left the train and returned home, while Perdue went all the way to Whiting in the hope of arresting Brown Bowen. But Bowen was not to be located. From the Whiting station, where Hardy and Campbell were released, Wes sent money with them to his wife who apparently needed it since their third and last child, Jane "Jennie" Hardin, was only a month old.

At Whiting, Hardin hoped for a quick release since he knew the rangers lacked warrants. He wrote, "my friends at Pollard, eight miles away, had formed a rescuing party with the sheriff at their head and expected to legally release me when the train came through . . . [and] stopped several minutes. But unfortunately the train passed through without stopping. . . ."[19]

Armstrong telegraphed Texas Adjutant General William H. Steele that a desperately fighting Hardin had been captured after some lively shooting. "This is Hardin's home [Whiting] and his friends are trying to rally men to release him," Armstrong stated. "Have some good citizens with [me] & we will make it interesting."[20]

Armstrong also wired telegrams to the press. Newspapers from New York to Chicago, and Tennessee to New Orleans, ran the story. The ranger had a strong sense of personal publicity.

The train chugged along, traveling slowly, periodically pausing to take on water. Hardin occasionally stepped outside for air, always in chains, much to the relief of the other passengers since John was wildly profane. Once outdoors, he sulked and frequently refused to climb back aboard. So the lawmen carried him on.[21]

At Decatur, Alabama, Hardin briefly saw, and described, his one golden opportunity to escape. The opening was cold and calculating, but all too fleeting even for John Wesley Hardin:

> I knew my only hope was to escape. My guards were kind to me but they were not most vigilant. By promising to be quiet, I had caused them to relax somewhat. When we got to Decatur, we had to stop and change cars for Memphis. They took me to a hotel, got a room, and sent for our meals. Jack [Duncan] and Armstrong were now getting intimate with me, and when dinner came I suggested the necessity of removing my cuffs and they agreed to do so. Armstrong unlocked the jewelry [manacles] and started to turn around, exposing his six-shooter to me, when Jack jerked him around and pulled his pistol at the same time. "Look out," he said, "John will kill us and escape." Of course, I laughed at him and ridiculed the idea. It was really the very chance I was looking for, but Jack had taken the play away just before it got ripe. I intended to jerk Armstrong's pistol, kill Jack Duncan or make him throw up his hands. I could have made him unlock my shackles, or get the key from his dead body and do it myself. I could then have easily made my escape. That time never came again.[22]

Texas Ranger detective Jack Duncan questioned Hardin, asking "And now, John, did you know that two men were sent out this way for you once before?" Hardin replied, "Yes, I know that." The detective continued, "And do you know that those men never came back to Texas?" Hardin emotionally responded, "Yes, I know that, and I know by God, they never will come back."[23]

The *Atlanta Constitution* suspected Hardin had killed two people in the Southeast. Within a week after Hardin's capture, the *Constitution* reported that "John Swayne [Swain] is a gambler and spends much time in Pensacola. He had killed one or two men here, as also has his brother-in-law Bowen. . . ."[24]

At Montgomery, Alabama, a worried Armstrong sent a flurry of telegrams insisting upon his warrants to Adjutant General Steele as well as Governor Hubbard. "What is the matter?" he cried. Fortunately, although Alabama Judge John B. Fuller waffled, he still refused to release Hardin because the authorities had charged him with the murder of Charles Webb. The *Austin Statesman* of August 29, 1877, reported the timely arrival of warrants, saying the paper work "enabled Lieut. Armstrong and Detective Duncan to start on their way, rejoicing with the Grand Mogul of Texas desperadoes."[25]

NOTES

1. W. J. Maltby to Maj. John B. Jones, June 17, 1874, Adjutant General's Papers, Archives, Texas State Library.

2. Hardin, *Life,* 109–110; *Victoria Advocate,* Sept. 8, 1877; Chuck Parsons, *The Capture of John Wesley Hardin,* College Station, Creative Publishing, 1978, 34.

3. Ibid., 110–111; A. J. Wright, "John Wesley Hardin's Missing Years," *Old West* (Fall, 1981), 6–7.

4. *Victoria Advocate,* Sept. 8, 1877.

5. General Correspondence, Adjutant General's Office, Texas State Archives, Austin.

6. Legislative Proceedings, Jan. 14–15, 1875, printed in the *Daily Democratic Statesman,* Jan. 15, 1875; also see *General Laws of the State of Texas,* Session of the 14th Legislature, Joint Resolution 1, Houston: A. C. Gray, 1875.

During a personal interview with John Wesley Hardin, the *Victoria Advocate* of Sept. 8, 1877, printed Hardin's denial that he had threatened Senator Stephens, or any legislative member. The newspaper closed with a comment that the Austin jail held some seventy dangerous prisoners, many as anxious to escape as Hardin. "It is not altogether improbable," the *Advocate* said, "that Mr. Hardin will yet have a chance to get at the Senator from Comanche."

7. Hardin, *Life,* 112; *Victoria Advocate,* Sept. 8, 1877; Jack DeMattos, "Gunfighters of the Real West: John Wesley Hardin," *Real West* (April, 1984), 48.

8. Hardin, *Life,* 112; Parsons, *Capture of,* 39.

9. Hardin, *Life,* 112–113; A. J. Wright, "A Gunfighter's Southern Vacation," *Quarterly of the National Outlaw and Lawman History Association,* Vol. VII, #3 (Autumn, 1982), 12–18.

10. *Mobile Register,* Nov. 12, 1876.

11. J. H. H. Swain to Mrs. Swain, June 6, 1877, Hardin Collection, San Marcos State University, San Marcos, TX.

12. Chuck and Marjorie Parsons, *Bowen and Hardin,* College Station: Creative Publishing Co., 1991, 72.

13. Ibid., 60.

14. Michael Whittington, "Six Telegrams That Tell a Story: The Arrest of John Wesley Hardin," *Quaterly for the National Association and Center for Outlaw and Lawman History,* Vol. XI, No. 2 (Fall 1986), 9.

15. Rick Miller, *Bounty Hunter,* College Station, Texas: The Early West, 1988; *Galveston News,* Aug. 23, 1895.

16. Chipley wrote Governor Hubbard on Aug. 28, 1877, and confirmed that Brown Bowen had indeed assaulted him, and had been almost beat to death in the process by his own weapon. The letter is on file with the governor's papers in the Texas State Archives, Austin; Also see Chuck and Marjorie Parsons, *Bowen and Hardin,* 74–76; Miller, *Bounty Hunter,* 84-86; *Pensacola Gazette* (reprinted from *The Advertiser and Mail,* Aug. 26, 1877; *Atlanta Daily Constitution,* Sept. 1, 1877; Hardin, *Life,* 115–116.

17. State of Florida vs. Martin Sullivan, Escambia County, Circuit Court, Criminal Records, Oct. 4, 187'7. A Florida grand jury indicted Sullivan for the killing, but nothing came of the trial. Other versions of the conflict have Mann reaching the depot passenger platform before deputies shot him dead.

18. Hardin to Jane Bowen Hardin, Aug. 25, 1877, Hardin Collection.

19. Hardin, *Life,* 120.

20. Telegram to Adj. General Steele, Aug. 23, 1877, Adj. General's Records, Texas State Archives. A total of six telegrams are on file in the Archives; *Dallas Morning News,* Aug. 22, 1895; *Galveston News,* Aug. 29, 1877; Whittington, "Six Telegrams," 9–11.

21. *Galveston News,* Aug. 23, 1895.

22. Hardin, *Life,* 121; Parsons, *Capture of,* 137.

23. *Atlanta Daily Constitution,* Sept. 1, 1877.

24. Ibid.

25. The telegrams from Armstrong to Duncan are in the Attorney General's file in the Texas State Archives; also see Parsons, *The Capture,* 59–60, and Miller, *Bounty Hunter,* 92–94.

★ 12 ★

RANGERS AND MOUNTIES DEFENDING THE CATTLEMAN'S EMPIRE

Andrew R. Graybill

With passage of the 1884 fence cutting legislation, state leaders in Austin had demonstrated their resolve to protect private property and to defend an industry of unquestioned economic value to the state. Officials charged the Texas Rangers with eradicating fence destruction, which became the primary mission of the force in the spring of 1884. This was not, however, the first time the Rangers had been considered for such a job. Two years before, Adjutant General W. H. King had proposed to use the force—albeit in a relatively nonconfrontational way—to mediate range conflicts before they reached the boiling point.[1] If such a plan was put into effect by King before the 1883 troubles, though, it did little good in bringing about tranquility between large and small ranchers on the cattleman's frontier: Rangers were investigating fence cutting cases less than six months after the adjutant general had filed his report.

There are at least two reasons why King and Governor John Ireland enlisted the Rangers to suppress fence cutting. First, the police had already proven their usefulness to the cattle industry by driving Native Americans from the state and dispossessing South Texas Mexicans of their livestock. More importantly, Austin had little faith in local law enforcement officials, many of whom reportedly backed the cutters. Governor Ireland, in fact, had said as much in his 1884 address to the state legislature, recommending that—in addition to the prosecution of wire cutters—the lawmakers levy a hefty penalty against any sheriff, deputy, or constable failing to investigate allegations of fence destruction.[2] His concerns were not unfounded, since Rangers and worried citizens alike wrote frequent letters complaining that local officials were in sympathy with the cutters and that juries would not convict men charged with such an offense.[3]

The state police, however, did not serve alone in their campaign against the wire cutters. Recognizing the difficulties inherent in apprehending the nippers, Ireland sought help from two detective agencies, Pinkerton's and Farrell's.[4] With $50,000 appropriated to him by the legislature, the governor lured operatives from Chicago and New Orleans, who upon their arrival in Texas were sworn in as Rangers and issued police credentials.[5] Once established, the detectives disappeared into the countryside, hoping to infiltrate wire-cutting gangs by posing as disgruntled cowmen. Having ingratiated themselves with suspected perpetrators, the agents set about collecting names and evidence to be used at trial before calling in the Rangers to make arrests. Although this procedure worked well in one case from May 1884, resulting in the apprehension of eight Runnels County nippers caught in the act, King tired of this complex and largely unsuccessful approach by early spring. Explaining that he had little confidence in the detectives and preferred the Rangers' more immediate and direct efforts, the adjutant general canceled undercover operations by the end of June.[6]

Fueling King's frustrations, no doubt, was the fact that—given the support of local communities for men charged with fence cutting—convictions were hard to come by even in the face of overwhelming evidence. One detective reported with disgust on court proceedings in Erath County, where a grand jury had refused to indict alleged cutters for the offense despite the presence of excellent witnesses. As the operative explained to the adjutant general, he learned only afterward that a leading anti-fence man had served on the jury, along with several others of like mind.[7] For his part, Ranger captain G. W. Baylor—a strapping Confederate army veteran placed in charge of the Frontier Battalion with the express purpose of ending the cutting—was no less exasperated. Noting the difficulty of winning convictions against alleged fence cutters, Baylor suggested that better results might be obtained by moving the trials to particularly embattled locales such as San Antonio, Waco, Austin, and Fort Worth. Repeated failures to secure jail time for the offenders were dispiriting, Baylor said, and he urged that the punishment of even a few men would bring about a more desirable end.[8]

By the middle of 1884, Ranger squads were taking more aggressive action to halt the cutting, as suggested by a case from Edwards County, seventy-five miles northwest of San Antonio. The previous October, rancher G. B. Greer of Green Lake had suffered a downed fence, and in July 1884 he contacted Governor Ireland to express his concern that the rebuilt enclosure had been targeted once again for destruction.[9] Greer requested a Ranger detachment for protection, but before the arrival of the police, cutters had snipped the wire in order to water their cattle at a small lake surrounded by the fence. Upon reaching Greer's spread two days later, the four-man Ranger unit hid a short distance from the water, where they later witnessed several men attempting to undo the rancher's repeated patch work. Emerging from their position, the police advanced on the cutters, who—according to the Rangers—ignored squad leader P. F. Baird's order to surrender, shouting instead for the Rangers to "come on & take us in you damned sons of bitches." After what Baird described as "quite a hot but short battle" of ten minutes, one cutter lay dead with two gunshot wounds to the chest and one to the head.[10]

Though no doubt satisfying to Greer and the Rangers alike, this success—along with the arrest of thirty-six cutters between 1 December 1883 and 30 November 1884 alone—did not put an end to fence destruction.[11] Most vexing, perhaps, was the assassination in February 1885 of Ben Warren—the prosecution's star witness in the

Runnels County case from the previous spring—which allowed a band of particularly active cutters to escape conviction. Such setbacks led one frustrated rancher to claim that the statute passed by the legislature was useless, and that stockmen in his part of north-central Texas had begun to despair of ever breeding fine-blooded cattle in separate pastures."[12] Stung by the criticism, King decided on a new approach in 1886, reviving undercover operations but with Rangers—and not private detectives—now serving as the infiltrators. Additionally, King resolved to focus police efforts on Brown County, the district with perhaps the most intractable fence cutting epidemic, and whose troubles reveal a wealth of information about the competing pastoral interests in central Texas in the mid-1880s as well as rare details about the cutters and their discontent.

Located near the geographical center of the state, Brown County developed rapidly as cattle country after its 1856 founding, with the number of animals rising from just under 4,000 to nearly 50,000 two decades later.[13] Most of the longhorns were owned by a handful of prominent cattlemen, who were among the first residents in the county. Like their counterparts throughout the state, these men responded to the arrival of settlers by fencing up their pastures, enclosing their own property as well as many of the county's 64,000 acres of appropriated school lands, a practice that infuriated farmers and small cowmen. Fence cutting thus began in the spring of 1883, and that fall a group of cutters razed two miles of a barbed-wire enclosure belonging to L. P. Baugh, one of the largest landowners in the county. They left behind a note that read: "Mr. Baugh, take down this fence; if you don't, we will cut it and if we cut it and a drop of the cutters' blood is spilled, your life will pay the forfeit."[14]

Baugh—who was legendary in Brown County for having nearly decapitated an Indian scout in the 1860s with a blast from his .8-gauge shotgun—did not take the threat lightly, and answered the message with one of his own: "You cowardly cur, this is my fence, and you let it alone."[15] When his fence was cut again one month later, Baugh approached Sheriff W. N. Adams and with his assistance organized a posse of twenty-six cattlemen, who visited the homes of suspected cutters and sternly warned them against any further fence destruction. This act so angered the small cowmen that 200 of them marched on Brownwood, the county seat, where they held a "Fence Cutters Convention" in the courthouse. Although Sheriff Adams managed eventually to disperse the men—and even wrangled a promise from their leaders to cease the cutting—tensions escalated once again in March 1885 when a grand jury indicted ten men for fence cutting on evidence supplied by Baugh. After two continuances, however, the charges were dismissed, lending credence to Ranger G. W. Baylor's complaint that the courts would not convict (or in this case, even try) alleged cutters.

It was at this point that the Baughs appealed directly to Adjutant General King, who dispatched Ira Aten, a young Ranger whom King had personally recruited earlier in the year for special duty in a fence-cutting case in Lampasas County. The twenty-four-year-old Aten had been inspired to join the force (over his parents' objection) by an episode he witnessed as a young boy: the death of the outlaw Sam Bass, killed by a Ranger squad in the town of Round Rock after a botched bank heist.[16] On his new assignment in Brown County, Aten quickly insinuated himself with the cutters (mostly young men who lived near the Baughs) and learned that they planned to cut a fence belonging to the family on the night of November 9, 1886. King promptly sent four Rangers from Company F to Brownwood, where they set an ambush in conjunction with the Baughs and some of their hired hands. What happened after the cutters arrived on the scene was a matter of some dispute, with Aten maintaining that the cutters fired first, even though one local history insists that the police cut down the perpetrators in the act of escape.[17] Whatever the case, two men—Amos Roberts and twenty-four-year-old Jim Lovell—were killed. Ironically, they were buried in a remote corner of the Baugh property.

In the end, a grand jury indicted seven cutters in February 1887, but the cases were transferred that fall to Bell County, more than one hundred miles away. This, according to the judge, was because "a fair and impartial trial cannot be had in Brown County because of the existing combination and influence on the part of influential persons in favor of the accused and against the State of Texas."[18] Such circumstances indicate broad support for the cutters in their struggle against the large cattlemen, as does the reminiscence of a Baugh relative, offered nearly seventy years after the gunfight on his family's property. As George Baugh explained to a local historian: "We have been criticized for the course the Rangers took, but the wirecutters were no angels, and something had to be done to make a man's life and property safe."[19] For his part, Aten said at the time that the deaths had "done more to suppress fence-cutting than any other thing" in Brown County, although his colleague Captain Scott believed that prospects for a "Gay Christmas" depended on another killing before the holiday.[20]

A closer look at Ira Aten's career as a detective sheds additional light on fence cutting in Texas, including the shift in Ranger tactics during the late 1880s and the mounting dilemmas faced by opponents of enclosure.[21] Following his 1886 success in Brown County, Aten traveled throughout the state on assignment, usually working alone. By the early autumn of 1888, however, he was ordered back to central Texas by Governor L. S. "Sul" Ross (himself a former Ranger), who commanded Aten to put an end to rampant fence cutting in Navarro County.[22] This time Aten took along fellow Ranger "Fiddling" Jim King, whose musical expertise they hoped to use to gain the cutters' confidence. Posing as newcomers to the region, the men were aided by the breakdown of their wagon outside of town, which wound up providing them with ample pretext to remain in the area indefinitely.[23]

Hoping to deflect any suspicion and also to meet some of the anti-fence men, the Rangers looked for work but found few opportunities, since the cotton crop that year was so poor that many people had simply abandoned the area. In the end, King and Aten secured positions baling and picking cotton, respectively, but at re-

duced pay. While waiting for the cotton season to begin, they bus-
ied themselves building a rock furnace around the gin, an activity
that afforded them the opportunity to meet some of the cutters. The
cover and access provided by these choices of employment are illu-
minating, for they suggest that some anti-fence men were forced by
economic insecurity to move back and forth between positions as
owner-operators and wage laborers. William Scott had made precisely this point about the Brown County gang in February 1887.
He described the homestead of that region's average cutter as consisting of "from one to two Hip Shot Crosseyed Bandy Shanked sore
backed good for nothing ponies, and a poor woman for a wife with
two to five poor little half starved and necked [*sic*] little children."²⁴
The heads of such families likely turned to wire cutting when it appeared to them that should the fences stay put, they would inevita-
bly become permanent wage workers.

Aten explained that the fence cutters in his region were generally "cowboys or small cow men" who owned somewhere between
15 and 200 cattle, with perhaps a hundred acres of land under cultivation. Although they targeted primarily the fences of area ranchers, they resented "grangers" —small farmers who often fenced up
their lands—just as much, for many of the cutters nursed a fierce
opposition to the very notion of enclosure, regardless of its purpose. In secret meetings of more than a hundred sympathizers, the
anti-fence men vented their indignation about the pasture men and
their supporters, on one occasion vowing to storm the local jail and
rescue a handful of compatriots caught in the act. While Aten dismissed such threats as mere bravado, he did confess to a friend that
he wished fellow Ranger detective John Hughes were with him in
Navarro County, for "it is awful risky business as these villains are
hard men."²⁵

One month into his Navarro County investigation, however,
Aten had soured on his mission. For one thing, he thought it impossible to gain the confidence of the wire cutters, because the anti-
fence men did not appear to need any help, and at any rate they were

wary of taking in anyone whom they did not know well. Without inside information, Aten knew that the execution of a successful Ranger ambush was unlikely. More troubling to him, though, was the clandestine nature of the work. As he explained in one letter, "We have had to tell ten thousand lies already & I know we wont get away with-out telling a million."[26] In addition, he loathed the prospect of actually destroying fences—essential if he and King were to establish any credibility—and found it "disgusting" to encourage the "good men" of the county to keep putting up their fences just so they could be cut down once again.[27] Still, he remained convinced that "nothing will do any good here but a first class killing & I am the little boy that will give it to them if they dont let the fence alone."[28]

This mixture of frustration and resolve led Aten to create what he called a "dynamite boom," an explosive device constructed from a shotgun packed with dynamite, gunpowder, and a blasting cap. Concealed underground, the contraption was designed to detonate when a cutter snipped the strand of barbed wire to which the "boom" was attached, triggering the cap and scattering "small pieces of that gun . . . all over Navarro County.[29] However, after Aten had set charges on all of the fences that had been cut in the previous year, Governor Ross learned of the plan and summoned him to Austin to explain. Aten later recalled that "while I was telling [Ross] of my experiences . . . that bald head of his got redder and redder, and when I had finished my story it was on fire." Ross did not order him to be court-martialed and shot, though, as Aten feared. Instead, the governor insisted that Aten return to Navarro County and remove the bombs, which the Ranger did by exploding them and thus terrifying the residents (cutters and noncutters alike) into believing that all the area fences were mined.[30] That ended fence destruction in the region, and Aten, who had sworn from the beginning of the operation that this would be his last mission, sold his belongings and left the area in mid-October. [31]

Similar conditions to those faced by the Texas Rangers also existed in Canada where the Northwest Mounted Police (NWMP, later to be called the Royal Canadian Mounted Police) ranged and worked. The frustration of settlers in western Canada reached a full boil in the early 1890s when Ottawa undertook a massive extension of the stock-watering reserve system, driven in large part by the demands of area ranchers. According to one historian, the government's action was the fulfillment of an "unwritten promise" between cattlemen and federal authorities which held that in exchange for accepting the complete cancellation of all closed leases by 1896, stockmen would receive expanded reserves.[32] Such an agreement exposes the conundrum faced by the Conservatives at the time. On the one hand, the party relied heavily on support from Alberta's ranching community and thus had to make large concessions to it, yet some members of the government recognized that waves of migration would be difficult to repress for much longer. As Deputy Minister of the Interior A. M. Burgess put it in 1887: "There can be no doubt that when an actual settler desires the land for the purpose of making his home upon it, it would be impossible, even if it were expedient, to keep him out."[33] The expanded reserves were Ottawa's attempt to seem responsive to farmer grievances while simultaneously advancing the big rancher's interests. Settlers, however, saw the plan as merely another handout to the cattlemen.

Beyond cementing their control of the region's scarce water supply, the extension of sequestered lands provided ranchers with a new weapon to use against the nesters: the NWMP. Until the expansion of the stock-watering reserve system in the 1890s, most squatting had taken place on leaseholds—lands privately held by individuals or companies, who were thus responsible for taking action against the interlopers. Therefore, eviction proceedings tended to go through the court system and usually resulted in an order for the squatter to desist. While the Mounted Police may have occasionally enforced such mandates, evidence supporting these assertions is spare. Rather, it seems that most squatters recognized the futility of their cause and simply abandoned the contested ground. With the extension of the reserve system, however, growing numbers of settlers now found themselves on public lands claimed by the government for the cattlemen, a circumstance that gave the NWMP (as a federal agency) unquestioned jurisdiction in the matter. While it seems unlikely that this feature was instrumental in the expansion of the reserves, it was clearly a perquisite for Alberta ranchers.

[William] Pearce [superintendent of mines for the Department of the Interior], for one, was determined to involve the Mounted Police in the new eviction proceedings because he believed it was imperative to send a strong and symbolic message that such practices would not be tolerated in cattle country. As he explained in an 1894 letter to the secretary of the Department of the Interior, "If this course [ejection by the NWMP] were taken in one or two cases it would undoubtedly effectually stop such attempts in the future."[34] Ranchers were no less interested in such a development, with the High River Stock Association urging the minister of the interior "that power be given the N.W.M. Police under the authority from the Superintendent of Mines, Calgary, to prevent & remove settlers attempting to take up land" near creeks or springs.[35] Such entreaties led the Department of the Interior in the spring of 1894 to retain police services in posting warning notices and even removing squatters from sequestered lands when necessary.[36]

For their part, police officials expressed skepticism about participating in the eviction campaign. Upon receiving a request from Secretary of the Interior John Hall to send a police detachment to destroy a collection of squatters' buildings near Calgary, NWMP comptroller Fred White wrote the deputy minister of justice to be certain "of the legality of [the squad's] action." White was subsequently informed by Hall that "there can be no doubt whatever both as to our having the power to do what is requisite and the propriety of exercising that power." Despite these assurances, White appears to have delayed issuing any orders to his force, since Pearce sent an angry letter to Hall several weeks later explaining that no action had been taken by the NWMP post at Calgary. The superintendent

of mines added that "weakening on the part of the Department . . .
would be fatal to the welfare of the stock interests."[37]

Police circumspection was not limited merely to concerns about
the authority of the force to remove offenders. Mountie reluctance
may have stemmed also from the sheer unpopularity of evictions
among the wider public, a sentiment confirmed by letters and petitions sent to Ottawa in support of several squatters.[38] Moreover, the
actual process of eviction could be highly unpleasant, as in the case
of Felix Thiboutott, a farmer who had spent an estimated $250 in
establishing himself and his family on lands deemed too close to a
spring. When on 21 January 1895 a deputy sheriff from the town
of Macleod—supported by a Mountie constable—began to empty
the furniture from Thiboutott's house in preparation for pulling it
down, the man's wife "declared herself ill and I believe went to bed,"
temporarily interrupting the proceedings. In the end, the family received permission to remove their shack to a distant corner of the
Alberta Ranche Company leasehold, far from the water source in
question. Pearce, however, was irritated by the compromise, insisting that "the easiest way of dealing with such cases is to eject squatters when they first attempt to settle on reservations."[39]

Perhaps the most intriguing source of police distaste for eviction may have been the fact that, on occasion, members of the force
who hoped to get a preretirement jump on ranching careers became squatters themselves, as suggested by one case from 1893.[40]
That summer the manager of the New Oxley Ranch applied to the
government for the purchase of some lands contained within the
company's leasehold, between the forks of the Belly and Kootenay
rivers. Upon making his investigation of the site, Pearce discovered
that NWMP staff sergeant Chris Hilliard illegally occupied the territory. The policeman defended his actions by expressing his intent
to leave the force and become "a bona fide settler." The case caused
considerable discomfort at NWMP headquarters, where top officials were forced to acknowledge that some officers in the field
looked the other way when men under their command acquired

property while serving in the force. Worried that allowing Hilliard to persist would send the wrong message and appear to give license to the police to flout the very rules they had been ordered to enforce, Mountie brass supported Ottawa's command for Hilliard to desist (though allowing him first to remove his buildings and fences).

Hilliard's case suggests several important differences between the circumstances and aspirations of men who served in the Mounted Police and those who were Rangers. First, Hilliard (and other Mountie squatters) must have had personal wealth or access to capital that would have financed the improvements he made to the land he hoped to acquire. Moreover, Hilliard's plan to become a rancher immediately after his discharge from the NWMP contrasts sharply with the prospects awaiting former Rangers, many of whom entered the employ of a rancher or syndicate after leaving the force. Instead of raising their own cattle, these ex-Rangers were far more likely to find themselves riding fences or stringing wire for a big outfit, just as many of them had done before their enlistment. Finally, the more itinerant nature of the Ranger force provided the Texas police with limited opportunities to scout prospective homesteading locations on which to eventually settle. Mountie detachments, on the other hand, often spent extended periods posted at permanent forts, allowing men like Chris Hilliard to identify and even prepare nearby areas for residence.

At any rate, notwithstanding their misgivings, the Mounted Police assisted in a number of squatter evictions between 1894 and 1896, complying with Ottawa's firm demands that they take such action. Although officials at the Department of the Interior noted that legal proceedings offered a viable means of effecting the squatters' removal from reserves, the minister of the interior had decided "that it would be in the public interest that the second of the methods"—eviction—be adopted.[41] While such a procedure no doubt had the symbolic value desired by Pearce, one historian has argued that it served also to "avert the attendant publicity of lengthy court battles," no small consideration given the unpopularity of the practice among many Albertans.[42] Tearing down offending structures proved to be more efficient and expedient.

Police involvement usually began with a request from Pearce (spurred by a rancher's complaint) to investigate the erection of a building or fence along a spring earmarked for stock-watering purposes. Provided that the Mountie detachment found that the squatter was indeed in violation of the law, the police were authorized to seize the ground "on behalf of Her Majesty" and raze or remove the illegal structures. Superintendent Sam Steele described the process matter-of-factly in his report for 1895: "Several evictions of settlers charged with illegally squatting have been conducted at the request of the Department of Interior. All parties had been previously warned that certain lands had been set aside by the department as 'stock watering reserves,' and the risks they ran by squatting without first obtaining proper authority had been explained to them."[43] Although on occasion members of the force showed some of their previous reluctance for the task—in one instance granting a squatter three weeks to harvest his crops before returning to evict him— they nevertheless faithfully executed their orders.[44]

In the end, the efforts of the Rangers and the Mounties to defend the cattleman's empire at the edges of the Great Plains produced different results. In Texas, fence cutting declined sharply throughout the remainder of the 1880s, with arrests plummeting from a high of thirty-six in 1884 to an average of only four per year for 1886 and 1887.[45] (Given the clandestine nature of the offense and the difficulty in apprehending cutters in the act, however, these figures must be read with caution.) Although Rangers and pro-fence men alike maintained that the occasional killing of a wire cutter was the most effective means of ending the destruction, it seems rather that Adjutant General King's new tactics deserve most of the credit. By using small Ranger squads to eradicate the offense in the handful of the most troubled counties—including Lampasas, Navarro, and especially Brown—King demonstrated both the resolve and the ability of the police to protect the ranchers' private property. Fear of Aten's "dynamite boom" was also significant, particularly its role in deterring would-be cutters in the area south of Dallas.

The dramatic decline in fence cutting led W. H. King to declare in 1888 that the epidemic had come to an end, and he gave credit to the police under his command, noting that "the efforts of the Rangers have had an immense and seemingly lasting effect."[46] To be sure, sporadic reports of fence destruction persisted into the following decade, as suggested by an impassioned letter from 1893 written by county judge (and future governor) John N. Garner, who asked for "three good Rangers" to wipe out the practice in his South Texas district.[47] Most other complaints at this time came from West Texas and especially the Panhandle, which in the 1890s experienced the ripples of westward migration that had produced such conflict in the central portion of the state. Yet most settlers arriving in those parts had witnessed the Ranger-assisted triumph of barbed wire further east and simply accepted the victory of enclosure as inevitable, leaving the large cattleman to breed and graze his stock unencumbered by the protestations and anonymous violence of the small Texas cowman.

Events took a dramatically different turn in Canada, where the forced removal of squatters by the NWMP came to an abrupt end with the victory of Wilfrid Laurier's Liberal Party in the 1896 parliamentary elections. Out of sheer political necessity, the Liberals had come to champion the rights of settlers who opposed Alberta cattlemen, almost all of whom backed the ruling Conservative Party, which had been in power since 1878. Ranchers expressed considerable anxiety over the change in leadership, exacerbated by Laurier's appointment of a new minister of the interior, Clifford Sifton, who—while not hostile to ranching interests per se—believed fervently in promoting farm settlement.[48] Sifton received staunch support from Frank Oliver, a Liberal M.P. from Edmonton (and later Sifton's successor at the Department of the Interior), who inundated him with memos opposing evictions and decrying the biased nature of the reserve system.

The reserves did not simply evaporate, since the Liberal government recognized the importance of the cattle industry to the financial health of the Dominion. Still, the Department of the Interior developed new policies with respect to the creation of reserves. In the first place, no longer could the mere recommendations of cattlemen or their associations serve as grounds for the alienation of a given tract. Prior to the establishment of any new reserves, officials were now required to conduct a thorough inspection of the lands in question in order to ascertain the possible existence of any private rights. Such inquiries led to decisions such as the one contained in a July 1897 letter from an interior official to Pearce (soon to be demoted to inspector of surveys), denying a request by the powerful Bar U Ranch for the government to evict a settler from prospective reserve land.[49] The upholding of the rights of squatters was "a complete reversal of earlier government policy."[50]

The tactics of the police in ejecting squatters from established stock-watering reserves experienced a seismic shift as well, a change initiated even before the end of 1896. As the deputy minister of justice explained in a November letter to his counterpart at the Department of the Interior describing appropriate police actions in the case of eviction, if "the squatter does not peaceably give up possession of the premises . . . it would not be proper to use force to remove him."[51] Indeed, the NWMP reverted to the pre-1894 practice of taking such matters before the court for reasons outlined by Comptroller Fred White in a 1905 letter to the secretary of the interior. White noted that "on one occasion, when it was thought that the Police were using their uniform, prestige and official position to frighten settlers . . . newspaper articles immediately appeared charging the Police Force with eviction similar to those in Ireland, and warning people against coming to Canada."[52] Negative publicity of this kind was anathema to the immigration policy of the new government.

The divergent outcomes for farmers and small ranchers in Texas and Alberta suggest a host of other key differences between the policies of government officials in Austin and Ottawa and their enforcement by the two constabularies. On the most fundamental level, the contrasting systems of land tenure in Texas and Canada distinguished their respective ranching empires. Although federal officials strongly desired to populate the North-West with whites loyal to the government, they were no less resolved to maintain tight control over those lands, and thus chose to lease rather than sell off vast portions of southern Alberta. This system permitted Ottawa to make changes to its land policy as circumstances required, such as the amending of lease laws and the opening of select townships for settlement in the mid-1880s. Although such moves did little to redress the basic imbalance between big syndicates and smaller ranchers and farmers, initiatives like these nevertheless allowed the federal government to seem responsive to the demands of settlers.

In Texas, by comparison, Reconstruction-era distrust of government and the powerful impetus of resource development fueled the state to divest itself of its public lands. In the wake of this liquidation, Austin retained little direct control over vast swaths of now private real estate, and could thus institute few proactive measures to reduce the tensions between big and small ranchers. In marked contrast to the Canadian example, Texas lawmakers only inserted themselves into the debate after the eruption of violence in 1883, and even then produced a decree—the anti-fence-cutting legislation of 1884—that clearly favored one interest at the expense of the other. Furthermore, the privatization of the state's public domain imbued Texas cattlemen with a powerful sense of entitlement, leading them to defend their claims with thickets of barbed wire (as was their right), even as the enclosure of the range created a sense of desperation among small cowmen and poorer homesteaders.

While the inequity of the Canadian lease system clearly irritated individuals of more modest means, both the fine print of the agreements (permitting cancellation) and the rhetoric of the government (promoting settlement) indicated a level of official flexibility totally absent in Texas. The Canadian elections of 1896 clearly demonstrate the importance of this political latitude. Because Alberta's land base remained under federal control, once the Liberals were in charge they could modify the government's positions on land use to suit their own constituency, attacking the entrenchment of the cattlemen by curtailing the stock-watering reserves. This was an impossible scenario with an alienated land base, as in Texas, where—even had the Populist moment occurred ten years earlier, in the mid-1880s—undoing the transfer of title in fee simple would have been a very tall order indeed, given the sanctity of private property.[53]

The timing and conditions of settlement played significant roles in determining the course of events in Texas and Alberta. At the southern end of the Plains, tensions between big and small ranchers erupted at the moment and in the zone of the abrupt transition from one pastoral system (the open range) to another (enclosure). People who had formerly relied upon a common resource now found themselves bitterly divided over its use, and in many cases (as in Brown County) the new order pitted neighbors against one another in an intensely personal conflict. Complicating matters was the fact that some cattlemen acted illegally, appropriating lands that did not belong to them along with the sections to which they were entitled by purchase, actions that fueled the irritation of the farmer and small cowman. Because the state government had largely divested itself from the contested lands, those who opposed enclosure directed their anger at the big ranchers, loosing their frustration on the barbed wire they blamed for their suffering.

In Alberta, on the other hand, Ottawa planted a large cattleman's empire well ahead of the tide of Eurocanadian settlement. By the time sizable numbers of white migrants arrived in the far reaches of the North-West, the dominance of the big rancher was an established (if resented) fact. Moreover, while they may have acted aggressively in pursuing the eviction of squatters, Canada's ranching elite rarely broke the laws set by Ottawa (save for the flouting of stocking guidelines and such), and they did not build structures to prevent trespass. (In this way, the "closure" of the Canadian range was actually the very act of keeping it open by preventing farmers from fencing up water or feed, which provides a neat inversion of the situation in Texas.) Thus it was that squatters in Alberta—unlike fence cutters in the Lone Star State—generally aimed their disappointment at the officials responsible for the land policy in the West and had few hallmarks of syndicate hegemony (such as a fence) on which to visit their rage.

These factors help to explain the higher levels of violence in Texas—where at least three people were killed—than in Canada, where there is little evidence of any gunplay (and certainly no fatal confrontations) between squatters and cattlemen. Aggravated by local conflict and despairing of any assistance from the state, disgruntled farmers and small cowmen in Texas took up the wire cutters in order to halt fencing. Part of their plan, no doubt, was to dissuade ranchers from enclosing land through the dissemination of fear and threats of violence, hence the nighttime raids, the menacing notes, and the brandishing of firearms. The ranchers, on the other hand, responded to the threats against life and property by resorting to force and, when that failed, calling upon the state to send in the Rangers, who entered a highly combustible situation after 1884. Armed with a mandate to eradicate the offense and—as explained by Ira Aten—a healthy fear of the fence cutters' hostility, the Rangers seem to have adopted a "kill or be killed" perspective in their dealings with the perpetrators.

None of these conditions obtained in western Canada. First, given the ranchers' roots in southern Alberta and their broad political influence, the best that the squatters could hope for was to establish a toehold in the region; directly challenging the power of the big cattlemen—as the fence cutters in Texas sought to do—was out of the question. Second, while it is hard to determine the extent of squatting on leaseholds or reserves, census figures suggest implicitly that the practice was much less widespread (and thus less troublesome to authorities) than fence destruction in Texas. While in 1881 there were an estimated 56,000 residents of the entire North-West

Territories (which comprised the present-day provinces of Alberta, Saskatchewan, and Yukon), Brown County alone had more than one-seventh that number.[54] Finally, the court system in Canada worked well enough to adjudicate many squatting cases; in Texas, the perceived inability of the state to win convictions against alleged cutters incited vigilantism and, in some instances, convinced the Rangers that shotguns were a more useful deterrent than the threat of legal action.

These observations alone, however, do not necessarily explain why the Rangers worked so diligently to suppress fence cutting. To a man, they appear to have hated the assignment, especially the secrecy and patience it required, not to mention the necessary deception of cutters and pro-fence men alike. Some members of the force even expressed the belief that just picking up a pair of nippers—no matter how essential to their disguise—made them as guilty as the cutters themselves. Additionally, the average Ranger likely had more in common socially and economically with the small cowmen and farmers who did most of the cutting than they did with those Texans who could afford spools of barbed wire. Aten, for instance, while on assignment in Navarro County, expressed his desire upon his retirement from the force to move to the Panhandle, where he would "settle down on a little farm [and] get to nesting."[55] Enclosing a few thousand acres and running a herd of fine-blooded stock, on the other hand, was probably beyond his monthly salary of fifty dollars.

One possible explanation for the loyalty of the police to the pro-fence men turns on the clandestine nature of the cutters' operations. As much as the Rangers disliked their own secrecy, they reserved a special scorn for the wire cutter who anonymously destroyed the property of others. Still more damning in the eyes of the police was the association of the anti-fence men with petty criminals. Rangers, for the most part, saw little justification behind the cutting and, in the words of Captain G. W. Baylor, attributed the destruction to horse, cow, and hog thieves who took advantage of the confusion

in order to enrich themselves.[56] That large sections of the population, including some local law enforcement officers, backed the
cutters was of little consequence; the nippers, according to Captain
William Scott, were "of the lowest order originating from a cross
between the Hiena and the Javiline Hog," raising their children to
become thieves and murderers.[57]

There were also clear economic advantages for Rangers who
defended pasture men. Just as George Durham took a position at
the King Ranch after his tour of duty in McNelly's unit, so, too, did
Rangers working in North and West Texas find employment with
some of the very cattlemen they had protected. In De Witt County
east of San Antonio, the owners of a large ranch convinced three
Rangers to quit the force and accept positions guarding their pasture, which had been targeted by fence cutters.[58] Aten, meanwhile,
did retire and move to the Panhandle. He never became a nester,
as he had hoped, but instead served as the sheriff of Castro County
until he tired of law enforcement work altogether. Despite his wife's
protestations, Aten then accepted an offer from the XIT Ranch,
where he—along with former Rangers Ed Connell and Wood Saunders—tracked cattle rustlers and kept watch over the Capitol Syndicate's 6,000 miles of fence.[59]

The support of Alberta ranchers by the Mounted Police is much
less difficult to fathom, given that former Mounties were among the
region's first cattlemen and that many more hoped to enter the business upon their retirement from the force. It stood to reason that
they would protect an industry that they had helped to found and
promote and which held the promise of future economic advancement. Much more than the Rangers, the Mounted Police—especially its officer corps—stood on relatively equal footing with members of the ranching community they served, and they developed
strong social ties to area stockmen through both work and leisure.
The occasional empathy they showed toward the squatters must be
read in the context of their class prejudices, and thus appears more

as a streak of paternalism than deep-seated ambivalence about the nature of their duties or the authority of the state to impose its will.

Despite these critical differences, the ranching empires that developed at opposite ends of the Great Plains in the 1870s and 1880s bore striking similarities to one another and thus illuminate the process of incorporation that transformed Texas and the Canadian North-West at the end of the nineteenth century. On the most fundamental level, each government decided to turn over vast amounts of public land to bonanza ranchers at virtually the same moment, and for nearly identical reasons. Politics played a role in both cases, since the ruling Conservative Party in Ottawa sought to reward one of its core constituencies, while in Texas an ideology of divestiture partly inspired the liquidation of the state's land base. More important in the capitals, however, were the prospective financial gains—such as the influx of foreign investment—of such an enterprise and especially the big rancher's strategic significance in establishing a beachhead for white occupation in areas previously beyond the control of Austin and Ottawa.

The land policies that facilitated these developments heavily favored wealthy individuals and corporations and placed smaller ranchers and homesteaders at both ends of the Plains in a similar predicament. In Texas, Austin's rapid (even aggressive) sale of the public domain left those who had depended on the free-grass system watching with dismay as rich syndicates erected miles of barbed wire fence around formerly communal pastures and water holes. Those who fenced up lands that did not belong to them further aggravated a tense situation, made still more desperate by the vagaries of the Texas climate. Farmers and small cowmen in Alberta fared little better, as the leaseholders took control of the best lands of southwestern Canada almost overnight and rigidly expelled outsiders. Like his Texas counterpart, the Canadian farmer became increasingly frustrated with his exclusion from the most attractive range, staked off by Ottawa as stock-watering reserves.

The perspectives and responses of the farmers and small cow-men in Texas and Alberta invite clear comparisons to the protests against enclosure in eighteenth- and nineteenth-century England. At the southern end of the Plains, farmers and small ranchers com-plained that a handful of wealthy individuals backed by foreign investors had seized more than their share of the public domain, by means both fair and foul. The rural poor objected less to the privatization of property than to the fact that a few people or cor-porations could control a disproportionate amount of real estate, barring the economic and social advancement of others. Likewise, Alberta farmers—or, more precisely, their advocates—attacked the perceived injustices of Ottawa's lease policy through explicit refer-ence to English colonial policy in Ireland. Such an analogy carried weight, since the provinces of Canada had only joined together in Confederation in 1867, and the ties to the British Empire and the Old World were still very strong. By likening the situation on the Canadian ranching frontier to the Irish experience of the eighteenth and nineteenth centuries, observers conjured images of landlords, tenants, and evictees—actors in a historical drama characterized by wealth for the few and destitution for the many.

When fence cutters and squatters challenged the control of the range by large cattlemen, Austin and Ottawa turned to their rural constabularies to enforce regulations favoring the "big man's frontier." Texas officials passed legislation that made fence cutting a felony (a statute still in force today), and charged the Rangers with eradicating the offense, initially backing their efforts with a $50,000 appropriation. Ottawa, on the other hand, sought more symbolic assistance from the Mounties. While the NWMP did, on occasion, forcibly remove squatters and tear down their improvements, the vigilance of the police in attending evictions and barn razings ex-ecuted by local law enforcement officials demonstrated the unwav-ering support of the distant federal government for large cattlemen. That they performed essentially the same task as the Rangers, how-ever, is quite clear: in the words of one historian, the Mounties were called upon "to man the final line of defense against the homestead-ers' advance.[60]

If, in the end, the Liberal triumph of 1896 marked a victory for farmers and small ranchers in Alberta, they would suffer once more with their Texas counterparts in the second and third decades of the twentieth century. This time, however, big cattlemen and govern-ment policies were not to blame; after all, a precipitous decline in beef prices and the brutal winter of 1906–7 had crippled the Cana-dian ranching industry, smoothing the path of the farmers' ascent.[61] Rather, the new political calculus in Ottawa—coupled with several years of abundant precipitation and the aggressive promotion of the West by boosters—convinced hundreds of thousands of settlers to head for the region straddling the provincial boundary between Alberta and Saskatchewan.[62] Although they had prevailed in their struggle for the lands of the former North-West, when the rain-fall reverted to its normal patterns, farmers in the Canadian West learned that William Pearce (though arrogant and sanctimonious) had been right all along about the unsuitability of the lands for in-tensive cultivation. It was a lesson that nesters in the Texas Pan-handle might also have understood. Having defied the odds to take up homesteads among their cattle-ranching neighbors, they could only watch as the dust storms of the 1930s swallowed their farms and their dreams.[63]

NOTES

1. See *Report of the Adjutant-General of the State of Texas,* February 28, 1882, 27.

2. State of Texas, *Message of Governor John Ireland.*

3. Examples abound. See, e.g., letter from F. N. Vallins to W. H. King, 14 April 1884, and letter from S. C. VanDevender to W. H. King, May 1884, TSLA, AGR, GC, box 401-404, folders 5 and 11.

4. The most complete history of the fabled Pinkerton Agency makes no mention whatsoever of the agency's extensive work in Texas in 1884. See Morn, *"The Eye That Never Sleeps."*

5. Letter from Alan Pinkerton to John Ireland, 11 March 1884, TSLA, AGR, GC, box 401-404, folder 1.

6. The Runnels County cutters were apprehended destroying part of a 90,000-acre enclosure on the property of Colonel T. L. Odum, a Texas legislator. See Utley, *Lone Star Justice*, 235–36. For King's misgivings about the detectives, see letter from W. H. King to G. R. Freeman, 11 April 1884, TSLA, AGR, GC, ledger 40l-631, 208-9. Letter from William Carlton to W. H. King, 10 June 1884, TSLA, AGR, GC, box 401-404, folder 16.

7. Letter from S. C. VanDevender to W. H. King, 3 May 1884, TSLA, AGR, GC, box 401-404, folder 11.

8. Letter from G. W. Baylor to W. H. King, 16 March 1884, TSLA, AGR, GC, box 401-404, folder 3.

9. Letter from G. B. Greer to John Ireland, 19 July 1884, TSLA, AGR, GC, box 401- 405, folder 5. That Greer appears to have been a sheep man may have provided the cutters with added incentive to destroy his fence, since sheep grazed the range much more closely than cattle. See letter from G. B. Greer to L. P. Sieker, 26 August 1884, TSLA, AGR, GC, box 401-405, folder 9.

10. Report of P. F. Baird, 8 August 1884, enclosed in letter from L. P. Sieker to W. H. King, 8 August 1884, TSLA, AGR, GC, box 401-405, folder 8.

11. For arrest figures, see *Report of the Adjutant-General of the State of Texas,* December 1884, 28.

12. Letter from D. D. Sanderson to John Ireland, 10 January 1885, TSLA, AGR, GC, box 401-406, folder 1.

13. This description of the cattle industry in Brown County relies on Havins, *Something about Brown,* esp. 33–40.

14. Havins, *Something about Brown, 37.*

15. There is some debate about whether the scout was an Indian or a white man dressed as an Indian. But in an interview, Baugh's great-nephew George insisted that the scout was indeed a white man, a fact that deterred his relative from scalping the dead man but did not keep him from displaying his effects in the Baugh home. The slain man had his revenge, though, as his clothes promptly infested the Baugh house with lice. See T. C. Smith, *From the Memories of Men,* 26–27.

16. Aten, *Six and One-half Years.*

17. Aten's account is contained in a letter to L. P. Sieker, 11 June 1887, Center for American History at the University of Texas, Austin, Walter Prescott Webb Papers (cited hereafter as WPW), box 2R289, vol. 11. Havins offers a different version of events in *Something about Brown, 39.*

18. Quoted in Havins, *Something about Brown, 40.*

19. Quoted in T. C. Smith, *From the Memories of Men, 29.*

20. See T. C. Smith, *From the Memories of Men;* and letter from William Scott to L. P. Sieker, 12 December 1886, TSLA, AGR, Ranger Records, box 401–1160, folder 4.

21. Aten's letters, particularly a set of five missives from 1888, have received ample attention from Ranger historians, including Webb, *The Texas Rangers;* Wilkins, *The Law Comes to Texas;* and Utley, *Lone Star Justice.* Indeed, they usually form the basis for any study of the Frontier Battalion's efforts to eradicate fence cutting, although in most cases the letters have been used (and with great effect) to add color to a narrative.

22. Aten, *Six and One-half Years,* 20-22.

23. Letter from Ira Aten to L. P. Sieker, 31 August 1888, TSLA, AGR, GC, box 401-412, folder 19.

24. Letter from William Scott to W. H. King, 14 February 1887, TSLA, AGR, GC, box 401-409, folder 14.

25. Letter from Ira Aten to L. P. Sieker, 31 August 1888, TSLA, AGR, GC, box 401-412, folder 19.

26. Letter from Ira Atcn to L. P. Sieker, 31 August 1888, TSLA, AGR, GC, box 401-412, folder 19.

27. Letter from Ira Atcn to L. P. Sieker, 17 September 1881, TSLA, AGR, GC, box 401-413, folder 4.

28. Letter from Ira Aten to L. P. Sieker, 31 August 1888, TSLA, AGR, GC, box 401-412, folder 19.

29. Letter from Ira Aten to L. P. Sieker, 8 October 1888, TSLA, AGR, GC, box 401-413, folder 6.

30. Aten, *Six and One-half Years,* 22.

31. Letter from Ira Aten to L. P. Sieker, 15 October 1888, TSLA, AGR, GC, box 401-413, folder 6.

32. Breen, "The Canadian Prairie West," 72. For evidence of the expansion of stock-watering reserves, see orders-in-council issued on the following dates: 12 October 1889, 7 November 1890, 6 October 1891, 28 May 1892, 18 July 1894, 21 May 1895, and 23 January 1896, all in NAC, RG 15, vol, 1204, file 141376, part II.

33. Quoted in Breen, *The Canadian Prairie West,* 56.

34. Letter from William Pearce to secretary of the Department of the Interior, 23 October 1894, NAC, RG 15, vol. 1204, file 141376, part II.

35. Petition from the High River Stock Association to the minister of the interior, 2 April 1894, NAC, RG 15, vol. 1241, file 352945.

36. Letter from A. M. Burgess to T. Mayne Daly, 30 April 1894, NAC, RG 15, vol, 1241, file 352945.

37. See letter from Fred White to deputy minister of the interior, 12 June 1894, NAC, RG 18, series A-1, vol. 116, file 72; letter from John Hall to Fred White, 18 June 1894, NAC, RG; 18, series A-1, vol. 116, file 72; and letter from William Pearce to John Hall, 27 July 1894, NAC, RG 15, vol. 1241, file 352945. It bears repeating that Pearce's Cato-like insistence concerning the protection of Alberta's stock interests was motivated to a great degree by his conviction that the region was simply not suited to farming.

38. See, e.g., letter from George B. Jonas to the minister of the interior, 19 June 1894; and petition to John Hall, undated, both in NAC, RG 15, vol. 1241, file 352945.

39. See letter from A. R. Cuthbert to S. B. Steele, 24 January 1895; letter, unaddressed, from R. Duthie, 12 March 1895; and letter from William Pearce to secretary of the Department of the Interior, 26 March 1895, all three in NAC, RG 15, 241, file 352945.

40. See NAC, RG 18, series A-l, vol. 101, file 23. For squatting by an ex-policeman, see letter from William Pearce to John Herron, 4 November 1895, NAC, RG 15, vol. 1204, file 141376, part II.

41. Letter from Lynwode Pereira to Fred White, 19 September 1895, NAC, RG 18, series A-I, vol. 116, file 72.

42. Breen, "The Canadian Prairie West," 73.

43. Canada, Parliament, "Report of the Commissioner of the North-West Mounted Police Force 1895," *Sessional Papers,* 1896, XXIX, vol. 11, no. 15, p. 38.

44. See monthly report of Sam Steele, November 1895, NAC, RG 18, series A-I, vol. 102, file 46.

45. See *Report of the Adjutant-General of the State of Texas,* December 1888, 47–48.

46. *Report of the Adjutant-General of the State of Texas,* December 1888, 41.

47. Letter from John N. Garner to W. H. Mabry, 13 November 1893, WPW, box 2R289, vol. 12.

48. Simon Evans, "The End of the Open Range Era," 72-74.

49. See letter from James A. Smart to Frank Oliver, 17 June 1897; and letter from Lynwode Pereira to William Pearce, 14 July 1897, both in NAC, RG 15, vol. 1204, file 141376, part III.

50. Simon Evans, "The End of the Open Range Era," 74.

51. Letter from A. Power to deputy minister of the interior, 21 November 1896, NAC, RG 18, series A-I, vol. 116, file 72.

52. Letter from Fred White to the secretary of the interior, 15 July 1905, NAC, RG 18, series B-1, vol. 1560, file 133.

53. For more on Populism in Texas, see Goodwyn, *Democratic Promise.*

54. Lower, *Western Canada,* 316; Havins, *Something about Brown,* 37.

55. Letter from Ira Aten to L. P. Sieker, 17 September 1888, TSLA, AGR, GC, box 401-413, folder 4.

56. Letter from G. W. Baylor to W. H. King, 16 March 1884, TSLA, AGR, GC, box 401- 402, folder 3.

57. Letter from William Scott to W. H. King, 14 February 1887, TSLA, AGR, GC, box 401-409, folder 14.

58. Gard, "The Fence-Cutters;" 9.

59. Duke and Frantz, *6,000 Miles of Fence,* 107.

60. Breen, "The Mounted Police," 135.

61. Simon Evans, "The End of the Open Range Era."

62. David C. Jones narrates the story of this migration and its outcome in his eloquent *Empire of Dust.* Figures from the appendix (pp. 254–56) indicate that between 1906 and 1921 the population of southwestern Saskatchewan jumped from 257,763 to 757,510, while southeastern Alberta grew from 185,195 to 588,454 over the same period. Alberta and Saskatchewan achieved provincial status in 1905.

63. See Worster, *Dust Bowl,* esp. the map on p. 30 for a sense of the damage in Texas.

RANGERS OF THE LAST FRONTIER OF TEXAS

James M. Day

A new era began in 1881, an era when most of the Ranger force turned from chasing Indians to hunting and arresting outlaws. The death in that year of Major John B. Jones marked a new era for the Texas Rangers and the Frontier Battalion which had been organized in 1874 and which existed until 1900 when the opinion of an attorney general took its power. No longer was a frontier line clearly evident in Texas. Farms and ranches, cities and towns, and railroads and roads that would become highways were everywhere in evidence, and they were prominent features over the entire state except in the Trans-Pecos country.

In the Trans-Pecos, civilization existed only in pockets scattered among the rugged mountains and canyons and the vast dry expanses. West Texas was an arid stretch where man had to adapt or die, ruggedly beautiful and charming, yet so deadly. By 1882, a railroad ran through its mid-section and stagecoach and wagon roads meandered through its mountain passes and across its deserts. The ranches were big of necessity and the towns and farms were small for the same reason. Far to the west lay the step-child of Texas—El Paso, the most populous city and county in the area.

The Trans-Pecos was the last frontier of Texas. It was here that the last Indian battle on Texas soil was fought on January 29, 1881.

A Texas Ranger force led by George Wythe Baylor surprised the remnants of an Apache band, fell upon it, and killed four braves, two women, and two children. In explaining the action, Baylor reported that all the Indians wore blankets and the Rangers could not discern their sex, but he added "the law under which the Frontier Battalion was organized don't [*sic*] require it." This battle in the Diablo Mountains west of Guadalupe Peak brought a change in Ranger ways. Thereafter they gave up the pursuit of Indians and tried to confine their chases to "desperate whites and villainous Mexicans" in an effort to keep law and order.

Baylor's Company A had brought permanent Ranger service to the region in 1879, and Lieutenant C. L. Nevill commanded Company E which operated out of Fort Davis beginning in August, 1880. The arrival on June 6, 1880, of Sergeant Ed Sieker leading a detachment of nine men from Company D at Fort Stockton was a momentous occasion, for Company D was to play the major role in Ranger service in the Trans-Pecos. At the time that Baylor retired from service in 1885, his unit headquarters had been moved from Ysleta to Alpine. His sergeant, James B. Gillett, had resigned in 1882 to become city marshal of El Paso, but he resigned that position in 1885 to move to Marfa. From 1890 to 1892 he was sheriff of Brewster County. When the battalion was reorganized in 1882, Company D was the unit remaining in the Trans-Pecos region and along the border from Brownsville to El Paso.

As the Ranger leaders retired, new ones had already been trained under the same order. One such man was Frank Jones of Travis County. Born in 1856, the son of Judge William Eastman Jones of Georgia and Elizabeth Reston of Tennessee, Frank Jones was living in Kendall County in 1873 when he enlisted in Company C of the Kendall County Minute Men. He served one year, until March 1, 1874, when he took his discharge. His Frontier Battalion service began in September 1 of that same year when he enrolled in Company A. In 1876 he transferred to Captain Pat Dolan's Company F and stayed about nine months. After a break in service, he joined

Company D commanded by Captain Dan Roberts on July 28, 1881. A month later he was promoted to corporal. When Captain Roberts retired in 1882, the newly promoted Captain L. P. Sieker took command of the company and Jones was promoted to sergeant. Later when Captain Sieker was appointed battalion quartermaster, Jones was appointed first lieutenant commanding Company D on September 1, 1885. He was promoted to captain on May 1 of the next year. He remained in service at that post and rank until his death.

Until 1890 Company D roamed the brush country of South Texas from Laredo to Brownsville, from Corpus Christi to San Antonio. They also had special assignments. The muster and payroll for March through May, 1887 shows that the company was stationed in Edwards County with Jones as captain and Ira Aten as first sergeant, and with twelve privates, one of whom was Bass L. Outlaw. Six men had been discharged in the three months period and three special Rangers were attached to the company. Pay ranged from $100 per month for Jones to $50 for Ira Aten to $30.00 for the privates. Special Rangers received no pay. The teamster received $20 per month. Into this company, on August 10, 1887 was enrolled, Rank and File Number 4, John R. Hughes. A strange and unusual connection of events tied Jones, Outlaw, and Hughes together until April 1894, by which time both Jones and Outlaw were dead, and Hughes was commander of the company. Their way of life was dangerous, exciting, and interesting as they attempted to tame the last frontier of Texas.

Frank Jones was not a tall man, standing only five feet, eight inches, but he was a man of great vitality. He was referred to as a Ranger's Ranger because he was always willing to set the example in leadership and energy. He had a dark complexion, dark hair, and brown eyes. When he signed on, he listed his occupation as "farmer." In the mid-eighties, about the time he made captain, he married a young lady named O'Grady from San Antonio, and they made their home at Boerne. Jones spent Christmas, 1887, at home and was back on duty when his wife became ill shortly after their daughter, Kathleen, was born. Mrs. Jones died, leaving him with a daughter to raise. After the funeral, he made arrangements for the care of his daughter and, saddened, he returned to duty.

His duty as captain consisted of dispatching detachments wherever trouble arose, seeing to the camp and the welfare of his men, and reporting to the adjutant general. The camp was moved from Edwards County to Webb County, to Duval County, to Rio Grande City and finally to Alpine in 1890. In November 1887, he asked permission to appoint a corporal to look after the men in camp because Sergeant Ira Aten was never there. He concerned himself with wood, water, flour, bacon, beans, beef, coffee, corn, and hay. Railroad passes and Mexican interpreters were also part of the job.

John R. Hughes was thirty-two years of age when he became a Ranger, and he did so in a rather unusual way. Born in Cambridge, Illinois on February 11, 1855, he had moved with his family to Dixon, Illinois; and on to Kansas City, Kansas, and then to Mound City, Kansas where his parents operated a hotel. At age fifteen he struck out for Indian Territory where he worked for Art Rivers, an Arkansas man who traded with the Choctaw Indians. Rivers was a crude man who provoked a fight with the Indians. In the melee one Indian struck Hughes, shattering the bones of the right arm which never healed properly and which never was strong again. From then on, although he never liked it, Hughes learned to use his left hand for the pistol. He mastered the use of his left shoulder for the rifle at which he became expert. He stayed on in the territory and learned Indian ways from the Osages. Horses were his main interest. Hughes liked horses: he studied them and decided to make his living from them.

Hughes with his brothers, Will and Emery, established the Long Hollow Ranch in Travis County which was six miles from Liberty Hill in Williamson County and thirty-three miles northeast of Austin. Their brand was a running H on the left shoulder of horses and on the left side of cattle. They ranched peacefully enough until April, 1886, a period of almost nine years. Then rustlers struck, taking sixteen head of their horses and their stallion, Moscow. The rustlers also took stock from the neighbors, so two weeks later, on May 4, 1886, Hughes took the trail to recover the horses. A long journey took him to the Silver City area of New Mexico, where the animals were located. Enlisting the aid of Sheriff Frank Swafford and a deputy, Hughes visited the ranch of the thieves. The gunfight following the confrontation brought death to four of the rustlers. Hughes and a man he hired returned to Travis County with seventy-seven of the horses, which were returned to their owners.

Friends of the rustlers who lived in the wilds of western Travis County would not leave Hughes alone. Ranger Sergeant Ira Aten told Hughes about the threats on Hughes' life. The two men thwarted an attempt on Hughes' life by a man named Roberts, and thereby they became fast, lifelong friends. They then followed Roberts almost to the Red River before they caught him and killed him in the gunfight that ensued. Then the friends went to Georgetown where Hughes enlisted as a Ranger private and they went on to the camp of Company D near Uvalde.

Hughes was tall, lithe, broad-shouldered and square-jawed, and those who knew him always mentioned his amazing dark brown eyes which dominated his whole appearance. His first assignments were routine. In early January, 1888, Captain L. P. Sieker ordered him to Edwards County to "look out for fugitives." He went by horseback in order to be more visible. In August he and a scout went into Frio and Duval counties looking for a wanted fugitive named Will Jacobs. They went through the "Allee Pasture," a piece of land owned by the Allee family in Duval county, looking for stolen cattle. They could not go farther because no one would guide them. Hughes said that "the whole country seems to live in dread of Allee and his crowd." In September Hughes was in charge of four men who were scouting in Cameron County. The scouting expeditions were endless and often barren.

Those were the days of the fence-cutting wars in Texas, and Hughes naturally was caught up in the turmoil as was most of the Ranger force. In order to discover who the cutters were, some of the Rangers went undercover. Hughes was one of those assigned to Navarro and McLennan counties. He left Wharton on May 14 and arrived in Corsicana the next day. The county judge was gone, but as Hughes reported to Captain Sieker, he asked to be kept informed if more Rangers were coming. His contact in Corsicana was C. S. West. Heavy rains followed and Hughes had made no headway by the nineteenth, but when the rains stopped, he made his move. By May 26, he was near Richland and was "undercover." He wrote Sieker:

> I am now staying with a man who is suspicioned [*sic*] of cutting wire and have almost gained his confidence. He talks freely to me about stealing cattle. He and I stold [*sic*] a stake rope a few days ago and expect to kill a beef as soon as we eat up what he had on hand when I came. Then if he knows who the wire cutters are I think he will tell me.

But there were too many undercover men around as Lee Hall had detectives on the case, and so did a Mr. Waller from Waco. As Hughes reported, someone "made a confidant of the wrong man and gave the whole thing away." By June 13 he was in Waco making arrangements to put up a pasture fence so he could go back to watch it. If that tactic failed, Hughes concluded:

> . . . it will be no use for me to work after them any more as they are the best organized band that I ever worked after. They keep spies out all the time. The big pasture men live in town and the people in the country are almost all in sympathy with the wire cutters.

For Hughes this proved to be a frustrating assignment.

While Hughes was learning his trade as a Ranger, Bass L. Outlaw was causing trouble wherever he went. He is a somewhat elusive character about whom few facts are known. Born in Georgia, he was of good family and had a good education, as attested by the letters he wrote. About five feet, four inches in height, he was wiry and well coordinated—a good athlete and a good pistol shot. His features were delicately refined with a receding chin—a face that did not go with the rest of him, symbolic perhaps of the confusion within him. His brother, E. B. Outlaw, who lived in Rector, Arkansas in 1894, stated that he had not seen Bass in twenty years. Rumor had it that Bass Outlaw was "Gone to Texas" because he had killed a man in Georgia. A study of his quarrelsome nature reveals that as a distinct probability.

Bass seemed to be at home in the Ranger camp, having enlisted in Company E in 1885 and transferring to Company D in 1887. In July 1888 he was in Hempstead having a row with Wharton County officials over money. Wade Jones, sheriff of Wharton County, asked the Rangers to guard the jail during a ticklish time, promising to pay $1.50 per day for the service. Outlaw volunteered and guarded the jail for eleven days before returning to Hempstead. Outlaw owed Jones $10.00, and he wrote to Jones asking him to deduct that sum from the $16.50 he had earned. The sheriff balked and so did the county judge, but when they appealed to Adjutant General W. H. King, the Ranger boss backed Outlaw, saying that the Rangers did not ordinarily charge for that kind of service, but if there was an agreement, the payment should be made.

Money was always one of Outlaw's problems. In August Outlaw was in Hempstead and was ill. He complained that Dr. Urban, who treated him, "was very liberal with his charges." Then when he went from Wharton to Hempstead he had a "rising" on his thigh and could not ride. Corporal Walter Durbin told him to take the train. Outlaw requested $3.35 for the train fare and $3.15 for the hotel bill. He frequently wrote Captain L. P. Sieker to advance money to pay bills.

After Ira Aten left Company D, Charles H. Fusselman became first sergeant and remained at that rank until he was killed on the east side of the Franklin Mountains on April 17, 1890. By then the affairs of the company had shifted from South Texas to the Trans-Pecos region, and Captain Jones was headquartered at Marfa. With Fusselman's death, Bass Outlaw was promoted to first sergeant. Evidence indicates that Outlaw was serious while on duty, but tended to cause trouble when off duty and drinking. Money continued to nag him. In a series of letters in 1891 and 1892 between Outlaw and Charley Murphy of Marfa, written on letterhead stationery from the Buckhorn Saloon in Alpine, he told the merchant clearly not to pry into his financial affairs. He did the same to Humphrey and Company.

Money was not his only problem. On November 3, 1891, in Alpine, Outlaw got drunk and tried to force his way into the Zamloch Show managed by C. E. Van Horne. Zamloch was forced to leave the stage to find the source of the noise and disturbance. Because Outlaw was the source of the noise, Zamloch ordered him out of the show. Outlaw left, but only after threatening Van Horne. The next day Outlaw met Van Horne and a lady in Marfa and made threats, using abusive language. When Van Horne complained to the governor, Jones investigated, and finding that the accusations were accurate, he reported them to Adjutant General W. H. Mabry.

Women were also a problem. On February 13, 1892 at Alpine, Outlaw was drunk again. He went to the house of J. M. Watts, a black man who ran a "low dive on the outskirts of town," pulled his gun on Watts and threatened to kill him. After Watts closed the door, Outlaw fired his Winchester but did no damage. Then he went to the house of Watts' prostitute and spent the night with her. Jones investigated the affair and reported Watts' statement to Mabry.

Trouble in line of duty finally was the undoing of Sergeant Bass Outlaw. When silver was discovered at Shafter, some seventy miles south of Marfa, a detachment of Rangers was stationed there to keep the peace. In December 1890 Outlaw was in charge of the detachment. A Mexican had been arrested by some citizens on a charge of theft. Outlaw released the suspect, saying there were no charges. When Sheriff Miller from Marfa arrived to take the man into custody, the sheriff and Outlaw had some sharp words. Miller told Jones that Outlaw was under the influence of liquor. Jones confronted Outlaw and threatened to discharge him, but several citizens were afraid of Outlaw and persuaded Jones to send him back to camp.

Bass Outlaw made his last mistake as a Ranger on September 17, 1892, when he got drunk in the saloon in Alpine. Jones was out of town. Outlaw was having a good time of it as he "shot up" the town. Sheriff Gillett heard the shots and came running. He read the "riot act" to Outlaw, ordered him to holster his pistol, and threatened him with instant arrest. Outlaw tried to brazen it out, but Gillett repeated his ultimatum in unmistakable terms. Outlaw laughed, said he was buying the drinks, and let a coin drop to the floor as he pulled the money from his pockets. It was a tense moment, one in which either man, or both, could die. Outlaw bent a little as if to recover the coin, then straightened suddenly as if to go for his gun, but he looked hard at the sheriff, checking to see if Gillett planned to shoot him. Gillett read the thoughts, gently smiled, picked up the coin, and tossed it on the bar with the admonition "Now you remember what I told you. It's a fine thing when a Ranger has to be ordered to keep the peace."

Frank Jones got back to Alpine the next morning and heard about his sergeant's misbehavior. He called Outlaw in and ordered his resignation, which Outlaw duly signed so he could receive his pay. He left headquarters furious at Gillett because he thought the sheriff had told Jones of the fracas. Outlaw went to Jackson's mercantile where he bragged about wanting to kill Gillett. He was still there when James Gillett arrived for a confrontation, the result of which was that Bass Outlaw admitted his error. The previous June, Jones had written that Outlaw "has at times drank [sic] to some excess but he's given me no trouble." He concluded, "He is a man of unusual courage and coolness and in a close place is worth two or three ordinary men. He has some fine traits and I have always felt a warm personal feeling for him." But that did not stop Jones from forcing his resignation. Outlaw went to El Paso and became a deputy United States marshal under former Ranger Dick Ware, one of the men who had shot Sam Bass. In December, twenty prominent persons asked that he be appointed a special Ranger and Jones agreed. One of those making the request was James B. Gillett.

While Company D was undergoing the Bass Outlaw ordeal, John R. Hughes was solidly doing his duty of enforcing the law. He had been made corporal at the time that Outlaw had been promoted to sergeant, and had replaced Outlaw at Shafter when the sergeant had the trouble with Sheriff Miller. Hughes and Outlaw worked together very little. Hughes set up a systematic process of infiltration whereby he located most of the employees and their friends who were stealing ore. He was responsible and courteous and the mine owners appreciated it, and rumor has it that he was handsomely rewarded. When Outlaw was discharged, Hughes was promoted to first sergeant. When the company moved to Ysleta in June, 1893, Hughes and a detachment of men remained at Marfa. The move of the headquarters of Company D to Ysleta on June 14 was probably precipitated by the recent marriage of Captain Jones to one Helen Baylor, who was divorced from James B. Gillett, and was the daughter of George Wythe Baylor. But there was also another reason. Above and below El Paso, where the Rio Grande spreads itself in its bed, a series of marshes and islands were formed. The areas, called bosques, were essentially unpopulated, and outlaws from Mexico, Arizona, New Mexico, and Texas, called The Bosque Gang, gathered there. Jones and his Rangers decided to move them out—even if they had to cross into Mexico in pursuit. Jones admitted to Mabry that he did this, but he said he would never do it near a settlement.

Below El Paso there was a place called "Tres Jacales," named for the three little huts located on Pirate Island, a stretch of land in midstream which alternately belonged to Mexico or the United States, depending on which side of the "island" the river ran. In June, 1893, the river was on the American side, but Jones paid no attention as he led his Rangers in pursuit of the three Olguin brothers. Jones plunged into a well-laid trap and he paid for it with his life. He died that day, June 30, in the line of duty, but on Mexican soil. His body was taken to Juarez and it took Masonic connections to have Jones' body returned days later. Sergeant Hughes went immediately from Marfa to the site and took command. It was left to him to report the incident to General Mabry, to recover Jones' personal effects, and to explain as best he could why being on Pirate Island in Mexican territory was not such a bad thing.

Then came a somewhat political battle over the appointment of a successor to Jones. Bass Outlaw, citing his extensive Ranger service, applied for the post. The county judge, an evangelist, and some eighty citizens of Brewster County petitioned Governor James Stephen Hogg in Outlaw's behalf. John R. Hughes also applied for the position and drew support from the leading citizens of Alpine and El Paso. Perhaps the most important telegram Hogg received was from the El Paso County Democratic chairman, who said simply, "Our people want Hughes." Although petitions, telegrams, and letters were created in great volume, the process was relatively short. Hughes applied for the captaincy on July 2, and was appointed on July 4, 1893. The fact that the process was political, even though the most meritorious man won, augured ill for the Ranger force.

Hughes' exploits as a Ranger are legion. The explanation of what he did rests on three interviews Hughes gave in later life. He was interviewed by a well-known journalist, L. A. Wilke, and the interviews were published in a true detective magazine. Then Dane Coolidge interviewed him and published his words in *Fighting Men of the West* in 1932. Finally Jack Martin did an extensive interview which led to the book *Border Boss* in 1942. All these works are good in the oral tradition but they cannot be considered completely reliable. However, they do point the way and they represent the nucleus of what is printed and available at this time.

There are many of Hughes' activities which merit retelling—one of his bulldog-like searches is notable. It concerns the killing of Ranger Sergeant C. H. Fusselman by Geronimo Parra on April 17, 1890. Hughes, a corporal, was at Marfa with Frank Jones when they received the message telling of Fusselman's death. Jones gave his permission and Hughes caught the train to El Paso. He chased the killers but lost the trail.

Three years later Hughes located Parra in prison in Santa Fe. He tried to have Parra extradited but failed. Then one day, some years later, Pat Garrett visited Hughes in El Paso. Hughes told Garrett about Parra and said he wanted to get the outlaw back in Texas. Garrett struck a deal with Hughes—"You get me Pat Agnew and I will get Parra for you." Hughes agreed.

The Ranger struck Agnew's trail which led down the Rio Grande to Del Rio and Carrizo Springs, and then doubled back to Pecos. Hughes caught his man on a ranch in the Big Bend near the border. After Hughes delivered Agnew to Garrett at Las Cruces, the two went to Santa Fe where Garrett managed to have Parra released to Hughes and himself. The three of them rode the train to Las Cruces, where Hughes took over and delivered Parra to El Paso. Hughes was a "mighty satisfied" man when Parra was convicted to hang for the killing of Fusselman.

Yet the drama was not ended. Parra and another murderer, Antonio Flores, were scheduled to hang on January 6, 1900. As Flores was taken from his cell, he brandished a knife and started stabbing jailer and former Ranger Ed Bryan in the stomach. The door to Parra's cell had been left open and he too had a knife which he plunged into a policeman named Christy and into Deputy Will Ten Eyck.

As Captain Hughes rushed into the struggle, he saw that Ten Eyck had managed to put Parra back into his cell. It took four men to subdue Flores, but they did it, then they placed the hood over his head and dropped Flores into eternity.

As Parra was brought out, Flores' body was handed up so the noose could be removed. It had become knotted in the drop and was difficult to untie. Parra had to watch the proceedings. Finally, the rope was retied and placed around Parra's neck and he went to his death at the end of the rope. Hughes said he felt satisfied that Sergeant Fusselman was avenged.

Hughes served the force admirably until his retirement in June, 1915, having been a Ranger captain for twenty-three years, the longest record in Ranger history. He retired because James Ferguson was elected governor and he was going to sell Ranger commissions. The old Ranger later said that Ferguson intended "to put me out of a job and let me starve." Hughes' remark was followed by a smile and he added "But I didn't starve." The fact is that Hughes was always a frugal man. He had saved his money and bought river bottom-land near Ysleta which increased in price when Elephant Butte Dam was built. Hughes sold the land and created the Citizens Industrial Bank in Austin. He led the Texas Centennial Parade in Dallas in 1936 and led many Sun Bowl parades in El Paso. He became something of a showman in his fine silver studded regalia. In 1940 he was selected by the *True Detective* magazine as the first recipient of the Certificate of Valor, an award inaugurated to call attention to the bravery of peace officers. Hughes drove his 1928 Model T Ford until he reached the age of ninety-two, when he committed suicide in the garage at the home of his niece in Austin. The date was June 4, 1942.

One more footnote needs to be added. Bass Outlaw went from bad to worse and started frequenting El Paso's houses of ill repute and the saloons, and was running with the "sporting crowd." On April 5, 1894 he went on a spree and was killed by the famed gunman, John Selman. In the process, Ranger Joe McKidrict, who was trying to separate the two, was also killed, and Outlaw, who was wounded, was arrested for murder. He died under arrest, saying, "Where are my friends?" It was left to Hughes to make the report to Adjutant General Mabry.

Captain Hughes, like Frank Jones before him, was a Ranger's Ranger.

REFERENCES

Coolidge, Dane. *Fighting Men of the West*. New York: E. P. Dutton, 1932.

Day, James M. "Clothed With Absolute Power: Masonry and the Texas Ranger, 1823–1893." *Transactions Texas Lodge of Research, June 18, 1978*. Waco: Texas Lodge of Research, 1978, 13:51–80.

———. "El Paso's Texas Rangers." *Password* 24:4 (Winter, 1979): 153–172.

El Paso Times, April 5, 1894; April 7, 1894; June 5, 1947.

Frost, H. Gordon. *The Gentleman's Club: The Story of Prostitution in El Paso.* El Paso: Mangan Books, 1983.

Gillett, James. *Six Years With the Texas Rangers, 1875–1881.* 1921. Reprint. Lincoln: University of Nebraska Press, 1976.

Havens, Paul. "Border Boss." *True Detective Mysteries* 34:3 (June, 1940); 34:4 (July, 1940); 34:5 (August 1940); 34:6 (September, 1940).

Hughes, John R. *The Killing of Bass Outlaw.* Ed. Morris Cook. Facsimile, Austin: the Brick Row Bookshop, 1953.

——. "The Wide Loop of a Ranger Noose," as told to L. A. Wilke. *Real Detective.* (September, 1936), 24–29, 82–85.

Hunter, J. Marvin. "The Killing of Captain Frank Jones." *Frontier Times* 6:4 (January, 1929): 145–149.

Martin, Jack. *Border Boss: John R. Hughes—Texas Ranger.* Reprint. Austin: State House Press, 1990.

Metz, Leon C. *John Selman: Texas Gun Fighter.* New York: Hastings House, 1966.

——. *Pat Garrett: The Story of a Western Lawman.* Norman: University of Oklahoma Press, 1974.

Parrish, Joe K. "Hanged By the Neck Until Dead." *Password* 3:2 (April 1958): 68–75.

Redman, Jack Duane. "General John B. Jones: Twenty Years of Service to Texas." Master of Arts thesis, University of Texas at El Paso, 1983.

Shipman Papers. (Folder 94), El Paso Public Library.

Sonnichsen, C. L. *Pass of the North: Four Centuries on the Rio Grande.* El Paso: Texas Western Press, 1968.

Sterling, William Warren. *Trails and Trials of a Texas Ranger.* 1959. Reprint. Norman: University of Oklahoma Press, 1968.

Texas Adjutant General Correspondence, 1888 (Archives Division, Texas State Library).

Texas Ranger Muster Rolls, 1887–1893 (Archives Division, Texas State Library).

"True Detective Valor Award for July: John R. Hughes of the Texas Rangers." *True Detective* (July 1940), 79.

Van Oden, Alonzo. *Texas Ranger's Diary & Scrapbook.* Ed. Ann Jensen. Dallas: the Kaleidograph Press, 1936.

Webb, Walter Prescott. *The Texas Rangers—A Century of Frontier Defense.* New York: Houghton Mifflin, 1935.

Wilkins, Frederick. *The Law Comes to Texas: The Texas Rangers, 1870–1901.* Austin: State House Press, 1999.

★ 14 ★

THE JESSE EVANS GANG AND THE DEATH OF TEXAS RANGER GEORGE R. BINGHAM

Chuck Parsons

The other three desperadoes were captured and lodged in jail at Fort Davis. Among those captured is Jesse Evans, one of the most notorious highwaymen now living. He operated in Colorado and New Mexico, and was known by all as a brave, daring robber, who defied the officers and took possession of whole towns when it suited his purpose. This was his first trip to Texas, and to be gobbled up by Gen. Jones' men, has no doubt disgusted him with Texas in general and the alert wide-awake Texas rangers in general.[1]

Western buffs readily recognize Jesse Evans, the desperado whose name will be forever linked with that of Billy the Kid. Virtually every book dealing with the Kid devotes some space to Evans. We are concerned here not only with the Texas crimes of Jesse Evans, but also the man whose death placed him behind the unforgiving walls of Huntsville State Prison: George R. Bingham, a Texas Ranger of Company D, Frontier Battalion, who was killed in action.

Although the printed material about the Kid is voluminous, our factual knowledge of Jesse Evans is limited. Two book-length biographies give recognition to the man. The first, *Jesse Evans: A Texas*

Hide-Burner, was written and published by the late Texas historian Ed Bartholomew.[2] The second, *Jesse Evans: Lincoln County Badman,* by Grady E. McCright and James H. Powell, focuses principally on his involvement in the Lincoln County War of New Mexico Territory.[3] Even with these two biographies and numerous articles dealing with Evans, he remains "one of the many enigmas relating to the Wild West."[4] Almost as if to prove that the outlaws attract much more attention than the lawmen, not even a single periodical article has been devoted to George R. Bingham.

Two descriptive lists in the Texas Adjutant General's Records provide scant information about Texas Ranger George R. Bingham. One identifies him as G. R. Bingham and a native of Missouri. His occupation prior to joining the service is given as a stock raiser. He was described as five feet nine inches tall, had a florid complexion, red hair, and blue eyes. His ranger companions knew him as "Red." He was born about the year 1852. This early list shows he was enlisted on 1 September 1878. A second descriptive list in the same grouping of records provides the same information, but adds that he was enlisted by Capt. D. W. Roberts in Company D in Kimble County, Texas.[5]

Ann L. Bingham, head of household, thirty-two, in the 5th Ward of St. Louis, is recorded by the Missouri census as living with three children: Laura, aged twelve; George, aged ten; and Charles, aged six years. All claimed Missouri as their place of birth.[6] The family has not been found on a census return of 1870.

What George R. Bingham did from his early years in Missouri until he entered Texas is a mystery. One published report stated he was in Denison, Grayson County, Texas, for a while prior to moving further west to locate in Menard County. The item, based on a special telegram from Austin, described Bingham as "a young man, a zealous and active officer and a lively and popular comrade. He came from Denison to Menard where he joined the rangers."[7]

His name first appears on the Frontier Battalion Company D Muster Rolls in August 1878. Captain Daniel Webster Roberts, an experienced frontiersman, recorded that he was enlisted on 6 August as a private.[8] Bingham's service records reveal that he first enlisted on 6 August 1878. The pay period ended on 31 August and he received thirty-four dollars for that service. In an apparent contradiction, the first descriptive list which accompanied the Muster Rolls states he was enlisted by Captain Roberts in Kimble County on 1 September 1878.[9]

Under Roberts were two sergeants: Warren Wesley Worcester and Lamartine Pemberton Sieker; two corporals: John W. Lawhon and Edward A. Sieker; and two dozen privates. Of this aggregate of twenty-nine men, only Roberts had earned fame fighting Indians. Sergeant L. P. Sieker later rose in the ranks to become Adjutant General and Quartermaster of the Frontier Battalion. His brother Ed served less time in the service but gained recognition as a dependable servant of the state. The privates, who remain little more than names on the muster roll, were A. E. Alexander, H. T. Ashburn, Victor Barry, Bingham, J. S. Brown, S. D. Coalson, L. H. Cook, M. G. Coyle, Frank Dejarnett, William Garrett, D. W. Gourley, W. T. Harris, John Hetherly, J. H. Moore, Jerry Roberts, S. E. Shannon, John Stengel, W. F. Sheffield, C. F. Wall, T. A. Weed, C. M. Wilkes, J. C. Webb, S. A. Henry and H. W. Merrill.[10]

The Monthly Returns prepared by the captains provide only a brief summary of the scouts made, arrests made and attempts to arrest during a given month. The summary only identifies the ranger who was in charge of the scout. It provides his name, how many men were with him, and the number of miles marched. Bingham was certainly on numerous scouts, but with few exceptions, his name rarely appeared in the monthly returns.

Bingham recognized the danger involved in hunting for fugitives. He had never drawn his pistol at another human being to force a surrender—until his last day. On 30 April 1880, Privates Bingham and J. W. Miller left Camp San Saba to travel to Fort Mc-Kavett, where they arrested William Beavers, Ben Ellis, John Shaw, and A. Handy. The men were charged with disturbing the peace, but after their arrest and delivery to authorities, the charges could not be sustained and they had to be released. This scout took but one day and only ten miles on horseback.[11]

Perhaps unknown to Captain Roberts and the rangers was that a reign of terror was beginning in the far off Pecos and Presidio Counties area of West Texas. On 26 January 1880, Pecos County Sheriff Harry Ryan had sent a lengthy telegram to Adjutant General John B. Jones expressing his fears:

> In a few days an attempt will be made to forcibly seize a heard [*sic*] of cattle in this county and take them to New Mexico & the result will be a cow war[.] Should the New Mexican party succeed it will be a precedent for band[s] of Lawless men to come from new Mexico and Rob cattle in Texas[.] When the fight begins life & property will be very insecure in the vicinity & in view of these circumstances I request that Capt [Junius] Peak be ordered to the Pecos where I will meet him. Answer so that I may know if I can depend on the Rangers.[12]

A "cow war" did not commence as Sheriff Ryan feared, but troubles escalated for the honest people of Presidio and Pecos Counties. In June 1879, burglars broke into the home of rancher George Crosson. They were captured but then escaped jail, and only one was re-captured and sent to Huntsville. The others were at large until May 1880. About the same time, George Claxson was murdered and robbed by unknown parties. Early settler Diedrick Dutchover lost fourteen head of horses to raiding Indians within a mile and a half from town. Juan Gutires was slain by Indians only a few miles from Fort Davis. Adolo Reiqis was murdered in late July 1879. His murderer was captured but then escaped jail and fled to Mexico. Perhaps most terrifying of all was the murder of W. H. Banks, the assistant jailer, who was murdered *inside the jail* on 23 November 1879. The murderers and prisoners who escaped also left Jailer A. McAfee near death, but he recovered from his wounds. There were numerous other examples of horses, cattle and sheep being stolen,

as well as burglaries and murders—by both Indians and white outlaws. One county official recorded outrages he was aware of and
mailed the list to the adjutant general's office in Austin.[13]

It was indeed a "deplorable state of affairs" in that section. To
the good citizens of Pecos and Presidio Counties the governor
could not act quickly enough. The *Statesman* of Austin reported
that the rangers were requested. "It seems" reported the *Statesman*,
"that large numbers of lawless men congregate around the cattle
camps in New Mexico, and from there raid into the state [of Texas]
and commit depredations."[14]

Governor Oran M. Roberts and Adjutant General John B. Jones
were acting upon the requests for Texas Ranger assistance. If there
had been doubt before, there wasn't after the most outrageous blow
from the lawless; the general merchandise store of Joseph Sender
and Charles Siebenborn in Fort Davis was robbed in broad daylight
on 19 May 1880 by a trio of thieves. The men were recognized as
Jesse Evans of New Mexico, and brothers Bud Graham alias Ace
Carr, and Charles Graham, alias Charles Gross. How many district
courts wanted Jesse Evans is undetermined, but the two Graham
boys had been indicted for murder in Williamson County, Texas.
While Evans and the Graham brothers were doing their work in
Sender & Siebenborn's store two others—John Gunter and another
Graham brother—acted as lookouts. Anyone who rode up was invited to take a drink with them to divert attention from the actual
robbery. The trio of thieves got away with a thousand dollars, plus
merchandise valued at one hundred dollars. They also robbed Edgar G. Glime and F. W. Ruoff, two men who happened to be in the
store at the time. The next day August Diamond's house was bur-
glarized "by unknown parties."[15]

The daring robbery of the Sender & Siebenborn store caused
concern as far away as El Paso. Two days following the robbery,
several merchants feared the robbers were headed their way to continue their depredations. On 21 May, men representing the firms of
Kettesen & Dayton, S. & W. Schutz, Ynocente Ochoa, and B. Schus-

ter & Co. telegraphed Adjutant General Jones that "a band of out-laws headed by one Jesse Evans of Lincoln Co. fame have robbed stores at Fort Davis in broad daylight yesterday & that they are on their way up here to commit probably the same outrage [.]" It was understood by this message that they wanted the rangers to come to their assistance.[16]

Pecos County Judge George Milton Frazer wanted ranger assistance as well. He telegraphed Governor O. M. Roberts on 24 May about the band of robbers camped near on the Pecos River. He explained that this was the same gang that had robbed Sender & Siebenborn's store and that the gang was committing more thefts. Attempting to make the Texas administrator act out of a sense of guilt, he stated he wanted ten rangers "to assist us to capture them" but if "you can't it will be useless to ever ask any assistance again."[17]

Jones sent ten rangers from Fort McKavett in Menard County to the Fort Davis area. They had thirty days' rations and funds to purchase forage and were ordered to report to Judge Frazer and "operate against out-laws." Jones advised Frazer of the orders given the rangers and that they would "come as rapidly as possible" and that he had no men any nearer than Fort McKavett.[18]

The rangers were from Captain Daniel W. Roberts' Company D of the Frontier Battalion with Sergeant Ed A. Sieker in charge. The men were George R. Bingham, Samuel A. Henry, Richard R. "Dick" Russell, and D. T. Carson. Later Sergeant L. B. Caruthers from Company E arrived to join in the work, but the names of the others are not recorded. They reached Fort Stockton on 6 June. Ten days later, Judge Frazer communicated to Governor Roberts that they had as yet "not been able to apprehend any of the robbers but will get them if he [Sergeant Sieker] is allowed to remain."[19]

The outlaws then boldly rode to Fort Stockton and remained there for several days. On 1 June, a little before sundown, Sheriff Harry Ryan and a posse surrounded Silverstein's Saloon. Carr was arrested, "suspected of being one of the party that robbed a store at Fort Davis a few days ago. He is also believed to be one of the

Peg Leg stage robbers, and a very dangerous character. A number of shots were fired during the progress of the arrest, but none took effect." Carr's friends made their escape.[20]

Judge Frazer, feeling anxious as the rangers had not yet arrived, telegraphed Jones on 3 June that "they should be here now" and advised that once they got there, there would be "plenty of work for them." Missing the irony of the situation that the citizens had already captured one of the robbers without the presence of the rangers, Frazer proudly announced that they had captured Carr and in addition left the other robbers afoot—as their horses had been captured. He believed they were "probably good to capture them if they do not get fresh horses before the rangers arrive." Nevertheless they captured no one but Carr and remained "in great fear and on the alert." Whoever wrote the report to the *Galveston Daily News* optimistically believed that the other gang members "w[ould] probably be captured soon." Carr was identified as one of the robbers by Joseph Sender and placed in jail "and a guard is on the lookout to prevent his escape or recapture by his friends."[21]

Once at Fort Davis, Sergeant Sieker had the responsibility of guarding Carr in the insecure Fort Davis jail. Since it was common knowledge that the rest of the gang was still in the area and would attempt to liberate Carr, Sergeant Caruthers ordered Sieker to take the prisoner to Fort Stockton, where the jail was more secure. Sieker and his detachment jailed Carr there on 18 June. Somehow the gang learned of the removal of the prisoner and made a plan to ambush the rangers in Limpia Canyon. Sieker suspected that might happen and took Carr by a different route to *durance vile*. Now the rest of the gang, identified as Evans, August Gross alias John Gunter, and Jesse and Charles Graham, "continued to skulk through the mountains near this place, . . . watching [for] an opportunity to release the prisoner."[22]

Sergeant Caruthers, who had arrived at Fort Davis the night of Sunday, 6 June, found everything "quiet now" but the people still wary and "always on the look out for the outlaws from Mexico and

the Pecos. . . ." He had learned there were "a great many outlaws congregated on the Pecos, from Lancaster up to Seven Rivers, a good
many of them are between the New Mexico line and Horsehead
Crossing and have been compelled to leave New Mexico." By then,
the citizens of Forts Davis and Stockton had offered a reward of
$1,100 for the others who had robbed Sender & Siebenborn's store.
He also reported the arrest of Carr, but pointed out that there had
been a gunfight with the citizens, "who only captured Bud, and let
the other two escape—in fact was badly managed by the aforesaid
parties." Believing the Graham brothers were wanted in Williamson
County he had wired for *capiases* to arrest them.[23]

Caruthers learned the gang planned to rob the stores of Ab-
bott and Davis and O. M. Keesey, but the attack was delayed because of Ace Carr's arrest. Caruthers also attempted to identify the
gang members. Bud Graham, alias Carr, was a brother of Charles
Graham, alias Charles Gross. Another brother was "Dolly" Graham alias George Davis. Graham, alias Davis, "being in town with
a commorade [*sic*] by the name of John Gunter, but I find he passed
in New Mexico, under the name of John Gross, but I think his real
name is August Gross of Fort Griffin, the third party in the robbery
here, one Jesse Evans, has several indictments against him in New
Mexico."[24] Further, Caruthers wrote, "the band [consisted of] some
twenty men last year, and that they have their agents here and in
Stockton, their agent here is Capt. Tyson, his real name is John Selman, who I find is Ind[icted] in Shackelford Co. I think from what
I can learn that he is Chief of the gang and as he was getting very
scarry [*sic*], I had him appointed Deputy Sheriff and Jailer as the
Jailer had just resigned."[25]

Caruthers apparently could not appreciate the irony of the situation of making John Selman a jailer, unless he believed Selman
would do his "duty" to prevent prisoners from escaping. Caruthers
had additional concerns. The outlaws constantly changed the location of their camps in the mountains. He had thought of a plan by
which, he believed, the outlaws would make an effort to escape jail

"and think it would have worked out all right, if the Sheriff (Captain Wilson) had not let all out on a drunk."[26]

Although at this point Caruthers would not arrest Selman, "because I know, that I could not hold him here," a week later he had him in custody. Apparently the arrest was made by Sergeant Sieker, although the details are unknown. Here Sieker complained of the small number of rangers he had, too few to guard the jailor or do any effective scouting.[27] Selman offered to identify the members of the Shackelford mob which had murdered his partner John M. Larn back in 1878, apparently in exchange for his freedom. Caruthers refused of course, and managed to keep Selman in custody even though a jail release was almost successful.[28] Carr "came very near making good his escape through the kindness of the jailer at Fort Davis, who has since been recognized as belonging to the same gang. He is known on the Pecos river as Jno. Smith, at Fort Davis as Jno. Liesen and in Shackelford County, where indictments are against him, as John Sellman [sic]."[29]

To reduce some of the pressure on his rangers, Sergeant Sieker wanted Selman to be delivered to Shackelford County and notified Georgia-born Sheriff William R. Cruger to that effect. Cruger wrote that he "would not answer for John Selman's life if I brought him here, and also that the charges against him could not be sustained by law." Thus, Selman was not wanted back in Shackelford County— and if he were delivered to county seat Albany, "nine chances to one that the mob will hang him."[30] To give Sieker and the authorities there some satisfaction, Adjutant General Jones ordered him to deliver Selman to Fort Concho, Tom Green County, and turn him over to the county sheriff there.[31]

Sergeants Sieker and Caruthers certainly had their work well defined: guard the jail, deliver Selman, watch suspected county officials for malfeasance, and scout the mountains for members of the Jesse Evans gang. The break they needed soon came.

On 29 June, someone informed them that some of the gang had been seen in the mountains in the vicinity of Presidio del Norte, almost one hundred miles south of Fort Davis. On the night of 1 July with Sergeant Sieker in charge, a scout was ready to begin the hunt for the Evans gang. Sieker selected Privates George R. Bingham, D. T. Carson, Samuel A. Henry, Richard R. Russell, and Sgt. Caruthers; they took Clato Herridio along as their guide. By the afternoon of the third, they were between fifteen and eighteen miles from Presidio del Norte, almost on the Rio Grande. Sergeant Sieker provided the best account of what happened then:

> When within 18 miles of that place, we discovered four men, with pack horse, going towards the rough mountains. We advanced on them, they commenced running & drew their guns & fired on us. We shot at them & a running fight lasted for 1-1/2 miles. When they run up a large mountain, we followed. As soon as we were on top of the mtn. we soon discovered they were concealed behind a ledge of rocks, as a solid volley was fired at our little band. As there were but three of us at that time, before we dismounted, a shot cut Carson's hat brim, and another passed under his leg, cutting his stirrup leather & wounding his horse in the side. They shot volley after volley at us, at forty yards range in open view & they behind the rocks. Carson shot one of the party in the side, but he was determined to "sell out," and kept firing, around our heads, very closely. When I saw him stick his head out to shoot, I shot him between the eyes, [the bullet] coming out at the back of his head. Bingham was to my left, and about 35 yards to the rear, when he was shot through the heart. We charged the party and took their stronghold. Then we had the advantage for the first time, and then they surrendered. Had I known Bingham was killed at that time, I should have killed them all. But we had disarmed them before we knew it. Then they prayed for mercy.[32]

Although initially the rangers outnumbered the outlaws, when the shooting started it was an even numbered affair—four outlaws and four rangers. Sergeant Caruthers was too far behind the rest of the group to participate. Private Henry was with the pack animal, riding a mule, as his horse had gone lame. Bingham had been shot and killed in the first volley from the outlaws' guns, leaving Sieker, Carson, and Russell to carry on the fight against the outlaw quartet.[33]

Carson had nearly been shot in the head and his horse was wounded, yet he continued to fight. Sieker maintained the presence of mind to get off a careful shot—under fire—and placed his bullet between the eyes of Jesse Graham. This demoralized the remaining three and with the odds even, they surrendered. The outlaws captured were identified as Charles Gross Graham, alias Charles Groves or Graves; August Gross, alias John Gunter; and Jesse Evans, "the noted New Mexico desperado." As soon as the fight was over and the prisoners secured—and Bingham's body discovered—Sieker sent guide Herridio to Presidio del Norte to request the services of a coroner.[34]

The next day Herridio and the coroner arrived, it was determined that "G. R. Bingham came to his death in the discharge of his duty—and that Jesse Graham came to his death by resisting arrest."[35]

The excitement of the fight gradually ebbed away, with two dead men, Carson's wounded horse, and two dead horses before them. They were all a mile and a half from the Presidio road, on top of a mountain, a mile above sea level. After the coroner finished with his examination, Bingham—and perhaps Graham—was provided with a temporary burial. "We buried him on the side of the road, and our little squad showed him all the respect we could. We formed and fired three volleys, over his grave, and with saddened hearts, we wound through mountain passes, to [Fort] Davis, arriving safely with our prisoners. The people are happy over our success, & will have Bingham's remains buried here."[36]

Sergeant Sieker kept his promise. On 11 February 1881, he and four men left camp in Musquiz Canyon to bury Bingham. He wrote in his monthly report they "disinterred him on 17th and sent him to Fort Davis where he was reinterred on 20th in town cemetery by Sergt Caruthers."[37] Today, George R. Bingham's remains still rest in the Pioneer Cemetery at the foot of Dolores Mountain in Fort Davis. This cemetery probably originated in the early to mid-1870s, and although not officially designated as a cemetery, it was used by people of all races and beliefs. Only a few stone markers remain there today.

Jesse Evans and the others paid for their crime of resisting the rangers. Not knowing that Bingham was killed at first fire, Sieker accepted their surrender. Had he known, the other three would have been shot as well, but instead of executing them, the prisoners were delivered to the jail in Fort Davis. On 7 July, Captain Neil Coldwell telegraphed Jones that the trio had had a "preliminary examination before Judge Duke on charge of murder of private Bingham & committed without bail." He further explained what his men would have to do, that it was "necessary that we guard jail until these men are tried in October[.] the arrest of these men will put a quietus on the trouble heretofore existing here except horse stealing by Mexican thieves which is likely to continue until broken up by Rangers." He estimated that if there were fifteen men stationed there, the country could be entirely free of thieves and fugitives from justice within three months. Five men would be needed to guard the jail and the others assigned to scout. Although the local populace could not produce enough dependable men to guard the jail, "citizens [were] much elated by [the] success of rangers & [said] that by their gallantry have broken the reign of terror here."[38]

By late September, Captain J. W. Graham of Georgetown had arrived in Fort Davis to see to his sons' defense. By the time court began on 4 October Mr. Graham had found an attorney who secured bond for them. Once out of their irons, the boys jumped bail and disappeared; their final demise is unknown. Jesse Evans was found guilty of participating in the robbery of Sender & Siebenborn's store, and was also found guilty of the murder of Bingham. He was sentenced to ten years on each count and was received at Huntsville on 1 December 1880 as prisoner number 9078. On 23 May 1882, Evans escaped from a work crew—what happened to him after that date is unknown.[39]

Captain Roberts may have had nothing more to say about the whole affair, but what Adjutant General John B. Jones wrote in 1880 is perhaps the finest eulogy that could be given to Bingham:

> The death of poor Bingham is much regretted but of course his fate is that which all take the chance of when they enter such service as we are engaged in.[40]

NOTES

1. *Daily Democratic Statesman* (Austin, Texas), 9 July 1880.

2. Ed Bartholomew, *Jesse Evans: A Texas Hide-Burner* (Houston: The Frontier Press of Texas, 1955).

3. Grady E. McCright and James H. Powell, *Jesse Evans: Lincoln County Badman* (College Station: Early West Series, 1983).

4. Leon Claire Metz, *The Encyclopedia of Lawmen, Outlaws and Gunfighters* (New York: Facts on File, Inc., 2003), 79.

5. Adjutant General Files, Texas State Archives. Hereafter cited as AGF, TSA.

6. Federal Census, St. Louis County, Missouri, 5th Ward, 19.

7. *Galveston Daily News,* 9 July 1880.

8. Company D Muster Rolls, Austin, AGF, TSA.

9. *Ibid.*

10. *Ibid.*

11. Monthly Record of Scouts, 30 April 1880, AGF, TSA.

12. Monthly Record of Scouts, AGF, TSA.

13. "Outrages and Indian Raids in Presidio Co. from June 1, 1879 to June 1, 1880" [1-2], AGF, TSA. This seven page document hereafter cited as "Outrages."

14. *Colorado Citizen* (Columbus, Texas), 10 June 1880, reprinting an item from an undated *Statesman.*

15. "Outrages"; Federal Census of Presidio County, 12 June 1880, 87.

16. Telegram to Adjutant General John B. Jones, 21 May 1880, AGF, TSA.

17. Judge G. M. Frazer, telegram to Governor O. M. Roberts, 24 May 1880, AGF, TSA.

18. Adjutant General John B. Jones, telegram to Judge G. M. Frazer, 25 May 1880, AGF, TSA.

19. Judge G. M. Frazer, telegram to Governor O. M. Roberts, 16 June 1880, AGF, TSA.

20. *Galveston Daily News,* 3 June 1880.

21. *Ibid.;* Captain Neal Coldwell, telegram to Adjutant General John B. Jones, 10 July 1880, AGF, TSA.

22. Captain Neal Coldwell, telegram to Adjutant General John B. Jones, 10 July 1880, AGF, TSA.

23. Sergeant Caruthers, telegram to Lieutenant C. L. Nevill, 8 June 1880, AGF, TSA.

24. Sergeant Caruthers, telegram to Adjutant General John B. Jones, 28 June 1880, AGF, TSA.

25. *Ibid.*

26. *Ibid.*

27. Semi-monthly return of Capt. D. W. Roberts, 1 July 1880, AGF, TSA.

28. Sergeant Caruthers, telegram to Adjutant General John B. Jones, 14 June 1880, AGF, TSA.

29. *Galveston Daily News,* 8 July 1880.

30. William R. Cruger, telegram to Adjutant General John B. Jones, 1 and 2 July 1880, AGF, TSA.

31. Adjutant General John B. Jones, telegram to Sergeant Sieker, 12 July 1880, AGF, TSA.

32. Sergeant Sieker, telegram to Governor O. M. Roberts, 21 July 1880, AGF, TSA.

33. Sergeant Sieker, telegram to Captain D. W. Roberts, 12 July 1880, AGF, TSA.

34. Captain Neal Coldwell, telegram to Adjutant General John B. Jones, 10 July 1880, AGF, TSA.

35. *Ibid.*

36. Sergeant Sieker, telegram to Governor O. M. Roberts, 11 July 1880, AGF, TSA.

37. Sergeant Sieker, telegram to John B. Jones, 28 February 1881, AGF, TSA.

38. Captain Neil Coldwell, telegram to Adjutant General John B. Jones, 7 July 1880, AGF, TSA.

39. Philip J. Rasch, "The Story of Jessie [*sic*] J. Evans," *Panhandle-Plains Historical Review* (1960).

40. Adjutant General John B. Jones, telegram to Captain Roberts, 14 July 1880, AGF, TSA.

THE STRUGGLE FOR THE INDIVIDUAL AND THE UNION, 1888–1903

Marilyn D. Rhinehart

Good bye, Mr. Gordon, we must leave you,
And you bet your life we're glad to go.
Something tells us we are needed—
To the Union Mines we'll go.
Yes the boys with picks are marching,
And we can no longer stay.
Hark! We hear our leaders calling
Good bye, we're away.

UNION BANNER

For fifteen years after the Texas & Pacific Coal Company purchased the Johnson assets, a core group of miners, most of Welsh, Scots, and Irish ancestry, led a protest movement that challenged the very heart of Colonel Hunter's system of operation in Thurber. Their lives most likely paralleled that of Gomer Gower and his family, as they migrated in and out of eastern, midwestern, and southwestern mining centers in the United States, following relatives and friends and operators' appeals for skilled workers. Many of these miners had probably worked underground in Erath and Palo Pinto counties some time before Hunter even invested in the mining industry there. Their mining experience dated to their childhoods, and from an early age they understood the usefulness of the strike, organization, negotiation, solicitation of help from local and distant allies, and emigration as tools of protest. Using such traditional resistance tactics, they laid the basis for a movement in Thurber that ultimately bridged ethnic and racial differences and assumed mass proportions in 1903.[1]

Ironically, their actions won success during William K. Gordon's tenure as general manager in Thurber. From the time Gordon went to work for Hunter in 1889, the civil engineer and self-taught geologist earned a reputation for fairness among the miners as he rose through company ranks as mining engineer, superintendent, assistant general manager, and then vice-president and general manager. He lived in the camp with his family and encouraged or at least quietly tolerated the residents' customs, as alien as they must have seemed. He continued and extended Hunter's attempt at welfare capitalism and gave every indication of being an enlightened and benevolent manager.[2]

Even company paternalism, however, could not overcome two important factors: the miners' individualistic impulse to have more control over their work and after-work lives and the mushrooming effect of the rise of the United Mine Workers' union in the Southwest. The result was the development of one of the most dramatic organizational episodes in Texas' early industrial history.

Labor organizations near the site of the Texas & Pacific Coal Company's mining operations had a history at least six years longer than that of the coal company itself. At least three Knights of Labor locals existed in Erath County between 1885 and 1888 (none specifically for coal miners), four in nearby Eastland County between 1883 and 1887, and nine in Palo Pinto County. The local at Gordon, just adjacent to Thurber, represented coal miners from 1882 to 1889.[3]

In 1884, a 186-day strike by 450 miners and laborers to protest a wage reduction closed the mines at Coalville. The walkout, which a

Knights of Labor local had called, failed, and the Gould railroad interests proceeded with a 14 percent wage cut. The railroad's mining operation in the area, however, did not survive the financial loss the strike precipitated; in 1886, Gould completely halted coal production there. Even so, the Gordon local still recorded over 200 members in a locale with a population under 1,000. When the Johnson brothers recruited the unemployed Coalville miners the same year the mines folded, they offered the workers a mining rate of $1.50 a ton, $.25 lower than they had received previously. This announcement prompted yet another strike.[4]

For two months the miners remained idle, until the Johnsons granted the local Knights of Labor Assembly the right to appoint a mine committee to negotiate with management in settling disputes. The brothers also agreed to remunerate the miners at the wage paid at Coalville. From that point, good relations between the miners' local and the company continued until William Johnson failed to meet the payroll in 1888, and the company changed hands. For the next four years, these workers agitated and organized in an effort to thwart the new owners' efforts to operate the mines without them.[5]

Hunter never professed any affection for assertive, organized workers and, as he established his domain in Thurber, refused to negotiate on any terms but his own. When the Texas & Pacific Coal Company took possession of the Johnson property, the Colonel immediately posted notices announcing more than a 30 percent cut in the mining rate and almost a 10 percent reduction in the day wage that the Johnson Company had paid. He further made clear his intention to operate the mines on the screened-coal rather than the mine-run basis.[6]

The Colonel also demanded, by Gower's account, that employees "renounce their allegiance to the Knights of Labor and promise not to participate in any sort of union organization efforts." This demand for a yellow dog contract had the same effect as "shaking a red shawl in the face of a bull." When a miners' committee sought a meeting with Hunter, he received them cordially enough but could not conceal his disdain for them. As the miners left, having gained no concessions from the Colonel, Gower recalled that Hunter admonished them: "I will make a dollar look as big as a wagon wheel to you s-o-bs before I get through with you." As a result, none of the old miners applied for Hunter's jobs, forcing him to send his confederates on recruiting tours to mining camps in Indiana, Illinois, Pennsylvania, Kentucky, Missouri, and Kansas.[7]

In a remarkable display of unity, the Johnson miners, in concert with Knights of Labor locals in various mining districts across the country, managed to impede company recruiting efforts for almost three months. Their means of operation were simple but effective. They sent representatives to mining districts and wrote letters to union newspapers. Gower recounted how he helped the local: "There was a sufficient number of us who sought employment in various parts of the country . . . to advise unsuspecting miners of the conditions in Texas. I, myself," he added, "though but an eighteen year old boy at the time, was assigned to the Belleville field in southern Illinois [where a sister and her family resided] for that purpose."[8]

Dan McLauchlan, recording secretary of Knights of Labor Local Assembly 2345, filed several reports on the miners' difficulties with the *Journal of United Labor,* a Knights of Labor publication (May 5, June 23, 1888). After the union committee's unsuccessful meeting with Hunter, McLauchlan claimed that the Texas & Pacific Coal Company was in the market for strikebreakers, who "would be glad to come here and work at any price." McLauchlan asked readers to stay away until a settlement had been reached—"until then," he wrote, "help us by giving Gordon, Texas, a wide berth" (October 25, 1888).

Another McLauchlan letter to the *Journal* (January 3, 1889) explained that working for Hunter meant accepting work at a reduced wage with no input from those who best understood the difficulty of working thin-veined mines. "We have not insisted upon the old price," McLauchlan concluded, "but simply ask that the matter be submitted to arbitration and we [be] given a chance to be heard. This is a poor place to come to for work . . . and all miners are requested to keep away." McLauchlan sent similar letters to another labor newspaper, the *National Labor Tribune* (October 13, October 20, December 15, December 22, 1888), a publication of the National Progressive Union of Miners.

The dispersal of information about conditions at the Johnson mines reaped immediate rewards. Moral and financial support from Knights of Labor locals in the nation's mining districts seriously impeded Hunter's effort to start production. Union members all over the country kept Thurber workers informed of company recruitment activities and sent their own representatives to dissuade miners from working for the Texas & Pacific Coal Company. When company trains arrived in the nation's mining districts, local assembly members infiltrated employment meetings, learned the time of return to Texas, and passed the information to Thurber's local. When the trains reached Fort Worth, a Knights delegation waited to persuade potential employees to leave and with Farmers' Alliance and Knights of Labor national assembly aid, to fund their return. Such activities kept the mines practically shut down until February, 1889, when company officials and Texas Rangers duped labor activists waiting for the train in Fort Worth. They managed to get over 170 miners—many of them black—past the union activists, but a third of these new employees subsequently refused to enter the mines and joined the Knights of Labor after hearing speeches at the Labor Hall.[9]

Frustrated in his initial attempts to import new employees, operate the mines, and maintain absolute control, Hunter resolved to crush the sulking miners. Much to his dismay, they congregated at an independently operated saloon in the area and at a meeting hall only a mile from company property on land the Knights of Labor had purchased in 1887. By the end of December, 1888, after gunfire showered the building where the Colonel and his lieutenants were in their offices, the general manager appealed to local and state officials for a contingency of Texas Rangers to be sent "to protect life and property at the mines." The *Dallas Morning News* reported on December 23 that ten of Captain McMurry's company of Texas Rangers had arrived at the mines three days earlier to handle a disturbance caused by the striking miners. Five days later, the paper noted, McMurry wired Adj. Gen. W. H. King in Austin that all was "quiet and orderly" around the mines.[10]

In January, the adjutant general himself visited the camp at Captain McMurry's request. His interview with the Knights of Labor committee convinced him of the sincerity of their pledge to help maintain order against the irresponsible few who had threatened Hunter. Nevertheless, agitation continued. In the interest of protecting Hunter's investment, Texas Ranger Company B maintained a visible presence in Thurber as the strikers continued their efforts to thwart Hunter's attempts to replenish the pits with imported miners. In May, McMurry wrote King that "through the workings of the Knights of Labor & the Strikers, the miners on yesterday demanded ten cents advance per ton on coal, besides several changes in the rules & regulations of the company—none of which Col Hunter says he will agree to—says he will shut down the mines first." McMurry expressed his reluctance to remove his men from the "hard case" in Thurber; "something like a 'slow fever,'" he thought, had started and was spreading there like an epidemic.[11]

In June, 1889, McMurry reported that thirty to forty strikers continued their agitation and were "very much annoyed on a/c of a number of them having been arrested for Rioting, Intimidation, [and] Carrying Pistols." On July 8, McMurry noted that John Clinton, a member of the miners' strike committee, had penetrated the enclosure and beaten two white miners, for which he was promptly detained.[12] Such reports, of course, further convinced state authorities of the accuracy of Hunter's claims against the striking workers.

The Knights of Labor local at Gordon regarded and reported the situation somewhat differently. In June, 1889, George W. Britton wrote the *Journal of United Labor* that the company had tried "all kinds of plans to get us into trouble." The first resulted in drunken men who did not belong to the Order shooting in the streets. "Then," Britton continued, "they [company officials] set up a big howl that the striking miners were rioting, and through that scheme they managed to get a company of State Rangers here. In place of them attempting to keep the peace they have been trying to get some of us into trouble, but so far," he added, "they have made a complete failure" (June 6, 1889). As for the "riot," Britton recorded the report of the Erath County Grand Jury on the matter (*Journal of United Labor,* June 6, 1889): "In regard to the rumored troubles at the coal mines, after a thorough investigation of the same, we are satisfied that there is not, nor ever has been, an organized body of men whose object was to intimidate Colonel Hunter or his employees either by force or threats in the discharge of their duty. The disturbance on December 12 or 13 that caused so much comment was made by a drunken, lawless element, for whose conduct the miners are not responsible."

Union committee members contended that, failing in its attempt to discredit the workers, the company had resorted to arresting the striking workers for vagrancy. "They have already arrested two of our members for a test case, and if they make it stick they say they will have us all behind the bars." Britton concluded with the comment that "if our trouble was settled, it would be but a short time till old 2345 would be booming again. We have had several struggles since we were first organized, but this is the worst we have ever had." Appeals for miners to stay away continued into August, 1889.[13]

Although other writers have contended that the Rangers acted as "referees" in the dispute between Hunter and the miners, it is clear that in the 1889–90 crisis, the underlying reason the adjutant general ordered the Rangers to Thurber was to remove the agitating miners or at least to maintain control over them for the company's benefit. As long as the Rangers remained, the striking miners knew they had little chance to succeed. Shortly before the Rangers left Thurber, McMurry told King, "the strikers still remain in force on the outside, praying for the Rangers to be moved away. They claim that they could soon get clear of 'old Hunter' and the Negroes [the largest number of miners recruited who remained at work], were it not for the Rangers."[14]

The captain's periodic reports, often written on Texas & Pacific Coal Company stationery, displayed an obvious bias against the strikers. McMurry described the Johnson miners' attempts to distribute literature and persuade imported workers to abandon their plans to work for Hunter: "It seemed that they were anxious to do some dirty work, although they possess an unusual amount of 'gall' they did not attempt to get on the train, and I imagine they were very much chagrined when the train did not halt at [the] Depot to give them an opportunity to deliver themselves of their inflammatory speeches and distribute their lying documents." Captain McMurry further charged that his men had been treated with disrespect by both the miners and their family members, although the Rangers by and large had minded their own business.[15]

In his annual report for 1889–90, the adjutant general also expressed sympathy for the company, repeating Hunter's contention that these "so-called strikers" had never been employed by the Texas & Pacific Coal Company but had made the claim to prevent other miners from assuming jobs at low wages in the mines. He also alluded to the economic impact the new business promised the area if development proceeded without impediment. "The opening of abundant beds of coal in this section of a quality to burn and to coke well, the necessary employment of hundreds of hands, the up-building and success of many local enterprises, the influx of population and," he added, "the creation of a home market for many local products; all these desirable things might be expected to begin and grow with the development of coal here, if the company was allowed to proceed peaceably in its enterprises, but to this the so-called strikers objected." King viewed the Rangers' role in moral terms. "Not only in its actual material results is this matter of vast importance, but even more so," he wrote, "in the moral influences exerted by the notice given to all dangerous or lawless combinations of every class and kind that labor shall be free in Texas and that when men will not work themselves they will not be allowed to combine against or violently interfere with those who will and do work."[16]

On several occasions, residents charged the Rangers with abusive acts. Covington A. Hall, general lecturer for the Knights of Labor, claimed in a letter to Atty. Gen. James S. Hogg that a "peaceful law abiding lot of citizens" at Thurber was "being abused, imposed upon and mystreated by a company of State Rangers." Hogg lacked jurisdiction in the matter but advised Hall to take his complaints to the governor. If Hall indeed followed Hogg's suggestion, it had no apparent impact on the Ranger presence there. In June, the strikers filed charges against at least two officers for disturbing the peace when they interfered with the striking miners' attempt to talk to several incoming strikebreakers. At least one of the lawmen was tried and found guilty but fined only one dollar. Despite these incidents, Gomer Gower described the Rangers overall as a "pretty decent bunch of fellows."[17]

Whatever their demeanor, the Rangers' purpose not only in Thurber but in various parts of the state when labor unrest erupted was indisputable. On January 15, 1887, the *National Labor Tribune* singled out Texas' adjutant general for special scorn. In a front-page article head-lined "THE ASININE GENERAL OF TEXAS," the paper ridiculed the statements of the adjutant general, in his annual report, on the subject of "oath-bound labor organizations, and the alleged necessity to maintain the militia in fighting shape to resist the encroachments of said organizations." There was no doubt that, while the Rangers remained in Thurber on the adjutant general's orders, Hunter held the upper hand.

In the process, the Colonel expended thirty thousand dollars in company funds and used the power at his disposal to attempt to drive the Johnson miners completely out of the area. A letter from an officer in the Palo Pinto Coal Mining Company to Gov. L. S. Ross demonstrated how far the colonel's influence extended. The company, "acting in unison with Col. Hunter," closed its mines in January, 1889. "Since then," he continued, "we have pretty nearly got rid of all the old miners." The Palo Pinto Coal Mining Company also utilized the Rangers' services with results similar to those in Thurber. "Capt. McMurray [McMurry] sent down three of the Rangers . . . and their presence wrought a marked effect on the men. We have given instructions to have a wire fence put around our village and as all the malcontents have moved about two miles away we don't anticipate any further trouble."[18]

In his fight against the Johnson miners, Hunter also took advantage of the acute problem of dual unionism then complicating organizational efforts in American mining districts. Apparently recognizing the heated jurisdictional battle that the fledgling Knights of Labor District Assembly 135 and the National Progressive [Miners] Union were waging, Hunter convinced representatives of the latter, which in 1890 formed the United Mine Workers, to declare the strike at Thurber over. The organization's willingness to do so reflected its leaders' reasoning that the possible employment of their members in Texas would open the district to successful unionization.[19]

In December, 1888, Hunter contacted the National Progressive Union's *National Labor Tribune,* which by then already had run several recruitment advertisements for the Texas & Pacific Coal Company as well as letters from Dan McLauchlan. Hunter requested that the Progressive Union send a representative to Thurber to investigate conditions at the mines. The union complied, and on Christmas Day, 1888, William Rennie arrived in Thurber. Met by Dan McLauchlan, John Clinton, and Hunter's son-in-law Edgar Marston, Rennie made a lengthy report to the *Tribune.* After meeting with Hunter and the miners' committee and examining the camp, he concluded that the company had not misrepresented the physical conditions around the mines to potential employees. Agreeing with Hunter's position on every point and accusing McLauchlan of spreading "barefaced falsehoods," Rennie concluded with the comment that he knew of "no mining camp where a miner can enjoy more advantages than at the mines of the Texas and Pacific Coal Company." His denunciation of McLauchlan reflected consolidationists' frustration with Knights of Labor locals that, they contended, acted too brashly and without the sanction of district leaders. "It is no wonder the K. of L. has got into bad repute," Rennie finished. Three weeks later the paper boasted about the ongoing movement of miners from DA 135 to the Progressive Union.[20]

Shortly after Rennie's trip, the *National Labor Tribune* (January 5, 1889) declared that under union rules a strike did not exist in Thurber; this opened the way for workers to accept employment there. This, the paper stated, would preserve the "Texas coal field" for unionization and save it from being overwhelmed by cheap Mexican labor. The local strikers, however, rejected the *Tribune's* decision and wrote letters to the *Journal of United Labor* (January 17) requesting continued support. In response, the Knights of Labor newspaper called for the *Tribune's* condemnation but took no further action.

In June, 1889, after submission of the local's case to the General Executive Board of the Knights of Labor to effect a settlement, Terence Powderly sent executive board member James J. Holland to confer with Hunter. Hunter told his stockholders that Powderly's adjutant found the company unyielding and already victorious, so the Knights of Labor called the strike "off." Holland claimed the company (which he mistakenly referred to as the Pacific Mining Company) "absolutely refused to treat with me." Accepting the fruitlessness of any further action, he sought employment for the strikers at another mine and recommended that the board terminate its sanction of the strike but continue to warn miners not to seek employment in Thurber. In November, 1889, the Assembly, at its thirteenth regular session, accepted Holland's report and approved his recommendation.[21] Many of the Johnson strikers did drift to other parts of the country, but problems at Thurber remained and activism continued.

In July, 1890, Hunter asked the Rangers to return to Thurber to forestall racial conflict. He claimed that the old strikers were fomenting trouble against the black miners Hunter had employed as strikebreakers the previous year. Fence cutting was the principal manifestation of the problem Captain McMurry reported. With the Rangers' assistance, however, Hunter and the fence held their ground, and within a month normal coal mining operations resumed. Even so, Gower recalled, although Hunter had discharged union members and black-listed former Johnson employees, the Colonel, in need of skilled miners, agreed in 1892 to reemploy some of them if they refrained from organizing activity. Whatever short-term promises they may have made, the organizational activity did not end, though no unions existed in the community in the 1890s.[22]

In response to the wage reductions that accompanied the 1893 depression in the major coal-producing states and threatened the western and southwestern coal fields, the United Mine Workers' fifth annual convention, in April, 1894, ordered a massive work stoppage. The general labor unrest of that year further heightened industrialists' fears of increased agitation and organization campaigns, employee walkouts, financial losses, and general social and economic chaos. Following in the footsteps of coal producers across the country, in March, 1894, the Texas & Pacific Coal Company reduced the tonnage rate that it paid pit workers from $1.15 to $1.00.[23]

Several months of disorder in the camp followed, capped by a threat on the Colonel's life supposedly made by the owners of a Palo Pinto County saloon just outside the camp fence. The arrest of several "agitators" at a late-night meeting further reflected the unrest in the village. Not surprisingly, in June, Hunter appealed to Adj. Gen. W. H. Mabry for assistance. "Owing to the troubled condition among the miners of the United States at this time, I ask you to appoint about five special rangers to assist in keeping peace at the mines." Hunter refused to admit that any strike had occurred in the pits, although the *Dallas Morning News* (June 6, 1894) reported a work stoppage, but he contended striking miners elsewhere "are sending their walking delegates in here in a clandestine manner."[24]

Hunter may have been correct. The previous month the newspaper in nearby Gordon recounted the story of a miner who claimed that law officers and company officials manhandled him. The *Texas Miner* (May 26, 1894) offered its own account of his "rather 'remarkable'" story. The company, the paper contended, based on its own investigation, knew that the individual in question and his two sidekicks had earned a reputation as agitators but hired them anyway. Law officers arrested them while the three shared drinks in the saloon with several black miners to whom they were delivering their pitch. "The officers simply took him [the complainant] in a hack and outside of camp, and warned him of the unhealthy condition of this camp for an agitator." A week later (June 2) the *Miner* wrote: "Some lazy, good-far-nothing scoundrels steal into camp under cover of night and try to make dissatisfaction with the men," but, the editor claimed, with little success. "Anarchists, agitators, you might as well understand, once and for all, that you cannot fool the Texas & Pacific Coal Company's miners." The June 9 issue of the newspaper similarly denied the existence of any discontent in the camp.

This episode reached a climax at the end of the first week of June, when the imported incendiaries (as the company considered them), one of whom was black, conducted a secret meeting inside the camp. William Lightfoot, hired by the company as an undercover officer to investigate the possibility of a strike, infiltrated the gathering at the Bruce & Stewart Saloon just outside the company compound. In an affidavit submitted to the justice of the peace (who had worked for the company), the captain described the situation. The saloon owners, he believed, held a grudge against Hunter because he had closed a road that allowed residents access from Thurber to the competing drinking establishment. Drawing the miners with an offer of free beer all day, the saloon owners encouraged speech making with the purpose of inciting a strike against the coal company.[25]

The following day the saloon owners and the black "agitator" called a meeting at the old Knights of Labor Hall to which they invited "certain miners in whom [they] had confidence." Light-foot recollected: "We met in the dark and had no light during the meeting except from a match which I struck to light a cigar." In the course of their speeches, the meeting's organizers urged the miners to strike (like their colleagues in mining districts throughout the country) to protest wage reductions instituted when the demand for coal remained high. In the meantime, law officers, on Lightfoot's information, surrounded the hall and arrested those inside for un-lawful assembly. Soon after this incident, the adjutant general's of-fice received at least twenty-five affidavits from a variety of Thurber-area residents, including Hunter, who claimed the miners had no complaints against the company. They blamed the saloon owners for encouraging drunkenness among the workers and providing a meeting place for a few malcontents.[26]

Gomer Gower also recalled the incident. Fearing that his em-ployees were planning to unionize, Hunter hired a spy, Gower re-lated, who identified himself as a member of the Knights of Labor and proposed to organize the workers. The better-informed in the group, Gower pointed out, immediately grew suspicious because they recognized that the Knights had relinquished their jurisdic-tion to the United Mine Workers. Others, however, expressed some interest, only to have their names reported to the Colonel. During a week's time, possibly at the same time the company solicited the affidavits mentioned earlier, Hunter and his legal staff questioned the miners at the Opera House. The workers apparently satisfied the company that not a single one was interested in organizing a union. "The whole affair was perfectly staged," Gower remembered, "with the Colonel, as always, dressed in his pleated white, spotless shirt plus trousers and coatless, presiding." Despite the intimidating scene, Gower explained, "the untutored miners, being well versed in the art of dealing with spies and evading the hypothetical ques-tion of the inquisitors, baffled the Colonel and his aides."[27]

While these events were transpiring, Adjutant General Mabry agreed to send several officers to investigate the trouble in Thurber. But in a confidential letter to Capt. William J. "Bill" McDonald, Mabry intimated Gov. James Hogg's apparent sympathy for the miners. Hogg recognized that the wage reduction, introduced at the very time that strikes elsewhere had forced an increase in the price of coal because of shortages, had prompted the difficulty at Thurber. "Under these conditions," Mabry wrote, "Gov. Hogg is averse to using the strong arm of the state to intimidate workmen whose wages may be below what justly can be paid them as living wages." While awaiting McDonald's report on the situation, Mabry continued that he expected his two representatives to maintain order, which, he counseled "you can best do . . . by going quietly to the leaders, and tell[ing] them that no lawless acts will be tolerated; that peace," he concluded, "and the majesty of the law will be preserved and maintained at all hazards."[28]

When the adjutant general received the officers' initial report, he rejected it because the report failed to recount events on both sides of the issue. This made it impossible for the state's chief executive and the adjutant general to understand the situation completely. "A full and impartial report of the grievances on the part of the men employed by the Coal Company, or other persons connected with the mines, is desired." Four days later, with an acceptable report in hand that claimed the miners had no real grievances except the presence of bothersome agitators, Mabry still refused to send any additional men. "Owing to the Governor's dislike to any appearance of coercion, until it is necessary to maintain peace, law, & order, no rangers will be sent to that point at present."[29]

Interestingly enough, in a personal letter to Mabry, Hunter expressed his satisfaction with the Ranger presence, albeit limited, in and around the camp. The *Texas Miner* (June 16, 1894) likewise applauded the Rangers' assistance. The paper attributed the "driving away [of] the cut-throat element of outside agitators and dynamiters who were terrorizing our miners and mine workers" to the prompt action taken by the governor and the adjutant general. Mabry's confidential orders notwithstanding, Ranger W. J. L. Sullivan reported to Thurber with two of his "boys" on June 12 (four days before Mabry refused to send the Rangers there in full force) "to help keep down a Strike at that plase [*sic*]." He also recorded the arrest of one person on June 20 "for threatening to blow up the coal mines."[30]

Hunter finally sought the posting of special law officers to the camp to ensure law and order. Within a month of the trouble at the saloon, secret investigator Lightfoot, followed several months later by Malcolm "Lit" Williams, initiated the procedures required for appointment as "Special Rangers" stationed in Thurber. Their monthly reports from the middle of 1894 through 1899 described no strike-related difficulties in the camp, despite the United Mine Workers' July 4, 1897, nationwide strike and stepped-up organizational activities throughout the Southwest.[31]

Agitation in Thurber, however, apparently did not cease. In April, 1896, the *Texas State Labor Journal* wrote a series of articles charging armed officers in the coal town with the robbery and intimidation of residents. The paper also blasted the company for cheating the miners out of their just wages by using the screen basis for weighing their coal output, docking them excessively for dirty coal, and charging unreasonable prices at the camp stores. At a mass meeting of purportedly five hundred to six hundred miners at the Opera House, a committee on resolutions drafted a series of statements refuting all of the labor paper's charges. According to a document of resolution that the committee sent to the adjutant general, the miners in attendance unanimously adopted the committee report. The committee head worked as a pit boss in Thurber and had contributed one of the affidavits claiming the miners had no complaints in 1894.[32] The accuracy and significance of this curious document are subject to question, considering the events that took place seven years later. Gower did not comment on it.

When Colonel Hunter retired in 1899 and turned the company over to Edgar Marston and William K. Gordon, the United Mine Workers of America had reached a turning point in its history. Although the union counted only 9,731 members in 1897, in the wake of the disastrous 1894 strike, the miners' organization called a work suspension on July 4, 1899. Over 100,000 miners responded, walking out of the pits in the nation's central mining district. Falling wages, the introduction of labor-saving machinery, unemployment, and the resulting effects on the coal-mining population had generated a greater militancy among miners, unionized or not, for which operators had not prepared.[33]

Plagued with overproduction, cutthroat competition, falling prices, and instability in the industry, mine owners in the Central Field agreed to meet in joint conference with representatives of miners' locals. They expected to find a joint solution to their problems and to establish the machinery that could forestall strikes. With this success and recognizing that the key to survival was a strong, national organization that would function as a counterforce to the operators, the United Mine Workers, under the leadership of John Mitchell, committed itself to an aggressive organizational effort. By 1899, union organizers had moved west of the Mississippi River and in that same year made important inroads in organizing the Southwest Field (including Arkansas, Indian Territory, and Texas).[34]

In Texas by 1900, the coal mines at Lyra, Strawn, Rock Creek, Alba, and Bridgeport, all within a seventy-mile radius of Thurber, could be counted as union camps. Gordon wrote Marston in January of that year that things were "quiet" with his miners after a spate of difficulty with the drivers. He expressed disappointment, however, that "Bennett over at Strawn [several miles northwest of Thurber] is allowing the Union to get a very strong foothold there. . . . Besides," he added, "it gives this organization a starting point in Texas, which could have been so easily prevented had he opposed it in its infancy."[35]

Thurber was one of the holdouts in the area, but the history of labor agitation there, the intensive organizational activity that apparently realized success in nearby mining camps and across the Southwest, and mine operators' recognition that districtwide union agreements could actually help stabilize the industry paved the way for Thurber's succumbing to the inevitable. Furthermore, although company officials may have felt some security in the large number of non-English-speaking immigrants in Thurber, whom employers typically regarded as docile and less inclined to join unions, the United Mine Workers early recognized the reality of sometimes militant multiethnic and multiracial mining populations and quickly adapted to them. In 1891, when the *United Mine Workers' Journal* began publication, it printed its weekly editions in a number of languages. Organizers who spoke foreign languages worked those areas with a high concentration of immigrant workers. Such a policy paid important dividends. "New" immigrant groups in Utah, Pennsylvania, and other mining centers actively supported strike calls and organization efforts. The miners' union also actively organized mixed locals to include not only immigrant but black laborers as well. [36]

With the intensification of union activity in Texas by 1900, organizers were working the Thurber mines surreptitiously, some even wearing disguises to penetrate the fenced compound. Peter Hanraty, president since 1900 of District 21, United Mine Workers of America, which claimed jurisdiction over the Southwest Coal Field, described his efforts to gain access to closed camps. Having succeeded in employing "guarrilo [guerrilla] warfare" against Oklahoma operators to force them to negotiate, he applied similar techniques in Texas:

> In May of last year [1903] I made my first trip to Texas for the
> purpose [of] looking over that field and to find out the conditions
> of the miners and to lay plans to organize them, Thurber . . . being
> the best fortified place against organized labor in the United States.

> I had to keep my identity unknowen and my movements very
> *secret,* for Fourteen Years the company had been very successful in
> keeping Organized Labor from getting a foothold there. . . . [A]fter
> making a thorough investigation and realizing the importance of
> organizing Thurber I layed my plans and set about to execute them.
> In June . . . I sent an Organizer there who spoke several different
> Languages, to work in the mines with instructions how to act, and
> after twelve days he left and told me it was impossible to Organize
> them. I then sent a Mexican there: what became of him I do not
> know, as he never reported, nor have I been able to locate him
> since. In Aug. I sent Tom Fenolio from Hartford to Thurber with
> Pacific [specific] instructions how to proceed; he went to work in
> the mines, and associated with the leading Italians and great credit
> should be given him for the able and fearless manner he worked
> among them. Arrangements were made for Labor-day celebration
> close to Thurber Junction but was changed to Lyra, invitations were
> sent to Thurber inviting the miners to participate.[37]

The company ordered activists discovered inside the town to vacate the premises, but smoldering discontent and "secret preparations" produced well-organized collective action by Labor Day, 1903. The union's stepped-up activity prompted the company to post an announcement, dated August 23 and written in four languages, that, effective October 1, the Texas & Pacific Coal Mining Company would increase the mining rate from $1.00 to $1.05 a ton and pay bonuses for production of anything over the miners' average monthly production of thirty tons. Additionally, the company proposed to delay the early-morning train departure from 6:30 to 7:00 and granted the miners a nine-hour day.[38]

Few miners failed to recognize what was afoot. A September 3 notice confirmed this perception. "For the information of all employees, notice is given that Thurber will remain a nonunion camp." Anyone who disagreed could "get a settlement at any time."[39]

The miners took these notices as a direct challenge. Fanning the fire were reports of the disappearance of a Mexican organizer (to whom Hanraty referred in his report) and rumors of the discovery of a murdered Mexican, his identification withheld by the company, in the area. Sensing the tension, Gordon took action. On August 30, 1903, the general manager wrote Gov. Samuel Willis Tucker Lanham for a contingent of three or four Rangers who, he felt, as the company's "guests" would "have a most quieting effect on the agitators." Claiming that 98 percent of the workers wanted no union, he charged union activists with fomenting discontent where none existed. Advised explicitly by Adj. Gen. John A. Hulen that their duty was "to keep the peace, and in no event [to] take sides with any faction that may possibly arise," the first group of Rangers arrived on September 5, after the mine workers' union had announced Hanraty's plans for the three-day picnic to begin on Labor Day. To defuse the union's effort, Gordon opened the Thurber Club, the private social retreat normally closed to the miners, for a grand barbecue in celebration of Labor Day.[40]

Not to be outdone, the United Mine Workers seized the opportunity of having the miners all together (some eleven hundred persons, not all miners, assembled there) and instructed a miner's son to ride among them spreading the word that a union organizer waited at Lyra to induct them into the organization. A massive Labor Day celebration at Lyra attracted a crowd of hundreds, although most of the Italians marked the celebration at Thurber, where Gordon had successfully outbid the union for an Italian band to entertain the crowd. At Lyra, after a short speech by Hanraty, a 2 1/2-hour discourse by international United Mine Worker organizer William Wardjon, and a liquor-free barbecue, about sixty miners from Thurber, very likely including members of the old Johnson miner group, joined the organization. Hanraty, Wardjon, and C. W. Woodman, secretary of the Texas State Federation of Labor, who had arrived in Lyra at midnight after an open-buggy ride in the pouring rain, received the new members and sent them back to the company town to "work quietly and wait." To the surprise of even the organizers, "the work of the sixty bore immediate fruit."[41]

On the following day, Thurber's as-yet largely unorganized miners presented Gordon with a set of demands. They called for a mining rate of $1.35 a ton, an increase in day wages, an eight-hour day, bi-weekly paydays, and recognition of the United Mine Workers of America. Although not among their written demands, the miners also made clear their sentiments that the fence and armed guards be removed.[42]

Gordon refused to meet the demands, and the miners boycotted the pits on Wednesday and marched to Lyra to meet union representatives. Wardjon, who had already returned to Fort Worth, made his way back to Lyra on the noon train, and on his arrival there heard a rousing cheer of "Wardjon, Wardjon" from those seeking union membership. "There," Wardjon related, "the men [fourteen hundred strong] congregated in a grove awaiting him—waiting for some one to tell them how to conduct a strike, how to become union men" (*United Mine Workers' Journal*, September 24, 1903).

Seven hundred miners joined the union on the spot, and organizers called another meeting for Thursday at the Palo Pinto Bridge, three miles from Lyra and Thurber. Unionized miners from Lyra led the procession and on their arrival at the bridge found nearly two thousand men and women representing not only miners and their families but brick workers, clerks, carpenters, teamsters, and laborers, all interested in unionization. As a posse of Rangers approached, the crowd, some standing, some seated on the ground, and others clinging to tree limbs, surrounded the speakers, fearing a confrontation. None occurred; the peace officers simply requested that the miners not set off any blasting powder, as was the custom during celebrations, and departed (*United Mine Workers' Journal*, September 24, 1903).

When asked who wanted to join the union, all those who were seated stood, and the organizers, with benefit of interpreters, proceeded to swear in the union's newest converts and to initiate steps to organize all the other company employees. Even local farmers expressed their intent to join a union. Wardjon counseled the miners not to return to work, draw any pay, or remove their tools from the mines until Hanraty advised them further, because under company rules workers had to vacate their homes one week after drawing their final pay. The miners then created a relief committee with all "races" represented, opened a commissary to aid those in need, and promised shelter to anyone forced out of his or her home.[43]

On Hanraty's return the district president told the strikers that if they did not want to work for the company under existing conditions, they should pick up their tools and leave the property. Hamaty explained: "If the company will not treat you as human beings, then leave them in peace. Lacking a say in what your wages are, you are not free men." So emerged the union's plan of action—an exodus, a massive "going away," a tactic that strikers had employed without much success in Indian Territory during the 1894 strike and that reflected an extension of the industrial worker's tradition of quitting as an expression of dissatisfaction.[44]

To succeed, the exodus had to be a peaceful one. "If anyone imposes upon you, let us know and we will see that you are protected under the law. But, let me tell you," Hanraty continued, "if you do anyone wrong, I will be the first to see that you are sent where you belong." The workers complied without exception. No violence or drunkenness aggravated the tense scene. To those ready to depart Thurber, the United Mine Workers offered shelter, assistance, new employment, and transportation and even promised to supervise the stock of those leaving if quarantine laws at their destinations would affect them. Gordon offered the miners train service to the mines, accompanied by Rangers, to collect their tools. All miners who requested their pay received it in cash. Tools that the company offered to purchase and personal property too cumbersome to transport sold cheaply.[45]

All together, at least five hundred miners left Thurber, most of them single Italians who sought employment elsewhere in the United States or who returned to Italy. The dramatic departure crippled the company, since only eight or nine men refused to strike, and the limited recruitment efforts initiated by the company had failed miserably. In one case, eighteen miners from Pennsylvania imported by the company marched to Lyra as soon as local residents described the situation in Thurber to them. Once there, union organizers convinced them to leave and paid their return passage. C. W. Woodman recalled that out of several trainloads of strikebreakers transported to Thurber, only three miners actually reached the camp. Others refused to work the mines on learning of the strike. The trio who continued the trip to the town finally joined the union and earned the nickname "the $30,000 men," since they were all that remained of the strikebreakers it had cost the company thirty thousand dollars to recruit.[46]

Almost two weeks into the strike, Edgar Marston arrived in Thurber in his private railroad car. Once there he met with the unshaven, unbathed Hanraty, Wardjon, and Woodman, who had been working and sleeping in a nearby wooded area during the crisis. Marston asked that the mine workers' union not call out the miners at Rock Creek, where a subsidiary of the Texas & Pacific Coal Company employed 150 men. In return he agreed to recognize the union at Rock Creek. The company having taken the first step, union officials promised not to transport any more workers from the area, inferring that Marston would recognize the union in Thurber if the employees halted their departures. Marston then agreed to participate in an upcoming Fort Worth meeting between Southwest Coal Field operators and union representatives.[47]

From September 23 to September 26, Marston met with national, regional, and local union leaders. They finally signed an agreement granting the miners an immediate 15 percent raise (to $1.15 a ton), biweekly paydays, and an eight-hour day for day laborers. The company also agreed to collect union dues, assessments, fines, and initiation fees, an agreement that subsequent payroll records confirm. The miners additionally received the right to have a checkweighman oversee the weighing of each miner's output and, although the screened mining system continued, the company narrowed the bars that determined the amount of coal retained for weighing. The company further agreed to pay for certain deadwork. In return, the union promised to return the workers to the mines and to solicit four hundred to five hundred miners, if needed, to replace employees who had departed permanently.[48]

The negotiations not only successfully addressed the miners' concerns about their work, the strike also influenced company policy in regard to those features of a company town that, even after Hunter's retirement, had continued to frustrate residents. The fence surrounding Thurber, the symbol of an autocracy that even in its paternalism affronted human dignity, came down. After the strike, the company allowed employees to live outside the town, tolerated independent merchants and peddlers, who freely advertised and sold their goods in the camp, and accepted residents' requests to seek the care of physicians other than those employed by the company if they so chose. Additionally, Marston's annual report for 1903 proposed that the mercantile company be operated more independently of the coal company, since the company stores served as a perennial topic at union meetings. [49]

Fifteen years of activism produced a victory in Thurber that both the individual and the union shared. The company won as well, for few serious labor difficulties threatened the mines' operation in the next twenty years. The events that occurred there, however, assumed a greater significance than the immediate impact on Thurberites. Similar scenes were played out in other bituminous and anthracite coal-mining regions across the United States. As a result, by the early 1900s, the United Mine Workers' Union was a powerful force in the Southwest and elsewhere. In Texas before the Thurber strike there were only three hundred organized miners. With the miners' success in Thurber and surrounding mining communities, "a powerful and militant organization" enforced the closed shop in Texas' mining district for over twenty years. By April, 1909, the total United Mine Workers' Union membership in Texas locals had reached twenty-two hundred.[50]

Thurber's miner activists constituted only one group of labor agitators in Texas who protested their working conditions in this same time period; longshoremen, railroad workers, cowboys, cotton handlers, and streetcar workers all expressed their discontent. The mine workers' locals, however, were an especially important group. Among the largest in the country, they played an influential role in the Texas Federation of Labor, which successfully fought the open shop movement in Texas until the 1920s. The state organization not only endorsed labor's traditional tactic, the strike, but also mobilized its resources to lobby successfully for legislation to protect Texas' industrial workers. Laws that the state legislature passed in the early 1900s, under pressure from organized labor, included prohibition of the use of coercion against employees who did not patronize company stores, institution of safety standards in mines, establishment of sixteen as the minimum age for mineworkers, a declaration of scrip payment as illegal, and passage of an anti-black-listing law. Gomer Gower declared that during this time "labor . . . was in the saddle in Texas." In the same period, Thurber could also lay claim to the distinction of being, in Gower's words, "one of the most pleasant mining communities in the country."[51]

NOTES

1. Gower, "Indian Territory Coal Miners," pp. 426–28, 434; *Immigrants in Industries*, "Bituminous Coal Mining," pp. 21-23; "The Bituminous Coal Mining Industry in the Southwest," pp. 10, 14–16. The "old" Johnson miners included men with names like Armstrong, Anderson, Brooks, Brown, Clinton, Curry, Cunningham, Duncan, Davis, Evans, Ford, Gentry, Grant, Hale, Hughes, Kelley, Lester, McLaughlin, McGee, McMillen, Moor, Mitchell, O'Neal, O'Connor, Pierce, Parker, Riley, Roark, Stewart, Scully, Thomas, Tudor, Williams, Weaver, and Young (Johnson Brothers Coal Mining Company, Ledger, 1887, Johnson Papers).

2. "William Knox Gordon," *Fort Worth and the Texas Northwest*, p. 155; Gower to Owens, Jan. 28, 1941, Gower Letters; Gordon, Jr., Biographical Data Information Sheet.

3. Garlock, *Guide to the Local Assemblies of the Knights of Labor*, pp. xxiv, 495–96, 505, 636.

4. Gower to Owens, Apr. 12, 1940, Gower Letters; *Third Annual Report of the Commissioner of Labor, 1887,* pp. 582-83, 806-807, 989; Gower to Gentry, Aug. 14, 1941, in Gentry, "Thurber," p. 228.

5. Gower to Gentry, Aug. 14, 1944, in Gentry, "Thurber," pp. 228–29; Gower to Owens, Nov. 4, Nov. 12, 1940, Gower Letters; Spoede, "William Whipple Johnson," pp. 57–59.

6. Gower to Gentry, Aug. 14, 1944, in Gentry, "Thurber," pp. 229–30.

7. Gower to Gentry, Aug 14, 1944, in Gentry, "Thurber," pp. 229, 230; Gower to Owens, Nov. 4, Nov. 12., 1940, Gower Letters; see *National Labor Tribune,* Dec. 22, 1888, for a letter from Dan McLauchlan; Annual Report, 1889, p. 3; *Texas & Pacific v.Lawson,* pp. 301, 318, 397–400; Journal A, Financial Material, Texas and Pacific Coal Company Records.

8.Gower to Owens, Nov. 4, 1940, Gower Letters; Gower to Gentry, Aug. 14, 1944, in Gentry, "Thurber," p. 230.

9. Gower to Owens, Nov. 4, 1890, Gower Letters; S. A. McMurry to W. H. King, Feb. 11, Feb. 17, Feb. 21, Apr. 6, 1889, General Correspondence, Adjutant General Records; Annual Report, 1889, pp. 3–4; Gower to Gentry, Aug. 14, 1944, in Gentry, "Thurber," pp. 230–31; *The Journal of United Labor,* Jan. 10, 1889, included a letter of thanks for donations to the local.

10.Annual Report, 1889, pp. 3, 4; *Dallas Morning News,* Dec. 21, Dec. 28, 1888; the *Stephenville Empire,* Dec. 221888; *Fort Worth Daily Gazette,* Dee. 23, 1888; J. L. Humphries to Gov. L. S. Ross, Dec. 13, 1888, S. A. McMurry to W. H. King, Dec. 20, 1888, General Correspondence, Adjutant General Records.

11. S. A. McMurry to W. H. King, May 8, May 23, 1889, Dec. 28, 1888 (telegram), General Correspondence, Adjutant General Records; *Fort Worth Daily Gazette,* Jan. 2, Jan. 6, 1889; Monthly Returns, Company B, Frontier Battalion, Dec. 31, 1888, Adjutant General Records.

12. McMurry to King, Apr. 6, June 6, July 8, 1889, General Correspondence, Adjutant General Records.

13. *The Journal of United Labor,* June 6, July 18, Aug. 1, 1889.

14. Gentry, "Thurber," p. 53; McMurry to King, July 2, 1889, General Correspondence, Adjutant General Records.

15. S. A. McMurry to W. H. King, Feb. 2, Feb. 17, 1889, General Correspondence, Adjutant General Records.

16. *Report of the Adjutant General of the State of Texas for 1888–1890,* pp. 26, 27, 28.

17. C. A. Hall to Attorney General Hogg, June 2, 1889, Mine Workers United, 1889–1940, Labor Movement in Texas Collection; Gower to Owens, Nov. 4, 1940, Gower Letters; J. S. Hogg to C. A. Hall, June 6, 1889, Mine Work-

ers United, 1889–1940, Labor Movement in Texas Collection; the *Journal of United Labor,* June 6, 1889.

18. J. G. Watkins to Governor Ross, Mar. 26, 1889, Harton Walker to W. H. King, Mar. 29, 1889, General Correspondence, Adjutant General Records; Annual Report, 1889, p.5.

19. *National Labor Tribune,* Jan. 12, 1889; "With so many miners needing employment is it not shameful that our efforts to secure a new union district should meet with obstruction among miners?"

20. *National Labor Tribune,* Oct. 20, Dec. 8, Dec. 15, Dec. 22, 1888, Jan. 5, Jan. 26, 1889.

21. Annual Report 1889, p. 5; Knights of Labor, *Proceedings of the General Assembly of the Knights of Labor of America Thirteenth Regular Session, November 12–20, 1889,* p. 9; *National Labor Tribune,* Jan. 19, 1889.

22. Telegram, R. D. Hunter to W. H. King, July 5, 1890, note, S. A. McMurry, July 7, 1890, S. A. McMurry to W. H. King, July 11, 1890, all in General Correspondence, Adjutant General Records; Gower to Gentry, Aug. 14, 1944, in Gentry, "Thurber," p. 232; Gower to Owens, Apr. 12, Nov. 4, 1940, Gower Letters.

23. Frank Julian Warne, *The Coal Mine Workers: A Study in Labor Organization,* pp. 212–14; Gower to Gentry, Aug. 14, 1944, in Gentry, "Thurber," p. 233.

24. *Dallas Morning News,* June 4, June 5, 1894; R. D. Hunter to W. H. Mabry, June 5, 1894, General Correspondence, Adjutant General Records.

25. *Dallas Morning News,* June 6, 1894; affidavit by William Lightfoot, June 18, 1894, General Correspondence, Adjutant General Records.

26. Affidavit by William Lightfoot, June 18, 1894, General Correspondence, Adjutant General Records; see also Harry W. Furman to W. H. Mabry, June 6, 1894, F. B. Boles, June 15, 1894, John R. Graves, June 15, 1894, Jas. Wassell, June 15, 1894, J. J. Caradine, June 16, 1894, W. F. Carman, June 16, 1894, W. K. Gordon, June 16, 1894, H. B. Hale, June 16, 1894, D. C. Heatherington, June 16, 1894, Evan Jones, June 16, 1894, Thomas W. Jordan, June 16, 1894, Joe Kendzora, June 16, 1894, Robt. McKinnon, June 16, 1894, J.F. Mann, June 16, 1894, W. H. Mann, June 16, 1894, Ben Matthews, June 16, 1894, Jas. Matthews, June 16, 1894, J. B. Pendleton, June 16, 1894, M. Ready, June 16, 1894, James R. Williams, June 16, 1894, Col. R. D. Hunter, June 18, 1894, Wesley Lewis, June 18, 1894, Andrew Ramage, June 18, 1894, S. P. Smith, June 18, 1894.

27. Gower to Gentry, Aug. 14, 1944, in Gentry, "Thurber," pp. 232, 233; Gower to Owens, Nov. 12, 1940, Gower Letters.

28. W. H. Mabry to W. J. McDonald, June 11, 1894, Letter Press Books, Apr. 26–July 4, 1894, Adjutant General Records.

29. Mabry to McDonald, June 12, June 16, 1894, in ibid.

30. Report, W. J. L. Sullivan, June 31, 1894, R. D. Hunter to W. H. Mabry, June 10, 1894, W. J. McDonald to W. H. Mabry, July 1, 1894, General Correspondence, Adjutant General Records.

31. J. W. Maddox to W. H. Mabry, July 2, 1894, N. A. Stedman to W. H. Mabry, July 2, 1894, E. A. Euless to W. H. Mabry, July 3, 1894, William Lightfoot to W. H. Mabry, July 7, Oct. 31, Dec. 6, 1894, Sept. 3, 1895, Robert H. Ward to the Adjutant General, Aug. 6, 1894, William Lightfoot and Lit Williams to W. H. Mabry, Feb. 6, Feb. 28, Mar. 31, May 5, June l, July 12, Aug. 3, Oct. 10, Nov. 6, 1895, Apr. 1, May 1, June 1, July 2, Aug. 9, Oct. 2, Nov. 30, 1896, Feb. 3, May 6, June 8, July 4, Aug. 2, Oct. 1, Dec. 2, 1897, William Lightfoot to W. H. Owens, Aug. 6, 1894, all in General Correspondence, Adjutant General Records; William Lightfoot, Application, July 26, 1894, Lit Williams, Application for appointment as a Special Ranger, Nov. 21, 1894, both in General Service Records, Adjutant General Records.

32. Resolutions dated May 1, 1896, Thurber, Texas. Affidavit by Robert McKinnon, June 16, 1894, General Correspondence, Adjutant General Records. George N. Beach, editor of the *Texas State Labor Journal* wrote Mabry, "Will you kindly inform me if there is a military organization in Thurber recognized or armed by the State! If so, when was it organized and by whom is it officered?" I located no reply in the Adjutant General's General Correspondence: George N. Beach to W. H. Mabry, Apr. 14, 1896.33Suffern, *Conciliation and Arbitration,* pp. 44–45.

34. Ibid., pp. 45, 50–51, 53–54.

35. W. K. Gordon to E. L. Marston, Jan. 10, 1900, William K. Gordon, Jr. Papers; C. W. Woodman, Secretary of the Texas State Federation of Labor, wrote J. E. Enness in Bridgeport, Texas, in 1902, asking the union there to assess its members $.25 to help support a lobbyist in Austin. Enness apparently refused, prompting Woodman to respond, with some understanding: "As you say, the drain on your treasury to support the miners has been heavy." This letter indicates both the existence of a state affiliated miners' union approximately sixty miles from Thurber in 1902, and labor upheaval that necessitated some financial response by the local union. In his letter Woodman also acknowledged receipt of $1.80 for the per capita membership assessment. The federation's annual tax was $.06 per member (C.W. Woodman Papers, Collection 163 [the Labor Archives, Special Collections, University of Texas at Arlington, Arlington, Texas], hereafter referred to as Woodman Papers).

36. Suffern, *Conciliation and Arbitration,* pp. 39, 45; Chris Evans, *History of United Mine Workers of America from the Year 1860 to 1890,* vol. 1, pp.

639, 641; Gutman, *Work, Culture, and Society in Industrializing America,* pp. 31, 124, 157–58; Allan Kent Powell, *The Next Time We Strike: Labor in Utah's Coal Fields, 1900–1903,* p. 53; Victor Greene, *The Slavic Community on Strike: Immigrant Labor in Pennsylvania Anthracite;* David Robert Wynn, "Trade Unions and the 'New' Immigration: A Study of the United Mine Workers of America, 1890–1910," pp. 109, 158–59, 161, 165, 171, 232, 248.

37. Report to the Delegates of the Sixth Annual Convention of District 23 (n.d.), Statements/Speeches P. Hanraty, Biographical Data, Pete Hanraty, untitled speech/ report on the organization of miners in Indian Territory, all in Peter Hanraty Papers (Oklahoma Historical Society, Oklahoma City), hereafter referred to as Hanraty Papers.

38. Gower to Owens, Apr. 12, 1940, Gower Letters; *Dallas Morning News,* Sept. 11, 1903; the *United Mine Workers' Journal,* Sept. 24, 1903. See Maroney, "The Unionization of Thurber, 1903," Allen, *Chapters in the History of Organized Labor in Texas,* pp. 96–98, Gentry, "Thurber," pp. 77–95, for the best secondary accounts of the strike.

39. *Dallas Morning News,* Sept. 11, 1903.

40. W. K. Gordon to S. W. T. Lanham, Aug. 30, 1903, John A. Hulen to J. H. Rogers, Sept. 3, Sept. 5, 1903, all in General Correspondence, Adjutant General Records; the *United Mine Workers' Journal,* Sept. 24, 1903; *Dallas Morning News,* Sept. 18, 1903; Gower to Owens, Apr. 12, 1940, Gower Letters.

41. *Dallas Morning News,* Sept. 11, 1903; Gower to Owens, Apr. 12, 1940. Gower Letters; *United Mine Workers' Journal,* Sept 17, 1903.

42.*United Mine Workers' Journal,* Sept. 17, 1903; *Dallas Morning News,* Sept. 11, 1903.

43. *Dallas Morning News,* Sept. 11, 1903; *United Mine Workers' Journal,* Sept. 24, 1903.

44. *Dallas Morning News,* Sept. 13, Sept. 20, 1903; untitled speech or statement by Pete Hanraty on organization of miners in Indian Territory, Hanraty papers; Hall, Korstad, Leloudis, "Cotton Mill People," p. 160.

45. *Dallas Morning News,* Sept. 12, 13, 14, 15, 18, 1903.

46. C. W. Woodman to Ben Owens, Apr. 22, 1940, Gower Letters; *Dallas Morning News,* Sept. 13, 17, 18, 1903.

47. Woodman to Owens, Apr. 22, 1940, Gower Letters; *Dallas Morning News,* Sept. 20, 1903.

48. Report to Delegates of the Sixth Annual Convention of District 21, Hanraty Papers; *Dallas Morning News,* Sept. 27, 1903; the *United Mine Workers' Journal,* Oct. 1, 1903; Texas &Pacific Coal Company Payroll Records, Nov., 1903, Texas and Pacific Coal Company Records; copy of Agreement between Miners and Operators in the Bituminous Mines of Texas, Sept. 16,

1903, William K.Gordon, Jr. Papers. Gordon's copy of the 1903 agreement includes a 15–17 percent tonnage rate increase for Thurber rather than the 35 percent described in some accounts. The miners originally demanded a 35 percent increase. Gower claims the increase was from $1.00 to $1.32 per ton. The agreement also provided for an eight-hour day for day labor.

49.Woodman to Owens, Apr. 22, Nov. 12, 1940, Gower Letters; Gentry, "Thurber," p. 110; John S, Spratt, Sr., *Thurber, Texas: The Life and Death of a Company Coal Town*, ed. Harwood P. Hinton, pp. 6–7.

50. Gentry, "Thurber," p. 100; see Allen, *Chapters in the History of Organized Labor*, for a full description of militant labor activity in late nineteenth-century Texas; *Sixteenth Annual Report of the Commissioner of Labor, 1901*, "Strikes and Lockouts," pp. 108, 252, 348; Texas State Federation of Labor, *Proceedings, 1904*, p. 17Gower Letters; *Union Banner*, Apr. 10, 1909.

51. Gower to Owens, Apr. 12, 1940, Gower Letters; Gower to Gentry, Jan. 18, 1945, in Gentry, "Thurber," p. 235; Maroney, "The Unionization of Thurber, 1903," p. 2; idem, "Organized Labor in Texas, 1900–1929," pp. 52, 59, 62, 65, 121; Allen, *Chapters in the History of Organized Labor in Texas*, pp. 98, 137; Woodman to Owens, Apr. 22, 1940, Gower Letters.

THE TEXAS RANGERS: A SELECTED BIBLIOGRAPHY

Harold J. Weiss, Jr. and Bruce A. Glasrud

Alexander, Bob. *Rawhide Ranger, Ira Aten: Enforcing Law on the Texas Frontier.* Denton: University of North Texas Press, 2011.

———. *Winchester Warriors: Texas Rangers of Company D, 1874–1901.* Denton: University of North Texas Press, 2009.

Anderson, Gary Clayton. *The Conquest of Texas: Ethnic Cleansing in the Promised Land, 1820–1875.* Norman: University of Oklahoma Press, 2005.

Brice, Donaly E. *The Great Comanche Raid: Boldest Indian Attack of the Texas Republic.* Austin: Eakin Press, 1987.

Carlson, Paul H., and Tom Crum. *Myth, Memory and Massacre: The Pease River Capture of Cynthia Ann Parker.* Lubbock: Texas Tech University Press, 2010.

Collins, Michael L. *Texas Devils: Rangers and Regulars on the Lower Rio Grande, 1846–1861.* Norman: University of Oklahoma Press, 2008.

Conger, Roger N., et al. *Rangers of Texas.* Waco: Texian Press, 1969.

Cool, Paul. *Salt Warriors: Insurgency on the Rio Grande.* College Station: Texas A&M University Press, 2008.

Cox, Mike. *The Texas Rangers: Wearing the Cinco Peso, 1821–1900.* New York: Tom Doherty Associates, 2008.

———. *Texas Ranger Tales.* Plano, TX: Republic of Texas Press, 1997.

Cutrer, Thomas W. *Ben McCulloch and the Frontier Military Tradition.* Chapel Hill: University of North Carolina Press, 1993.

Davis, John L. *The Texas Rangers: Images and Incidents.* San Antonio: Institute of Texan Cultures, 1991.

Day, James. *Rangers of Texas.* Waco: Texian Press, 1969.

De Soucy, M. David, and Marshall Trimble. *Arizona Rangers, 1901–1909.* Charleston, SC: Arcadia Publishing, 2008.

Durham, George (as told to Clyde Wantland). *Taming the Nueces Strip: The Story of McNelly's Rangers.* Austin: University of Texas Press, 1962.

Exley, Jo Ella Powell. *Frontier Blood: The Saga of the Parker Family.* College Station: Texas A&M University Press, 2001.

Fehrenbach, T. R. *Comanches: The Destruction of a People.* New York: Alfred A. Knopf, 1974.

———. *Lone Star: A History of Texas and the Texans.* New York: Macmillan, 1968.

Ford, John S. *Rip Ford's Texas.* Ed. Stephen B. Oates. Austin: University of Texas Press, 1963.

Gard, Wayne. *Frontier Justice.* Norman: University of Oklahoma Press, 1949.

———. *Sam Bass.* New York: Houghton Mifflin Co., 1936.

Gillett, James B. *Fugitives from Justice: The Notebook of Texas Ranger Sergeant James B. Gillett.* Austin: State House Press, 1997.

———. *Six Years with the Texas Rangers, 1875 to 1881.* Ed. M. M. Quaife. 1921. Repr., New Haven, CT: Yale University Press, 1925.

Glasrud, Bruce A., and James M. Smallwood, eds. *The African American Experience in Texas: An Anthology.* Lubbock: Texas Tech University Press, 2007.

Graybill, Andrew R. *Policing the Great Plains: Rangers, Mounties, and the North American Frontier, 1875–1910.* Lincoln: University of Nebraska Press, 2007.

Greer, James K. *Colonel Jack Hays: Texas Frontier Leader and California Builder.* New York: E. P. Dutton & Co., 1952.

Gwynne, S. C. *Empire of the Summer Moon: Quanah Parker and the Rise and Fall of the Comanches. . . .* New York: Scribner, 2010.

Hardin, Stephen L. *The Texas Rangers.* London: Osprey Publishing Ltd, 1991.

———. *Texian Iliad: A Military History of the Texas Revolution, 1835–1836.* Austin: University of Texas Press, 1994.

Hatley, Allen G. *Bringing the Law to Texas: Crime and Violence in Nineteenth Century Texas.* LaGrange, TX: Centex Press, 2002.

———. *The Indian Wars in Stephen F. Austin's Texas Colony, 1822–1835.* Austin: Eakin Press, 2001.

———. *Texas Constables: A Frontier Heritage.* Lubbock: Texas Tech University Press, 1999.

Hornung, Chuck. *Fullerton's Rangers: A History of the New Mexico Territorial Mounted Police.* Jefferson, NC: McFarland, 2011.

———. *New Mexico's Rangers: The Mounted Police.* Charleston, SC: Arcadia Publishing, 2010.

Hughes, W. J. *Rebellious Ranger: Rip Ford and the Old Southwest*. Norman: University of Oklahoma Press, 1964.

Ivey, Darren L. *The Texas Rangers: A Registry and History*. Jefferson, NC: McFarland & Co., 2010.

Jenkins, John H., and Kenneth Kesselus. *Edward Burleson: Texas Frontier Leader*. Austin: Jenkins Publishing Co., 1990.

Jennings, Napoleon Augustus. *A Texas Ranger*. New York: Charles Scribners, 1899.

Johnson, David. *The Mason County "Hoo Doo" War, 1874–1902*. Denton: University of North Texas Press, 2006.

Kilgore, D. E. *A Ranger Legacy: 150 Years of Service to Texas*. Austin: Madrona Press, 1973.

Knowles, Thomas W. *They Rode for the Lone Star: The Saga of the Texas Rangers—The Birth of Texas—The Civil War*. Dallas: Taylor Publishing Co., 1999.

Martin, Jack. *Border Boss: Captain John R. Hughes, Texas Ranger*. San Antonio: Naylor, 1942.

McCaslin, Richard B. *Fighting Stock: John S. "Rip" Ford of Texas*. Fort Worth: Texas Christian University Press, 2011.

Metz, Leon. *John Wesley Hardin: Dark Angel of Texas*. El Paso: Mangan Books, 1996.

Miletich, Leo N. *Dan Stuart's Fistic Carnival*. College Station: Texas A&M University Press, 1994.

Miller, Rick. *Sam Bass and Gang*. Austin: State House Press, 1999.

Moore, Stephen L. *Savage Frontier: Rangers, Riflemen, and Indian Wars in Texas*. Vol. 1, 1835–1837. Plano, TX: Republic of Texas Press, 2002.

———. *Savage Frontier*. . . . Vol. 2, 1838–1839. Denton: University of North Texas Press, 2006.

———. *Savage Frontier*. . . . Vol. 3, 1840–1841. Denton: University of North Texas Press, 2007.

———. *Savage Frontier*. . . . Vol. 4, 1842–1845. Denton: University of North Texas Press, 2010.

Morris, John Miller. *A Private in the Texas Rangers: A. T. Miller of Company B, Frontier Battalion*. College Station: Texas A&M University Press, 2001.

Oates, Stephen B. *Visions of Glory: Texans on the Southwestern Frontier*. Norman: University of Oklahoma Press, 1970.

O'Neal, Bill. *The Bloody Legacy of Pink Higgins*. Austin: Eakin Press, 1999.

———. *Reel Rangers: Texas Rangers in Movies, TV, Radio, and Other Forms of Popular Culture*. Waco: Eakin Press, 2008.

———. *The Arizona Rangers.* Austin: Eakin Press, 1987.

———. *War in East Texas: Regulators and Moderators.* Lufkin, TX: Best of East Texas Publishers, 2006.

Paine, Albert Bigelow. *Captain Bill McDonald, Texas Ranger: A Story of Frontier Reform.* New York: J. J. Little & Ives Co., 1909.

Paredes, Américo. *"With His Pistol in His Hand": A Border Ballad and Its Hero.* Austin: University of Texas Press, 1958.

Parsons, Chuck. *John B. Armstrong: Texas Ranger and Pioneer Ranchman.* College Station: Texas A&M University Press, 2007.

———. *Captain John R. Hughes, Lone Star Ranger.* Denton: University of North Texas Press, 2011.

———. *The Texas Rangers.* Mt. Pleasant, SC: Arcadia Press, 2011.

———. *The Sutton-Taylor Feud: The Deadliest Blood Feud in Texas.* Denton: University of North Texas Press, 2009.

———. and Marianne E. Hall Little. *Captain L. H. McNelly—Texas Ranger—The Life and Times of a Fighting Man.* Austin: State House Press, 2001.

Prassel, Frank R. *The Western Peace Officer: A Legacy of Law and Order.* Norman: University of Oklahoma Press, 1972.

Preece, Harold. *Lone Star Man: Ira Aten, Last of the Old Texas Rangers.* New York: Hastings House, 1960.

Raymond, Dora N. *Captain Lee Hall of Texas.* Norman: University of Oklahoma Press, 1940.

Reid, Samuel C., Jr. *The Scouting Expeditions of McCulloch's Texas Rangers. . . .* Philadelphia: G. B. Zieber, 1847.

Rhinehart, Marilyn D. *A Way of Work and a Way of Life: Coal Mining in Thurber, Texas, 1888–1926.* College Station: Texas A&M University Press, 1992.

Roberts, Daniel W. *Rangers and Sovereignty.* San Antonio: Wood Printing and Engraving, 1914.

Robinson, Charles M. III. *The Men Who Wear the Star: The Story of the Texas Rangers.* New York: Random House, 2000.

Samora, Julian, Joe Bernal, and Albert Peña. *Gunpowder Justice: A Reassessment of the Texas Rangers.* Notre Dame, IN: University of Notre Dame Press, 1979.

Sinise, Jerry. *George Washington Arrington. . . .* Burnet, TX: Eakin Press, 1979.

Smallwood, James M. *The Feud That Wasn't: The Taylor Ring, Bill Sutton, John Wesley Hardin, and Violence in Texas.* College Station: Texas A&M University Press, 2008.

Smith, David P. *Frontier Defense in the Civil War: Texas' Rangers and Rebels.* College Station: Texas A&M University Press, 1992.

Sonnichsen, C. L. *I'll Die Before I'll Run: The Story of the Great Feuds of Texas.* New York: Harper & Brothers, 1951.

———. *Ten Texas Feuds.* Albuquerque: University of New Mexico Press, 1957.

Spellman, Paul N. *Captain J. A. Brooks: Texas Ranger.* Denton: University of North Texas Press, 2007.

———. *Captain John H. Rogers, Texas Ranger.* Denton: University of North Texas Press, 2003.

Spurlin, Charles D. *Texas Volunteers in the Mexican War.* Austin: Eakin Press, 1998.

Stephens, Robert W. *Captain George H. Schmitt Texas Ranger.* Dallas: Privately published, 2006.

———. *Texas Ranger Sketches.* Dallas: Privately published, 1972.

Thompson, Jerry. *Cortina: Defending the Mexican Name in Texas.* College Station: Texas A&M University Press, 2007.

Utley, Robert M. *Lone Star Justice: The First Century of the Texas Rangers.* New York: Oxford University Press, 2002.

Webb, Walter Prescott. *The Story of the Texas Rangers.* Austin: Encino Press, 1957.

———. *The Texas Rangers: A Study in Frontier Defense.* Boston: Houghton Mifflin Co., 1935.

Weiss, Harold J., Jr. *Yours to Command: The Life and Legend of Texas Ranger Captain Bill McDonald.* Denton: University of North Texas Press, 2009.

Wilkins, Frederick. *Defending the Borders: The Texas Rangers, 1848–1861.* Austin: State House Press, 2001.

———. *The Highly Irregular Irregulars: Texas Rangers in the Mexican War.* Austin: Eakin Press, 1990.

———. *The Law Comes to Texas: The Texas Rangers, 1970–1901.* Austin: State House Press, 1999.

———. *The Legend Begins: The Texas Rangers, 1823–1845.* Austin: State House Press, 1996.

CONTRIBUTORS

Bob Boze Bell is Executive Editor of *True West* Publishing. As a noted speaker, writer, and illustrator, he continues to publicize the real and fictional Wests. Some of his books on Old West outlaws and lawmen, from Billy the Kid to Wyatt Earp, have become classics.

Donaly E. Brice is a well-known archivist at the Texas State Archives and a Fellow of the Texas State Historical Association. An acknowledged expert on the Great Comanche Raid and a Reconstruction desperado, Cullen Montgomery Baker, Brice also co-authored *The Governor's Hounds: The Texas State Police, 1870–1873.*

Paul H. Carlson is professor emeritus of history at Texas Tech University. He is a Fellow of both the Texas State Historical Association and the West Texas Historical Association. Carlson has won numerous teaching awards, earned research and writing honors, and is co-author of *Myth, Memory and Massacre: The Pease River Capture of Cynthia Ann Parker.*

Michael L. Collins is Regents Professor of History at Midwestern State University. He authored a study of Theodore Roosevelt and the American West. Another memorable narrative is entitled *Texas Devils: Rangers and Regulators on the Lower Rio Grande, 1846–1861.*

Tom Crum has had an impressive judicial and historical career. As a retired state district judge and a past president of both the West Texas and East Texas historical associations, he has combined the study of law, history, and folklore. Crum has published numerous articles and is co-author with Paul Carlson of a book about the recapture of Cynthia Ann Parker and the myths therein.

James M. Day had a varied career, from being Director of the Texas State Archives to joining the faculty of the University of Texas at El Paso. A noted expert in the fields of English, history, and folklore, he won many awards with his publications. Two of his books are worth noting: a study of the literature of the Texas Meir expedition and a biography of Ranger Captain Clint Peoples.

Bruce A. Glasrud is professor emeritus of history at California State University, East Bay, and retired dean of Arts and Sciences at Sul Ross State University. A specialist in minorities in Texas, Western, and Southern history, Glasrud is the author/editor or co-author/editor of twenty books.

Andrew R. Graybill earned a doctorate in history from Princeton University. His field of study is transnational borders in North America, including Rangers and Mounties. Graybill published *Policing the Great Plains: Rangers, Mounties, and the North American Frontier, 1875–1910*. He taught at the University of Nebraska at Lincoln and is currently the director of the Clements Center at Southern Methodist University.

Stephen L. Hardin is professor of history at McMurray University in Abilene, Texas. He is the author of *The Texas Rangers*, the award-winning *Texian Iliad: A Military History of the Texas Revolution, 1835–1836*, and the editor of *Lone Star: The Republic of Texas, 1836–1846* (1998). Distinguished for his readable style and his accessible approach to history, Dr. Hardin is a Fellow of the Texas State Historical Association, an inductee of the prestigious Texas Institute of Letters, and a member of Western Writers of America.

W. J. Hughes earned his Ph.D. degree in history at Texas Tech University and taught at Mankato State College in Minnesota. His eye for details in historical research can be seen in the biography, *Rebellious Ranger: Rip Ford and the Old Southwest*.

Richard B. McCaslin is professor and chair, Department of History, at the University of North Texas. McCaslin earned his Ph.D. at the University of Texas and is a Fellow and Board member of the Texas State Historical Association. Among his numerous publications are *Fighting Stock: John S. "Rip" Ford of Texas*, *Tainted Breeze: The Great Hanging at Gainesville, Texas*, and *At the Heart of Texas: One Hundred Years of the Texas State Historical Association*.

Leon Metz has become one of the foremost experts on the history of Old West outlaws and gunmen. Among his many publications are two standard works in the field: *Pat Garrett: The Story of a Western Lawman* and *John Wesley Hardin: Dark Angel of Texas*. Metz has served as an archivist and is past president of Western Writers of America.

Rick Miller is a lawyer and a former local chief of police. He received his juris doctorate from Baylor University and served as county attorney of Bell County. An acknowledged expert on outlaws and lawmen in the Old West, Miller has published two noted biographies: *Sam Bass & Gang* and *Bloody Bill Longley: The Mythology of a Gunfighter*. He also has been a pioneering voice in developing several outlaw-lawman organizations.

Stephen L. Moore is a sixth generation Texan who specializes in Texas and World War II military history. Prodigious research went into his esteemed four-volume history of Rangers, riflemen, and the Indian wars during the Republic years—*Savage Frontier: Rangers, Riflemen, and Indian Wars in Texas*.

Stephen B. Oates, a prominent and award-winning scholar who taught at a number of institutions of higher education, holds a Ph.D. degree from the University of Texas. Known for his vivid narratives and insightful analyses, Oates published several books on Texas history in his early career. He authored *Confederate Cavalry West of the River* and edited *Rip Ford's Texas*. His articles have been collected and republished in *Visions of Glory: Texans on the Southwestern Frontier*.

Chuck Parsons arrived in Texas after a teaching career and eighteen years as a secondary school principal in the upper Midwest. Since then he has concentrated on researching and writing about Texas outlaws, lawmen, feudists and Texas Rangers of the Old

West. The author of such works as *Captain John R. Hughes: Lone Star Ranger, The Sutton-Taylor Feud,* and *John B. Armstrong,* Parsons also contributes regularly to journals/magazines such as the *Journal of South Texas, True West,* and the *Journal* of the Wild West History Association.

Marilyn D. Rhinehart earned her Ph.D. in American history from the University of Houston. After serving as a member of the faculty and administration at North Harris College in Houston, she accepted a position as Executive Vice President of Academic Affairs at Johnson County Community College, near Kansas City. Rhinehart has emphasized in her writings Texas, labor history, and the United States at the turn of the twentieth century. Her book, *A Way of Work and a Way of Life: Coal Mining in Thurber, Texas, 1888–1926,* has been well-received.

David E. Screws earned a master's degree in history from the University of Texas, Permian Basin while a resident in Midland. His *Journal of Big Bend Studies* article originally was prepared while working on his degree. Screws subsequently moved to the Corpus Christi area where he taught for a while.

Harold J. Weiss, Jr. is professor emeritus of history at Jamestown Community College, Jamestown, New York. He has published articles on western law and order in numerous journals. Weiss is the author of a highly acclaimed biography: *Yours to Command: The Life and Legend of Texas Ranger Captain Bill McDonald.*

SOURCE CREDITS

Bob Boze Bell and Rick Miller, "Bad Day at Round Rock," *True West* 40.5 (July 2002): 34–36. Reprinted by permission of the authors and courtesy *True West* magazine.

Harold J. Weiss, Jr., "The Texas Rangers Revisited: Old Themes and New Viewpoints," *Southwestern Historical Quarterly* 97 (April 1994): 621–640. Reprinted by permission of the author and courtesy *Southwestern Historical Quarterly*.

Stephen L. Hardin, "'Valor, Wisdom and Experience': Early Texas Rangers and the Nature of Frontier Leadership," *Osprey Military Journal* 4.2 (2002): 50–56. Reprinted by permission of the author and courtesy of Osprey Publishing.

Donaly E. Brice, "The Great Comanche Raid of 1840," *South Texas Studies* (1996): 75–107. Reprinted by permission of the author and courtesy Victoria College *South Texas Studies*.

Stephen L. Moore, "The Deadly Colts on Walker's Creek," in *Savage Frontier: Rangers, Riflemen, and the Indian Wars in Texas, 1842–1845* (Denton: University of North Texas Press, 2010): IV, 139–154, 235–237. Reprinted by permission of the author and courtesy the University of North Texas Press.

Stephen B. Oates, "*Los Diablos Tejanos*," *American West* 2 (Summer 1965): 41–50. Reprinted by permission of the author.

Michael L. Collins, "The Callahan Expedition," in *Texas Devils: Rangers and Regulars on the Lower Rio Grande, 1846–1861* (Norman: University of Oklahoma Press, 2008), 73–88, 270–272. Reprinted by permission of the author and courtesy of the University of Oklahoma Press.

W. J. Hughes, "Rip Ford's Indian Fight on the Canadian," *Panhandle Plains Historical Review* 30 (1957): 1–26. Reprinted courtesy of the *Panhandle Plains Historical Review*.

Richard B. McCaslin, "Rangers, 'Rip' Ford, and the Cortina War," in *Fighting Stock John S. "Rip" Ford of Texas* (Fort Worth: TCU Press, 2011): 82–98, 294–297. Reprinted by permission of the author and courtesy of TCU Press.

David E. Screws, "Hispanic Texas Rangers Contribute to Peace on the Texas Frontier, 1838–1880," *Journal of Big Bend Studies* 13 (2001): 27–36. Reprinted courtesy of the *Journal of Big Bend Studies*.

Paul H. Carlson and Tom Crum, "The 'Battle' at Pease River and the Question of Reliable Sources in the Recapture of Cynthia Ann Parker," *Southwestern Historical Quarterly* 113 (July 2009): 32–52. Reprinted by permission of the authors and courtesy *Southwestern Historical Quarterly*.

Leon Metz, "Capturing the Grand Mogul," in *John Wesley Hardin: Dark Angel of Texas* (El Paso: Mangan Books, 1996): 158–172, 320–321. Reprinted by permission of the author.

Andrew Graybill, *Policing the Great Plains: Rangers, Mounties, and the North American Frontier, 1875–1910.* (Lincoln: University of Nebraska Press, 2007): 138–157, 233–236. Reprinted by permission of the author and courtesy *Agricultural History* and the University of Nebraska Press.

James M. Day, "Rangers of the Last Frontier of Texas," *Password* 45 (Winter 2000): 159–174. Reprinted courtesy of the El Paso Historical Society.

Chuck Parsons, "The Jesse Evans Gang and the Death of Texas Ranger George R. Bingham," *Journal of Big Bend Studies* 20 (2008): 75–87. Reprinted by permission of the author and courtesy of the *Journal of Big Bend Studies*.

Marilyn D. Rhinehart, "The Struggle for the Individual and the Union, 1888–1903," in *A Way of Work and a Way of Life: Coal Mining in Thurber, Texas, 1888–1926* (College Station: Texas A&M University Press, 1992): 71–91, 134–138. Reprinted by permission of the author and courtesy of Texas A&M University Press.

INDEX